D0376495

EXPLORING FAMILY THEORIES

EXPLORING FAMILY THEORIES

SUZANNE R. SMITH
RAEANN R. HAMON
BRON B. INGOLDSBY
J. ELIZABETH MILLER

New York   Oxford
OXFORD UNIVERSITY PRESS
2009

OXFORD

UNIVERSITY PRESS

Oxford University Press, Inc., publishes works that further
Oxford University's objective of excellence
in research, scholarship, and education.

Oxford New York
Auckland Cape Town Dar es Salaam Hong Kong Karachi
Kuala Lumpur Madrid Melbourne Mexico City Nairobi
New Delhi Shanghai Taipei Toronto

With offices in
Argentina Austria Brazil Chile Czech Republic France Greece
Guatemala Hungary Italy Japan Poland Portugal Singapore
South Korea Switzerland Thailand Turkey Ukraine Vietnam

Copyright © 2009 by Oxford University Press, Inc.

Published by Oxford University Press, Inc.
198 Madison Avenue, New York, New York 10016
http://www.oup.com

Oxford is a registered trademark of Oxford University Press

All rights reserved. No part of this publication may be reproduced,
stored in a retrieval system, or transmitted, in any form or by any means,
electronic, mechanical, photocopying, recording, or otherwise,
without the prior permission of Oxford University Press.

Library of Congress Cataloging-in-Publication Data
Exploring family theories / Suzanne R. Smith . . . [et al.].—2nd ed.
p. cm.
Originally entered under: Ingoldsby, Bron B. and published: Los
Angeles, CA: Roxbury Pub., c c2004.
Includes bibliographical references and index.
ISBN 978-0-19-537771-2 (alk. paper)
1. Family—Research.   2. Interpersonal conflict—Research.
3. Interpersonal communication—Research.   4. Symbolic interactionism.
I. Smith, Suzanne R., 1968–   II. Ingoldsby, Bron B. Exploring family
theories.
HQ519.E96 2009
305.85—dc22
2008033899

Printing (last digit): 9 8 7 6 5 4 3 2 1
Printed in the United States of America
on acid-free paper

To Bron Ingoldsby
Father, husband, scholar, beloved friend

The original idea for this book came from Bron Ingoldsby who loved the teaching and research of theory. Bron's ability to think about concepts and apply them in unique and creative ways is one of the many reasons he was an incredible teacher and a successful scholar. His drive and passion for this book is what got his coauthors through the first edition of this manuscript, and what inspired us to continue with the second edition despite the pain it brought to write it without him by our sides.

However, we most remember Bron for his quick wit, infectious laugh, and dry sense of humor. He was one of those rare individuals with whom each and every person who knew him felt a special connection. For us, he was a best friend, a sympathetic colleague, and an admirable man who fought cancer with dignity and grace. He is greatly missed.

Acknowledgments

Life has a way of bringing about unexpected joys and sorrows, and the writing of the current edition of this text was influenced by one of each. It is with deepest sorrow that we acknowledge the death of Bron Ingoldsby, the first author of this text in the first edition. He was the driving force behind this book, and the inspiration we needed to get it written when time was scarce and nerves were frayed. On the other hand, Beth Miller has had the wonderful experience of becoming a mother since the last edition was written and is enjoying the beauty of motherhood and its numerous positive stressors. Because of these two events, these authors were not able to participate in the writing of this second edition. However, Raeann Hamon and Suzanne Smith would like to acknowledge that the three original authors were equal collaborators in the first edition, and their work is obviously the foundation on which this second edition has been built. Thus, this edition would not have been possible without the time and talents of Bron and Beth in the first edition.

We would like to collectively thank Sherith Pankratz at Oxford University Press for guiding us through this process. In addition, thanks to the many colleagues who graciously gave of their time and expertise in reviewing the book as we sought information to inform our revisions for the second edition. Raeann and Suzanne would also like to thank our departments for their support throughout this project. Specifically, we would like to thank the Human Development Department at Washington State University Vancouver, Vancouver, Washington, and the Human Development and Family Science Department at Messiah College, Grantham, Pennsylvania. We would also like to thank our friends and family for their patience as we worked nights and weekends to complete this project.

Finally, we again pay tribute to the originators of the theories themselves, many of whose works are included in this text. We acknowledge the important contributions of today's family researchers that continue to enhance our understanding of family theories and recognize that their scholarship will expand our knowledge of families and further our ability to apply that knowledge in its proper theoretical context. Finally, we recognize those students reading this book who will one day write their own text on family theories based on the ideals of those before them but enlightened by their own educational and research experiences.

CONTENTS

About the Authors

Suzanne R. Smith is Associate Professor of Human Development at Washington State University Vancouver where she serves as the Associate Chair and Program Director. She earned her PhD from the University of Georgia. Dr. Smith's primary area of research is parent–child relationships, but she has spent significant time over the last decade living with and researching the Hutterites. She has served as president of both the Northwest Council on Family Relations and the Teaching Family Science Association, as well as being a member of the board of the National Council on Family Relations.

Raeann R. Hamon is Distinguished Professor of Family Science and Gerontology and Chair of the Human Development and Family Science Department at Messiah College in Pennsylvania. Dr. Hamon earned her PhD from Virginia Tech. A Certified Family Life Educator, she teaches courses on family theories, family life education, marital relationships, and aging. Her research is related to Bahamian families, intergenerational relationships, families in later life, and issues related to the discipline of family science.

Bron B. Ingoldsby was Associate Professor of Family Life at Brigham Young University in Provo, Utah. He earned his PhD from the University of Georgia. Dr. Ingoldsby was a recognized scholar in the area of cross-cultural family relationships and an active member of the National Council on Family Relations. He lost his valiant battle to cancer in October, 2006, and is survived by his wife and twin daughters and their families.

J. Elizabeth Miller is Associate Professor of Family and Child Studies at Northern Illinois University. She also served as Director of Teaching Assistant Training and Development in the Graduate School, Northern Illinois University. She earned her PhD from the University of Georgia. Her primary research is in the areas of work and families and teaching from a feminist perspective. Dr. Miller is active in the National Council on Family Relations and was chair of the Women's Caucus of the American Association of Higher Education.

INTRODUCTION

"Why do you do that?" "Why does our family insist on doing things that way?" Questions about people's behavior are the essence of social science inquiry. The focus may be on individuals, families, social groups, communities, or cultures. In order to engage in the process of social science inquiry, you need two things: research and theory. Before we enter into a discussion of social science theory, and specifically family theory, we first need to have a general discussion about theory.

WHAT IS THEORY?

A theory is a tool used to understand and describe the world. More specifically, a theory is a general framework of ideas and how they relate to each other and can be used to answer questions about particular phenomena. The usefulness of a theory is measured by its ability to describe or predict some event or behavior.

You probably are familiar with many theories already, such as the theory of evolution, the theory of relativity, the theory of the big bang, and the theory of plate tectonics. There are also theories that describe human activities, such as music theory, economic theory, and the theory of language. The theory of plate tectonics, for example, describes the earth's surface as huge sections of the earth's solid crust floating on a molten, liquid inner core. It predicts *where* volcanoes and earthquakes will most likely occur, that is, where these sections of crust rub against or bump into each other. It does not, however, predict *when* volcanoes will erupt or earthquakes will happen. But earth scientists can use the theory as a basis for research and data collection so that they can someday predict when earthquakes will occur.

The degree to which a theory helps us to generate questions—its *heuristic* value—is also important. A theory can help us decide what to research; the results of that research can lead to the development of new theories, which again leads to new research. Such a beneficial relationship is called a symbiotic relationship. Research poses questions and then tries to answer them by making observations and collecting data. When enough data have been collected, patterns emerge, and a theory is developed to try to explain the patterns that are observed. Thus, theory helps us explain "what's going on" and can allow us to *predict* "what's going to happen" when certain conditions are present.

A theory can also change the way we view and understand the world. Take, as an example, Einstein's Theory of Relativity. Before Einstein, the world was viewed as being made up of discrete objects—matter (such as protons, neutrons, and electrons) and energy (such as electricity and heat). Things were described as *absolutes*, and the speed of light was "absolutely" the fastest speed that anything could reach. Einstein looked at this theory and asked the question: "What if I were traveling in a rocket at the speed of light?" This question led him to develop his theory of relativity ($e = mc^2$), which stated that matter and energy were two forms of the same thing, linked together by the speed of light, and that time was relative, depending on how fast you could travel in relation to the speed of light.

Where Do Theories Come from?

Theories generally don't emerge fully formed all at once. Instead, they build slowly over time, as scholars gather data through observation and analysis of evidence, relating concepts together in different ways. This type of reasoning, moving from specific bits of information toward a general idea, is known as *inductive reasoning*. Once the theory exists, scholars use the general ideas of the theory to generate more specific questions, often in the form of research questions, thereby moving in the opposite direction. Taking a general idea from a theory and testing it to tease out the details is known as *deductive reasoning*. Both kinds of thinking patterns are common in theory construction and development, and they demonstrate the linkage between research and theory once again.

However, as one can see from the figure, "The cycle of theory building," theories are not stagnant. Theories help us to formulate questions that we test via research. The research generates data, which filter back into the cycle and help us to further refine the theory. As our theoretical ideas change, so do our research questions. It is also important to remember that theories do not exist in a cultural vacuum, but that they are the product of humans and their experiences. As humans redefine their values, their theories are influenced by those changes. This is particularly evident in theories of social science but can be seen in natural science theories as well. After all,

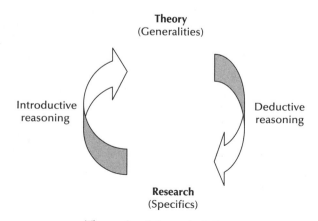

The **cycle** of theory building.

it was once believed that the world was flat and that the earth was the center of the universe.

Radical changes or shifts in scientific views are known as *paradigm shifts* (Kuhn 1970). These shifts occur after significant data have been gathered that do not fit the current theory. Thus, a new theory is needed to explain the data. According to Kuhn, in the natural sciences, paradigm shifts change science dramatically, as did Einstein's Theory of Relativity or the fact that Columbus did not, in fact, fall off the end of the earth.

In the social sciences, paradigm shifts are not as obvious because we do not evaluate our theories from the standpoint of truth but rather on how useful they are. We, as scholars, cannot define what is true for all humans or families, so neither can our theoretical perspectives. At times, significant changes in culture or human experience can change theoretical perspectives in radical ways. However, generally, social theories are not discarded as they are in natural science but are instead used to explain more specific social phenomena from different perspectives.

Many of the world's greatest minds, those whose ideas literally changed the way we understand the world, were theoreticians. For example, we live in a post-Freudian world: Freud's theories revolutionized our understanding of the mind, sexuality, and how we deal with stress. Karl Marx suggested that communism is an alternative to social injustice and oppression and is a method by which all humans could achieve a humane and equitable life. Freud and Marx brought about significant shifts in the way we thought about issues in society and human behavior that are still valued today, although we do not believe every aspect of Freudian psychology, and Marx's Communist Manifesto had its limitations. Similarly, Piaget brought about another paradigm shift in the area of cognitive development with his insight that children think in ways that are qualitatively different from adult processes. His theory has undergone modifications, and many researchers still use his work as a basis for their research, but some of them have also gone beyond his work and expanded it. In this way, we evaluate theories based on the aspects of those theories that are useful.

How Are Theories Developed?

Bengtson et al. (2005) likened theorizing to putting together the pieces of a puzzle. Each puzzle piece is comprised of a bit of family research data. Alone and disorganized, the pieces do not make sense and are perplexing. However, when assembled in a meaningful way, the puzzle provides a more coherent image or picture. Thus, theories are ideas or abstractions that make sense of the data. They are intellectual constructs that are subject to change as new puzzle pieces or evidence is introduced. Nevertheless, they have identifiable components that make up their structure. *Assumptions* are the beliefs that are taken for granted or believed to be true. They form the foundation underlying the theory. *Concepts* are the terms and specific ideas used in building the theory. *Propositions* are statements that demonstrate how concepts fit together in a context. They are the relationships between the concepts, the "glue" holding the theory together. Thus, theory is based on assumptions and should be composed of clearly defined concepts that fit together in the form of propositions. For these propositions to be useful, they should be specific enough to lead scholars to be able to describe, explain, and predict phenomena and to be able to ask questions that would guide their research in deductive ways. The theories should also be flexible enough to be able to grow and change so that new information can feed back into the theory, causing it to adapt and change in an inductive feedback loop; but the theory also needs to be general enough to apply to a wide variety of specific cases. In short, the usefulness of a theory is determined by its ability to describe more, rather than less, detail; to predict with more, rather than less, accuracy; and to apply to a broader rather than a more narrow, range of specific cases.

It is also true that theories have a certain point of view, or lens. Depending on our emphasis, the perspective may be more broad (macro) or more narrow (micro). The lens we choose is often a function of the question we are asking, and so, again, a theory's usefulness depends on the subject at hand. In the social sciences, human situations are complex, and it is difficult to find one theory that can explain or predict every emotion, behavior, interaction, process, and event. Because of this, social theories are those lenses that we can use to help us to interpret or focus on the components of human interactions, which allow us to do so in conceptual ways.

Although theories are abstract, they do serve important purposes in our under- standing of social phenomena. Theories provide a general framework for understanding data in an organized way as well as showing us how to intervene (Burr 1995). In social sciences, it is rare to find anyone who believes that there is only one way to under- stand social phenomena, particularly those as complicated as individuals and families. Thus, the frustrating but truthful response to many questions in social science is, "It depends." Indeed, it does depend on one's point of view, but that is not the same as one's opinion. For example, someone may believe that divorce sets a bad example for children. As scholars, we know that divorce is too complex to be labeled as merely *good* or *bad* and that questions about the effects of divorce on children cannot be easily answered. We need more complex ideas to analyze such situations, and we need to consider multiple elements within families to study aspects of divorce, its develop- ment, and its effects. To decide which theory to turn to, we consider the usefulness of the theory, or how well it enables us to answer the questions at hand. How "well" a theory does in explaining a situation depends on the researcher's point of view, or lens. Thus, two social scientists may each choose a different theory to explain the same situation.

Each theory allows us to look at different aspects of family life: One theory might suggest that we focus on the roles that people play, whereas another suggests that we focus more on the individual's gains and losses. Taking on the lens of the theory enables us to see how the world looks from that perspective. Each theory has underlying basic assumptions that focus the lens, just as each has concepts and propositions that guide what we analyze. Each theory has been developed within a historical context, and has asked different questions; thus, each theory has a different research history. Because of this, each theory can give us a different answer to our question; thus, "It depends."

THEORY IN HISTORICAL PERSPECTIVE

It can be interesting to trace the evolution of theory building and see how theories have become more sophisticated and accurate over time. Some of the earliest scien- tific writings of the Western world come from the golden age of Greek civilization. Thinkers such as Aristotle were what we call armchair philosophers. That is, they simply presumed that their ideas, if logical or rational, had to be true. Therefore, no effort was made to test them empirically. As a result, many of their ideas were later found to be incorrect. It was Galileo, for instance, who centuries later tested Aristotle's beliefs concerning weights and gravity. He, like many others, found that the truth is sometimes counterintuitive. Some of Aristotle's other ideas cannot even be called rational. For example, it is reported that he believed a woman could increase her chances of having a male child if she conceived it under a full moon and north wind after drinking lion's blood!

During the Renaissance, a number of key philosophers developed theories about the nature of children. John Calvin, a Protestant minister, felt that they were born evil and, therefore, needed to be forced into acting appropriately. Jean-Jacques Rousseau took the opposite position: that they were born good and therefore needed very little adult intervention. John Locke stood in the middle with his view that children are born as "blank slates," neither good nor bad, but empty vessels to be filled by proper environmental training. Most modern parenting theories and approaches derive from these basic theoretical frameworks.

A number of very important human development theories emerged in the late 1800s and early 1900s from the works of men that we will call intuitive geniuses. We have the theory of evolution by Darwin, which has resulted in a dramatic paradigm shift in biology and related fields. Freud and his followers, such as Erik Erickson, took their clinical data and extrapolated elaborate theories of the mind that transformed psychology. Jean Piaget's careful observations and questions revolutionized our understanding of how we think. Each of these scholars built upon the data available to him or her, with original and imaginative thinking.

By 1900, positivism was the dominant approach to science and theory building. It is based on the belief that "reality," or "truth," can be measured and understood independent of the observer. Behaviorism and most of the theories in this book are built on the tradition of careful measurement of empirical data. Newtonian physics makes the same assumptions. The idea is that there are repetitive and predictable patterns of behavior or action that can be found, measured, and explained in an organized way.

In recent years, we have seen the rise of postmodernism. Social scientists have drawn on Einstein's Theory of Relativity and on chaos theory, which developed from quantum mechanics. In this view, there is no reality independent of the observer, and individual actions cannot be predicted. However, general patterns can be discerned.

Many of the ideas of former theoreticians, including some presented in this text, have become so well known as to seem mundane. As a result, there may be a temptation to say, "Well, that is just common sense. Everyone knows that or could think of it on his or her own." Generally, that is the case because hardworking scholars have developed those very ideas, and they are so good that the public has come to know and accept them. As a result, we are changed and enriched by the contributions of the theoreticians.

FAMILY THEORY

Why study family theory? The family is certainly the most important and enduring of all human social groupings. What, then, could be more fascinating than the attempt to understand family dynamics? Nothing impacts our personality and happiness more than our family relationships. Why is kinship always the center of any human society? How do these interactions work, and why are they so influential in our lives?

Because there are so many perspectives to consider, it is not a simple thing to develop a coherent theory of family interaction. Social science is made even more difficult because we are attempting to understand ourselves. Whereas in the natural sciences we are examining objects and life forms that are less complex than we are, in human development we do not have the advantage of a higher intelligence than the subject in order to get a good *metaperspective*. With groups like families, there is the added complexity of looking beyond the individual to the relationships between individuals. All of this makes family theory development difficult at best.

We are also hindered by the difficulty of not even having a good and commonly accepted definition of the term *family*. Anthropologist George Murdock (1949) surveyed the world's cultures and came up with this definition:

> The family is a social group characterized by common residence, economic cooperation, and reproduction. It includes adults of both sexes, at least two of whom maintain a socially approved sexual relationship, and one or more children, own or adopted, of the sexually cohabiting adults. (p. 1)

His work (described in greater detail in our chapter on structural functionalism) has generated a half century of ongoing scientific and political debate on what we mean when we say family. As we will see, each theory has its own variation on the definition.

This is also a good example of why we need more than one family theory. First, there is more than one type and one definition of family. Second, even if you agree on how to define the family, you may disagree on which particular aspect of their interactions or behaviors on which you should focus your attention. Finally, each theory offers an insight that others cannot provide because of their different lenses.

The purpose of this text is to provide a basic introduction to the major theories pertaining to the family among professionals today. Each addresses different aspects of family life and answers different questions. Humans are extremely complex, and it is difficult to analyze ourselves; therefore, every theory will be imperfect. But each one brings us closer to understanding and being able to make positive change where needed in family life. Each theory has its own basic assumptions and concepts and is a product of its own historical context as well. Each is used in answering specific research questions that other theories may not answer or may answer differently. It will be up to you to try on the lens of each theory and determine how well you think it explains human and family behavior.

TEXT ORGANIZATION

We will discuss nine theories about the family that have been widely used and accepted over the past fifty years. We present these nine theories in a loose chronological order. It is difficult to be precise, as most of them experienced a gradual emergence and some have long histories as general social theories before they were used to study family as a specific social phenomenon. Our order of placement is determined by the time in which significant publications discussing the theory from a family perspective appeared.

Symbolic interaction theory is one of the first and most influential theories in the field of family science. Its roots stem from the pragmatic philosophers of the early 1900s and is based on the belief that we construct our own realities. Events and relationships take on different meanings based on an individual's perceptions and the context of a situation. Symbolic interaction continues to be a very popular family theory today.

Shortly after the Depression and World War II and in the infancy of family theory building, several other theories took center stage. Structural functionalism, which comes from sociology and anthropology, takes a macro view of the family within culture. It looks at the family through the lens of asking what the family does to justify its existence in society.

Family development theory applies basic-stage theory from psychology to families. It considers how families change over time in response to normative family events. Although its widespread use comes later, family stress theory, which looks at how the family as a system deals with challenging situations or events, was developed while studying family reactions to the Depression, and later to wartime during World War II.

In the late 1950s and early 1960s, several theories took more of an inside look at family communication and interaction. First, family systems theory derives from communication and clinical work. It makes a micro analysis of how family members relate to each other in a complex world of multicausality. Next, conflict theory comes from a sociological perspective and focuses on how people and families create stability and instability in their relationships due to differences in status. Then, social exchange theory takes its inspiration from behaviorism and economics in analyzing family decision making as a rational process of choosing between rewards and costs.

Our final two theoretical approaches began to receive significant notice in the 1970s. Feminist theorists began their investigations with the perspective that women's experiences are central to our understanding of families and focused on the influences of social situations and politics. Most recently, the biosocial perspective, with its roots in the work of Charles Darwin, maintains as its general premise that humans are driven by innate structures, but that the family and cultural environment influence their behaviors.

Each chapter begins with a fictional vignette to introduce a way of using that particular theory for understanding an aspect of family life. It is followed by a brief history of the development of the theory, and then an explanation of the basic assumptions that undergird the theory. The primary terms and concepts used in understanding the theory are provided. The usefulness of each theory is highlighted by examples of research and application within the particular framework. Every theory is critiqued, with its principle problems and strong points. Finally, the reader is provided with a series of questions and exercises designed to relate the implications of the theory to the vignette and to the personal and family life of the student.

A highlight of this book is the integration of research with theory. After each chapter, a professional research article has been included. Each research article illustrates how new information about families is gained when researchers used theories to guide their effort. Whereas, in the first edition of this text, a classic article was included at the end of each chapter, for this edition, we've chosen more contemporary readings with one exception. The Epilogue links the chapters together, using a conceptual model for comparing and contrasting the theories. This model indicates how each can be useful for understanding and guiding intervention for particular situations from its viewpoint.

Once again, anyone can collect facts, but being a scholar requires understanding them in a way that allows for research, testing, comprehension, and practical application. In order to be useful, data must be ordered within a theoretical framework. Which will you enjoy the most and find the most useful? There is only one way to find out!

REFERENCES

Bengtson, V., A. C. Acock, K. R. Allen, P. Dilworth-Anderson, and D. M. Klein. 2005. Theory and theorizing in family research: Puzzle building and puzzle solving. In *Sourcebook of family theory and research*, ed. V. L. Bengtson, A. C. Acock, K. R. Allen, P. Dilworth-Anderson, and D. M. Klein, 3–33. Thousand Oaks, CA: Sage Publications.

Burr, W. R. 1995. Using theories in family science. In *Research and theory in family science*, ed. R. D. Day, K. R. Gilbert, B. H. Settles, and W. R. Burr, 73–88. Pacific Grove, CA: Brooks-Cole.

Kuhn, T. S. 1970. *The structure of scientific revolutions* (2nd ed.). Chicago: Univ. of Chicago Press.

Murdock, G. P. 1949. *Social structure*. New York: Free Press.

1

Symbolic Interactionism Theory

Keiko and Thanh are leaving the house to attend a cocktail party sponsored by Thanh's company. It's important that he be there because he's up for a big promotion this year and wants to make sure those in charge know who he is and can connect his face with his name because his name is so unusual in the United States. Keiko is tired from working all day and getting the children taken care of before they leave the house, so she is dreading the party. Thanh, however, is very excited.

They are greeted at the door by the company vice president and a very loud band. Thanh introduces his wife with pride and accepts champagne for both of them to sip as they mingle in the crowd. He is really in his element, speaking to everyone he passes, introducing his wife, and keeping his hand on the small of her back to make sure she feels comfortable and included. Because she doesn't know anyone there, he wants to make sure she is close so he can introduce her to everyone and make her feel like a part of the group. He is enjoying the music and expensive champagne and can't wait for the dancing to begin. Thanh says to his wife, "Isn't this the best party you've ever been to?! And can you believe who all is here—all the important people, and I've gotten to talk to all of them. I can't imagine a more perfect evening."

As Keiko looks at him, he knows something is wrong. He asks, "Aren't you enjoying yourself?" She doesn't know what to say to him. After all, the place is too loud and too crowded, and people are drinking way too much. She wonders how he can stand knowing that everyone he speaks to is judging both of them. And why does he have to be so controlling of her? Everywhere they go, he is right by her side, as if he does not trust her to go out on her own for fear she will say something that would make him look bad. It is one of the worst nights of her life! How can two people in the same place have such different opinions about what is going on?

So, who was right—was it the best party they had ever been to or a night of being controlled and judged? Was the party incredible or incredibly boring? The answer to those questions, according to symbolic interactionism, is that they are both right. People define situations based on their own personal experiences and sense of self. Thus, two people can be in the exact same situation and have different interpretations of what is going on in that situation. We'll learn more about this as we discuss this multifaceted and exciting theory.

HISTORY

Important Early Contributions

Of all the theories discussed in this text, symbolic interactionism has probably had the greatest impact on the study of families. Not only is this theory rich in history because it has been in use since the early 1900s, but it is still one of the most commonly used theoretical perspectives in the field today, perhaps because it continues to develop (Fine 1993). The longevity and popularity of this theory is due in part to its emphasis on a conceptual framework that is not only rich in content but also adaptable to any time period. It is also due to the fact that symbolic interactionism was uniquely born out of both qualitative and quantitative research (LaRossa and Reitzes 1993).

Unlike most theories, there is no one person who is most commonly associated with its development. Thus, the historical review of symbolic interactionism will be longer than most of those in this text because there are many people whose work needs to be reviewed in order to fully understand the basic assumptions of this theory. While who is covered in this section will vary from one writing to the next, this discussion is based on the guidance of LaRossa and Reitzes (1993).

Symbolic interactionism has its earliest roots in the United States in the pragmatic philosophers of the early 1900s, such as William James, John Dewey, Charles Pierce, and Josiah Royce (Vander Zanden 1987). Not only were these scholars themselves influential in the development of the theory, but perhaps more important, they trained their students who in turn became the primary contributors to the assumptions and concepts that make this theory what it is today. The pragmatists did, however, contribute four important ideas that laid the foundation for the development of symbolic interactionism.

The first important contribution of the pragmatists was to view the world as something that was always changing rather than a static structure whose history is predetermined. Second, the pragmatists argued that social structure is not something that is fixed in time but rather is constantly changing and developing. Third, they were perhaps the first to suggest that meaning comes not from objects themselves but from our interactions with objects. For example, the meaning of a table depends on the person who is viewing or using the table at the time. Finally, "they exhibited an ideological commitment to progress and to democratic values" (La Rossa and Reitzes 1993, 136) that could be advanced through science. Thus arose the notion that we could use research to figure out how society, and people, grow and change and how they do so within the confines of a democratic society that is always evolving.

These four ideas came about at a time in history when people were desperate for information about how the changing structure of society was going to affect them. This was the time of the industrial revolution, when people were going from working at home on the farm to working at the factory, which also meant moving from rural areas to urban areas closer to work (Mintz and Kellogg 1988). Certainly, all of these changes left people feeling like they had little or no control over their lives anymore, which meant they certainly had little control over society. However, the idea of symbolic interactionism allowed people to feel as if they gained back a little more of that control because it is based on the idea that people are not victims of some predetermined course of history but instead are able to change how things happen in society through communication and interaction (LaRossa and Reitzes 1993).

Not only did these ideas appeal to society in general, but they were also accepted by scholars, as these ideas were grounded in research. Symbolic interactionism provided the means by which to study social interactions in a scientific fashion. It was at this time that people began to study the family just as a scientist would study a specimen or an astronomer would study a constellation (LaRossa and Reitzes 1993). This empirical position is still appealing to researchers today and continues to be one of the greatest strengths of the theory (Burnier 2005).

Principal Scholars

As was previously stated, one thing that makes symbolic interactionism unique is that it is a combination of the efforts of many different researchers. Although there are many people who made important contributions to the development of this theory, we will focus on just a few: George Herbert Mead, Charles Horton Cooley, William Isaac Thomas, and Herbert Blumer.

George Herbert Mead. George Herbert Mead, whose primary contributions focused on the self, is probably the most recognized of all those who have influenced symbolic interactionism. He believed that we learn about ourselves through interactions with others that are based on gestures (Mead 1934/1956). A gesture can be thought of as any action that causes a response or reaction in another person. We can all think of a few finger gestures that are sure to create a response in others, but Mead used the term more broadly to include such things as language and facial expressions as well. We develop a sense of self-consciousness when we can anticipate how other people will respond to our gestures. Because of this, it takes interactions with others to fully develop a sense of self.

How does this process take place? Mead (1934/1956) believed there were two stages people follow to develop a sense of self. In the first, the *play stage*, the child tries to use gestures to practice the behaviors associated with different roles, such as that of mother, father, firefighter, or teacher (Vander Zanden 1987). For example, if you have ever watched preschool children play house, you have probably seen a girl imitate things she has seen her mother do, such as cooking dinner, changing a baby's diaper, or helping another child with homework. Boys, on the other hand, if they are in the dramatic play area at all, are likely to be doing such things as pretending to drive the family to an event or organizing a play activity for the children. During this dramatic play experience, children are able to imagine the attitudes of the mother or learn to take the perspective of another person. During this stage, children usually assume the role of only one person at a time.

In the second stage, however, children begin to take on the perspective of many people at one time and to see how the individual fits within that group (Mead 1934/1956). This is called the *game stage*, and you can use almost any childhood game as a good example. For instance, when you play soccer, you have to think about not only what you are doing on the field, or the purpose of your position, but also about what everyone else on the field is doing. Another good example is that of the family. During this stage, children can understand what each person's role in the family is, including their own, and how the behavior of one family member affects the interactions of other family members.

The final step in this process is being able to anticipate how one's behaviors affect not only those in our immediate environment but also in society at large. Mead (1934/1956) called this being able to take the role of the "generalized other," which means understanding social norms and expectations so that one can guess how other people will react to a specific gesture or interaction. An example of this is the young man who nervously looks around as he purchases a pornographic magazine. Although he is of legal age, he has internalized the social perception that viewing pornography is lewd and engaged in only by sexual deviants. He is apprehensive that someone he knows will come into the store and see him buying this magazine, thus forming a bad opinion about him.

Finally, Mead (1934/1956) believed that the self is not a thing but rather a process based on constant movement between the "I" and the "me." The "I" is the spontaneous acts we engage in, which are unpredictable and unstable. The "me" (the social self), on the other hand, is those learned roles that are determined by interactions with others. In other words, the social self (or "we") is all of our learned experiences, whereas the "I" is our immediate reaction to situations. As Robinson (2007) suggested, the "I" is the response of the individual to the "me," which is a reflection of the social world in which we live and interact.

Charles Horton Cooley. Many of the researchers who developed symbolic interactionism focused on the self. For example, Charles Horton Cooley is perhaps best known for his idea of the "looking-glass self," which is based on the premise that individuals think about how they appear to others, make a judgment about what the other person thinks about them, and then incorporate those ideas into their own concept of self (Longmore 1998). For this process to take place, we must interact with others. Cooley (1956) believed that most of this learning took place during face-to-face interactions with others, especially in small groups, which he called primary groups. What distinguishes a primary group from other people that we come into contact with? We do not expect any self-gain or reward from interacting with those in our primary group (Beames 2005). The best example of a primary group is a family. Thus, it is in our families that we learn about ourselves because families teach us about social expectations for behavior, things that we are good at, and many other thoughts and behaviors that come together to make up who we are.

William Isaac Thomas. So when did the concepts included in symbolic interactionism first start being used in family studies? Most believe it was when William Isaac Thomas (and Floarian Znaniecki) wrote *The Polish Peasant in Europe and America* (1918–1920). This book was one of the first to state that the family has a role in the socialization process (LaRossa and Reitzes 1993). It pointed out that families construct their own realities so that one's culture, or social structure, influences both family and individual behavior.

Thomas is also well-known for coining the phrase *definition of the situation*, which is another foundation of symbolic interactionism. According to this idea, you cannot understand human behavior without also understanding the subjective perspectives of the people involved in the interaction. For example, parents are often faced with two siblings who carried on a conversation and then came to the parents for a "final ruling." It becomes obvious during the parents' conversations with each of the siblings that although they were both a part of the same conversation, each person had a different interpretation of what was said by the end of the discussion. This is because each sibling's reaction to the conversation was based on his or her individual, subjective, experience. Thomas took this idea further in what is called the Thomas theorem, which states that "if people define situations as real, they are real in their consequences" (LaRossa and Reitzes 1993, 140). Thus, each sibling in the conversation above makes comments based on his or her own interpretation, making each person's subjective opinion valued. So, if they were to ask their parents, "Whose point of view is right?" then, according to Thomas, the parents' answer would be, "They both are because your point of view is based on your interpretation of the conversation, taking into account your own personal experience." This is probably not the answer the disagreeing siblings want to hear!

Herbert Blumer. It should be obvious at this point that there are many people who have influenced the development of symbolic interactionism. In fact, there are many more than can be discussed here, but one thing we haven't covered yet is who was the first person to use the phrase *symbolic interactionism*, and that was Herbert Blumer. He is also credited with developing the three primary premises of symbolic interactionism, which will be discussed momentarily. Many people consider Blumer to be synonymous with symbolic interactionism (Fine 1993). Therefore, the influence of Herbert Blumer (1969) cannot be overlooked in a historical discussion of this theory.

BASIC ASSUMPTIONS

Perhaps the best way to understand symbolic interactionism is to review the seven basic assumptions of this theory as developed by many researchers in this field, although they are based on three overarching themes which were originally developed by Blumer (1969). Most people who use symbolic interactionism rely on the three themes developed by Blumer which will be discussed below. However, LaRossa and Reitzes (1993) organized these themes around other basic assumptions of the theory and for this reason the organizational structure they used will be followed here. All of these assumptions spring from the idea that we understand and relate to our environment based on the symbols that we know or those that we learn.

First Overarching Theme

The first overarching theme (Blumer 1969) is that meaning is a central element of human behavior that cannot be overlooked. This is best explained by reviewing the three assumptions that developed from this primary belief.

People will react to something according to the meaning that the thing has for them. In other words, people live in a symbolic environment and will respond to something based on their definition of that symbol. A cigarette, for example, is a symbol of relief from withdrawal for one person and a "death stick" to another. Thus, the first person would pick up a cigarette and light it, whereas the second person would probably destroy it.

We learn about meaning through interactions with others. This assumption is drawn from the work of Allen and Doherty (1998). While different researchers in this area have varying beliefs about the origins of meaning, most would agree that meaning is learned and processed through our social interactions. People make value judgments about which symbols are positive and negative, and react to them based on these values. Where do we learn about these values? Through interactions with others.

As people come into contact with different things and experiences, they interpret what is being learned. In other words, people are both actors and reactors. We are not passive people who simply respond to the world around us; instead, we are active people who choose which parts of the environment to respond to. So, if we enter a room in which we are uncomfortable, rather than simply stand there and feel nervous, hoping someone will come talk to us, we can actively seek out someone we know and go talk to them to put ourselves at ease. In this case, we are taking an active part in controlling our environment.

Second Overarching Theme

The second overarching theme has to do with our self-concept. Because humans are active social beings who interact with others based on their meaning of the situation, they must have a sense of self for this to take place.

A human infant is asocial. This means that infants are not born with predetermined ideas about who they are but rather develop these as they interact with people along the way. An example of this is the notion of the looking-glass self (Cooley 1956), which was discussed previously. A social interactionist, then, would not say that a child has misbehaved because of a mischievous temperament but rather that this child has learned and interpreted this behavior as a result of his or her interactions with the environment.

Once individuals develop a sense of self, this will provide motivation for future behavior. Because humans are reflexive, they will always reflect on what they experience and use this as a guide for future behavior. This process entails not only a sense of self but also a sense of how others view you. For example, people often respond to a situation based not only on their own beliefs and values but also on how they think others will perceive that behavior (whether positively or negatively). This reflexive process takes an understanding of the self as well as the generalized other discussed earlier. For example, a group of college students who took part in a ten-week expedition to Ghana found themselves not only more self aware after the experience, but also more comfortable interacting with people they did not know as a result of both this new self-awareness and the experience itself (Beames 2005).

Third Overarching Theme

The final overarching theme moves from a discussion of the self to a discussion of society. Whereas the previous themes and their underlying assumptions have focused on more individual aspects, this theme is based on the idea that infants are not born into a social vacuum. Instead, the environment of an infant has symbols and values that were assigned at birth. One only has to go into a nursery to see an example of this. If the room is decorated in pinks and is filled with dolls, what do we assume? We presume, of course, that the infant is a girl. Parents have often used the color pink and dolls as symbols of what is feminine or as an example of the types of things infant girls will come to value.

Individuals are influenced by society. Individuals are influenced not only by their own self-concept, and the values, symbols, and beliefs of their families but also by the cultural norms and values of the society in which they live. Perhaps the changing nature of fathering behaviors best exemplifies this. Whereas just a generation ago it was unusual for men to show physical affection to their children, it is now common for this to take place in today's families. This is because of the changing societal expectations of fathers, which state that both parents should show their children they love them not only with words but also with actions such as hugs (Smith 1996).

People learn the rules and values of society through everyday interaction within that culture. What is the best way to learn about life in Japan? Although it is helpful prior to a visit to that country to read about their cultural norms so you do not begin your stay there offending people, the best way to learn about Japanese individuals and families is to spend some time living among them. You can learn many things during these common, daily experiences that can never be taught in a book.

PRIMARY TERMS AND CONCEPTS

So how do the ideas of all those early pioneers and the basic assumptions given above come together in a practical way to allow us to use and make sense of symbolic interactionism? Again, because of the history of this theory, it is difficult to summarize it in a succinct way that will encompass all of its diverse parts. Thus, perhaps the best way to proceed is to discuss some of the primary concepts used in this theory and how they relate to the things we have already reviewed. There are numerous terms and concepts associated with this theory, many of which have been covered within the previous discussion. Terms commonly associated with symbolic interaction include, but are not limited to, symbols, interaction, gestures, social norms, rituals, roles, salience, identities, social act, and definition of the situation. Some of these are covered below.

Symbols

The title of this theory combines two terms that are of utmost importance in this theory: symbols and interaction. Anything can be thought of as a symbol, with language being the most powerful example (Flint 2006). Symbols are the products of social interaction. This means that we are not free to use symbols in any way we choose. Rather, their meaning is given to us by the way we see others using them. Thus, the meaning of a symbol in one situation may not be the same in a different situation. For example, how often have you seen professional basketball players swat each other on the butt as they come off the court for a time out? Now, what if you saw a man and woman walking down the street, and the man reached over and swatted the woman on the butt. Does the action of hitting the person on the butt represent the same thing in each of these situations? Obviously not. We would assume in the basketball example that it is symbolic of encouragement or praise, whereas it might be evidence of intimacy in the example of the couple on the street. How you define the symbol is based on the context of the situation or the current environment, and it is something you learn from interacting with others in this environment.

Interaction

It is difficult to talk about the word *symbols* without also talking about *interaction*, as the two terms are dependent upon each other. Interaction, therefore, is a social behavior between two or more people during which some type of communication takes place causing each person to react to the situation and, as a result, modify his or her behavior (Burr et al.1979). This communication can be verbal, but it can also be nonverbal.

Gestures

Gestures, a good example of nonverbal communication, are acts that represent something else (Vander Zanden 1987). We all know some popular, and some not so popular, hand gestures that are used in the United States, such as touching the thumb and forefinger together in a circle to represent that something is OK. These gestures and symbols are meaningless if there is not someone around to interpret and react to them, thus making interaction a necessary part of socialization.

Social Norms

If interactions with others teach us what symbols and gestures mean, this also means that interactions teach us appropriate social norms. Social norms can be defined as expectations about how to act in a given situation. Is your behavior with your friends the same when you are with your parents as it is when you are alone together? My guess is your behavior changes in each of those situations, based on what are appropriate interactions for each of those environments. Interactions with each of these groups, our parents and our friends, teach us what behaviors they find acceptable, and we adapt our behavior based on the social norms followed within each situation.

Rituals

These ideas come together in families in the form of rituals. For example, think about how your family celebrates holidays such as Thanksgiving. Many of us have elaborate rituals, such as who sits where at the table, who is in charge of carving the turkey, and whether or not a prayer is said before the meal and, if so, who says the prayer, and so on. Do you eat your big meal in the afternoon or evening? Who does the cooking? Who does the cleaning? What happens after the meal? Each family has its own social norms for how they interact with each other during holidays and which symbols and gestures are an appropriate part of those rituals. Problems can arise when individuals marry and attempt to negotiate which family's rituals will be carried out in the new married couple's household because people often enter into marriage assuming their family's traditions will be continued. Thus, it would be good to talk about this before marriage takes place so that you can decide which behaviors to adopt.

Roles

Another thing that can influence our behavior in any social situation is our self-defined role. A role is a set of social norms for a specific situation, or "part." Think about actors in a play, each playing a character or a role. The same is true of each of us in life. What are some roles you play? Maybe you are a son or daughter, brother or sister, roommate, athlete, or even a husband or wife. Are the expectations for each of these roles the same? Not only do the expectations differ across roles they can also differ across people who have the same role. For example, all of you reading this book right now are probably doing so not because of some burning desire to know more about family theories but because it was assigned to you in one of your courses in your role as a student. Some people think the role of a student is to read assigned chapters prior to class, participate in class discussion, study for exams, and complete assignments on time. Others, however, see their role as a student as enjoying an active social life, perhaps playing a sport, attending class when it is convenient, and completing assignments when they have time. For still others, the role of student means attending class and completing assignments when time permits after working a forty-hour week and taking care of a family as well. The bottom line is that each person defines for him- or herself what is appropriate behavior for each role he or she plays.

Salience

So how do you decide which of your roles is most important, or which one is going to get the most of your time? According to Stryker (1968), we divide our time among each of our roles based on the amount of salience that role has in our lives. The more salient or important a role is to us, the more time we invest in this role. In the previous example the first student described probably sees his or her role as student as the most salient at the moment, meaning he or she identifies most with the role of a student and will perform those tasks associated with that role first. A student might not go home on a long weekend to see his parents, for example, in order to finish a big paper due the following week at school. One possible explanation for this is that he sees his role as student as more important right now, or more salient, than his role as a son.

Although each individual defines for him- or herself the behaviors associated with a role, there are also social norms or expectations for roles. This does not mean, however, that roles are static—we have evidence in many of our family roles that these do indeed change over time (LaRossa and Reitzes 1993). Perhaps the best example of this is the role of mothers and fathers. Although traditionally dads were responsible primarily for the financial support of the family, and mothers were responsible for the care of the house and children, this is changing in today's society as more women enter the workforce and more men become highly involved fathers. Therefore, roles help us anticipate or predict behavior, but we must never forget that they are also both individual and social constructions.

Because the idea of roles is easy to discern in families, and thought by many scholars to be of utmost importance, an entire theory has emerged based on the idea that families interact based on the assignment of roles. For example, historically males preformed the "instrumental role"—being the financial provider for the family—while females performed the "expressive role"—taking care of the house and children (Parsons and Bales 1955). As you can guess, this notion came under attack by feminist scholars, who asserted that it did not account for the role of power and inequality in gendered or socially constructed relationships (Osmond and Thorne 1993). Thus, while role theory is still used today in many ways to discuss the various roles that individuals play within families, it has also changed from its original form to include more modern notions of families.

Identity

As you can probably guess, those roles that are most salient for us are also those that most likely define our identity. There are several points to take into consideration here. First, this is a mental process in that our mental events determine our behavior. Once we have figured out what something means, we use that definition to determine our future behavior. This determination is made based on its relevance to our identity. Thus, those roles that are most salient to us, or which best identify who we think we are, are given priority in our lives. It is those interactions in which we choose most often to engage and indeed at which we most often attempt to excel (McCall and Simmons 1978).

It is here where we come full circle in our discussion of this theory. Socialization begins with the individual who is born asocial. Humans begin to learn about their environment, and themselves, through interactions with others, including family, friends, and school. These environments are symbolic representations of meaning. In other words, we are born into a culture and thus must learn what the social norms of a culture are through interaction with others in the same culture. Through this process, people learn about themselves and others, and learn not only which roles and behaviors are deemed most socially acceptable but also those that best represent who each of us is as an individual. This helps us decide which roles are most salient to us, or which best form our sense of identity. This in turn influences our future interactions with others, as we interpret our own behaviors, and those of others, based on these beliefs. Because of this, some people respond to one thing in a situation while others in the same situation respond to something entirely different. Our world is, after all, socially constructed.

COMMON AREAS OF RESEARCH AND APPLICATION

There are many areas of research that have used the concepts and assumptions of symbolic interactionism, beginning with the work of the early founders previously discussed. While some have suggested that the use of symbolic interactionism showed a drop in usage in the 1960s and 1970s (Fine 1993), its use since that time, and even recently, is widely evident. For example, it was used as the theoretical framework for dissertations on topics such as the meaning of television to viewers (Sohar 2006), relationship issues such as fidelity (Vaillancourt 2007) and dating styles (Rankin 2006), and an exploration of the role of religion in affirming sexual orientation (Mcqueeney 2006). In addition to being used by developing scholars and in new fields of research, this is a theory that is still widely used today in areas such as transition to parenthood (LaRossa and LaRossa 1981), issues unique to African American families (Allen and Doherty 1998; Hollingsworth 1999), and studies of the self such as how accurate people are in perceiving how they are viewed by others (Cook and Douglas 1998; March 2000). This theory is also mentioned often in studies concerning family relationships or how families cope with tragedies such as death or living with Alzheimer's disease. We will review briefly an emergent area of research which is based on the digital age. Interestingly, this theory is also being used widely today outside of family studies in fields such as marketing, which uses it to assesses the meaning products have for the consumer (Flint 2006), and social work, which uses it to inform their practices across all systems (Forte 2004). Finally, whereas this theory was originally used to explain the changing family role associated with industrialization, it is currently being used to explain how families are dealing with the increasing number of women with young children entering the workforce and how this is affecting family and individual roles, perceptions of self, and social norms.

African American Families

Think about the first overarching theme we discussed, which states that meaning is an important element of human behavior that cannot be overlooked. The research on African American families is a good example of this theme, as it is based on the fact that although Blacks and Whites are raised in the same geographical areas in the United States, their lives are often very different. This is because different ethnic groups often teach different roles and values. For example, whereas household work is often divided based on traditional gender roles in White families, the same is not usually true in Black families. Specifically, while traditional White families define cooking and cleaning as behaviors associated with the role of wife and/or mother, in African American families these behaviors are typically performed based on work hours and type of tasks first rather than specified gender roles (McLoyd et al. 2000).

The Digital Age

The second overarching theme was more focused on the development of the self. Recent research exploring the role of the self when communicating online suggests that the development of the "I" and the "me" as described by Mead (1934/1956) exists online just as it does offline. Venues such as blogs, MySpace, and eBay's "all about me" pages allow individuals to react to people and environments in cyberspace (the "I") while learning cyber social rules and norms (the "me"). Because of the fast-paced and fluid nature of the online environment, the "I" is constantly redefined as it interacts with the "me" (Robinson 2007). Additional research on online social relationships suggest that developing a socially constructed sense of community is desired, whether this is done online or offline (Fernbeck 2007). Thus, some people are using the online community as a means of developing the sense of community they are missing offline.

The Role of Intercultural Interactions

The final overarching theme focused on the role of society. An interesting study by Beames (2005) focused on youth who took part in a ten-week expedition to Ghana where they lived among and worked with the people of the area. It was found that students developed a greater appreciation for the things they took for granted in their country of origin, such as running water, toilets inside that flush, and the ability to go to a grocery store and buy almost any food you can imagine. Thus, their interactions in a society different than theirs taught them that how we think about and use symbols changes from one culture to the next, that social norms and rituals vary greatly around the world, and that learning about yourself can help you better interact in any society (Beames 2005).

Methodological Issues

A final strength of symbolic interactionism, which has led to its continued use, is its acceptance of both qualitative and quantitative methodologies. This means that researchers are not limited to one means of data collection, such as giving people a survey to find out how they feel about a certain topic. This theory also supports the use of observations, interviews, and, as you would guess, interactions with others in order to gain a deeper understanding of how people come to define their realities. Thus, its history is rich with people who have used a variety of methods to determine what makes individuals and families interact as they do.

CRITIQUE

Although symbolic interactionism has been used for many decades, there are obviously those who have concerns about the theory and its usage. We will review some of the most common criticisms of this theory below. Keep in mind during this discussion that these comments are often directed toward an individual using symbolic interactionism ideas rather than the theory in general. Stryker (1980) provided a summary of the criticisms of this theory, a few of which will be reviewed here. First is the idea that people find the key concepts confusing because they are difficult to define and thus difficult to test using research. However, as both LaRossa and Reitzes (1993) and Stryker (1987) noted, there has been a plethora of work in this area over the last several decades to address this problem. Thus, while perhaps this was true at the time of Stryker's original writing, this is no longer as valid today.

A related criticism is that the ideas and concepts of individual scholars in this field have not been combined into one central theory. In other words, whereas most theories have a basic set of assumptions, lists of concepts, and organized guidelines, some believe this does not exist in the same sense for symbolic interactionism. Some authors have attempted to develop these theories, but there is no agreement as there is with other theories covered in this text. Thus, for some scholars this theory does in fact have specific guidelines and assumptions, but for others these are not well-developed enough to meet their needs; it depends on your school of thought. Further, while some scholars see this as a strength, since it allows them to pick and choose among the various concepts relevant to their particular research, many would say this is indeed a flaw with the theory in general. This makes it difficult to describe the theory to others in a logical fashion and test the central tenets of the theory, because they are so diverse.

Stryker's (1980) third criticism is that symbolic interactionism does not give enough attention to either the importance of emotions or the role of the unconscious. Although few would argue with this statement in a general sense, there are some aspects of this theory which do, in fact, address this issue. Cooley (1956), for example, stated that people have feelings about themselves, or emotions, that drive the looking-glass self. Similarly, recently researchers have started to study the role of emotions in many individual and family contexts using the basic assumptions of symbolic interactionism. Thus, while this criticism holds true of many aspects of this theory, it does not for others.

A fourth criticism, offered by researchers such as Goffman (1974), is that symbolic interactionism places too much emphasis on the ability of individuals to create their own realities and doesn't pay enough attention to the fact that we live in a world that we do not create ourselves. Thus, while you can spend a lot of time researching how individuals feel about and deal with being distanced from their families and sent to war, the bottom line is the soldiers still must cope with a hostile environment, and their families must still cope with the absence of a loved one. The point to remember from this is that while concepts such as the definition of the situation are valid and important, one cannot neglect an assessment of the physical realities of the environment as well.

Similarly, Stryker noted in his 1987 writing that the role of power is often neglected by the use of symbolic interactionism. For example, while two people can interpret the same situation in different ways, in the current social and political environment it is likely that one of those people holds more power than the other. Stryker suggests that this point is often neglected in the framework of symbolic interactionism.

A current criticism of this theory is its lack of attention to the role of biology. Although there are some scholars who attempt to address the genetic inheritance factor within this framework, as a general rule symbolic interactionists are more concerned with biology only as it pertains to cognition, which in turn influences social interactions (LaRossa and Reitzes 1993).

Finally, it is best to think of symbolic interactionism as a framework for organizing or influencing research rather than as a completely integrated theory in and of itself. While there are obviously some problems with this approach, symbolic interactionism also has some valid strengths that have contributed to its duration in the field. One example is that the theory is able to grow and change with the times, meaning that it is just as applicable today as it was when it began in the 1920s. Another strength of the theory is the focus on family interactions and the role individuals play in those social acts. In other words, one cannot look at any situation as being static but rather must recognize that each person in that situation is viewing things from his or her own perspective and acting with the hope of influencing the outcome of the interaction. Finally, symbolic interactionism reminds us that we are all social beings, playing roles and learning from each other.

APPLICATION

Now that we have covered symbolic interactionism in its entirety and evaluated its strengths and weaknesses, let's see how well you understand this theory by answering some questions as they pertain to our married couple discussed at the beginning of this chapter as well as how they pertain to your own lives.

1. Using the concepts and language of symbolic interactionism, explain how the spouses discussed in the short story at the beginning of this chapter could have such different opinions about the cocktail party they attended.

2. Think about what roles you play. Make a list of them and the behaviors and responsibilities of each of those roles. Which of those roles is most salient for you? How does this influence your behavior?

3. Describe a situation you have been in recently that was similar to the one given at the beginning of this chapter. What was the specific setting? How did you react to the situation? How did the other people involved respond? How did your identity influence your behavior in this situation?

4. What are the social norms for the college or university you attend? How are these norms similar to or different from those of your family? How did you discover what those social norms were? How did you respond initially? List ways your behavior has changed as a result of these social norms and your interactions with others within the college environment.

5. Explain how the concepts of the "I" and the "me" are exemplified in your sample reading. Then, explain how the generalized other is used in the reading.

REFERENCES

Allen, W. D., and W. J. Doherty. 1998. "Being there." The perception of fatherhood among a group of African-American adolescent fathers. In *Resiliency in African-American families*, ed. H. I. McCubbin, E. A. Thompson, A. I. Thompson, and J. A. Futrell, 207–244. Thousand Oaks, CA: Sage.

Beames, S. 2005. Expeditions and the social construction of the self. *Australian Journal of Outdoor Education* 9(1): 14–22.

Blumer, H. 1969. *Symbolic interactionism: Perspective and method.* Englewood Cliffs, NJ: Prentice-Hall.

Burnier, D. 2005. Making it meaningful: Postmodern public administration and symbolic interactionism. *Administrative Theory & Praxis* 27(3): 498–517.

Burr, W., G. K. Leigh, R. D. Day, and J. Constantine. 1979. Symbolic interaction and the family. In *Contemporary theories about the* family, ed. W. R. Burr, R. Hill, F. I. Nye, and I. I. Reiss. Vol. 2, 42–111. New York: Free Press.

Cook, W. L., and E. M. Douglas. 1998. The looking-glass self in family context: A social relations analysis. *Journal of Family Psychology* 12(3): 299–309.

Cooley, C. H. 1956. *Social organization.* Glencoe, IL: Free Press.

Fernbeck, J. 2007. Beyond the diluted community concept: A symbolic interactionist perspective on online social relations. *New Media Society* 9(1): 49–69.

Fine, G. A. 1993. The sad demise, mysterious disappearance, and glorious triumph of symbolic interactionism. *Annual Review of Sociology* 19: 61–87.

Flint, D. J. 2006. Innovation, symbolic interaction and customer valuing: Thoughts stemming from a service-dominant logic of marketing. *Marketing Theory* 6(3): 349–362.

Forte, J. A. 2004. Symbolic interactionism and social work: A forgotten legacy. Part 2, *Families in Society* 85(4): 521–531.

Goffman, E. 1974. *Frame analysis: An essay on the organization of experience.* New York: Harper and Row.

Hollingsworth, L. D. 1999. Symbolic interactionism, African American families, and the transracial adoption controversy. *Social Work* 44(5): 443–453.

LaRossa, R., and M. M. LaRossa. 1981. *Transition to parenthood: How infants change families.* Beverly Hills, CA: Sage.

LaRossa, R., and D. C. Reitzes. 1993. Symbolic interactionism and family studies. In *Sourcebook of family theories and methods: A contextual approach,* ed. P. G. Boss, W. J. Doherty, R. LaRossa, W. R. Schumm, and S. K. Steinmetz, 135–163. New York: Plenum Press.

McCall, G. J., and J. L. Simmons. 1978. *Identities and interactions: An examination of human associations in everyday life.* Rev. ed. New York: Free Press.

McLoyd, V. C., A. M. Cauce, D. Takeuchi, and L. Wilson. 2000. Marital processes and parental socialization in families of color: A decade review of research. *Journal of Marriage and the Family* 62: 1070–1093.

March, K. 2000. Who do I look like? Gaining a sense of self-authenticity through the physical reflections of others. *Symbolic Interactionism* 23(4): 359–373.

Mcqueeney, K. 2006. "Who I am in God and who God is in me": Race, class, gender, and sexuality in lesbian- and gay-affirming Protestant congregations. PhD diss. *Dissertation Abstracts International* 67(4-A): 1377.

Mead, G. H. 1934/1956. *On social psychology: Selected papers.* Ed. A. Strauss. Chicago: Univ. of Chicago Press.

Mintz, S., and S. Kellogg. 1988. *Domestic revolutions: A social history of American family life.* New York: Free Press.

Osmond, M. W., and B. Thorne. 1993. Feminist theories: The social construction of gender in families and society. In *Sourcebook of family theories and methods: A contextual approach,* ed. P. G. Boss, W. J. Doherty, R. LaRossa, W. R. Schumm, and S. K. Steinmetz, 591–623. New York: Plenum Press.

Parsons, T., and R. Bales, eds. 1955. *Family, socialization, and interaction process.* Glencoe, IL: Free Press.

Rankin, L. A. 2006. Ideal dating styles and meanings of romantic relationships among White and Latino high school students: A multi-method approach. PhD diss. *Dissertation Abstracts International* 67(3-B): 1733.

Robinson, L. 2007. The cyberself: The self-ing project goes online, symbolic interaction in the digital age. *New Media Society* 9(1): 93–110.

Smith, S. R. 1996. A qualitative investigation of how men come to define themselves as fathers. PhD diss., University of Georgia, Athens.

Sohar, K. 2006. A qualitative investigation of "Daily Show" viewers: Symbolic constructions of identification and credibility. PhD diss. *Dissertation Abstracts International,* 66(9-A): 3142.

Stryker, S. 1968. Identity salience and role performance: The relevance of symbolic interaction theory for family research. *Journal of Marriage and the Family* 30: 558–564.

———. 1980. *Symbolic interactionism: A social structural version.* Menlo Park, CA: Benjamin/Cummings.

———. 1987. The vitalization of symbolic interactionism. *Social Psychology Quarterly* 50(1): 83–94.

Thomas, W. I., and F. Znaniecki. 1918–1920. *The Polish peasant in Europe and America.* Vol. 5. Boston: Badger.

Vaillancourt, K. T. 2007. Reconstructing the meaning of fidelity: A qualitative inquiry into swinging relationships. PhD diss., *Dissertation Abstracts International* 67(8-A): 3182.

Vander Zanden, J. W. 1987. *Social psychology*. 4th ed. New York: Random House.

SAMPLE READING

Klunklin, A., and J. Greenwood. 2006. Symbolic interactionism in grounded theory studies: Women surviving with HIV/AIDS in rural northern Thailand. *Journal of the Association of Nurses in AIDS Care* 17(5): 32–41.

This reading addresses some of the issues we have covered in this chapter, such as the role of the generalized other and the "I" and "me" components of the self as experienced by HIV/AIDS wives and widows in the rural north of Thailand.

SAMPLE READING

Symbolic Interactionism in Grounded Theory Studies: Women Surviving with HIV/AIDS in Rural Northern Thailand

---

Areewan Klunklin, PhD, RN
Jennifer Greenwood, RN, RM, DipN, RNT, DipEd, MEd, PhD

Although it is generally acknowledged that symbolic interactionism and grounded theory are connected, the precise nature of their connection remains implicit and unexplained. As a result, many grounded theory studies are undertaken without an explanatory framework. This in turn results in the description rather than the explanation of data determined. In this report, the authors make explicit and explain the nature of the connections between symbolic interactionism and grounded theory research. Specifically, they make explicit the connection between Blumer's methodological principles and processes and grounded theory methodology. In addition, the authors illustrate the explanatory power of symbolic interactionism in grounded theory using data from a study of the HIV/AIDS experiences of married and widowed Thai women.

Key words: symbolic interactionism, grounded theory, HIV/AIDS in Thailand, HIV/AIDS in women

It is generally acknowledged that symbolic interactionism and grounded theory are connected (Benoliel, 1996; Strauss & Corbin, 1990), but the precise nature of such connections remain implicit and unexplained. In this report, the authors make explicit and explain these connections. First, they make explicit the connection between Blumer's (1969) methodological principle of direct examination of the social world and the methodological components of grounded theory. Second, the authors make explicit the connections between Blumer's methodological processes of exploration (depiction)

JOURNAL OF THE ASSOCIATION OF NURSES IN AIDS CARE, Vol. 17, No. 5, September/October 2006, 32–41
doi: 10.1016/j.jana.2006.07.005
Copyright © 2006 Association of Nurses in AIDS Care

and inspection (analysis) and constant comparative analysis, theoretical sampling, and the development and validation of codes, categories, and theories. Third, using data derived from a symbolic interactionist grounded theory study into the HIV/AIDS experiences of married and widowed northern Thai women, the authors show the utility of symbolic interactionism as an explanatory framework in grounded theory.

Symbolic interactionism allowed the authors to explain rather than merely describe the relationship of the preemptive strategies used by participants to avoid hurtful discrimination and the distancing strategies used by noninfected people to protect themselves from potential infection. In addition, symbolic interactionism reminded the authors, with considerable force, of the importance of symbolic meaning in social life and that symbolic meaning attaches to differential value systems rather than to social facts, events, and actions per se.

SYMBOLIC INTERACTIONISM

The theoretical basis for grounded theory is derived from the social psychological theory of symbolic interactionism (Benoliel, 1996; Chenitz & Swanson, 1986; Holloway & Wheeler, 1996; Morse & Field, 1996; Stern, 1994), which is a theory of human group life and human conduct (Blumer, 1969). Symbolic interactionism and its related research methods were developed at the University of Chicago School of Sociology between 1920 and 1950. Symbolic interactionism constituted a challenge to the "hegemony of functionalism" (Bowers, 1988; p. 33).

Functionalism views the social world as a whole unit or system composed of interrelating, functioning parts. Parts are generated and adapted based on their functional utility to the whole. Analysis of parts (e.g., individual roles, social groups, and organizations) is significant only in relation to their consequences for the whole. Individuals learn or internalize their functional expectations (roles) through socialization; individuals are determined, therefore, rather than determining (Merton, 1973).

Researchers in the functionalist tradition frame their studies on the functionalist theory of social life; in other words, they begin with a theoretical framework, posing their research questions or problems in terms of the theoretical framework. These questions or problems are then converted into hypotheses, and a study is designed to test these hypotheses (Blumer, 1969). Theories in the functionalist tradition, therefore, are hypotheticodeductively derived from grand theories that are logically derived (what researchers now term *armchair theorizing*).

Social interactionism, a "barbaric neologism" first coined by Blumer in 1937 (Blumer, 1969, p. 1) differs substantially from functionalism in both theoretical perspective and research methods. Symbolic interactionism is theoretically focused on the acting individual; the individual is regarded as determining rather than determined and society is constructed through the purposive interactions of individuals and groups. The theories of symbolic interactionism are empirically and (primarily) inductively derived. The central concepts of symbolic interactionism include the self, the world, and social action (Charon, 1995).

The Self

The self is constructed through social interaction, first with significant others (i.e., those directly responsible for socialization) such as mother, father, and then others in progressively widening social circles. Significant others are important to self-concept because of their confirmatory and validitory feedback on actions and responses (de Laine, 1997). Through interaction with people more generally, the attitudes of the wider community are internalized as the "generalized other," and these interactions then function as an instrument of the self's social control. Religious systems, the legal system, and social norms are elements out of which the generalized other is constituted (de Laine, 1997). Such systems or norms are historical creations linked to contemporary situations; they are therefore subject to social change (de Laine, 1997). For instance, community attitudes to HIV infection change as the community's HIV-related knowledge increases.

Self identity emerges in and through social interaction and is modified as definitions of self, the other, and the situations encountered change (de Laine, 1997). The self is composed of two components, the "I" and the "Me" (Mead, 1934). The I is the active, dynamic interpreting component of the self; it is the reflector, interpreting cues and synthesizing them with the other components of the self. The I relates cues to components of the Me (Bowers, 1988).

The Me is the object of self-reflection, which can be defined to "myself" and others. It is the object of personal, internal conversations and represents "my" self-image. Each individual has multiple Me's, such as mother, person with AIDS (PWA), daughter, seamstress. These multiple Me's can exist simultaneously or consecutively and change over time. Who "I" am at any given time depends on the Me that is called forth by the context in which the I finds itself (e.g., when the child of a Me is diagnosed as HIV-positive, the Me that is mother becomes dominant).

The World

The world in social interactionist theory refers to a world of symbols, but this world is the "object world" (Blumer, 1969). Not all objects are symbols; objects become symbols when meaning is assigned to them by the designator, I. An object is anything that can be designated to the self and reflected upon, such as physical objects (e.g., houses), social objects (e.g., families), and abstract objects (e.g., culture). Symbols, which for the symbolic interactionist include both verbal and nonverbal behaviors, designate objects in the social world (Bowers, 1988). A common language provides people with a stock of readymade linguistic symbols. Behaviors can be interpreted in relation to gestures, timing, facial and body movements, and intonation. What this implies is that objects possess no inherent or intrinsic meaning; meaning is derived from how others act toward objects, and these meanings are represented symbolically in action and in language. Such symbols indicate to others how particular individuals will act toward the object in question and allow them to adapt or adjust their own actions accordingly. Symbolic interactionism, then, refers to the social processes by which individuals are continuously designating symbols to each other and to themselves.

Participants in social life are continually attempting to determine how others are interpreting their actions to predict their responses and adapt or revise their own courses of action. Feedback from others indicates the relative accuracy of such assessments and whether the chosen course of action should be revised or maintained.

Joint Action

Joint action is accomplished, in particular social contexts, through a complex series of processes whereby participants fit their courses of appropriate action together (Blumer, 1969). Joint action involves each participant attempting to take the role of the other to determine how objects are being designated (to enable prediction of behavior); to select an appropriate action, verbal or nonverbal; and to evaluate from feedback how the selected action is being interpreted by others (Bowers, 1988). Joint action, or meaningful human interaction, is always designed and conducted in complex, dynamic social contexts; to understand it, therefore, requires its observation and interpretation in those complex social contexts. Symbolic interactionism views meanings as social products that are created through the defining activities of people as they interact. The meaning of objects to a particular person arises fundamentally out of the way the objects are defined by those with whom he or she interacts.

Therefore, symbolic interactionists are insistent that social life must be studied through "firsthand observation" (Blumer, 1969, p. 38) of the everyday lives of people in social spheres. Naturalistic inquiry is the only research mode through which to gain an understanding of subjects' realities, the realities of the objects designated as their designator understands them (Bowers, 1988).

Blumer (1969) asserts that the study of social life requires two processes: exploration (depiction) and inspection (analysis). Exploration is a flexible procedure that enables the researcher to become familiar with the sphere of social life that is the focus of the study. Exploration also ensures that subsequent interpretations remain grounded in empirical reality. The line of inquiry, data determination, and analyses all respond flexibly to what is to be found in the empirical data. Inspection essentially refers to establishing the validity of the data analysis. The researcher conceptualizes the data and then carefully examines it for evidence of empirical instances of those conceptualizations.

SYMBOLIC INTERACTIONISM AND GROUNDED THEORY

The theoretical framework of symbolic interactionism guides the principles of grounded theory (Benoliel, 1996, Strauss & Corbin, 1990), yet the specific links between them remain largely implicit. In this section, therefore, the authors will attempt to make such linkages explicit.

According to Blumer (1969), the methodological stance of symbolic interactionism is that of direct examination of the empirical social world. This involves confrontation with the empirical world that is accessible to observation and analysis, the determination of data through disciplined examination of that world, the raising of abstract problems regarding that world, the relating of categories derived from those data, the construction of hypotheses relating to such categories, the weaving of such propositions into a theoretical scheme, and the testing of the categories, propositions and theory constructed by renewed examination of the empirical world. These methodological principles are precisely those recommended by Glaser and Strauss (1967), Glaser (1978), Strauss (1987), and Strauss and Corbin (1990, 1998) in relation to grounded theory methodology (see Table 1).

Table 1. Symbolic Interactionism—Grounded Theory Methodology

Symbolic interactionism	Grounded theory
Direct observation of empirical world	Participant observation; interviewing; document analysis; videotaping, etc.
Determination of data through disciplined observation	Observation; interviewing guidelines; theoretical sampling
Raising of abstract problems	Analytic, methodologic, personal memoing
Construction of categories	Open coding; axial coding; theoretical coding; properties, dimensions
Construction of theoretical scheme	Core category; categories; subcategories; properties, dimensions; memos; diagrams
Testing of categories	Theoretical sampling; theoretical saturation; literature review; group analysis; member checks

Another more subtle point of association between symbolic interactionism and grounded theory relates to Blumer's (1969) twin research components of exploration (depiction) and inspection (analysis). Blumer's exploration component, or the component that enables the researcher to respond flexibly to what is found in the data, is clearly a function of purposive and theoretical sampling and constant comparative analysis. Indeed, it would be impossible to be flexibly responsive to what is to be found in data in the absence of constant comparative analysis and theoretical sampling. Similarly, Blumer's inspection component, the component in which the researcher conceptualizes (theorizes) the data, then checks those conceptualizations against the data, is strictly consistent with Glaser and Strauss's (1967), Glaser's (1978), Strauss's (1987) and Strauss and Corbin's (1990, 1998) views on the development and validation of analytic elements (i.e., codes, categories and theories). Grounded theory, therefore, is usefully construable as the method of symbolic interactionism.

THE RESEARCH METHOD

The method of grounded theory that was used in this study generally follows that described by Glaser and Strauss (1967) and Glaser (1978, 1992). This research aimed to explore the impact of HIV infection on married or widowed women diagnosed with HIV/AIDS and to understand how they coped with HIV/AIDS. It was conducted in Chiangmai province where HIV infection is highest in women (Cash, Anasuchatkul, & Busayawong, 1995). The researcher chose one subdistrict about 30 kilometers from Chiangmai for a number of reasons. First, the site provides an opportunity to recruit participants from among the infected women who were members of a PWA group. Second, the area consists of rural villages close to the city, where villagers are mainly farmers. Third, there was an active leader of the PWA group who was very cooperative. Finally, the participants were willing to share their experiences. A purposive sample of 24 married or widowed rural women with both symptomatic and asymptomatic disease was included. The age of the participants ranged from 20 to 45 years. Data determination included interviews using interview guidelines and participant observation. The number of interviews conducted with each participant varied from one to four; however, most participants were interviewed at least twice (Foddy, 1993), with the two interviews 3 to 6 weeks apart. Reinterviewing allowed the clarification, elaboration, and verification of information obtained at first interview or cross-checking of information acquired from other sources. In addition, the researcher undertook participant observation when interviewing respondents in their own homes. Field notes were kept of such observations (Russell, 1999), and these helped to inform data analysis. All interviews were conducted in Thai, transcribed in Thai, and analyzed using Thai Ethnograph (Qualis Research, Colorado Springs, CO). The researcher undertook data entry herself; it was very arduous and time-consuming. Data were analyzed using constant comparative method and analysis, and theoretical sampling was facilitated by memoing and diagramming until saturation of categories was achieved. Ethnograph in a qualitative study is useful for analyzing the large amount of textual data. However, in terms of the grounded analytical approach, the computer program cannot assist with the creativity and intuitive nature of qualitative research (Stroh, 2000). For this reason, the researcher not only analyzed the data manually after using the Ethnograph program but also translated six full interviews into English to confirm the credibility of the emergent categories in this study. The study also incorporated group analysis in English (which took place in Australia to reduce researcher bias and enhance analytic validity) as well as "member checks" in Thai (conducted in Thailand) of the substantive theory (Denzin & Lincoln, 1994).

The study was approved by the Human Research Ethics Committee of the University of Western Sydney, Australia (where the principal investigator was enrolled as a PhD student) even though the data were to be determined in Thailand. The study was also approved in northern Thailand by the principal medical officer of the public hospital at which most participants were recruited. Verbal consent is customary in northern Thailand. Consent was obtained from each participant before each episode of data determination.

RESULTS

The basic social problem experienced by participants was surviving with HIV/AIDS, which subsumed a range of physical, psychoemotional, sociocultural, and economic problems. These problems resulted directly from the pathophysiological consequences of the disease but, more particularly, from the social constructions of HIV/AIDS in rural northern Thailand.

The Sociocultural Implications of HIV/AIDS

HIV/AIDS is perceived by northern Thais not only as an incurable infectious disease, but because it is seen as being transmitted through dubious or "bad" behaviors such as intravenous drug use and sexual activity, it is seen as unclean or stigmatizing.

Northern rural Thais live in tightly knit communities in which the closeness of their dwellings reflects the closeness of their social relationships. This closeness, however, impacts negatively on people with HIV/AIDS infection; they have an infectious disease from which relatives and friends fear contagion. Through a range of strategies, therefore, neighbors and friends seek to remove themselves from the risk of infection. Such strategies are perceived by people with HIV/AIDS as social discrimination (Danziger, 1994; Gilmore & Somerville, 1994; Joint United Nations Programme on HIV/AIDS & World Health Organization [UNAIDS], 2005; Songwathana, 1998; Suksatit, 2004). It is also clear that people with the visible signs of HIV infection are subjected to the worst discriminatory practices (Suksatit, 2004; Weitz, 1990).

Northern Thai women with HIV/AIDS infection expect to experience at least some discrimination. They understand how others construe HIV/AIDS through their shared culture by imaginatively taking the role of the generalized Thai village "other." Indeed, at least one participant (P 21) admitted to ostracizing PWA herself before she became infected. Participants not only understood the behaviors and perceptions of the other, but also how to fit their actions to the actions of the other (Blumer, 1969). These women knew, therefore, how HIV/AIDS was designated in northern Thai villages and adjusted their behavior appropriately to concur with this designation.

Discrimination, as examined in this study, took many forms and led to participants feeling different and unworthy. First they were "looked at" very pointedly by village neighbors, and second, they were "kept at a distance" by neighbors, friends, and even some family members. In addition, PWA were looked at and kept at a distance both on an everyday basis and episodically at culturally significant events. The family members of PWA, particularly their children, were also targets of discrimination.

Being looked at. When participants described themselves as "being looked at," they were referring to very pointed looks, the sort they did not elicit before they became known as PWA. Being looked at in this particularly pointed way was to ensure that PWA recognized that they had been designated as undesirable in villagers' object worlds and, because of their shared enculturation, PWA did recognize that they had been designated in this way. Such looks provided the context in which the Me as PWA became painfully salient: "They looked at me as unusual . . . The villagers looked at me. I felt uncomfortable" (P 21).

Being kept at a distance. Having looked at PWA in accordance with their designation as abnormal, infectious human objects and to ensure that they appreciated their new designation as ostracized people, villagers used a variety of strategies to avoid the risk of infection from such objects. These strategies were related to both everyday and episodic activities and were all aimed at protecting themselves by keeping their distance from possible infection. "Being kept at a distance" led to the denial of even mundane, everyday courtesies to PWA; even water was withheld. (In rural Thai villages, houses normally have a jar of water and dipper outside that visitors use to refresh themselves): "Some villagers reject me very much. They don't give me any water. They tell me that the dipper doesn't work. I know myself they don't want me to use their dipper. They hide their dipper" (P 16).

Also, on an everyday basis, shopkeepers, particularly those who sold food, kept PWA at a distance. They did this because they were afraid of becoming infected or because they were afraid other customers would stop frequenting their shops: "They reject me. Shopkeepers in some shops tell me to pick the goods by myself and put money on the table. They don't receive money from my hand" (P 16).

Keeping their distance from PWA and food prepared or handled by PWA also extended into culturally significant events such as marriages and funerals:

> At [my husband's] funeral, many neighbors came. But no one ate the food. They also stayed away from his coffin...uh...some covered their mouths and noses with a handkerchief. Someone said she was scared the disease was spread by air (P 21).

Families of PWA being kept at a distance. The sociocultural implications of HIV/AIDS also affected the families of PWA; people attempted to keep their distance from the children of PWA and incredibly, their dogs. The most common means of keeping the children of PWA at a distance was to require their withdrawal from school:

> My son was not allowed to go to school. A teacher said that my son might catch the disease from his father. She said that my son might bite other students and cause them to catch the disease. If the school took my son, all other parents would take their children out of the school. My son, therefore, had to withdraw from that school (P 17).

And even when children were allowed in school, subtle stigmatization persisted; the personal utensils and equipment of the children of PWA were kept at a distance: "My child can come back to school again. But she has to separate her stuff, for example, her glass, her spoon" (P 21).

Joint Action: An Example

Being looked at and being kept at a distance by noninfected associates were strategies meant to inform PWA that they had been designated by such associates as infectious and "dirty." This designation, however, enabled PWA to interpret, or render mean-ingful, both the actual and expected distancing behaviors of their associates and, in light of these interpretations and expectations, to plan their own appropriate responses to them. HIV/AIDS is still designated as a seriously stigmatizing disease in northern Thailand; when people become infected they know from their internalization of the generalized, cultural other that they should expect to experience social discrimination and ostracism. They also know that they can expect others in their families to expe-rience discrimination. To avoid such expected discrimination, they "hide out with HIV/AIDS." Hiding out was an appropriate response; indeed, its appropriateness is such that it constituted a mirror image of being kept at a distance. As will become clear in the ensuing discussion, the anticipation of being looked at and especially being kept at a distance by noninfected associates allowed participants to keep them-selves and their family members at a distance by hiding out.

Hiding out with HIV/AIDS is a psychologicomotivational orientation that refers to any active strategies used by participants to protect themselves, their children, and their husbands from the discrimination associated with HIV. Clearly, however, the more obvious the manifestations (e.g., lesions) or results (e.g., death) of the disease and the degree of discrimination and ostracism expected, the more participants concentrated on concealing their disease and that of other family members.

What this implies is that the presence of visible and readily recognizable HIV/AIDS-related lesions and symptoms facilitates or expedites the recognition of their bearers as PWA. Participants knew this and accordingly tried to conceal their lesions. Participants found it prudent, in light of the expected distress and discrimination the revelation of the diagnosis would entail, to protect themselves, their children, and their husbands. They told lies to hide out or distance themselves from the truth. They also altered their activities to hide out or distance themselves socially or to physically conceal their own diagnosis or that of close family members from people who they expected would react negatively from the moment the diagnosis was confirmed.

Protecting Herself and Her Husband

Participants told lies and altered their activities to protect the family unit from probable discrimination. They knew that their husbands' positive diagnosis would entail ostracism for themselves, too. They behaved similarly when both partners were infected:

> I talked with my husband, and we decided to quit our jobs. We worked at the same shop in the city. He was a salesman and I was the housekeeper. We could earn around 5,000 baht a month. We decided to quit our jobs at the shop because we were afraid people would reject us if they knew we had AIDS. So we didn't tell the owners of the shop that we got AIDS. They asked us why we were leaving. I told them a lie. I said I wanted to go home (P 10).

Protecting Her Children

Many parents and schoolteachers were afraid that children would become infected through contact with the children of HIV-positive parents. To avoid infection, parents withdrew their children from school. In addition, teachers who feared infection or multiple withdrawals from their school refused to admit the children of HIV-positive people or, if already admitted, to require their withdrawal. Thus, the children of HIV-positive people experienced discrimination. If mothers were unable to shield their children from discrimination, they felt guilty for failing them (Brown et al., 1996). Therefore, to protect their children, HIV-positive mothers lied about their disease:

> When my daughter was two and a half years old, I took her to school near our house. She went to school for around 3 months. The principal of the school told me to withdraw my daughter because four to five students had withdrawn from the school because of her. Two to three months later, the Head asked me to tell my story to other students' parents at one of their meetings. I went there and told them that I had AIDS but I lied about my daughter. I told them I had never tested her blood because I really wanted her to go to school. That's why I told a lie because I knew my daughter had AIDS (P 21).

Parents also found schools that would enroll their children, even if it meant traveling long distances in searing heat: "I send my child to school at [another village]. That school accepted my son; though it is far from home, it is good for my son to study" (P 18).

Protecting Herself

Participants protected themselves from hurtful discrimination, by "avoiding social contact" with people who reacted negatively to them and by "being clean and covered." Avoiding social contact had three dimensions. The first was engaging in almost reclusive behavior, the second was limiting their activities in the village, and the third was resigning from paid employment. Being clean and covered had two dimensions; these were covering skin lesions, dark skin, and weight loss (the common and easily recognized manifestations of advanced disease) and always presenting themselves in public as clean. Both of these strategies are appropriate responses in a culture that still designates HIV/AIDS as a "dirty" disease.

Avoiding social contact. Avoiding social contact includes almost reclusive behavior; some participants chose to withdraw almost entirely from village life to protect themselves from hurtful discrimination. Participants recognized that such hurtful behavior was designed precisely to ensure that they did keep their physical distance (hide out). They also recognized that they had been designated as unworthy, dirty, and infectious: "I live alone. I didn't mix with them. I joined some parties sometimes... I know what I should do" (P 3). "Although other villages treat me badly, I don't care. I live with my son and don't mix with other people" (P 4). "I live only in my house with my daughter. I do not care about anyone. I do not go to join any activities in the village" (P 10).

In addition, participants protected themselves from hurtful rejection by limiting their activities in their villages. Knowing that friends and neighbors still believed that HIV/AIDS can be transmitted in food and food utensils, they selectively avoided engaging in the preparation and cooking of food, both on an everyday basis and at special ceremonial functions. Participants contributed to such events (as all women are traditionally expected to do) by washing and cleaning up. Some participants were so sensitive to the attitudes of others that they refused to eat out at all, always preferring to eat at home.

Participants also chose to hide from possible hurtful discrimination by not going to the temple and by shopping in distant villages where their diagnoses were not known. Participants also made important employment choices to avoid discrimination. They chose to leave factory work to work at home. They also chose not to avail themselves of gainful employment outside their homes.

Being clean and covered. As already indicated, participants tried to conceal the obvious and commonly recognized manifestations of their disease because the degree of discrimination they experienced was associated with visible HIV/AIDS-related symptoms: "I always wear a long-sleeved shirt and pants to cover the nodules on my arms and legs" [she shows her skin lesions on both arms and legs] (P 17).

They also tried to conceal the "dirtiness" of their disease: "When I go anywhere, I will take a bath and put on clean clothes so that others will not think that I am dirty" (P 20).

DISCUSSION

A number of points are worthy of note in the above analyses. First, both PWA and the noninfected share a common understanding of how HIV/AIDS is designated in Thai culture: as a potentially lethal, highly contagious, and dirty disease. This common understanding is a function, as already indicated, of their shared enculturation, and it enables them to fit their behaviors together in joint action. Being "looked at" by noninfected persons is to ensure that PWA understand their designation in the shared object world. It is because PWA expect to be looked at in this very particular way that they strive to hide the most obvious manifestations of their disease by being "clean and covered." They also ensured that any obvious HIV/AIDS-related lesions were covered, because levels of discrimination were associated with the easily recognized or well-known HIV/AIDS symptoms. In both respects, participants behaved as other PWA (Suksatit, 2004; Weitz, 1990) and as cancer sufferers did when cancer was considered a dirty disease (Moneyham et al., 1996). Being clean is to counteract villagers' construal of them as dirty, and being covered is to minimize or limit the amount of being looked at they must face. These behaviors are a perfect fit. In addition, being kept at a distance helps noninfected villagers protect themselves from infection, and hiding out is the PWA response to its expectation.

Second, and related, the behaviors associated with being kept at a distance and hiding out are virtual mirror images; they are almost identical behaviors, and this has some interesting implications. Being kept at a distance is consistent with other HIV/AIDS-related literature. PWA typically experience abandonment and social rejection (Fife & Wright, 2000; Suksatit, 2004). Because they both result in social isolation, financial hardship, and serious inconvenience for PWA, it cannot be the behaviors that are associated with being kept at a distance per se that are problematic for PWA, but what these behaviors mean. For PWA, being kept at a distance subsumes a range of behaviors that mark them as unworthy, lesser people and that evoke the Me that is the PWA. However, when these same behaviors are chosen by PWA themselves (albeit with the same apparently unfortunate consequences), they enable PWA to avoid the hurtful, discriminatory behaviors that mark them as "other." These same behaviors, therefore, mean something different to PWA when they are self-imposed: they mean the exercise of the PWA's self-determining "I."

Implications for Further Nursing Research

The focus of this study has been HIV/AIDS-infected wives and widows in the rural north of Thailand; research into the experiences of other PWA populations in the rural north, therefore, would be useful. Comparative research into the experiences and needs of infected children with parents and those who are orphaned could usefully be undertaken. Another important group whose experiences and needs require investigation is grandparents who, increasingly, are required to support two generations of PWA in their families. Finally, and because the experiences of PWA are directly attributable to community construals of HIV/AIDS, research into the impact of a range of different HIV/AIDS educational programs on the well-being of PWA is needed.

SUMMARY

Symbolic interactionism is theoretically focused on the acting individual, and the individual is regarded as self-determining rather than determined; society is constructed through the purposive actions of individuals and groups. The self is constructed through social interaction and includes the internalization of the beliefs and attitudes of "the generalized other." The self has two components, that is, the "I," the agentic component, and the "Me," the subject component. Individuals and groups interact in object worlds in which meanings are designated symbolically in verbal and nonverbal behaviour. Grounded theory is the method of symbolic interactionism. The methodological principles of grounded theory are consistent with the exploration and inspection components of symbolic interactionism. As an explanatory framework, symbolic interactionism really does enable analysts to explain rather than merely describe the behaviors of interactors in local, object worlds.

REFERENCES

Benoliel, J. Q. (1996). Grounded theory and nursing knowledge. *Qualitative Health Research*, 6, 406–428.

Blumer H. (1969). *Symbolic interactionism: Perspective and method.* Englewood Cliffs, CA: Prentice-Hall.

Bowers, B. J. (1988). Grounded theory. In B. Sarter (Ed.), *Paths to knowledge: Innovative research methods for nursing* (pp. 33–60). New York: National League for Nursing.

Brown T., Sittitrai W., Phadungphon C., Carl G., Sirimahachaiyakul W., Jittangkul D., et al. (1996). Risk factors for non-condom use in commercial sex context in Thailand. (Abstract No. Tu.C.2660). *Proceedings of AIDS Research in Thailand, 1993–1997.* Bangkok, Thailand: AIDS Division, Department of Communicable Disease Control, Ministry of Public Health.

Cash K., Anasuchatkul B., & Busayawong W. (1995). *Experimental educational interventions for AIDS prevention among northern Thai single migratory factory workers* (Women and AIDS Research Program, Research Rep. No. 9). Chiangmai, Thailand: Faculty of Education.

Charon J. M. (1995). *Symbolic interactionism.* London: Prentice-Hall.

Chenitz, W. C., & Swanson, J. M. (1986). Qualitative research using grounded theory. In W. C. Chenit, & J. M. Swanson (Eds.), *From practice to grounded theory: Qualitative research in nursing* (pp. 3–15). Menlo Park, CA: Addison-Wesley.

Danziger, R. (1994). The social impact of HIV/AIDS in developing countries. *Social Science and Medicine, 39,* 905–917.

Denzin, N. K., & Lincoln, Y. S. (1994). Introduction: Entering the field of qualitative research. In N. K. Denzin, & Y. S. Lincoln (Eds.), *Handbook of qualitative research* (pp.1–17). Newbury Park, CA: Sage.

de Laine M. (1997). *Ethnography: Theory and applications in health research.* Sydney, Australia: Maclennan & Petty.

Fife, B. L., & Wright, E. R. (2000). The dimensionality of stigma: A comparison of its impact on the self of persons with HIV/AIDS and cancer. *Journal of Health and Social Behavior, 41,* 50–67.

Foddy W. (1993). *Constructing questions for interviews and questionnaires: Theory and practice in social research.* Cambridge, UK: Cambridge University.

Gilmore, N., & Somerville, M. A. (1994). Stigmatization, scape-goating and discrimination in sexually transmitted diseases: Overcoming "them" and "us." *Social Science and Medicine, 39,* 1339–1358.

Glaser B. G. (1978). *Theoretical sensitivity.* Mill Valley, CA: The Sociology Press.

Glaser B. G. (1992). *Basics of grounded theory analysis.* Mill Valley, CA: The Sociology Press.

Glaser B. G., & Strauss A. L. (1967). *The discovery of grounded theory: Strategies for qualitative research.* New York: Aldine De Gruyter.

Holloway I., & Wheeler S. (1996). *Qualitative research for nurses.* London: Blackwell Science.

Joint United Nations Programme on HIV/AIDS & World Health Organization (UNAIDS). (2005). *HIV-related stigma, discrimination and human rights violations: Case studies of successful programmes.* Geneva, Switzerland.

Mead, G. H. (1934). *Mind, self and society.* Chicago: The University of Chicago Press.

Merton, R. (1973). *The sociology of science.* Chicago: The University of Chicago Press.

Moneyham, L., Seals, B., Demi, A., Sowell, R., Cohen, L., & Guillory, J. (1996). Perceptions of stigma in women infected with HIV. *AIDS Patients Care and STDs, 10,* 162–167.

Morse, J. M., & Field, P. A. (1996). *Nursing research: The application of qualitative approach* (2nd. Ed.). London: Chapman & Hall.

Russell, C. (1999). Participant observation. In V. Minichicllo, G. Sullivan, & K. Greenwood (Eds.), *Handbook for research methods in health sciences* (pp. 431–448). Sydney, Australia: Addison Wesley Longman.

Songwathana P. (1998). *Kinship, karma, compassion and care: Domiciliary and community based care of AIDS patients in southern Thailand.* Unpublished doctoral dissertation, University of Queensland, Brisbane, Australia.

Stern P. N. (1994). Eroding grounded theory. In J. M. Morse (Ed.), *Critical issues in the qualitative research methods* (pp. 212–224). London: Sage.

Strauss, A. L. (1987). *Qualitative analysis for social scientists.* New York: Cambridge University Press.

Strauss A. L., & Corbin J. (1990). *Basics of qualitative research.* London: Sage.

Strauss A. L., & Corbin J. (1998). *Basic of qualitative research: Techniques and procedures for developing grounded theory* (2nd ed.). Newbury Park, CA: Sage.

Stroh, M. (2000). Computers and qualitative data analysis: To use or not to use...? In D. Burton (Ed.), *Research training for social scientists: A handbook for postgraduate researchers* (pp. 226–243). London: Sage.

Suksatit B. (2004). *Stigma perception and health promoting self-care ability of young adults with HIV/AIDS.* Unpublished master's thesis, Mahidol University, Bangkok, Thailand.

Weitz, R. (1990). Living with the stigma of AIDS. *Qualitative Sociology, 13,* 23–38.

Areewan Klunklin, PhD, RN, is in the Faculty of Nursing at Chiang Mai University, Thailand.

Jennifer Greenwood, RN, RM, DipN, RNT, DipEd, MEd, PhD, is adjunct professor of nursing at James Cook University, Edmonton, Alberta, Canada.17, No. 5, September/October 2006, 32–41.

2

STRUCTURAL FUNCTIONALISM THEORY

Ralph and Alice have been married for about twenty years. Ralph feels that they have a good thing going. He works in construction and is able to provide well for his family. He was able to offer Alice this sense of security when they got married. He is also handy around the house, fixing things as they break or wear out and keeping the place looking nice.

Alice is attractive and a good sexual partner. Rather than working outside the home, she has kept the house clean and meals prepared, and focused her time on the rearing of their four beautiful children. The kids have always appreciated her help with schoolwork and her ability to attend and support their various activities. They have been representative of the traditional, nuclear Western family.

Recently, Alice has grown restless and less satisfied. She would like to get a part-time job in order to have some spending money that she could control. And she would like Ralph to spend more time talking with her instead of working on some project in the garage. Ralph feels that things are just fine the way they are—why do they have to change?

But things are changing. With the children growing up and moving out, the family structure is reverting back to that of a couple. Alice has more free time than she had in the past and would like to focus on some of her own interests. Ralph can see the point of using some of his salary to hire someone to make home repairs—but in order to give him more time to watch sports on TV, not to use it for the womanly tasks of shopping and talking about feelings!

Ralph wants both of them to do what they are supposed to do: He works as the provider and she takes care of him. Alice feels that it makes more sense for them both to provide and nurture.

HISTORY

Functional theory, as it is often called, is based on the "organic analogy." This is the idea, developed by early social philosophers such as Comte and Durkheim, that society is like the human body. While the body is made up of various parts such as the organs and muscles and tissues that need to work together for it to be healthy, society is also comprised of many parts that must function together in order to work properly. Each part needs to be in a state of *equilibrium*, or balance. Just as the human body has evolved over time, so has society. Comte introduced "positivism"—the view that social science should be based on empirical observations—into social thought. He also focused on terms that later became popular in functional theory like solidarity and consensus, which refer to the interconnectedness of social life and the source of its unity. Durkheim was also concerned with how social systems are integrated and hold themselves together (Kingsbury and Scanzoni 1993).

The writings of social anthropologist Alfred Radcliffe-Brown (1952) were pivotal in establishing a field of comparative sociology, with structural functionalism as its most important tool. His essay on understanding the role of the mother's brother in certain societies helped to supplant social Darwinism with the new and, at the time, relatively sophisticated framework of structural functionalism.

The leading thinker of functionalism in America was Talcott Parsons (1951), who believed that behavior was driven by our efforts to conform to the moral code of society. The purpose of such codes is to constrain human behavior in ways that promote the common good. The purpose of an organism is to survive. In order for a society to survive, the subsystems (the family and other institutions) must function in ways that promote the maintenance of society as a whole. This is similar to how a person's organs must function in interrelated ways in order to maintain good health.

For Parsons (1951), the key to societal survival was the shared norms and values held by its individual members. Deviation from those norms leads to disorganization, which threatens the survival of the system. Because the family is the key system in society, divorce, teen rebellion, non-marital sex, and single parenthood all threaten the structure or the functions of the family and therefore need to be avoided.

By the 1950s, functionalism had become the dominant paradigm in sociology, and it has had a tremendous impact on family studies. For example, family research since the 1930s has adopted the organic model, with its many studies on marital quality and adjustment. Family stability is assumed to be critical to childhood outcomes, and because marital satisfaction is central to that stability, it must be one of the most important research questions in the field. Further, the existence of any social structure, such as the family, is explained by the functions it carries out for the greater society (Kingsbury and Scanzoni 1993).

The social upheaval of the 1960s led many to criticize functionalism for its inability to deal with change. Parsons (1951) did not see deviant behavior as contributing to positive change, whereas others, such as Merton (1957), did recognize the role of conflict in maintaining equilibrium or leading to a new relationship status. Other writers (Goode 1969) strove to raise the level of theoretical rigor in the discipline. Parsons ignored these ideas, feeling that change always came from the outside (such as industrialization leading to the preeminence of the nuclear family) and that children only learned culturally approved values in the family. He also called on Freudian ideas to support his claim that there were biologically driven roles (instrumental and expressive) that men and women should fulfill within the ideal structure of the nuclear family.

As a result, structural functionalism fell into disfavor with scientists after the 1970s. Holman and Burr (1980) declared it to be a "peripheral" theory with very little to contribute to contemporary thinking. Nevertheless, its organic model and the concept of the family needing to stay in balance are important assumptions in more modern family theories, such as stress and systems theories (Kingsbury and Scanzoni 1993).

In addition, the case has been made (White, Marshall, and Wood 2002) that a considerable amount of present-day family research uses family structure without explicitly recognizing it as a key variable. They concluded, using Canadian data on childhood outcomes, that parenting processes are more important than family structure. There are contemporary scholars, such as Wallerstein and Blakeslee (1989) and Popenoe (1996), who argued that the intact nuclear family is still an important component in healthy child rearing.

Perhaps more important is the fact that family structure continues to play a role in political decision making. White, Marshall, and Wood (2002) indicated that politicians, in making decisions about single parents and welfare, for instance, often overestimate the importance of family structure in creating their policies.

BASIC ASSUMPTIONS

One common criticism of structural functionalism is that it never reached the long-term popularity and usage it could have because its terms, beliefs, and basic assumptions were never fully developed into what we would consider a formalized "theory" (Lane 1994). For this reason, listing the basic assumptions of this theory is difficult, as it depends on which author's work you reference. Thus, we will discuss only two basic assumptions that all who use this framework would agree are central components of the theory itself.

The function of families is to procreate and socialize children. Structural functionalism is basically a theory of social survival. Its key idea is that families perform the critical functions of procreation and socialization of children so that they will fit into the overall society. Theorists ask themselves what is needed for a society to maintain itself and then what institutions or subgroups within that society are providing them. They conclude that the intact nuclear family of husband, wife, and their children is the ideal structure. This is the configuration of individuals in the modern world that works best in meeting the needs of its members as well as those of the larger society. That is, it functions best.

All systems have functions. Theoretical work has focused principally on the functions carried out by the family and what these functions accomplish. Although other functions are mentioned, the procreation and socialization of children are central. The main function of any social system, including the family, is simply to maintain its basic structure.

Parsons (1951) concluded that the best way to do this was for husbands and wives to play certain roles. Males need to be *instrumental*, which means that they are the ones who provide for the family. Because of this, their abilities should be focused on meeting the physical needs of family members in terms of food, shelter, education, and income. By contrast, females are to be *expressive*, meaning that they meet the emotional needs of family members by being nurturing and smoothing out problems in relationships. According to this theory, the biological imperatives of motherhood predispose women for this "indoor" work, whereas the greater physical strength of men leads them naturally into the provider role (Winton 1995).

PRIMARY TERMS AND CONCEPTS

Structure

The structure refers to the composition of the family, or what members make up the family institution within a particular society. Is it a nuclear or single-parent family? Is the marriage intact, or has there been a death or divorce? Structure can also be used to describe the framework of a society or an organization.

Function

What services do the family provide to society? The family exists for the functions that it serves, which in turn enhance the survival of the larger group. We best understand the purpose of any organization by examining what it does, or its functions.

Instrumental

Tasks that need to be performed within a family to ensure its physical survival are instrumental in nature. The focus is placed on providing the material needs of the family members, and it is often assumed from historical analysis that males are best suited for these tasks. This would include earning a family income, paying the rent, and providing for transportation and clothing.

Expressive

The human relationship interactions necessary for the psychological satisfaction of the family members are expressive in nature. They include love, communication, and support and are generally assumed, due to biology, to be tasks best suited for females. Thus, mothers are often thought to be better able to meet the emotional needs of children than fathers.

Equilibrium

The assumption here is that any human system will resist change. Even though change comes gradually, family members tend to function best when things are in balance. Parsons (1951) felt that this is best achieved when the members share the same values and goals and when they carry out differentiated roles—that is, each spouse fulfilling a different role, such as an instrumental husband and an expressive wife (Winton 1995).

The Benchmark Family

The benchmark family refers to the traditional intact nuclear family of a husband, wife, and their children, with the husband as breadwinner and the wife as homemaker.

(Yes, Ward, June, Wally, and Beaver Cleaver may come to mind here!) Many Americans consider most relationship patterns that differ from this ideal as less desirable, or even deviant, by comparison (Kingsbury and Scanzoni 1993).

Deviant Behavior

Merton (1957), expanding on the original principles of structural functionalism, developed a typology of deviant behavior to show how behaviors that deviate from the social norms can still play a useful role in the theory, and in society for that matter. His typology was based on five categories which will be reviewed below: conformity, innovation, ritualism, retreatism, and rebellion. The examples for each of these are drawn from Kingsbury and Scanzoni (1993), but you could also use examples based on wives or mothers or children in their respective roles.

Conformity

Nondeviance is the same as conformity. For instance, a husband/father is a good provider and does so in the approved manner of hard work and achievement. In this case, he has conformed to the social norm of being the family breadwinner.

Innovation

In the category of innovation, the man accepts the goal of material success but attains it in an illegal or otherwise socially unacceptable manner. He is, therefore, both conforming and deviant. An example of this would be the corporate lawyer who uses privileged information for his own economic gain.

Ritualism

Ritualism refers to a man who gives up on success but still works hard. Therefore, no matter how hard he tries, he will not meet his wife's expectations of him as a provider. Why does he continue to try? Because that is his nature, or his ritual.

Retreatism

Retreatism refers to the husband who rejects both the normative goals and the means to obtain them. Drug addicts and homeless people are examples of individuals who might fall into this category. They avoid both the rewards of society and the frustrations that come with trying to attain them. In other words, they retreat from cultural norms.

Rebellion

Rebellious individuals are like those in the previous category, except that they also attempt to create a new social structure. They might argue that material success is corrupting and that we should focus on spiritual or other goals instead. This last category in particular allows functionalism to deal with change in ways that Parsons (1951) could not.

COMMON AREAS OF RESEARCH
AND APPLICATION

Structural functionalism has been most useful in guiding comparative research about the family, chiefly as it is carried out by anthropologists and sociologists who were searching for any universalities in family life. It has also been used to explore cultural variations among families and societies. This research has provided the foundation upon which much of modern family science is built. Even though this framework has basically not been used since the 1960s or 1970s (Lane 1994), it still influenced much of the work done in the field both prior to and since that time. Below are some of the key areas of knowledge attained, thanks to the structural functionalism framework.

Family Structure

George Murdock (1949) surveyed 250 societies described in the "Human Relations Area Files," an immense collection of ethnographic field notes on cultures around the world. From this, he concluded that what he called the nuclear family was the basic social structure for humans everywhere. It consists of a husband, wife, and their children. This was the minimal structure, and it was the norm in one-fourth of the societies surveyed. The others were either polygamous or extended but had a nuclear family at the core.

Family Functions

Historical analysis demonstrates that, across time, the family has provided many important functions for society. In modern times, many of these functions—religion, health care, protection, education, and entertainment—have been taken over by other institutions. Today we have churches, the medical establishment, the police, public and private schools, movies, and other entities to meet these needs. As these kinds of changes occur, the family adapts and focuses on what it does best (Ingoldsby and Smith 1995).

Murdock (1949) concluded that there were four essential functions that the family provides for all societies. The first is *sexual*. All societies have found that this powerful impulse must be restrained in order to avoid chaos. However, it must not be over-regulated or personality problems and an insufficient population would result. The compromise found everywhere is marriage. Although sexual relations do occur outside of marriage, most sexual expression occurs in marriage, and it is the one context in which sexual behavior is always socially acceptable.

The second function is *reproduction*. This follows naturally from the fact that marriage is the primary sexual relationship in all societies. While many children are born out of wedlock, the majority are born according to society's preference, which is within the family. Such children are usually privileged in terms of acceptance, inheritance, and other factors.

The third function is *socialization*. In addition to producing children, the family must care for them physically and train them to perform adult tasks and adopt the values deemed appropriate by their particular culture. As Lee (1982) pointed out, this is much more than just learning occupational skills. It involves language skills and the transmission of culture as well. All societies depend on the family to love and nurture their children so that they will become civilized.

The final function is *economic*. This does not mean that the family is the economic unit of production, although it has been in many times and places. Here Murdock (1949) was referring to the division of labor by gender: "By virtue of their primary sex differences, a man and a woman make an exceptionally efficient cooperating unit.... All known human societies have developed specialization and cooperation between the sexes roughly along this biologically determined line" (7). In other words, because males have greater physical strength and females bear the children, marital pairs have found that their survival is enhanced if they divide responsibilities according to their capacities.

In addition, the functions of rituals and behaviors within the family are also analyzed. Each culture has its own approaches to birthing, parenting, sexual taboos, and other matters. A productive way of understanding these family rules is to investigate what functions they each serve for the family and the society at large.

Origin of the Family

The questions of how and when the family originated among humans is presently considered to be beyond the reach of science. However, there have been many philosophical and theoretical speculations, and the large majority of them have come to the same basic conclusion: The structure of the family developed as the result of the economic division of labor. Social and technological changes have reduced this traditional (expressive/instrumental) division of labor proposed by the functionalists (Ingoldsby and Smith 1995), but the argument that economic efficiency and sexual attraction are the basis for marriage and family life is still a powerful one. As Lee (1982) explains:

> The family originated among human beings because a certain division of labor between the sexes was found to be convenient or efficient and maximized the probability of survival for individuals and groups...the logic here implies that the origin of sex roles...coincided with the origin of the family. (54)

Family Universality

Functionalists have wanted to determine if the family exists worldwide as a social institution. If it does, then it can be said that the family may be necessary for the survival of human society. However, if it can be demonstrated that there exists even one culture without the family as we define it, then it must be concluded that although the family unit is common, there are viable alternatives. Murdock's (1949) research convinced him that the nuclear family is universal and necessary for human social life:

> No society, in short, has succeeded in finding an adequate substitute for the nuclear family, to which to transfer these functions. It is highly doubtful whether any society ever will succeed in such an attempt, utopian proposals for the abolition of the family to the contrary notwithstanding. (11)

Stephens (1963) described the work of Edith Clarke in Jamaica, and Melford Spiro with the Israeli kibbutz, which tells a different story. Clarke argued that fathers are missing from lower-class Jamaican families and thus the structure is a mother–child dyad rather than the father–mother–child triangle of the nuclear family. Similarly, Spiro's work gives the impression that the socialization and economic functions are not provided by the family in the kibbutz. Despite these studies, careful review by scholars has rejected these arguments and found in favor of Murdock's ideas instead.

However, Lee (1982) demonstrated that there are a few stable societies, such as the Nayar of India, in which biological fathers do not live with or provide for their families or help socialize their children. Mother–child dyads, typically with help from other male relatives, do exist as the norm in a few places and function much like single-parent families do in the modern Western world. By means of comparison, divorce can be said to provide the important function of enabling adults to escape from difficult relationships, and single parenting may become a necessary adaptation to that situation. In these other societies, however, mother-only parenting is the preferred family structure, even though the couple remains married.

A case could also be made that there are other functions beyond Murdock's four that are emerging as important family contributions to society. The principal one would be providing companionship and emotional support to its members. While love is not yet found to be essential for marriages everywhere, it is playing an ever greater role in urban, industrialized societies (Ingoldsby and Smith 1995). Given that in 2007 more than half of the world's population was living in cities, this is becoming increasingly important (Population Reference Bureau 2007).

Marital Structure

Students are often surprised to learn that historically polygyny (plural wives) is the preferred marital structure in over three-fourths of all societies. This is the case in spite of the fact that the relatively balanced sex ratio results in most people practicing monogamy. The temptation has always been to blame polygyny on the male sex drive, although functionalists make a very convincing case that it is actually about economics. Societies that engage in light agriculture and animal husbandry tend to prefer polygyny because the labor of women and children creates wealth and, therefore, these families are better off than monogamous ones. By contrast, polyandrous (multiple husbands) unions, which are very rare, appear to be adaptations to economic poverty due to living in a harsh environment (Ingoldsby and Smith 1995).

Working Women

Early functionalists found working mothers to be destabilizing and, therefore, a threat to quality child rearing. Political conservatives who continue to take that position blame uncaring and greedy mothers in a materialistic society. However, structural functionalism tends to look to outside forces, particularly economics, to explain change—for example, the rise in the number of working mothers since the 1960s has resulted from the shift in the United States from a manufacturing to a service economy. Because these new salaries are much lower than those paid for skilled factory work, couples have found it necessary for both of them to work outside the home in order to maintain a middle-class lifestyle. In this way, many valued supports for their children, such as music lessons and sports activities, can continue to be provided. This theory always encourages us to look to larger societal forces to explain changes in the family as it adapts only when there are other factors which require change in order for the family to reestablish equilibrium.

Use by Other Fields of Study

While there are probably many similar fields of study which have benefited from the earlier work of structural functional theorists, one field which frequently used this approach was political science (Lane 1994). In fact, Groth (1970) suggested that "among the recent approaches to the study of politics one of the most stimulating as well as influential has been structural functionalism" (485). It is useful for this field because it stimulates research, can fit together pieces of the puzzle which seem very different, and can help to compare two areas or types of politics which on the surface seem very different. Silverman and Gulliver (2006) further stated that it allows for a comparative analysis of different political systems, and aides in the cross-cultural comparison of diverse political structures.

One interesting area of research, especially given the current "graying of America," is in the relationship between aging and cumulative advantage/disadvantage (CAD). CAD is based on the principle that some people are more advantaged when it comes to resources, where they live, financial status, health, and so on, and that the gap between those who are advantaged and those who are not is widening. It also suggests that this is not purely a matter of individual characteristics or abilities but is also reliant on the society in which one lives and the structures set forth in that society. Thus, it makes sense that structural functionalism might be applied to develop a better understanding of CAD because it is focused on figuring out how structures which are in place meet the functions needed by a system (Dannefer 2003).

Finally, Chilcott (1998) wrote an interesting article asserting that structural functionalism could be modified to help analyze the school systems. If you consider the school itself as a system, with people such as principals, teachers, and students each playing roles within that system, you could use this framework to better understand why that system does and does not work. You could also research how those roles work together to form an integrated whole. Thus, you can see from this brief review of the literature that while structural functionalism itself has not been used much in research in recent years, it has been influential in many different ways and modified for many uses over the years making it an important component of the history of family theories.

CRITIQUE

A number of problems have contributed to the general decline in the acceptance of and use of structural functionalism. The main ones are listed below (see Kingsbury and Scanzoni [1993] and Winton [1995] for a more detailed description).

First, very few scientific ideas can be completely free of the dominant values of society, and structural functionalism is no exception. Historically, it developed in a conservative time and, therefore, values traits that were popular at the time, such as structure, stability, and unity. As political views and cultural values have changed, support of the theory has waned.

At a deeper level, the theory is criticized for confusing "function" with "cause." Even though it may be possible to demonstrate that families perform certain functions that are necessary to society, it does not necessarily serve as a causal explanation for why families exist. The theory does not do a good job of explaining the historical process of how family types come to exist in a given society.

Chilcott (1998) also suggested that structural functionalism does not adequately account for change. Because it is based on a static model of society, explaining change becomes difficult. Similarly, he states that dysfunction is not dealt with in a way that is helpful. Both of these, however, have been addressed by people who use this theory as a basis from which to start rather than as their only theoretical framework.

Functionalism also focuses on a macroanalysis of large social systems and assumes that maintaining a steady state is important. Many other theorists feel that understanding the interpersonal struggles that go on in family life are critical and that disagreement must be assumed to be intrinsic to family life.

Finally, some theorists have made the mistake of assuming that just because something is functional, it deserves to be maintained. Feminists in particular have been offended by the notion that women should always perform expressive tasks because this is seen as hurting their status in the system. Therefore, the status quo is dysfunctional for women, even if it has been functional for the rest of the family or the overall society in some times and places. This can be further expanded to include the notion that this theoretical model would be problematic when applied to same sex relationships. This has been the most damaging critique of the theory.

However, structural functionalism has a number of strengths that result in its usefulness in family studies today. As mentioned previously, the organic analogy is still used in other more current theoretical approaches. Family systems theory takes the basic concepts of equilibrium and roles and successfully applies them to a microanalysis of family relationships.

As the research examples in the chapter demonstrate, the theory is very useful for cross-cultural scholarship. No other framework has been as successful in providing us with an understanding of different family forms and why they work at various times and in various places. An example would be the relationship between marital structure (monogamy, polygyny, etc.) and economy (Lee 1982).

Finally, as Pittman (1993) explains, "the presumed moralism allegedly undergirding functionalism with a conservative, consensus-based, status quo bias, is almost certainly the product of the period of theory development (1940s and 1950s) rather than inherent to the theory itself" (221). For example, the theory itself does not demand that all families need to be nuclear, with the husband acting instrumentally and the wife expressively. Researchers using this framework have simply noted the historical and comparative success of this approach in many societies. As times and circumstances—such as social views and economic structures—change, other structures or functions may prove to be more useful. Equilibrium can change and, therefore, be understood as dynamic. The basic theory is neutral in that it looks at stability but does not necessarily value it as superior to other possible forms. More modern interpretations of the theory have attempted to integrate conflict and change into the paradigm.

APPLICATION

1. Think about the couple described at the beginning of the chapter. How much can we learn about a family just by analyzing its structure and the functions that are performed?

2. Write a short paper listing every member of your own family of origin. What was its basic structure? Who performed the instrumental and expressive tasks? Were there other roles necessary to a calm functioning of the family, and if so, who carried them out?

3. Think back to a time of family crisis. What changes were taking place, and was a new and different equilibrium reached? Did anyone play a rebellious role in the crisis, and if so, how did that turn out? How strong were societal forces for things to remain the same?

4. How typical are the families that you know? What percentage do you think meet the criteria for being a benchmark family as described earlier in the chapter? How well, in comparison, do you feel the less traditional families function?

5. After reading the following article on love, discuss how dating and mate selection behaviors were handled in your family as you were growing up. In what ways did your parents try to control love?

REFERENCES

Chilcott, J. H. 1998. Structural functionalism as a heuristic device. *Anthropology & Education Quarterly* 29(1): 103–111.

Dannefer, D. 2003. Cumulative advantage/disadvantage and the life course: Cross-fertilizing age and social science theory. *The Journals of Gerontology: Series B: Psychological Sciences and Social Science* 58B(6): S327.

Goode, W. J. 1969. The theoretical importance of love. *American Sociological Review* 34: 38–47.

Groth, A. J. 1970. Structural functionalism and political development: Three problems. *The Western Political Quarterly* 23(3): 485–499.

Holman, T., and W. Burr. 1980. Beyond the beyond: The growth of family theories in the 1970's. *Journal of Marriage and the Family* 42: 729–742.

Ingoldsby, B., and S. Smith. 1995. *Families in multicultural perspective*. New York: Guilford.

Kingsbury, N., and J. Scanzoni. 1993. Structural-functionalism. In *Sourcebook of family theories and methods: A contextual approach*, ed. P. G. Boss, W. J. Doherty, R. LaRossa, W. R. Schumm, and S. K. Steinmetz, 195–217. New York: Plenum.

Lane, R. 1994. Structural-functionalism reconsidered: A proposed research model. *Comparative Politics* 26(4): 461–477.

Lee, G. 1982. *Family structure and interaction: A comparative analysis*. Minneapolis: University of Minnesota Press.

Merton, R. K. 1957. *Social theory and social structure*. Glencoe, IL: Free Press.

Murdock, G. P. 1949. *Social structure*. New York: Free Press.

Parsons, T. 1951. *The social system*. New York: Free Press.

Pittman, J. 1993. Functionalism may be down, but it is not out: Another point of view for family therapists and policy analysts. In *Sourcebook of family theories and methods: A contextual approach*, ed. P. G. Boss, W. J. Doherty, R. LaRossa, W. R. Schumm, and S. K. Steinmetz, 218–221. New York: Plenum.

Popenoe, D. 1996. *Life without father*. New York: Free Press.

Population Reference Bureau. 2007. *World population data sheet*. http://www.prb.org (accessed January 8, 2007).

Radcliffe-Brown, A. 1952. *Structures and function in primitive society*. Glencoe, IL: Free Press.

Silverman, M., and P. H. Gulliver. 2006. "Common sense" and "governmentality": Local government in southeastern Ireland, 1850–1922. *Journal of Royal Anthropology* 12: 109–127.

Stephens, W. 1963. *The family in cross-cultural perspective*. New York: Holt, Rinehart, & Winston.

Wallerstein, J., and S. Blakeslee. 1989. *Second chances: Men, women, and children a decade after divorce*. New York: Ticknor and Fields.

White, J., S. Marshall, and J. Wood. 2002. Confusing family structures: The role of family structure in relation to child well-being. Paper presented at the North West Council on Family Relations, Vancouver, British Columbia, Canada.

Winton, C. 1995. *Frameworks for studying families*. Guilford, CT: Duskin Publishing Group.

SAMPLE READING

Goode, W. J. 1969. The theoretical importance of love. *American Sociological Review* 34: 38–47.

This chapter concludes with a copy of the classic article by William Goode in which he takes a historical and cross-cultural look at love and analyzes its function in society and family life. He concludes that it must generally be controlled, to varying degrees, in the interest of mate selection processes that contribute to societal goals of chastity, social and kinship structure, and economics.

SAMPLE READING

THE THEORETICAL IMPORTANCE OF LOVE*

William J. Goode
Columbia University

Love is analyzed as an element of social action and therefore of social structure. Although the romantic complex is rare, a "love pattern" is found in a wide range of societies. Since love is potentially disruptive of lineages and class strata, it must be controlled. Since its meaning is different within different social structures, it is controlled by various measures. The five principal types of "love control" are described. Disruptions are more important to the upper social strata, who possess the means for control. Therefore these strata achieve a higher degree of control over both the occurrence of love relationships and the influence of love upon action.

Because love often determines the intensity of an attraction[1] toward or away from an intimate relationship with another person, it can become one element in a decision or action.[2] Nevertheless, serious sociological attention has only infrequently been given to love. Moreover, analyses of love generally have been confined to mate choice in the Western World, while the structural importance of love has been for the most part ignored. The present paper, views love in a broad perspective, focusing on the structural patterns by which societies keep in check the potentially disruptive effect of love relationships on mate choice and stratification systems.

TYPES OF LITERATURE ON LOVE

For obvious reasons, the printed material on love is immense. For our present purposes, it may be classified as follows:

1. Poetic, humanistic, literary, erotic, pornographic: By far the largest body of all literature on love views it as a sweeping experience. The poet arouses our sympathy

---

*This paper was completed under a grant (No. M-2526-S) by the National Institute of Mental Health.

and empathy. The essayist enjoys, and asks the reader to enjoy, the interplay of people in love. The storyteller—Bocaccio, Chaucer, Dante—pulls back the curtain of human souls and lets the reader watch the intimate lives of others caught in an emotion we all know. Others—Vatsyayana, Ovid, William IX Count of Poitiers and Duke of Aquitaine, Marie de France, Andreas Capellanus—have written how-to-do-it books, that is, how to conduct oneself in love relations, to persuade others to succumb to one's love wishes, or to excite and satisfy one's sex partner.[3]

2. Marital counseling: Many modern sociologists have commented on the importance of romantic love in America and its lesser importance in other societies and have disparaged it as a poor basis for marriage, or as immaturity. Perhaps the best known of these arguments are those of Ernest R. Mowrer, Ernest W. Burgess, Mabel A. Elliott, Andrew G. Truxal, Francis E. Merrill, and Ernest R. Groves.[4] The antithesis of romantic love, in such analyses, is "conjugal" love; the love between a settled, domestic couple.

A few sociologists, remaining within this same evaluative context, have instead claimed that love also has salutary effects in our society. Thus, for example, William L. Kolb[5] has tried to demonstrate that the marital counselors who attack romantic love are really attacking some fundamental values of our larger society, such as individualism, freedom, and personality growth. Beigel[6] has argued that if the female is sexually repressed, only the psychotherapist or love can help her overcome her inhibitions. He claims further that one influence of love in our society is that it extenuates illicit sexual relations; he goes on to assert: "Seen in proper perspective, [love] has not only done no harm as a prerequisite to marriage, but it has mitigated the impact that a too-fast-moving and unorganized conversion to new socio-economic constellations has had upon our whole culture and it has saved monogamous marriage from complete disorganization."

In addition, there is widespread comment among marriage analysts, that in a rootless society, with few common bases for companionship, romantic love holds a couple together long enough to allow them to begin marriage. That is, it functions to attract people powerfully together, and to hold them through the difficult first months of the marriage, when their different backgrounds would otherwise make an adjustment troublesome.

3. Although the writers cited above concede the structural importance of love implicitly, since they are arguing that it is either harmful or helpful to various values and goals of our society, a third group has given explicit if unsystematic attention to its structural importance. Here, most of the available propositions point to the functions of love, but a few deal with the conditions under which love relationships occur. They include:

    (1) An implicit or assumed descriptive proposition is that love as a common prelude to and basis of marriage is rare, perhaps to be found as a pattern only in the United States.

    (2) Most explanations of the conditions which create love are psychological, stemming from Freud's notion that love is "aim-inhibited sex."[7] This idea is expressed, for example, by Waller who says that love is an idealized passion which develops from the frustration of sex.[8] This proposition, although rather crudely stated and incorrect as a general explanation, is widely accepted.

(3) Of course, a predisposition to love is created by the socialization experience. Thus some textbooks on the family devote extended discussion to
the ways in which our society socializes for love. The child, for example,
is told that he or she will grow up to fall in love with some one, and early
attempts are made to pair the child with children of the opposite sex.
There is much joshing of children about falling in love; myths and stories
about love and courtship are heard by children; and so on.

(4) A further proposition (the source of which I have not been able to locate)
is that, in a society in which a very close attachment between parent and
child prevails, a love complex is necessary, in order to motivate the child
to free him from his attachment to his parents.

(5) Love is also described as one final or crystallizing element in the decision
to marry, which is otherwise structured by factors such as class, ethnic
origin, religion, education, and residence.

(6) Parsons has suggested three factors which "underlie the prominence of the
romantic context in our culture": (a) the youth culture frees the individual
from family attachments, thus permitting him to fall in love; (b) love is a
substitute for the interlocking of kinship roles found in other societies, and
thus motivates the individual to conform to proper marital role behavior;
and (c) the structural isolation of the family so frees the married partners'
affective inclinations that they are able to love one another.[9]

(7) Robert F. Winch has developed a theory of "complementary needs" which
essentially states that the underlying dynamic in the process of falling in
love is an interaction between (a) the perceived psychological attributes of
one individual and (b) the complementary psychological attributes of the
person falling in love, such that the needs of the latter are felt to be met
by the perceived attributes of the former and *vice versa*. These needs are
derived from Murray's list of personality characteristics. Winch thus does
not attempt to solve the problem of why our society has a love complex,
but how it is that specific individuals fall in love with each other rather
than with someone else.[10]

(8) Winch and others have also analyzed the effect of love upon various institutions or social patterns: Love themes are prominently displayed in the
media of entertainment and communication, in consumption patterns, and
so on.[11]

4. Finally, there is the cross-cultural work of anthropologists, who in the main
have ignored love as a factor of importance in kinship patterns. The implicit understanding seems to be that love as a pattern is found only in the United States, although
of course individual cases of love are sometimes recorded. The term "love" is practi-
cally never found in indexes of anthropological monographs on specific societies or in
general anthropology textbooks. It is perhaps not an exaggeration to say that Lowie's
comment of a generation ago would still be accepted by a substantial number of
anthropologists:

But of love among savages?...Passion, of course, is taken for granted; affection,
which many travelers vouch for, might be conceded; but Love? Well, the romantic sentiment, occurs in simpler conditions, as with us—in fiction....So Love

exists for the savage as it does for ourselves—in adolescence, in fiction, among the poetically minded.[12]

A still more skeptical opinion is Linton's scathing sneer:

> All societies recognize that there are occasional violent, emotional attachments between persons of opposite sex, but our present American culture is practically the only one which has attempted to capitalize these, and make them the basis for marriage.... The hero of the modern American movie is always a romantic lover, just as the hero of the old Arab epic is always an epileptic. A cynic may suspect that in any ordinary population the percentage of individuals with a capacity for romantic love of the Hollywood type was about as large as that of persons able to throw genuine epileptic fits.[13]

In Murdock's book on kinship and marriage, there is almost no mention, if any, of love.[14] Should we therefore conclude that, cross-culturally, love is not important, and thus cannot be of great importance structurally? If there is only one significant case, perhaps it is safe to view love as generally unimportant in social structure and to concentrate rather on the nature and functions of romantic love within the Western societies in which love is obviously prevalent. As brought out below, however, many anthropologists have in fact described love *patterns*. And one of them, Max Gluckman,[15] has recently subsumed a wide range of observations under the broad principle that love relationships between husband and wife estrange the couple from their kin, who therefore try in various ways to undermine that love. This principle is applicable to many more societies (for example, China and India) than Gluckman himself discusses.

THE PROBLEM AND ITS CONCEPTUAL CLARIFICATION

The preceding propositions (except those denying that love is distributed widely) can be grouped under two main questions: What are the consequences of romantic love in the United States? How is the emotion of love aroused or created in our society? The present paper deals with the first question. For theoretical purposes both questions must be reformulated, however, since they implicitly refer only to our peculiar system of romantic love. Thus: (1) In what ways do various love patterns fit into the social structure, especially into the systems of mate choice and stratification? (2) What are the structural conditions under which a range of love patterns occurs in various societies? These are overlapping questions, but their starting point and assumptions are different. The first assumes that love relationships are a universal psychosocial possibility and that different social systems make different adjustments to their potential disruptiveness. The second does not take love for granted, and supposes rather that such relationships will be rare unless certain structural factors are present. Since in both cases the analysis need not depend upon the correctness of the assumption, the problem may be chosen arbitrarily. Let us begin with the first.[16]

We face at once the problem of defining "love." Here, love is defined as a strong emotional attachment, a cathexis, between adolescents or adults of opposite sexes, with at least the components of sex desire and tenderness. Verbal definitions of this emotional relationship are notoriously open to attack; this one is no more likely to satisfy critics than others. Agreement is made difficult by value judgments: one critic would exclude anything but "true" love, another casts out "infatuation," another objects to "puppy love," while others would separate sex desire from love because sex presumably is degrading. Nevertheless, most of us have had the experience of love, just as we have been greedy, or melancholy, or moved by hate (defining "true" hate seems not to be a problem). The experience can be referred to without great ambiguity, and a refined measure of various degrees of intensity or purity of love is unnecessary for the aims of the present analysis.

Since love may be related in diverse ways to the social structure, it is necessary to forego the dichotomy of "romantic love–no romantic love" in favor of a continuum or range between polar types. At one pole, a strong love attraction is socially viewed as a laughable or tragic aberration; at the other, it is mildly shameful to marry without being in love with one's intended spouse. This is a gradation from negative sanction to positive approval, ranging at the same time from low or almost nonexistent institutionalization of love to high institutionalization.

The urban middle classes of contemporary Western society, especially in the United States, are found toward the latter pole. Japan and China, in spite of the important movement toward European patterns, fall toward the pole of low institutionalization. Village and urban India is farther toward the center, for there the ideal relationship has been one which at least generated love after marriage, and sometimes after betrothal, in contrast with the mere respect owed between Japanese and Chinese spouses.[17] Greece after Alexander, Rome of the Empire, and perhaps the later period of the Roman Republic as well, are near the center, but somewhat toward the pole of institutionalization, for love matches appear to have increased in frequency—a trend denounced by moralists.[18]

This conceptual continuum helps to clarify our problem and to interpret the propositions reviewed above. Thus it may be noted, first, that individual love relationships may occur even in societies in which love is viewed as irrelevant to mate choice and excluded from the decision to marry. As Linton conceded, some violent love attachments may be found in any society. In our own, the Song of Solomon, Jacob's love of Rachel, and Michal's love for David are classic tales. The Mahabharata, the great Indian epic, includes love themes. Romantic love appears early in Japanese literature, and the use of Mt. Fuji as a locale for the suicide of star crossed lovers is not a myth invented by editors of tabloids. There is the familiar tragic Chinese story to be found on the traditional "willowplate," with its lovers transformed into doves. And so it goes—individual love relationships seem to occur everywhere. But this fact does not change the position of a society on the continuum.

Second, reading both Linton's and Lowie's comments in this new conceptual context reduces their theoretical importance, for they are both merely saying that people do not *live by* the romantic complex, here or anywhere else. Some few couples in love will brave social pressures, physical dangers, or the gods themselves, but nowhere is this usual. Violent, self-sufficient love is not common anywhere. In this respect, of course, the U.S. is not set apart from other systems.

Third, we can separate a *love pattern* from the romantic love *complex*. Under the former, love is a permissible, expected prelude to marriage, and a usual element of courtship—thus, at about the center of the continuum, but toward the pole of institutionalization. The romantic love complex (one pole of the continuum) includes, in addition, an ideological prescription that falling in love is a highly desirable basis of courtship and marriage; love is strongly institutionalized.[19] In contemporary United States, many individuals would even claim that entering marriage without being in love requires some such rationalization as asserting that one is too old for such romances or that one must "think of practical matters like money." To be sure, both anthropologists and sociologists often exaggerate the American commitment to romance;[20] nevertheless, a behavioral and value complex of this type is found here.

But this complex is rare. Perhaps only the following cultures possess the romantic love value complex: modern urban United States, Northwestern Europe, Polynesia, and the European nobility of the eleventh and twelfth centuries.[21] Certainly, it is to be found in no other major civilization. On the other hand, the *love pattern*, which views love as a basis for the final decision to marry, may be relatively common.

WHY LOVE MUST BE CONTROLLED

Since strong love attachments apparently can occur in any society and since (as we shall show) love is frequently a basis for and prelude to marriage, it must be controlled or channeled in some way. More specifically, the stratification and lineage patterns would be weakened greatly if love's potentially disruptive effects were not kept in check. The importance of this situation may be seen most clearly by considering one of the major functions of the family, status placement which in every society links the structures of stratification, kinship lines, and mate choice. (To show how the very similar comments which have been made about sex are not quite correct would take us too far afield; in any event, to the extent that they are correct, the succeeding analysis applies equally to the control of sex.)

Both the child's placement in the social structure and choice of mates are socially important because both placement and choice link two kinship lines together. Courtship or mate choice, therefore, cannot be ignored by either family or society. To permit random mating would mean radical change in the existing social structure. If the family as a unit of society is important, then mate choice is too.

Kinfolk or immediate family can disregard the question of who marries whom, only if a marriage is not seen as a link between kin lines, only if no property, power, lineage honor, totemic relationships, and the like are believed to flow from the kin lines through the spouses to their offspring. Universally, however, these are believed to follow kin lines. Mate choice thus has consequences for social structure. But love may affect mate choice. Both mate choice and love, therefore, are too important to be left to children.

THE CONTROL OF LOVE

Since considerable energy and resources may be required to push youngsters who are in love into proper role behavior, love must be controlled *before* it appears. Love relationships must either be kept to a small number or they must be so directed that they do not run counter to the approved kinship linkages. There are only a few institutional patterns by which this control is achieved.

1. Certainly the simplest, and perhaps the most widely used, structural pattern for coping with this problem is child marriage. If the child is betrothed, married, or both before he has had any opportunity to interact intimately as an adolescent with other children, then he has no resources with which to oppose the marriage. He cannot earn a living, he is physically weak, and is socially dominated by his elders. Moreover, strong love attachments occur only rarely before puberty. An example of this pattern was to be found in India, where the young bride went to live with her husband in a marriage which was not physically consummated until much later, within his father's household.[22]

2. Often, child marriage is linked with a second structural pattern, in which the kinship rules define rather closely a class of eligible future spouses. The marriage is determined by birth within narrow limits. Here, the major decision, which is made by elders, is *when* the marriage is to occur. Thus, among the Murngin, *galle*, the father's sister's child, is scheduled to marry *due*, the mother's brother's child.[23] In the case of the "four-class" double-descent system, each individual is a member of *both* a matri-moiety and a patri-moiety and must marry someone who belongs to neither; the four-classes are (1) ego's own class, (2) those whose matri-moiety is the same as ego's but whose patri-moiety is different, (3) those who are in ego's patri-moiety but not in his matri-moiety, and (4) those who are in neither of ego's moieties, that is, who are in the cell diagonally from his own.[24] Problems arise at times under these systems if the appropriate kinship cell—for example, parallel cousin or cross-cousin—is empty.[25] But nowhere, apparently, is the definition so rigid as to exclude some choice and, therefore, some dickering, wrangling, and haggling between the elders of the two families.

3. A society can prevent widespread development of adolescent love relationships by socially isolating young people from potential mates, whether eligible or ineligible as spouses. Under such a pattern, elders can arrange the marriages of either children or adolescents with little likelihood that their plans will be disrupted by love attachments. Obviously, this arrangement cannot operate effectively in most primitive societies, where youngsters see one another rather frequently.[26]

Not only is this pattern more common in civilizations than in primitive societies, but is found more frequently in the upper social strata. *Social* segregation is difficult unless it is supported by physical segregation—the harem of Islam, the zenana of India[27]—or by a large household system with individuals whose duty it is to supervise nubile girls. Social segregation is thus expensive. Perhaps the best known example of simple social segregation was found in China, where youthful marriages took place between young people who had not previously met because they lived in different villages; they could not marry fellow-villagers since ideally almost all inhabitants belonged to the same *tsu*.[28]

It should be emphasized that the primary function of physical or social isolation in these cases is to minimize informal or intimate social interaction. Limited social contacts of a highly ritualized of formal type in the presence of elders, as in Japan, have a similar, if less extreme, result.[29]

4. A fourth type of pattern seems to exist, although it is not clear cut; and specific cases shade off toward types three and five. Here, there is close supervision by duennas or close relatives, but not actual social segregation. A high value is placed on female chastity (which perhaps is the case in every major civilization until its "decadence") viewed either as the product of self-restraint, as among the 17th Century Puritans, or as a marketable commodity. Thus love as play is not developed; marriage is supposed to be considered by the young as a duty and a possible family alliance. This pattern falls between types three and five because love is permitted before marriage, but only between eligibles. Ideally, it occurs only between a betrothed couple, and, except as marital love, there is no encouragement for it to appear at all. Family elders largely make the specific choice of mate, whether or not intermediaries carry out the arrangements. In the preliminary stages youngsters engage in courtship under supervision, with the understanding that this will permit the development of affection prior to marriage.

I do not believe that the empirical data show where this pattern is prevalent, outside of Western Civilization. The West is a special case, because of its peculiar relationship to Christianity, in which from its earliest days in Rome there has been a complex tension between asceticism and love. This type of limited love marked French, English, and Italian upper class family life from the 11th to the 14th Centuries, as well as 17th Century Puritanism in England and New England.[30]

5. The fifth type of pattern permits or actually encourages love relationships, and love is a commonly expected element in mate choice. Choice in this system is *formally* free. In their 'teens youngsters begin their love play, with or without consummating sexual intercourse, within a group of peers. They may at times choose love partners who they and others do not consider suitable spouses. Gradually, however, their range of choice is narrowed and eventually their affections center on one individual. This person is likely to be more eligible as a mate according to general social norms, and as judged by peers and parents, than the average individual with whom the youngster formerly indulged in love play.

For reasons that are not yet clear, this pattern is nearly always associated with a strong development of an adolescent peer group system, although the latter may occur without the love pattern. One source of social control, then, is the individual's own teen age companions, who persistently rate the present and probable future accomplishments of each individual.[31]

Another source of control lies with the parents of both boy and girl. In our society, parents threaten, cajole, wheedle, bribe, and persuade their children to "go with the right people," during both the early love play and later courtship phases.[32] Primarily, they seek to control love relationships by influencing the informal social contacts of their children: moving to appropriate neighborhoods and schools, giving parties and helping to make out invitation lists, by making their children aware that certain individuals have ineligibility traits (race, religion, manners, tastes, clothing, and so on). Since youngsters fall in love with those with whom they associate, control over informal relationships also controls substantially the focus of affection. The results of such control are well known and are documented in the more than one hundred studies of homogamy in this country: most marriages take place between couples in the same class, religious, racial, and educational levels.

As Robert Wilkman has shown in a generally unfamiliar (in the United States) but superb investigation, this pattern was found among 18th Century Swedish farmer adolescents, was widely distributed in other Germanic areas, and extends in time from the 19th Century back to almost certainly the late Middle Ages.[33] In these cases, sexual intercourse was taken for granted, social contact was closely supervised by the peer group, and final consent to marriage was withheld or granted by the parents who owned the land.

Such cases are not confined to Western society. Polynesia exhibits a similar pattern, with some variation from society to society, the best known examples of which are perhaps Mead's Manu'ans and Firth's Tikopia.[34] Probably the most familiar Melanesian cases are the Trobriands and Dobu,[35] where the systems resemble those of the Kiwai Papuans of the Trans-Fly and the Siuai Papuans of the Solomon Islands.[36] Linton found this pattern among the Tanala.[37] Although Radcliffe-Brown holds that the pattern is not common in Africa, it is clearly found among the Nuer, the Kgatla (Tswana-speaking), and the Bavenda (here, without sanctioned sexual intercourse).[38]

A more complete classification, making use of the distinctions suggested in this paper, would show, I believe, that a large minority of known societies exhibit this pattern. I would suggest, moreover, that such a study would reveal that the degree to which love is a usual, expected prelude to marriage is correlated with (1) the degree of free choice of mate permitted in the society and (2) the degree to which husband-wife solidarity is the strategic solidarity of the kinship structure.[39]

LOVE CONTROL AND CLASS

These sociostructural explanations of how love is controlled lead to a subsidiary but important hypothesis: From one society to another, and from one *class* to another within the same society, the sociostructural importance of maintaining kinship lines according to rule will be rated differently by the families within them. Consequently, the degree to which control over mate choice, and therefore over the prevalence of a love pattern among adolescents, will also vary. Since, within any stratified society, this concern with the maintenance of intact and acceptable kin lines will be greater in the upper strata, it follows that noble or upper strata will maintain stricter control over love and courtship behavior than lower strata. The two correlations suggested in the preceding paragraph also apply: husband-wife solidarity is less strategic relative to clan solidarity in the upper than in the lower strata, and there is less free choice of mate.

Thus it is that, although in Polynesia generally most youngsters indulged in considerable love play, princesses were supervised strictly.[40] Similarly, in China lower class youngsters often met their spouses before marriage.[41] In our own society, the "upper upper" class maintains much greater control than the lower strata over the informal social contacts of their nubile young. Even among the Dobu, where there are few controls and little stratification, differences in control exist at the extremes: a child betrothal may be arranged between outstanding gardening families, who try to prevent their youngsters from being entangled with wastrel families.[42] In answer to my query about this pattern among the Nuer, Evans Pritchard writes:

> You are probably right that a wealthy man has more control over his son's affairs than a poor man. A man with several wives has a more authoritarian position in

his home. Also, a man with many cattle is in a position to permit or refuse a son to marry, whereas a lad whose father is poor may have to depend on the support of kinsmen. In general, I would say that a Nuer father is not interested in the personal side of things. His son is free to marry any girl he likes and the father does not consider the selection to be his affair until the point is reached when cattle have to be discussed.[43]

The upper strata have much more at stake in the maintenance of the social structure and thus are more strongly motivated to control the courtship and marriage decisions of their young. Correspondingly, their young have much more to lose than lower strata youth, so that upper strata elders can wield more power.

CONCLUSION

In this analysis I have attempted to show the integration of love with various types of social structures. As against considerable contemporary opinion among both sociologists and anthropologists, I suggest that love is a universal psychological potential, which is controlled by a range of five structural patterns, all of which are attempts to see to it that youngsters do not make entirely free choices of their future spouses. Only if kin lines are unimportant, and this condition is found in no society as a whole, will entirely free choice be permitted. Some structural arrangements seek to prevent entirely the outbreak of love, while others harness it. Since the kin lines of the upper strata are of greater social importance to them than those of lower strata are to the lower strata members, the former exercise a more effective control over this choice. Even where there is almost a formally free choice of mate—and I have suggested that this pattern is widespread, to be found among a substantial segment of the earth's societies—this choice is guided by peer group and parents toward a mate who will be acceptable to the kin and friend groupings. The theoretical importance of love is thus to be seen in the sociostructural patterns which are developed to keep it from disrupting existing social arrangements.

NOTES

1. On the psychological level, the motivational power of both love and sex is intensified by this curious fact: (which I have not seen remarked on elsewhere) Love is the most projective of emotions, as sex is the most projective of drives; only with great difficulty can the attracted person believe that the object of his love or passion does not and will not reciprocate the feeling at all. Thus, the persona may carry his action quite far, before accepting a rejection as genuine.

2. I have treated decision analysis extensively in an unpublished paper by that title.

3. Vatsyayana, *The Kama Sutra*, Delhi: Rajkamal, 1948; Ovid, "The Lovers," and "Remedies of Love," in *The Art of Love*, Cambridge, Mass.: Harvard University Press, 1939; Andreas Capelanus, The Art of Courtly Love, translated by John J. Parry,

New York: Columbia University Press, 1941; Paul Tuffrau, editor, *Marie de France: Les Lais de Marie de France*, Paris: L'edition d'art, 1925; see also Julian Harris, *Marie de France*, New York: Institute of French Studies, 1930, esp. Chapter 3. All authors but the first *also* had the goal of writing literature.

4. Ernest R. Mowrer, *Family Disorganization*, Chicago: The University of Chicago Press, 1927, pp. 158–165; Ernest W. Burgess and Harvey J. Locke, *The Family*, New York: American Book, 1953, pp. 436–437; Mabel A. Elliott and Francis E. Merrill, *Social Disorganization*, New York: Harper, 1950, pp. 366–384; Andrew G. Truxal and Francis E. Merrill, *The Family in American Culture*, New York: Prentice-Hall, 1947, pp. 120–124, 507–509; Ernest R. Groves and Gladys Hoagland Groves, *The Contemporary American Family*, New York: Lippincott, 1947, pp. 321–324.

5. William L. Kolb, "Sociologically Established Norms and Democratic Values," *Social Forces*, 26 (May, 1948), pp. 451–456.

6. Hugo G. Beigel, "Romantic Love," *American Sociological Review*, 16 (June, 1951), pp. 326–334.

7. Sigmund Freud, *Group Psychology and the Analysis of the Ego*, London: Hogarth, 1922, p. 72.

8. Willard Waller, *The Family*, New York: Dryden, 1938, pp. 189–192.

9. Talcott Parsons, *Essays in Sociological Theory*, Glencoe, Ill.: Free Press, 1949, pp. 187–189.

10. Robert F. Winch, *Mate Selection*, New York: Harper, 1958.

11. See, e.g., Robert F. Winch, *The Modern Family*, New York: Holt, 1952, Chapter 14.

12. Robert H. Lowie, "Sex and Marriage," in John F. McDermott, editor, *The Sex Problem in Modern Society*. New York: Modern Library, 1931, p. 146.

13. Ralph Linton, *The Study of Man*, New York: Appleton-Century, 1936, p. 175.

14. George Peter Murdock, *Social Structure*, New York: Macmillan, 1949.

15. Max Gluckman, *Custom and Conflict in Africa*, Oxford: Basil Blackwell, 1955, Chapter 3.

16. I hope to deal with the second problem in another paper.

17. Tribal India, of course, is too heterogeneous to place in any one position on such a continuum. The question would have to be answered for each tribe. Obviously it is of less importance here whether China and Japan, in recent decades, have moved "two points over" toward the opposite pole of high approval of love relationships as a basis for marriage than that both systems as classically described viewed love as generally a tragedy; and love was supposed to be irrelevant to marriage, i.e., noninstitutionalized. The continuum permits us to place a system at some position, once we have the descriptive data.

18. See Ludwig Friedländer, *Roman Life and Manners under the Early Empire* (Seventh Edition), translated by A. Magnus, New York: Dutton, 1908, Vol. 1 Chapter 5, "The Position of Women."

19. For a discussion of the relation between behavior patterns and the process of institutionalization, see my *After Divorce*, Glencoe, Ill.: Free Press, 1956, Chapter 15.

20. See Ernest W. Burgess and Paul W. Wallin, *Engagement and Marriage*, New York: Lippincott, 1953, Chapter 7 for the extent to which even the engaged are not blind to the defects of their beloveds. No one has ascertained the degree to which various age and sex groups in our society actually believe in some form of the ideology.

Similarly, Margaret Mead in *Coming of Age in Samoa*, New York: Modern Library, 1953, rates Manu'an love as shallow, and though these Samoans give much attention to love-making, she asserts that they laughed with incredulous contempt at Romeo and Juliet (pp. 155–156). Though the individual sufferer showed jealousy and anger, the Manu'ans believed that a new love would quickly cure a betrayed love (pp. 105–108). It is possible that Mead failed to understand the shallowness of love in our own society: Romantic love is, "in our civilization, inextricably bound up with ideas of monogamy, exclusiveness, jealousy, and undeviating fidelity" (p. 105). But these are *ideas* and ideology; behavior is rather different.

21. I am preparing an analysis of this case. The relation of "courtly love" to social structure is complicated.

22. Frieda M. Das, *Purdah*, New York: Vanguard, 1932; Kingsley Davis, *The Population of India and Pakistan*, Princeton: Princeton University Press, 1951, p. 112. There was a widespread custom of taking one's bride from a village other than one's own.

23. W. Lloyd Warner, *Black Civilization*, New York: Harper, 1937, pp. 82–84. They may also become "sweethearts" at puberty; see pp. 86–89.

24. See Murdock, *op. cit.*, pp. 53 ff. *et passim* for discussions of double-descent.

25. One adjustment in Australia was for the individuals to leave the tribe for a while, usually eloping, and then to return "reborn" under a different and now appropriate kinship designation. In any event, these marital prescriptions did not prevent love entirely. As Malinowski shows in his early summary of the Australian family systems, although everyone of the tribes used the technique of infant betrothal (and close prescription of mate), no tribe was free of elopements, between either the unmarried, and the "motive of sexual love" was always to be found in marriages by elopement, B. Malinowski. *The Family Among the Australian Aborigines*, London: University of London Press, 1913, p. 83.

26. This pattern was apparently achieved in Manus, where on first menstruation the girl was removed from her playmates and kept at "home"—on stilts over a lagoon—under the close supervision of elders. The Manus were prudish, and love occurred rarely or never. Margaret Mead, *Growing Up in New Guinea*, in *From the South Seas*, New York: Morrow, 1939, pp. 163–166, 208.

27. See Das, *op. cit.*

28. For the activities of the tsu, see Hsien Chin Hu, *The Common Descent Group in China and Its Functions*, New York: Viking Fund Studies in Anthropology, 10 (1948). For the marriage process, see Marion J. Levy, *The Family Revolution in Modern China*, Cambridge: Harvard University Press, 1949, pp. 87–107. See also Olga Lang, *Chinese Family and Society*, New Haven: Yale University Press, 1946, for comparisons between the old and new systems. In one-half of 62 villages in Ting Hsien Experimental District in Hopei, the largest clan included 50 percent of the families; in 25 percent of the villages, the two largest clans held over 90 percent of the families; I am indebted

to Robert M. Marsh who has been carrying out a study of Ching mobility partly under my direction for this reference: F. C. H. Lee, *Ting Hsien. She-hui K'ai-K'uang t'iao-ch'a*, Peiping: Chuung-hua p'ing-min Chiao-yu ts'u-chin hui, 1932, p. 54. See also Sidney Gamble, *Ting Hsien: A North China Rural Community*, New York: International Secretariat of the Institute of Pacific Relations, 1954.

29. For Japan, see Shidzué Ishimoto, *Facing Two Ways*, New York: Farrar and Rinehart, 1935, Chapters 6, 8; John F. Embree, *Suye Mura*, Chicago: University of Chicago Press, 1950, Chapters 3, 6.

30. I do not mean, of course, to restrict this pattern to these times and places, but I am more certain of these. For the Puritans, see Edmund S. Morgan, *The Puritan Family*, Boston: Public Library, 1944. For the somewhat different practices in New York, see Charles E. Ironside, *The Family in Colonial New York*, New York: Columbia University Press, 1942. See also: A. Abram, *English Life and Manners in the Later Middle Ages*, New York: Dutton, 1913, Chapters 4, 10; Emily J. Putnam, *The Lady*, New York: Sturgis and Walton, 1910, Chapter 4; James Gairdner, editor, *The Paston Letters, 1422–1509*, 4 vols., London: Arber, 1872–1875; Eileen Power, "The Position of Women," in C. G. Crump and E. F. Jacobs, editors, *The Legacy of the Middle Ages*, Oxford: Clarendon, 1926, pp. 414–416.

31. For those who believe that the young in the United States are totally deluded by love, or believe that love outranks every other consideration, see: Ernest W. Burgess and Paul W. Wallin, *Engagement and Marriage*, New York: Lippincott, 1953, pp. 217–238. Note Karl Robert V. Wilkman, *Die Einleitung Der Ehe. Acta Academiae Aboensis (Humaniora)*, 11 (1937), pp. 127 ff. Not only are reputations known because of close association among peers, but songs and poetry are sometimes composed about the girl or boy. Cf., for the Tikopia, Raymond Firth, *We, the Tikopia*, New York: American Book, 1936, pp. 468 ff.; for the Siuai, Douglas L. Oliver, *Solomon Island Society*, Cambridge: Harvard University Press, 1955, pp. 146 ff. The Manu'ans made love in groups of three or four couples; cf. Mead, *Coming of Age in Samoa*, *op. cit.*, p. 92.

32. Marvin B. Sussman, "Parental Participation in Mate Selection and Its Effect upon Family Continuity," *Social Forces*, 32 (October, 1953), pp. 76–81.

33. Wilkman, *op. cit.*

34. Mead, *Coming of Age in Samoa*, *op. cit.*, pp. 97–108; and Firth, *op. cit.*, pp. 520 ff.

35. Thus Malinowski notes in his "Introduction" to Reo F. Fortune's *The Sorcerers of Dobu*, London: Routledge, 1932, p. xxiii, that the Dobu have similar patterns, the same type of courtship by trial and error, with a gradually tightening union.

36. Gunnar Landtman, *Kiwai Papuans of the Trans-Fly*, London: Macmillan, 1927, pp. 243 ff.; Oliver, *op. cit.*, pp. 153 ff.

37. The pattern apparently existed among the Marquesans as well, but since Linton never published a complete description of this Polynesian society, I omit it here. His fullest analysis, cluttered with secondary interpretations, is in Abram Kardiner, *Psychological Frontiers of Society*, New York: Columbia University Press, 1945. For the Tanala, see Ralph Linton, *The Tanala*, Chicago: Field Museum, 1933, pp. 300–303.

38. Thus, Radcliffe-Brown: "The African does not think of marriage as a union based on romantic love, although beauty as well as character and health are sought in the choice of a wife," in his "Introduction" to A. R. Radcliffe-Brown and W. C. Daryll Ford, editors, *African Systems of Kinship and Marriage*, London: Oxford University Press, 1950, p. 46. For the Nuer, see E. E. Evans-Pritchard, *Kinship and Marriage Among the Nuer*, Oxford: Clarendon, 1951, pp. 49–58. For the Kgatla, see I. Schapera, *Married Life in an African Tribe*, New York: Sheridan, 1941, pp. 55 ff. For the Bavenda, although the report seems incomplete, see Hugh, A. Stayt, *The Bavenda*, London: Oxford University Press, 1931, pp. 111 ff., 145 ff., 154.

39. The second correlation is developed from Marion J. Levy, *The Family Revolution in China*, Cambridge, Harvard University Press, 1949, p. 179. Levy's formulation ties "romantic love" to that solidarity, and is of little use because there is only one case, the Western culture complex. As he states it, it is almost so by definition.

40. E.g., Mead, *Coming of Age in Samoa, op. cit.*, pp. 79, 92, 97–109. Cf. also Firth, *op. cit.*, pp. 520 ff.

41. Although one must be cautious about China, this inference seems to be allowable from such comments as the following: "But the old men of China did not succeed in eliminating love from the life of the young women.... Poor and middle-class families could not afford to keep men and women in separate quarters, and Chinese also met their cousins.... Girls ... sometimes even served customers in their parents' shops." Olga Lang, *op. cit.*, p. 33. According to Fried, farm girls would work in the fields, and farm girls of ten years and older were sent to the market to sell produce. They were also sent to towns and cities as servants. The peasant or pauper woman was not confined to the home and its immediate environs. Morton H. Fried, *Fabric of Chinese Society*, New York: Praeger, 1953, pp. 59–60. Also, Levy (*op. cit.*, p. 111): "Among peasant girls and among servant girls in gentry households some premarital experience was not uncommon, though certainly frowned upon. The methods of preventing such contact were isolation and chaperonage, both of which, in the 'traditional' picture, were more likely to break down in the two cases named than elsewhere."

42. Fortune, *op. cit.*, p. 30.

43. Personal letter, dated January 9, 1953. However, the Nuer father can still refuse if he believes the demands of the girl's people are unreasonable. In turn, the girl can cajole her parents to demand less.

Reprinted from: William J. Goode, "The Theoretical Importance of Love." In *American Sociological Review*, pp. 38–47. Copyright © 1969 by The American Sociological Association. Reprinted with permission.

3

Family Development Theory

John and Natasha Morrison were looking forward to their retirement in a few years. Their eldest daughter, Tamara, was just finishing law school and was pregnant with her first child. John Jr., their only son, was doing well in college and planning a career in communications. Their youngest daughter, Kamika, would soon be graduating from high school. With her college tuition safely tucked away in an education IRA, they were hoping to take retirement in their early sixties. As a couple with active professional careers and three children, they had often dreamed of an extended vacation but had been too busy to take one. They planned to take a grand world tour when they retired.

Natasha's parents, who lived nearby and saw the family regularly, came to visit for Father's Day. The family sat around the picnic table out back and reminisced about the changes in their lives over the years. When the children were young, they all had the same kinds of activities and friends. Now it was as if they were all in their own separate worlds. It was difficult to find time together because each person was so busy and focused on his or her own life. John and Natasha were worried about John's father, who lived 500 miles away and was in poor health. Tamara and her husband were busy getting ready for their first child and establishing their professional careers. Johnny was beginning to show signs of seriousness about a girlfriend for the first time in his life. Kamika was hardly ever at home anymore, staying busy with her friends and after-school activities. She was particularly interested in dance and recently had made a new friend, Matt, who also wanted to be a dancer.

Everyone gathered around the table to watch John open his Father's Day presents. Kamika seemed very excited. "Daddy, I have the greatest surprise for you! You'll be so excited. I'm so very sure! I'm going to go to New York to be a dancer! I've been accepted into a little company in New York where they will train me, and Matt and I are moving there in a month! Isn't that just great?"

HISTORY

Family development theory emerged in the late 1940s, corresponding with the development of the field of family science. It was one of the first family-focused theories,

64

with a separate identity from psychology or sociology. Psychology-based theories, with their narrower emphasis on individuals, did not fully explain what happened in families with competing individual needs. Sociology-based theories, focused on society and culture, were too broad in their analysis. Thus, family development theory originated from the critiques of these two perspectives.

Evelyn Duvall and Ruben Hill (1948) pointed out that families were social groups that were influenced by developmental processes, in the same way that individuals were. Like individuals, families experienced life cycles, with clearly delineated stages, each of which required the accomplishment of specific tasks. But families needed to be studied as a dynamic unit, not as a collection of individuals. According to family developmental theorists, the family life cycle had two major stages—expansion and contraction. During expansion, children are born and raised, whereas during contraction, children leave the family home. This "cycle" of expansion and contraction gave rise to the term *family life cycle* (Duvall 1957).

In 1948, Duvall and Hill first presented their version of the family life cycle in which they identified tasks that would be accomplished by both parents and children. These tasks were grouped into eight stages of development across the family life cycle. Later versions of the theory went beyond the demarcation of stages and tasks and began to focus on changes within the family over time, including transitions and social roles. Duvall later codified these in a textbook, *Family Development*, first published in 1957. Updated and republished many times (Duvall 1957 and the revised editions 1962, 1967, 1971, 1977), this was one of the most widely used textbooks on the subject for the next thirty years. Thus, Duvall's eight stages of the family life cycle are the best-known stages of the family development theory.

Other theorists, building on the foundation laid by Duvall and Hill (1948), worked to expand these concepts. In 1964, Roy Rodgers (1964) developed a version of the theory with twenty-four different stages, but its complexity overshadowed its usefulness. Rodgers (1973) further expanded the concept of family interaction by focusing on three dynamics across the family career. He emphasized that families were influenced by institutional norms, by the expectations that arise from the family itself, and by the expectations that arise from the individuals within the family. In contrast, Joan Aldous (1978, 1996) suggested that family development should be considered in only four stages, because families are often in several stages of parenting at the same time. She further recommended the use of the term *family career*, rather than *family life cycle*, because families did not return to the way they had been at the beginning of their lives.

In the 1970s and 1980s, some family scholars criticized family development theory because it lacked scientific testability. In 1973, Wesley Burr, a renowned theorist and researcher, reviewed many of the major issues in family studies, including the family life cycle. In his book Burr (1973) wrote: "It has not yet been proved that the family life cycle will turn out to be a very useful concept in deductive theories" (219). His concern with the theory was that the concepts and variables were not well defined and so could not be properly tested in empirical research. Addressing these concerns, James White published a book in 1991 entitled *Dynamics of Family Development: A Theoretical Perspective* in which he outlined specific testable propositions and variables for family development theory. White is considered one of the major proponents of family development theory today.

At about the same time, a new variant of family development theory—life course perspective—was being described. The life course perspective went beyond the life cycle view by including additional variables such as multiple views of time (ontogenetic, generational, and historical), micro- and macro-social contexts, and increasing diversity over time (Bengtson and Allen 1993).

BASIC ASSUMPTIONS

Families undergo stages of development, just like individuals. Family development theory focuses on the developmental stages of the family as well as the individual. Transitions from one stage to the next are usually related to changes in individual development. For example, newly married couples, couples with preschoolers, couples with teenagers, and couples whose children have moved out of the home clearly are in different stages of development and have different tasks to accomplish. Family stress is usually greatest at transition points between developmental stages.

There are tasks associated with each stage of development. This concept is taken from psychologically based developmental theories (e.g., Havighurst 1948). Tasks are defined on the basis of normative expectations. Each stage is delineated by a set of tasks that must be accomplished to prepare adequately for the next stage of development. Failure to complete a task does not necessarily preclude moving to the next stage of development but may limit a family's optimal functioning at the next level. For example, parents who pay too much attention to raising their children and not enough to their own relationship may find that they encounter problems with their relationship after the children leave home.

Development is reciprocal. The individual development of each family member influences other family members as well as the overall development of the family. The family's development influences the critical periods of individual development as well. Because there is reciprocity in the interaction of the family and individual development, it is necessary to consider them in concert.

Families must be viewed in multiple levels of analysis. Family development theory requires that family life be considered in the multiple contexts of the society, the family, and the individual. The social context and/or historical period influence both the processes within the family and the developmental issues encountered by individuals within the family.

Families should be viewed over time. One of family development theory's core assumptions is that families are not static but change over time. This "change over time" is the primary focus of the theory. How and when families change, what they accomplish at different points of time, and why they change can be known only if one studies families over time.

PRIMARY TERMS AND CONCEPTS

Family

Duvall (1977) proposed that the family is composed of "interacting persons related by ties of marriage, birth, or adoption, whose central purpose is to create and maintain a common culture which promotes the physical, mental, emotional, and social development of each of its members" (5). The dynamics of the family may change over time, dependent on the needs of the individuals, the relationships between them, and the impact of society on the family. These variables determine the components of the developmental tasks and are dependent on the family "tempos and rhythms."

Normative Events

Rather than focusing on crises in families, family development theorists focus on the things that happen more normatively with the passage of time, such as marriages, childbirth, developmental and educational milestones.

Stages

Probably the most unique aspect of family development theory is its focus on the stages of the family life cycle. These stages are periods of "relative equilibrium in which consensus about the allocation of roles and rules of procedure is high" (Hill 1986, 21). In the model developed by Duvall and Hill, stages are the result of major changes in family size, changes in the developmental age of the oldest child, or changes in the work status of the breadwinner (Hill 1986).

Each stage of development is related to behaviors or tasks that would normally be expected to occur during that stage. Norms govern both group and individual behavior, often defining the roles that people play. It is important to note that these norms are socially defined and change over time as cultural mores change. So, too, static norms regulate behavior and expectations within a particular stage, while process norms regulate timing and sequencing of expectations and behaviors.

Tasks

The concept of tasks in family development theory is derived from a similar concept of tasks, as defined by Havighurst (1948, 1953), in individual developmental theory. According to Havighurst, developmental tasks occur at particular points in development in response to either physical maturation or cultural pressure or changes. The individual must respond by developing new abilities, roles, or relationships. If the challenge of development is met positively, then the individual will be happier and have more success with later stages of development. If not, then, as with other stage theories of development (e.g., Erikson and Piaget), we would predict that the individual would be less successful.

Using this model, Duvall and Hill (1948) incorporated specific tasks for each of the eight stages of the family life cycle. These tasks focus on what the family, as a unit, must accomplish, while taking into account the individual needs of the parents and children. For example, Duvall (1957, 1977) outlined the tasks (as an individual) that a child would have to achieve to develop optimally. She further linked those individual tasks to the tasks that the family must achieve as it assimilates the individual child into its unit. Thus, when a newborn moves into the toddler stage, the family must create a safe physical environment for the toddler to explore. Later, when a young adult enters into the launching phase, the family's task is to provide a secure base but recognize that the young adult's reliance on the family may be more economic than physical. Each stage of development requires the family to change and accommodate the needs of the children as they age (Duvall 1977).

Timing

When something happens has an impact on family life. In other words, it makes a difference to the family when a child is born, or when someone retires, or when someone moves out of the house. This is particularly apparent when there are multiple events occurring at or near the same time. So, too, social prescriptions exist about *when* individuals and families are to engage in particular behaviors or accomplish certain tasks. Pressure exists for family life events to occur "on time" rather than "off time" (Neugarten, Moore, and Lowe 1965). The life course perspective theorists introduced the concept of different qualities of time into family development theory. *Ontogenetic time* refers to the time one recognizes as one grows and changes through one's own lifetime (one's personal awareness of time—like an "internal clock"). *Generational time* refers to how one's time is experienced within one's social group (as in one's family or in a cohort). *Historical time* refers to how time is experienced in the social context or greater historical period (e.g., living during the Great Depression in contrast to being a baby boomer; Bengtson and Allen 1993). Thus, one can experience one's adolescent period as a unique stage in one's developmental history (ontogenetic). But it might matter whether that adolescence was experienced during the turbulent Vietnam era or the late 1990s (historical). Similarly, it might make some difference if one becomes a first-time parent at the age of seventeen or at the age of forty-four (generational).

Change

Something changes when it undergoes a transformation from one state to another. (For example, John and Natasha Morrison's experience of family, noted at the beginning of this chapter, will be different when the last child, Kamika, graduates from high school and moves to New York, leaving them with their home all to themselves.) Family development theory proposes that family relationships are not static but rather change over time. Catalysts for change can be either internal (such as biological growth) or external (through interaction with the environment). The nature of this interaction is reciprocal—that is, the organism both elicits and responds to stimuli in its environment.

Change comes with varying levels of acknowledgment and acceptance by family members. Individual changes become the catalyst for family change, causing shifts from one family stage to another. Changes in personal roles within the family are often the result of individual changes and transitions from one stage to the next.

Transitions

One cannot study change without studying transitions. Transitions are the processes that form a bridge between the different states when something changes. In family development theory, transitions are the shifts in roles and identities encountered with changes in developmental stages (Hagestad 1988). (For John and Natasha Morrison, their experience of moving into the middle years may be dependent upon their sense of success in their parenting roles as well as the degree to which they nurtured their own marital relationship in previous stages.) Ease of transition is dependent on the resolution of the stages beforehand, or the degree to which the stage is perceived to be a crisis. As families shift from one stage to the next, their roles, behaviors, and tasks are reallocated in accordance with their new stage. Some families move easily from one stage to the next and some do not. Depending upon how prepared they are for the new stage, families will respond to the change as either a crisis or as an opportunity (Rapoport 1963). Some developmental transitions, such as when one's child begins school, are easy to recognize. Other transitions, such as identifying exactly when a child becomes an adolescent, are more difficult for the family to pinpoint and to accommodate. Furthermore, crises can create critical transitions—that is, those that occur in addition to normally expected transitions, such as an unexpected pregnancy. Focusing on transitions helps us to understand what families go through as they move from stage to stage (Duvall 1988).

COMMON AREAS OF RESEARCH AND APPLICATION

The Family Life Cycle

Evelyn Duvall's eight-stage model (see table 3.1) is the most well-known version of the family development theory. As with all stage theories, there are specific tasks associated with each stage. The chart provided by Duvall and Miller (1985)[1] provides a delineation of those eight stages.

Stage 1: Establishment phase—courtship and marriage. Stage 1 is known as the *establishment phase* because couples are focused on establishing their home base. There are many tasks associated with the establishment phase of relationships, and as in individual developmental models, the accomplishment of future tasks relies heavily on the successful negotiation of the previous stage's tasks. If couples can blend their individual needs and desires, find workable solutions to conflicts, and maintain good communication and intimacy patterns, then they are better able to handle the tasks associated with the next stages.

In the United States, the establishment phase generally begins with some form of courtship. Courtship is the personal preparation for marriage consisting of three general tasks. Duvall (1977) lists these tasks as (1) readying oneself for the roles of husband or wife, (2) disengaging from close relationships that might compete with the marriage, and (3) reprioritizing, so the couple's interests are more important than those of the individual. The degree to which one is successful at addressing these tasks during courtship predicts success during marriage.

Individuals thinking about forming a couple need to learn about each other's desires, dreams, expectations, and style of living. They need to find out more about each other's habits and hobbies, ways of interacting with their friends and families, and likes and dislikes, from foods to movies to household decorations. In addition to these pragmatic considerations, couples also have to develop intellectual and emotional communication patterns, patterns of behaviors and preferences, and a jointly workable philosophy of life and set of values. Some couples, frequently encouraged by clergy or

Table 3.1 Stage-Sensitive Family Developmental Tasks Through the Family Life Cycle

Stages of the family life cycle	Positions in the family	Stage-sensitive family developmental tasks
1. Married Couple	Wife Husband	Establishing a mutually satisfying marriage Adjusting to pregnancy and the promise of parenthood Fitting into the kin network
2. Childbearing	Wife-mother Husband-father Infant daughter or son or both	Having, adjusting to, and encouraging the development of infants Establishing a satisfying home for both parents and infant(s)
3. Preschool age	Wife-mother Husband-father Daughter-sister Son-brother	Adapting to the critical needs and interests of preschool children in stimulating, growth-promoting ways. Coping with energy depletion and lack of privacy as parents
4. School age	Wife-mother Husband-father Daughter-sister Son-brother	Fitting into the community of school-age families in constructive ways Encouraging children's educational achievement
5. Teenage	Wife-mother Husband-father Daughter-sister Son-brother	Balancing freedom with responsibility as teenagers mature and emancipate themselves Establishing postparental interests and careers as growing parents
6. Launching Center	Wife-mother-grandmother Husband-father-grandfather Daughter-sister-aunt Son-brother-uncle	Releasing young adults into work, military service, college, marriage, and so on with appropriate rituals and assistance Maintaining a supportive home base
7. Middle aged Parents	Wife-mother-grandmother Husband-father-grandfather	Refocusing on the marriage relationship Maintaining kin ties with older and younger generations
8. Aging Family Members	Widow or widower Wife-mother-grandmother Husband-father-grandfather	Coping with bereavement and living alone Closing the family home or adapting it to aging Adjusting to retirement

Source: Duvall, and Miller, 1985 *Marriage and Family Development* 6th ed. Boston Allyn and Bacon: Copyright © 1985 by Pearson Education. Reprinted by permission of the publisher.

marriage educators and counselors, participate in a marriage preparation program in order to be certain that the most important issues have been discussed.

Once these topics are explored, the marriage ceremony is an outward and clearly demarcated symbol of status change for couples. It receives both legal sanction and public recognition and, in many instances, religious validation. Before cohabitation became more common, the marriage ceremony also signaled the end of individuals living separately.

The new marital tasks for the couple include developing systems for acquiring and spending money, establishing daily routines, and creating a satisfying sex life. Both partners must also create new and appropriate relationships with relatives and old friends while establishing new friendships as a couple.

Many of the tasks associated with early marriage focus on the establishment of a home suitable for children. Some of these tasks include developing family-planning strategies, agreeing on the timing of pregnancy, arranging for the care of the baby, acquiring knowledge regarding parenthood, and adapting the home to accommodate children. It used to be that couples did not have much control over when they became pregnant. Today, however, couples can use contraceptives to choose the "best" time to become pregnant. But with this choice comes the responsibility for the couple to determine, and to agree, when the so called "best" time is.

Stage 2: Childbearing families—families with infants. The arrival of an infant brings about a new set of tasks for the family to face. The family must expand both physically and emotionally. New roles of "father" and "mother" appear. The couple must now negotiate how they will share the new responsibilities of caring for the child and must reallocate previously assigned household responsibilities.

Infants are completely dependent on their parents for food, clothing, shelter, and medical care. Parents are also responsible for nurturing their infant's cognitive and emotional needs. Infants require a safe and stimulating environment, which can include car seats, diapers, cribs, and toys. The couple might have to expand their household space by moving to a new home or rearranging their current space and how they use it.

All of this, of course, costs money, which places an additional financial demand on the family. These stressors can be damaging to the couple's relationship, so the couple must continue to practice effective communication strategies to maintain a strong bond. They should also remember to pay attention to their own relationship while they attend to their infant's needs.

Stage 3: Families with preschool children. In families with more than one child, it is not uncommon for the firstborn to be only a few years old when the next child is born (Glick 1977). In addition to adapting to the even greater physical needs of two (or more) children, the family must also adjust to the individual differences and temperaments of the children. Preschoolers need structure in their play and activities, and they benefit from intensive parental involvement. Infants also need a lot of physical attention, with diaper changes and feedings, as well as emotional and cognitive nurturing.

Just as in Stage 2, there are the issues of additional physical space and additional financial demands. The more children there are, the more difficult it becomes for the couple to meet their own developmental needs and continue to grow as a couple. Despite the demands on the resources of time, energy, and money, the couple still needs to spend time together doing such things, for example, dining out once a week or twice-yearly vacations away. Regardless of the activity, it is just as important to the relationship to spend some time focusing only on their marriage as it is to focus on their roles as parents.

Stage 4: Families with school-aged children. School is the first public social system that children encounter outside the immediate family. This is significant because families give up some authority over their children to the school. Their parenting skills and their children's behaviors are judged in this public forum. School represents an expansion of the family to other social systems that influence the family in significant ways.

The child's individual development drives the family at this stage. Trying out new activities is a major task of the school-aged child. Families with school-aged children must provide for their children's activities outside of school, which often include sports, music, and religious and social interactions. Parents must work to develop relationships with teachers, religious leaders, and parents of other children. They must develop strategies for accomplishing tasks around the home, particularly if schedules require the parents and children to be away from home more frequently (e.g., evening ball games and weekend birthday parties) and find ways to appropriately delegate family tasks to various family members. Parents must also determine what the appropriate expectations are for their children (who may be at different developmental stages) for helping around the house, developing responsible behavior, watching television, or listening to music. While it is relatively easy to recognize appropriate music for a preschooler, it is more difficult to figure that out for a ten-year-old. And ten-year-olds bring additional issues to the families because they are influenced by their friends and by television. Because these issues require parental decisions, R-rated movies may be prohibited in one ten-year-old's household but may be allowed at her friend's house. One reason for this may be that as their children's physical autonomy increases, many parents increase their level of parental monitoring.

Stage 5: Families with adolescents. As in Stage 4, individual development drives the family in Stage 5. Adolescence is a time of rapid physical (sexual), cognitive, and psychosocial change. According to Erik Erikson, adolescents need to achieve their own identities separate from their families, and they do so by "trying on" different identities until they find one that "fits" (identity achievement). If identity is not achieved, then the adolescent will remain in a confused state without a clear sense of self (role diffusion). Parents must allow adolescents to establish their own separate identities, which sometimes may be in conflict with the family's values and ideas. Duvall (1957) states that open communication helps parents and adolescents learn from each other and helps to bridge the generations.

The adolescent may express a need for more space, both physical and emotional, more freedom to choose activities, and more activities to do, along with the need for more money to do those things. In addition, many adolescents and their parents have concerns about their futures, including the cost of tuition for college or technical training.

Adolescents are able to share more of the responsibilities of family living, perhaps cooking meals, making repairs around the house, or looking after younger children. This enables many parents to work longer hours and earn more money without having to spend money on child care for the younger children. Thus, families can find ways to develop cooperative and symbiotic interactions.

Stage 6: Families with young adults—the launching stage. When we look at the *launching stage*, we see the beginning of the cycle of contraction of the nuclear family—that is, when family size begins to shrink as the children grow up and move out of the home. This stage begins when the oldest child leaves home and ends when the last child has left. Obviously, this may take some time if there are many children or if the children are widely spaced.

Whenever one member leaves the family, the family must adapt, and this includes reallocating responsibilities, duties, and roles among the family members who remain at home. At times, there is a reallocation of physical facilities and resources, such as when bedrooms are shifted after the oldest child moves away. More frequently, there is a reallocation of financial resources, because the oldest child's move may entail tuition, room and board at a university, a large wedding, or supplementing the oldest child's finances until he or she "gets situated."

As the children leave the physical home, communication patterns change. Daily casual communication around the dinner table gives way to a phone call once a week. The nature of the communication also changes. It moves from conversation about everyday events to crisis management and questions about how to cope with being on one's own. When good communication patterns have been established in previous stages between parents and children, young adults can rely on their parents to support them during the launching stage.

With launching comes an ever-widening family circle where friends and new family members enter into the family setting. From a roommate who visits on Thanksgiving to a potential life partner, young adults' relationships bring a new dimension into the family structure. Similarly, their new interactions may also bring divergent life philosophies into the family. Reconciling these differences can bring about major family changes.

Stage 7: The middle years. The middle years refers to the time after all the children have launched but before the parents retire. In the 1950s, when this theory was first developed, couples generally had their children in their early twenties, and those children were launched by the time the parents were in their middle to late forties. The couple had about ten or fifteen years to accomplish the tasks of the middle years.

One of those tasks is ensuring security for later years by increasing retirement accounts. The couple must reallocate household responsibilities once again, as now they are no longer serving as "shuttle services" for their busy teens. They need to work to maintain a comfortable home but may look for a smaller one that requires less maintenance and space, given that their children have moved out. Although the children are not physically there, emotional ties still exist, of course, so parents must develop new methods of extended family contacts, which can include increased phone contact, e-mail, or visits. Their children begin to have children during this stage, and now the couple can begin to develop relationships with their grandchildren.

So what is a couple to do when they stop being caretakers of their children? For many couples, this is a major transition, as they have just lost the job of parenting that they had for twenty to twenty-five years. Those couples who neglected their own couple relationships during their child-rearing years, expending their energies raising and supporting a family, are at risk during this time. When the children are gone, they may realize that they are no longer really acquainted with their partner. Now, couples might look to this time as an opportunity to renew their relationship with their partner and become more involved in community life by pursuing political office, volunteer work, or mission work. They may also simply indulge themselves, for example, by eating out more frequently, because it is "just the two of them." Most important, the couple must work to maintain their own communication, as they consider what they want to accomplish during the remainder of their lives.

Stage 8: Aging family members. According to Duvall (1957 [rev. ed. 1977]), this last stage "begins with the man's retirement, goes through the loss of the first spouse, and ends with the death of the second" (385). This stage includes the task of adjusting to retirement, including the reduced income that retirement frequently brings. If there is illness or physical limitation, couples may seek a new home arrangement that is more satisfying or safe, such as a retirement village, long-term care facility, or moving in with one of their children. All such transitions require a shift in household routines.

Aging adults continue to spend time with their adult children and their grandchildren. Some of these couples may need to care for their elderly relatives as well as their grandchildren. The "sandwich generation" faces many challenges as they deal with their multiple responsibilities.

As the couple ages, they encounter death of family and friends more frequently. Older relatives die, and then friends of their own generation whom they may have known for years, or even decades, begin to die. As they face bereavement, the couple must prepare for their own death and the death of their partner. The family cycle is complete when the last partner dies.

The Family Career

Aldous (1978, 1996) built on the concept of the family life cycle but noted that not all families followed the cycle from beginning to end, as in the case of divorced or remarried families. She preferred the term *"family careers"* to indicate that families followed stages that were somewhat predictable but not cyclical in nature. Moreover, she combined Duvall's (1957) stages of parenting into one stage because parents often were in several stages of parenting at the same time (depending upon the ages of their children). Thus, Aldous's family career had only four stages—the establishment of the marital relationship, the parental role, the return to the couple relationship, and the aging couple.

Aldous's model did not focus exclusively on the family, however, but went further to include dimensions of family interdependency and social networks. For example, in addition to her analysis of the family career, she also considered the parent-child career and the sibling career, and how these interactions changed over the life span of the family. Expanding on the sibling career, Cicerelli (1994) indicated that the sibling relationship was, for many individuals, likely to be the longest bond experienced in their lifetime.

The Dynamics of Family Development

White (1991) and his colleagues (Rodgers and White 1993; Watt and White 1999) expanded the family development theory to provide a more contextualized perspective.

The stages of family development are driven not only by the ontogenetic development of the individuals but also by the contexts in which the development occurs. These changing contexts make the family development stages dynamic rather than static. This perspective still takes into account stages over time but recognizes that, in this social context, all families do not follow the exact same path at the exact same time (White 1991). Understanding the family as a dynamic process encourages researchers to see fluidity and interrelationships between the process of development, the individual, and the context of the development (Fuller and Fincham 1994).

Interestingly, Watt and White (1999) found that the family development perspective created a structure for analyzing how computer technology pervades family life. Through each family developmental stage, computers serve as inexpensive tools for education, recreation, and communication. For example, computers impact mate selection by creating a "space" for cyberdating. Computers assist newly married couples with financial planning and career enhancement. When children leave the home, computers can help parents fill the "empty nest" with e-mail or allow them to pursue educational and occupational interests.

It is not enough, according to White (1991), to simply note that computers are used differently in each stage, but use must also be studied based on the context. For example, are boys more likely to use computers than girls? Does this create a hierarchical status in the family? What might be the effect of spending long hours on the computer? How is family life affected? And—more to the point of development theory—does it matter to the family *when* those hours are spent? Is there a different effect if a young adult, early in his or her married career, spends hours on the computer, compared with an older retired adult? These are all interesting questions to consider.

The Life Course Perspective

Bengtson and Allen (1993) expanded the theory with the "life course perspective," which addressed some of the issues not addressed in the "life cycle perspective." The life course perspective incorporated changes over time (and over the life course), identified three different "kinds" of time (ontogenetic, generational, and historical), and included the social context in which the changes occurred. They also highlighted an additional component—the meanings that individuals attach to the changes throughout their life course.

The life course perspective has a number of advantages over the family life cycle perspective in that it takes into account primarily the complexity of family and individual change over time. Each element of the theory adds richness to our understanding of how families exist in time, space, context, and process. It enhances our understanding of the social meanings that people give to their own developmental and family life (Bengtson and Allen 1993).

Let us look at widowhood as an example. As individuals, we mourn the deaths of those we love in a multitude of ways. Thus, we have an *individual response* to death. Now let's put it into a *time context*. Is the death of a spouse experienced differently depending on how old one is? Is grieving affected by our age? (Some people believe that as one ages, death is easier to accept, although it is difficult to gather hard data on that fact.) What about *family context*? Is the death of a spouse processed differently if the children are grown? Is the death processed differently if the spouses spent most of their time together (as in a family-run business) versus less time together? Next, let's consider the *social context*. Is the death processed differently if both partners worked and neither was totally dependent on the other for family income? Finally, let's consider the "meaning" associated with death. Is the death processed differently if the death is the result of a long illness? Is it different for those who ascribe religious meanings to death and "eternal life"?

Following the life course perspective encourages us to consider the multiple social contexts of family development, just as we know that many social contexts influence us individually. Although our families are our primary socialization agent, we are also influenced by our peers, our schooling, our faith systems, our government, and our culture. The diversity of that culture also should be included in any analysis of the life course, as the differences of our ethnic, racial, geographic, and religious heritage play out in our families and in our lives (Bengtson and Allen 1993).

Carter and McGoldrick Model

Family development theory has found support in family therapy, particularly when it defines family more broadly (e.g., remarried families, multigenerational families, gay and lesbian families) and is expanded to include varied developmental trajectories. Carter and McGoldrick (1999) analyzed the individual, from a therapy perspective, in terms of his or her place in the larger context of the family life cycle. Their model is based upon developmental stages, but it also encompasses different levels—the individual, family, and social context—within those stages. As a therapeutically focused model, the emphasis includes how problems or symptoms develop in individuals and families over time, particularly in response to major life transitions.

At the individual level, it includes a focus on such things as individual temperament, class, and genetic makeup as well as change over time. The family level of analysis might include an exploration of family secrets, expectations, emotional climate, patterns of relating, ethnicity, and negotiation skills. Both the individual and the family issues are always considered within the larger sociocultural context (e.g., existence of homophobia, racism, or classism), and how this changes over time.

Carter and McGoldrick provide an example. The birth of a child is naturally a taxing event on a couple, producing "the normal stresses of a system expanding its boundaries at the present time" (Carter and McGoldrick 1999, 7). If there was excessive turmoil in the family of origin for one or both of the parents, then there might be heightened anxiety for the couple as new parents. Relational distress might also arise if there is a mismatch between the temperaments of the parents and the new child. Finally, additional disorder might be introduced if the child is born during a time of political upheaval, such as when the parents might be refugees living outside their own country.

The model is useful in exploring life cycle stressors and how these interact with family stories, themes, triangles, and roles over time. It further emphasizes a balance between connectedness and separateness, as individual identity is understood in relation to significant people, relationships, and contexts.

The Systemic Family Development Model

Most recently, a new model has been proposed that incorporates aspects of family systems theory, family stress theory, and a multigenerational perspective of family development theory (Laszloffy 2002). It addresses two perceived shortcomings in the original theory: the assumption that all families develop similarly (universality) and the bias toward a single generational experience/focus of the life cycle (labeling a stage, for example, the *launching stage* emphasizes the parental experience whereas naming it *launching* and *leaving* acknowledges this multigenerational interchange). The systemic family development (SFD) model proposes, just like other developmental theories, that families experience transitions and shifts in family roles. Unlike other theories, though, which attempt to generalize patterns of family development over time, SFD states that each family's developmental pattern is unique. An analysis of a family must account for the combination, specific to the family being analyzed, of all of the factors influencing the family, including socioeconomic status, race, religion, gender, sexual orientation, politics, and sociocultural values. Laszloffy describes the family as a layer cake, with each layer representing a generation within the family. Each layer is at a different stage within the family cycle (aged adults, parents, adolescents, preschoolers, and others), having to deal with its own issues and developmental tasks. Laszloffy argues that in order to fully describe the family, one must study the interrelationships between the layers and describe the complexities that result from the family dealing with emerging stressors.

From a systems perspective, families are process oriented. While there is a great deal of variability in the timing and type of family stressors they encounter, all families experience stressors and the need to change and adapt. Therefore, even normative developmental transitions cause stress for the family unit. The family's response to its stressors will vary according to its resources, as predicted by stress theory. The more difficult the transition is, the more intense the stress. If the family has many resources, and the developmental transition is normative (and therefore expected), it will be easier to handle the transition. When the family successfully negotiates the transition, stress is relieved, and the family returns to stability.

The SFD model provides a way for family scholars to view the family in multiple developmental cycles concurrently while respecting the various social contexts (e.g., race, ethnicity, and socioeconomic status) that influence development. It allows us to investigate the influences across generations as well as within generations. It may also prove to be an important research tool because scholars can use the same theory to explain a family both at a point in time (a cross-sectional view, or the vertical slice of the cake) and over a span of time (a longitudinal view, or a layer of the cake).

CRITIQUE

A primary criticism of family development theory is that it best describes the trajectory of intact, two-parent, heterosexual nuclear families. For example, Duvall's (Duvall and Miller 1985) eight-stage model was based on a nuclear family, assumed an intact marriage throughout the life cycle of the family, and was organized around the oldest child's developmental needs. It did not take into account divorce, death of a spouse, remarriage, nonmarried parents, childless couples, or cohabiting couples. In so doing, it "normalized" one type of family and invalidated others. Today's family experiences and structures are more varied. For example, launching comes later in life for many families and is less complete than when Duvall first described these stages (Qualls 1997). Similarly, Dykstra and Hagestad (2007), in examining the impact of being childless on older adults, expose the way in which parenthood is deemed to be a critical "organizer of the life course and a major factor in social integration" (1275) in family development, disadvantaging those who do not have children, whether by choice or circumstance. Slater and Mencher (1991), too, acknowledge the exclusion of lesbian families from most family life cycle models and the need to afford such families rituals which delineate important markers of family life and connect them to larger society.

Family development theory was also criticized by many as being only descriptive but not heuristic (research generating). Critics said it lacked a sense of usefulness as a theory because it had little predictive power. It described only one particular kind of family (middle class, heterosexual, lifelong couples and their children), and it did not provide much insight into what governed their patterns of behavior (Bengtson and Allen 1993; Burr 1973; Falicov 1988). In fact, in the early 1980s, some researchers pronounced it a "minor" theory (Holman and Burr 1980). Because of these criticisms, White (1991) worked to formalize the theory in a more scientific way, with testable propositions that could be used to predict family functioning.

Mattessich and Hill (1987) worked to expand the theoretical structure, but it was still deemed too descriptive and broad (Aldous 1990). In other words, the theory suffered from trying to explain too much and so could only explain things simply so as to avoid being overwhelmingly complex. Further, while family development theory described the stages of the family life cycle, it did not describe the relationship between the stages or how they formed a total pattern of the family's development (Breunlin 1988).

In addition, early renderings of family development theory failed to include family identity factors such as race, socioeconomic status, ethnicity, and family structure (Bennett, Wolin, and McAvity 1988; Dilworth-Anderson and Burton 1996; Winton 1995). Bengtson and Allen's (1993) development of the life course perspective specifically includes these factors and lends itself to testable hypotheses. Carter and McGoldrick's (1999) family therapy perspective actually includes even more family identity structures (e.g., stepfamilies, divorcing families, never-married families, multigenerational families) and ethnic and racial differences. Laszloffy's (2002) systemic family development model broadens the theory's scope to include not only families of different structure, race, ethnicity, and sexuality but also multiple generations of families at the same time. The continued viability of family development theory will depend upon its ability to incorporate diverse families and varied family experiences.

APPLICATION

1. Using the scenario of the Morrison family at the beginning of the chapter:
   a. Identify the different life cycle stages represented by the Morrison family. Note the different tasks that each must accomplish.

    b. Identify the assumptions in the scenario.

    c. Analyze the tasks that each family member must accomplish in terms of different social and personal constraints. Can some tasks be avoided altogether? Must some tasks be addressed within a limited time frame?

    d. Indicate how the concept of change can be seen in this vignette. How do you think the family might cope with these changes?

    e. Indicate how this family provides examples of the effect of social changes.

2. Think of an intimate relationship either you or people close to you have been in. How has being in the intimate relationship changed this person? What kinds of changes have you noticed? What kinds of changes are noticed by your family and friends? Can you identify any of the establishment tasks in this relationship?

3. Draw a picture of your family at the time you entered it; when you were in elementary school; when you graduated from high school; your family as it is today; and your family as you expect it to be five years from now.

    f. How did your family change over time?

    g. Compare and contrast your drawings and reflections with others in class.

4. In the Sample Reading, White (1991) concluded that women in full-time dual-earner relationships are less satisfied with work–family balance than are males. In light of what you know about family development theory, why do you think this is?

NOTE

1. The edition that Duvall edited with Brent Miller was the last edition of Duvall's *Family Development* textbook. She died in 1998.

REFERENCES

Aldous, J. 1978. *Family careers: Developmental change in families.* New York: Wiley.
———. 1990. Family development and the life course: Two perspectives on family change. *Journal of Marriage and the Family* 52: 571–583.
———. 1996. *Family careers: Rethinking the developmental perspective.* Thousand Oaks, CA: Sage.
Bengtson, V. I., and K. R. Allen. 1993. The life-course perspective applied to families over time. In *Sourcebook of family theories and methods: A contextual approach*, ed. P. G. Boss, W. J. Doherty, R. LaRossa, W. J. Schumm, and S. K. Steinmetz, 469–499. New York: Plenum.
Bennett, L. A., S. J. Wolin, and K. J. McAvity. 1988. Family identity, ritual and myth: A cultural perspective on life cycle transitions. In *Family transitions: Continuity and change over the life cycle*, ed. C. J. Falicov, 211–234. New York: Guilford.
Breunlin, D. C. 1988. Oscillation theory and family development. In *Family transitions: Continuity and change over the life cycle*, ed. C. J. Falicov, 133–155. New York: Guilford.
Burr, W. R. 1973. *Theory construction and the sociology of the family.* New York: Wiley.
Carter, B., and M. McGoldrick. 1999. *The expanded family life cycle: Individual, family and social perspectives.* 3rd ed. Needham Heights, MA: Allen and Bacon.

Cicerelli, V. 1994. The sibling life cycle. In *Handbook of developmental family psychology and psychopathology*, ed. L. L' Abate, 44–59. New York: Wiley.

Dilworth-Anderson, P., and L. M. Burton. 1996. Rethinking family development theory. *Journal of Social and Personal Relationships* 13: 325–334.

Duvall, E. M. 1957 and the revised editions 1962, 1967, 1971, 1977. *Family development*. New York: Lippincott.

———. 1988. Family development's first forty years. *Family Relations* 37: 127–134.

Duvall, E. M., and R. L. Hill. 1948. *Reports of the committee on the dynamics of family interaction*. Washington, DC: National Conference on Family Life.

Duvall, E. M., and B. C. Miller. 1985. *Marriage and family development*. 6th ed. New York: Harper and Row.

Dykstra, P. A., and G. O. Hagestad. 2007. Roads less taken: Developing a nuanced view of older adults without children. *Journal of Family Issues* 28:1275–1310.

Falicov, C. J. 1988. Family sociology and family therapy contributions to the family developmental framework: A comparative analysis and thoughts on future trends. In *Family transitions: Continuity and change over the life cycle*, ed. C. J. Falicov, 3–51. New York: Guilford.

Fuller, T. L., and F. D. Fincham. 1994. The marital life cycle: A developmental approach to the study of marital change. In *Handbook of developmental family psychology and psychopathology*, ed. L. L'Abate, 60–82. New York: Wiley.

Glick, P. C. 1977. Updating the life cycle of the family. *Journal of Marriage and the Family* 39: 5–13.

Hagestad, G. 1988. Demographic change and the life course: Some emerging trends in the family realm. *Family Relations* 37: 405–410.

Havighurst, R. J. 1948. *Developmental tasks and education*. Chicago: Univ. of Chicago Press.

———. 1953. *Human development and education*. New York: Longmans and Green.

Hill, R. 1986. Life cycle stages for types of single parent families: Of family development theory. *Family Relations* 35: 19–30.

Holman, T. B., and W. R. Burr. 1980. Beyond the beyond: The growth of family theories in the 1970s. *Journal of Marriage and the Family* 42: 729–742.

Laszloffy, T. A. 2002. Rethinking family development theory: Teaching with the systemic family development (SFD) model. *Family Relations* 51: 206–214.

Mattessich, P., and R. Hill. 1987. Life cycle and family development. In *Handbook of marriage and the family*, ed. M. B. Sussman and S. K. Steinmetz, 437–469. New York: Plenum.

Neugarten, B., J. Moore, and J. Lowe. 1965. Age norms, age constraints, and adult socialization. *American Journal of Sociology* 70: 710–717.

Qualls, S. H. 1997. Transitions in autonomy: The essential caregiving challenge. *Family Relations* 46: 41–46.

Rapoport, R. 1963. Normal crises, family structure and mental health. *Family Process* 2: 68–80.

Rodgers, R. 1964. Toward a theory of family development. *Journal of Marriage and the Family* 26: 262–270.

———. 1973. *Family interaction and transaction: The developmental approach*. Englewood Cliffs, NJ: Prentice-Hall.

Rodgers, R. H., and J. M. White. 1993. Family developmental theory. In *Sourcebook of family theories and methods: A contextual approach*, ed. P. G. Boss, W. J. Doherty, R. LaRossa, W. R. Schumm, and S. K. Steinmetz, 225–254. New York: Plenum.

Slater, S., and J. Mencher. 1991. The lesbian family life cycle: A contextual approach. *American Journal of Orthopsychiatry* 61: 372–382.

Watt, D., and J. M. White. 1999. Computers and the family life: A family development perspective. *Journal of Comparative Family Studies* 30: 1–15.

White, J. M. 1991. *Dynamics of family development: A theoretical perspective*. New York: Guilford.
Winton, C. A. 1995. *Frameworks for studying families*. Guilford, CT: Dushkin Publishing.

SAMPLE READING

White, J. M. 1999. Work-family stage and satisfaction with work-family balance. *Journal of Comparative Family Studies* 30(2): 163–175.

Using family development theory, White tests three theoretical hypotheses based on work-family staging. He discovered that a number of factors determined how satisfied respondents were with the balance between their job and their family life.

SAMPLE READING

WORK-FAMILY STAGE AND SATISFACTION WITH WORK-FAMILY BALANCE

*James M. White**

INTRODUCTION

Work and Family Stage

Family development theory (Hill & Rodgers, 1964; Rodgers, 1973; Aldous, 1978; Mattessich & Hill, 1987; White, 1991; Rodgers & White, 1993) posits that each stage of the family is marked by a different set of norms or expectations. In addition, family development theory proposes that the sequencing and timing of family stages is prescribed by sequencing and timing norms for family development. It is important to recognize that concurrent with roles played at any stage of family development, there are also roles that family members play within the normative venue of other institutions such as work and education.

The interaction of one's work career and *the* family career has been mainly examined by the stress, conflict, and imbalance it brings to the juggling of multiple roles and role demands (e.g., Menaghan, 1989; Menaghan & Parcel, 1990). Although the debate between role expansion theory and role strain theory is far from resolved, it does seem likely that there is some truth to both perspectives (Tiedje, et al., 1990). Regardless of these particular theoretical debates, there are well documented effects for female participation in work and family roles on such variables as satisfaction with parenting and perceived stress (see Menaghan & Parcel, 1990).

Mattessich and Hill (1987) suggest that one somewhat underdeveloped aspect of family development theory is the specification of how stages of the family career interact with stages of other social institutions. White (1991) and Rodgers and White (1993) suggest that family stage sequences are synchronized with work and educational stage

*Family Science, 2205 East Mall, University of British Columbia, Vancouver, British Columbia V6T 1Z4, Canada.

Work-family stage and satisfaction with work-family balance
James M White
Journal of Comparative Family Studies; Spring 1999; 30, 2; Research Library pg. 163

sequences by means of cross-institutional sequencing norms. These authors suggest that the stage sequences of the family career must be synchronized with the stage sequences of other careers such as the work career and educational career. If the sequencing of family stages are not synchronized with the sequencing of work and educational stages then the result is for the family or individual to be thrown "off-time" in one or more of these institutions. Although the positive effects for being out of synchrony within and between institutional careers has yet to be demonstrated, the detrimental effects for being out of synchrony within and between institutions has been documented by several studies (e.g., Morgan & Riridfuss, 1985; Hogan, 1978, 1980; White, 1987, 1991).

White (1991) argues that timing and sequencing norms between institutions not only prevent the pile up of stress by avoiding too many simultaneous expectations but that the institutions of a society are geared toward accommodating the normative and most frequent pattern of career development. Menaghan (1989) cites two arguments for the "protective effects" of normative sequencing of roles. First, social institutions are coordinated with expected and frequent patterns. Second, the impact of one's problems seem less significant when they are the "normal problems" of persons in a certain stage such as young mothers as opposed to unique and unshared problems.

Voydanoff (1987) proposes a similar idea in regard to the synchronization of work and family stages. Voydanoff identifies the traditional synchronizing of work and family stages, *traditional simultaneous staging*, as follows: establishment family—novitiate work, new parents—early work career, school age family—middle work career, postparental family—late career, and aging family—post exit work stage. However, Voydanoff notes that this traditional synchronization of family and work careers relies on the segregated gender roles of male provider and female homemaker. She argues that when traditional simultaneous staging is adapted to dual-earner families it is prone to work-family role overloads and role imbalance.

Voydanoff's argument in regard to the stage sequencing of one and two-earner families can be extended. It seems that the traditional pattern is not just a poor adaptation for the two earner family but is currently out of synchrony with other social institutions. In the past, the traditional family-work sequencing pattern where the mother spent significant amounts of time out of the labor force, was undoubtedly synchronized with the timing and sequencing norms of other institutions. In the context of contemporary North American society, it seems doubtful that this pattern is synchronized with the normative changes which have occurred in both education and work. It seems more likely that today's traditional one earner family is less synchronized with other social institutions than two earner families. Indeed, a stay at home mother is likely to find herself socially isolated since most other mothers are at work and find that her children have no neighborhood playmates since potential playmates are in various forms of alternative care. In the current economic and social environment, social institutions appear increasingly geared toward the two earner family. As a result of the greater synchronization of two earner families, we would expect that satisfaction with work and family would be higher for members of these families.

Voydanoff (1987) maintains that there are two staging strategies used by two earner families in order to reduce role overload and work-family imbalance. The first strategy is *sequential staging* (pp. 90–93). Sequential staging is where work stages and family stages are sequenced by the female so that they are not experienced simultaneously thus reducing the need to meet role demands for work and family stages at the same time. Voydanoff points out that this is the most popular sequencing pattern. Females often leave the labor force for a short period of time and most re-enter within two years after the first birth (Voydanoff, 1987, p. 91). The second strategy is *non-traditional simultaneous* staging.[1] In simultaneous staging both work and family stages are experienced concurrently, however, there is deviation from the traditional stage synchronization. This form of simultaneous staging is more likely to demand a symmetrical division of labor (p. 93). As a deviation from traditional simultaneous sequencing, the non-traditional pattern may be accomplished by means of the couple delaying parenthood. Another means is for the couple to dyadically synchronize work stages so that the husband and wife are at different points in their work careers when they start their family. As Voydanoff points out, husbands and wives at different work career stages might have less competition with each other in regard to work and work related resources.

Balancing Work and Family

The traditional family balanced work and family interaction by gender segregated roles. In recent times, compelling economic and ideological reasons have rapidly propelled mothers into the work place and this has been accompanied by the markedly slower entry of male workers into domestic and nurturing roles (Ferree, 1990; Pleck, 1984). Although there has been some research into the husband's participation in home life (Coltrane & Ishii-Kuntz, 1992), most of the research has focused on the worker-mother role (Menaghan & Parcel, 1990). The reason for this is not simply the rate at which changes have occurred for female roles but the ramifications this shift has for the organization of the family including spousal well-being, child develop-ment, and household division of labor. Indeed, many authors feel that adding work demands to continuing home responsibilities presents role overload or role conflict for females.

There are two perspectives on the balance of female work and family roles. The role conflict perspective suggests that female participation in the roles of worker and mother are especially likely to result in strain and conflict (Voydanoff, 1987). The second perspective is that role expansion is linked to heightened resources and experi-ences useful in successfully completing multiple roles (Marks, 1977; Thoits, 1983). More recently these two perspectives have been tied together as a typology (Tiedje, et al., 1990). These researchers found mothers' feelings about the effect of work on their relationship with their children partitioned into two independent factors, enhancement and conflict. They suggest that research in this area might be best served by a focus on the relative *balance* between role enhancement and role conflict. The assessment of balance between work and family encompasses both the positive and negative aspects inherent in this complex situation. Since satisfaction measures reflect the subject's comparison of the ideal and actual, they are relative measures. Thus, those mothers satisfied with the balance between work and family might not all share just one mixture of enhancement and conflict.

Theoretical Hypotheses

The discussion of work-family stage sequencing raises several important dimensions for our understanding of the articulation of work and family demands. First, Voydanoff

(1987) and White (1991) sensitize us to the possibility that an entire sequence of stages may have an overall effect on work-family balance. Second, some authors suggest that the duration within any one family-work stage may have effects on work-family balance (Rodgers & White, 1993). Third, each specific work-family stage may have effects on work-family balance. Indeed, the more immediate effects of the current work-family stage are most likely to be tied to the current satisfaction with work-family balance since it is this immediate stage which present current difficulties for the family. It is this third range of effects which the present study investigates.

There are several theoretical hypotheses which may be derived from the discussion of work-family staging. First, there is the relatively straightforward hypothesis that dual earner families would have higher work-family balance than one earner families. This hypothesis can be derived by combining arguments by Voydanoff (1987) and White (1991). Sequencing and timing deviations in the family career are most often linked to cross-institutional adaptation to the stage sequencing and timing norms of other institutions. In this case, the traditional work and family stage sequencing is viewed as out of synchronization with institutions of work and education. As a result, there would be greater dissatisfaction with the balance between work and family for these families than dual earner families.

Second, there is the hypothesis that sequential staging for two earner families would have greater work-family balance than non-traditional simultaneous staging. The rationale here is that since sequential staging allows for relatively clear role definition and less overlap with work roles since they are sequenced, there would be lower work-family balance in two-earner families pursuing non-traditional simultaneous staging than those following the sequential staging. The most obvious current stage for those pursuing dual earner sequential staging would be those families where the mother works part time because these mothers represent neither traditional one-earner families nor do they represent non-traditional simultaneous sequencing where mothers do both roles full time and simultaneous.

Third, among those families with part time working mothers (sequential stage sequencing) and full time working mothers (non-traditional simultaneous stage sequencing), those couples who delay parenthood and or have couple work stage heterogeneity would have higher work-family balance than those not following these strategies.

METHODS

Sample

The data used in this study were collected by Statistics Canada as part of their annual General Social Survey of Canada (GSS). The 1990 GSS focused on the area of family and friends. The target population for the 1990 GSS was all Canadians fifteen years old and older. Certain subgroups were not sampled such as residents of the two territories, institutionalized inmates, residents of Indian Reserves and members of the Canadian Armed Forces. Furthermore, other groups such as those without telephones (estimated at less than 2%) were excluded due to the sampling procedures.

The sampling procedure for the 1990 GSS was complex. The sample was stratified by province and data collected by two different methods of Random Digit Dialling. The complexity of the sampling involved in the 1990 GSS necessitated a complex weighting procedure. Statistics Canada recommends a separate weighting procedure for analyses of variance such as regression and ANOVA which involves computing a new weight by dividing the final population weight by the average weight. This weighting procedure is used in the subsequent analyses.

The sample released in the microdata tapes contains 13,495 cases. For the purposes of this analysis, a subsample is selected which has the characteristics of being currently married, at least one of the spouses is employed in a job or business, and there is at least one child under the age of fifteen years residing in the home. The entire subsample contained 6759 currently married respondents, 6902 respondents or their spouse worked at a job or business, and 3641 had at least one child under 15 years of age living at home. The joint distribution of these three characteristics creates a subsample for analyses composed of 2757 cases.

MEASURES

Satisfaction with work-family balance. The dependent variable in this study is the respondent's satisfaction with the balance between work and family life. Work-family balance is measured by a four point Likert-type response to the question "Are you satisfied or dissatisfied with the balance between your job or main activity and family and home life?" This item is one of eight items assessing various dimensions of satisfaction. Some previous research (Tiedje, et al., 1990) has suggested that satisfaction with work-family balance contains an "optimism" component. The present study does not control for such a component in the work-family balance measure. However, it seems reasonable that such an "optimism" component would also surface in other measures of satisfaction. Furthermore, it is useful to examine the correlations with the satisfaction measures for work, family, and marriage to make sure that the work-family balance item measures something other than satisfaction with one of these areas. For currently married respondents, the bivariate correlations between satisfaction with work-family balance and satisfaction with work (0.325), satisfaction with immediate family (0.183) and satisfaction with marriage (0.183) are relatively modest. These correlations do not suggest a strong common component.

Family-work stage. The independent variables in this study are the three family-work stages implied by Voydanoff's (1987) discussion of work-family sequencing strategies. Although Voydanoff discusses family-work sequences, it is clear from her discussion that families move through *stages*. This study concentrates on the effect of the current family-work stage on work-family balance. Each family-work sequencing pattern implies a relatively unique cross-sectional family-work stage. These family-work stages can be hypothesized to have a direct effect on how satisfied respondent's are with the balance between work and family.

One earner families are linked to Voydanoff's traditional simultaneous stage. The conceptual characteristics of this stage are that (1) the female is home and family based, and the male work based; and (2) it is characterized by only one earner. The measures used to construct this stage are (1) that the female respondents identify their main activity as a "housekeeper" or that male respondents list that as the main activity for their spouse; and (2) it is a male one earner family. Thus, this family-work stage is called the *Traditional single earner family*.

Voydanoff (1987) proposes two family-work sequencing strategies for two earner families. One of the staging sequences for two earner families is non-traditional simultaneous stage sequencing. Simultaneous sequencing entails the simultaneous enactment of both family and work roles. The stage which corresponds to this pattern is where the mother of a dual earner family works full time. In this study we simply refer to this family-work stage as *Full time dual-earner* family.

The third sequencing stage is sequential stage sequencing. The conceptual characteristics of this work-family sequencing stage are: (1) it is a dual earner family; and (2) the female is sequencing roles rather than attempting them simultaneously. Since there is no way in the present study to determine who is out of the labor force for extended rather than short periods of time, the measures used to construct this stage are: (1) it is a dual earner family where (2) the female works less than twenty hours per week. In this study, this family-work stage is called the

Part time dual-earner family. In addition to the stage sequencing patterns Voydanoff (1987) proposes that the timing of parenthood and couple work stage heterogeneity may be a significant factor within sequential stage sequencing and non-traditional simultaneous stage sequencing. In this study, delayed parenthood is indicated by a dummy variable where one equals all those who have had children after 25 years of age. The mean age for the first births for the sample is slightly over twenty-five years so the measure of delayed parenthood would represent all those above the mean. Voydanoff (1987) suggests that couple work stage heterogeneity might reduce husband-wife competition. In addition, being at different points in work careers may free up time for one spouse to deal with family responsibilities. The way in which couple work stage heterogeneity is measured in this study is by the age difference between spouses. A dummy variable was assigned one for all those couples whose ages differ by six or more years. This represents about 20% of those currently married.

Control Variables. Several known variables related to work-family balance are included in the analyses. These are total family income, number of children under fifteen years of age, regular alternative care for children, satisfaction with the way housework is shared and respondents education level (Voydanoff, 1988; Voydanoff & Donnelly, 1989; Menaghan & Parcel, 1990; Hanson & Ooms, 1991).

RESULTS

Work-Family Balance

The dependent variable is the respondents satisfaction with the balance between work and family. The mean score for the sample is 3.27 with a standard deviation of 0.80 and the median is 3.0. The measure of work-family balance is significantly related to gender, $F(1, 2737) = 16.1, p < .000$. The mean for male work-family balance is 3.21 whereas the mean for females is 3.33. Gender differences are also found on a number of other related satisfaction measures. Males are less satisfied with their jobs than females ($M_m = 3.40$, $M_f = 3.48$) and less satisfied with their immediate family ($M_m = 3.66$, $M = 3.68$). Females are less satisfied than males with the way housework is shared ($M_f = 3.32$, $M_m = 3.65$), and less satisfied with their marriage partner (M_f 3.75, $M_m = 3.80$).

Hypothesis 1 This hypothesis is that dual earner families would have higher work-family balance than one earner families. A two-way analysis of variance only partially supports this hypothesis. In general, the mean work-family balance is higher for single earner families than for two earner families, $F(1, 2629) = 18.5$, $p < .000$. However, there is a significant interaction between the factors of type of family earner and gender $F(1, 2629) = 28.9$. $p < .000$. Females in one earner families have higher work-family balance than males ($M_f = 3.47$, $M_m = 3.18$) and females in two earner families have lower work-family balance than males ($M_f = 3.18$, $M_m = 3.23$). As Table 1 shows, the interaction of gender and type of family earner remains relatively unchanged when covariates are added to the model.

Hypothesis 2. This hypothesis is that the part time dual-earner stage families would have greater work-family balance than families in the full time dual-earner stage. The analyses supports this hypothesis. The mean work-family balance for full time dual earners is 3.18 whereas the mean for part time dual earners is 3.40. As in Table 1, Table 2 shows there is an especially strong effect for satisfaction with the way housework is shared. However, again there are strong interaction effects. When the control variables are entered first, sequencing pattern and gender remain strongly related to work-family balance. The relation between gender and stage with work-family balance can best be interpreted by examining Table 3. Table 3 contains the cell means for the 2x3 design. Note that females in traditional one-earner families have higher work-family balance than males in such families. A similar gender difference exists between females and males in full time dual-earner families. On the other hand, females in full time two earner families have lower satisfaction with work-family balance than males. Table 3, suggests that most, though not all, of the difference between the full time and part time dual earner

Table 1. The Relationship between Type of Family Earner and Gender on Work/Family Balance Controlling for Covariates

Variable	Sum of SQS	DF	F	Prob. F
Covariates				
Family Income	124	1	0.208	.649
Childcare	12.78	1	21.45	.000
No. Child < 15	1.43	1	2.39	.122
Sat. Housework	60.88	1	102.1	.000
Educ. Level	7.17	1	12.03	.001
Main Effects				
Earner	2.66	1	4.47	.035
Gender	17.44	1	29.26	.000
Interaction				
Earner × Gender	18.13	1	30.40	.000

Note: Difference between F ratios for two models is the result of more missing cases for one or more covariates.

Table 2. The Relationship between Stage and Gender on
Work/Family Balance Controlling for Covariates

Variable	Sum of SQS	DF	F	Prob. F
Covariates				
Family Income	0.00	1	0.000	.998
Childcare	12.44	1	21.32	.000
No. Child < 15	1.54	1	2.64	.104
Sat. Housework	53.36	1	91.47	.000
Educ. Level	4.68	1	8.02	.005
Main Effects				
Stage	7.71	2	6.61	.001
Gender	21.59	1	37.02	.000
Interaction				
Stage × Gender	29.57	1	25.07	.000

Table 3. Cell Means for Work/Family
Balance by Stage and Gender

	Gender	
Stage	Male	Female
Traditional		
Single-earner	3.17	3.55
	(513)	(583)
Full time		
Dual-earner	3.22	3.15
	(580)	(644)
Part time		
Dual-earner	3.30	3.51
	(74)	(68)

Note: ( ) contains cell frequency.

stages on work-family balance scores is due to the high satisfaction of females in the part time stage.

Hypothesis 3. This hypothesis is that families in the full time or part time dual-earner stage, that have delayed parenthood or have couple work stage heterogeneity (age difference), would have higher work-family balance than those not following these strategies. An analysis of variance for each stage, indicated no statistically significant relationships for the age difference between partners or delayed parenthood on work-family balance.

DISCUSSION

Two of the three hypotheses received partial support. The results of the data analysis suggest support for hypotheses 1 and 2:

    1. For hypothesis 1, the relationship between type of earner in the family and work-family balance is different for males than it is females. Females in one earner families are more satisfied with work-family balance than males. In two earner families, males are more satisfied with work-family balance than females.

    2. For hypothesis 2, females in both the traditional single-earner and the part time dual-earner stages are more satisfied with work-family balance than males. Females in the full time dual-earner stage are less satisfied than are males with the balance between work and family.

    Voydanoff (1987) suggested that the traditional sequencing of work and family where roles are segregated by gender, would result in role overload for two earner families. An extension of this argument is that the traditional sequencing pattern for work and family is no longer synchronized with other social institutions timing and sequencing norms (White, 1991). At a broader level this implies that we should expect dual earner families to be more synchronized with institutions and expectations. Furthermore, we would also expect that one earner families would have lower work-family balance that two earner families as a consequence of the greater institutional and normative synchrony of dual earner families compared to the "anachronistic" single earner families.

    The finding that the work-family balance is significantly higher for one earner families raises doubts about these theoretical expectations. The work-family balance for single earner families is significantly higher than dual-earner families. If we further examine this finding, we find that an analysis of the cell means for the interaction between gender and earner, reveals that much of the main effect for single-earner families on work-family balance is attributable to the high score on work-family balance for females in one earner families.

    The analyses for hypothesis 2 present a similar finding. Again, the theoretical expectation is that among dual-earner families the part time dual-earner families would be more satisfied with work-family balance than the full time dual earners because sequencing of roles provides clear roles and mitigates against role overload. Consistent with the findings for hypothesis 1, both males and females in the part time dual-earner family have the higher work-family balance than those in the full time dual earner stage. Females in this part time dual-earner stage score almost as high on work-family balance as females in the traditional single-earner stage.

    The persistent gender difference in regard to satisfaction with work-family balance suggests that males are most satisfied when wives assume the part or full time role of worker in addition to that of mother. Mothers on the other hand are more satisfied with the balance between work and family when they are either full time homemakers or the number of hours committed to the job is reduced below twenty hours per week. It would seem that the current economic and social norms, at least as indicated by the labor force participation of mothers, favors mothers remaining in the labor force. However, this norm appears to be carried by males whose satisfaction (difference between ideal and actual) is lower when mothers are not in the labor force either part or full time.

These findings lead to three different, though not mutually exclusive, interpretations. One interpretation is that, given the percentage of mothers with small children in the labor force, females might be seen as conforming to predominantly male norms and general social and economic pressures in regard to their behavior when this is contrary to the subjective ideals they hold for work-family balance. A second interpretation is in regard to normative change. White (1991) suggested that when norms change, often aggregate behavior changes first followed by actors expectations. It may be that female expectations (ideals) for the balance between work and family are in the process of change and have not yet synchronized with their behavior. This would suggest that females are adapting their ideals to fit the behavior patterns in which they already participate. Menaghan argues that "...the impact of specific role combinations varies with their normative expectedness" (1989, p. 711). It should be added, however, that the norms for the sequencing of work and family are in some degree of flux. Menaghan point out that "When enough people share a role pattern, or adopt a new pattern, other institutions begin to change, albeit slowly, and supportive organizations, political advocacy groups, and institutional expectations may emerge or alter in response to the bad fit between old institutional patterns and new lifestyles." (1989, pp. 711–712) Thus, even though the labor force behavior of mothers appears to indicate a strong norm for full time work participation concurrent with parenthood, there may also be a degree of subjective *anomie* in regard to these roles.

The finding that female satisfaction with work-family balance is highest when females are in the more traditional sequencing patterns (single earner and part time dual earner) is somewhat at odds with the extent of labor force participation of mothers with children under three years of age (estimated at over 50%). However, a third interpretation is that for some females, the sequencing of work and family stages (and its relationship with female satisfaction with work-family balance) is well attuned to the relatively rapid changes in the timing and sequencing norms of other institutions. Females and males are expected to spend longer periods of time getting more education. The age for brides and groom in both Canada and the U.S. continues to climb. The delay of marriage is undoubtedly tied to both longer periods of education and also to time required for the establishment of a work career. This delay in marriage shortens the time for childbearing so as a result fewer children are spaced more closely together. With the closer spacing of children family demands become both more concentrated and of shorter duration than previously. Thus, the sequencing patterns where females spend significant time at home as opposed to work (traditional one earner and part time dual-earner stages), might be an adaptation to these changes which enhances work-family balance. Due to the tight spacing and small size of families, the duration of time spent out of the labor force is reduced from that required for larger families with more years between siblings. That sequential stage sequencing (part time dual-earner stage) is an adaptation to contemporary realities is further indicated by the finding that this pattern is the only one where there is high satisfaction with work-family balance for both males and females.

CONCLUSION

This study indicates that work and family balance might remain tied to more traditional work-family career stages. The findings reported here are both strong and consistent. The area of work-family career synchronization is one in which gender differences are important. The fact that most mothers still carry the lion's share of the work load for child care and domestic chores, suggest that females are balancing a qualitatively and quantitatively different set of demands than males. This study suggests that, although females can and do juggle these many demands, the greatest satisfaction with the balance between work and family roles exists when females reduce the time and commitments at work when children are at home. Male satisfaction seems to be geared more to female participation in the labor force. However, this should not conceal the fact that there seems to be relatively high satisfaction on work-family balance for both males and females when females participation in the labor force is somewhat reduced, as in part time dual earner families.

In any examination of work and family, researchers are always limited by the rapid social change taking place in today's economy and families. This undoubtedly interjects cohort and period effects into both longitudinal and cross-sectional research in this area. The current study is not immune to these threats. If we were to repeat this research today we would find "family work place benefits" in many workplace situations and "flex time" available to those with family responsibilities. Such changes would entail significant period effects. Furthermore, families may move through work-family stages and some of the differences we see in this study might be due to the process of moving through different stages. The current cohort of parents might have experienced a greater frequency of female role models balancing the complex demands of work and family. In addition, the current cohort might have a higher value on father's participation in the family. These changes would represent significant cohort effects.

Despite these potential limitations, in this study the effects for the current work-family stage on satisfaction with work-family balance are quite consistent and strong. If there is a movement through these stages than this research would suggest that when mothers re-enter the labor force full-time, they would experience declines in their satisfaction with the balance between work and family. Such a conclusion would be limited to the period and cohort captured in this research as well as the obvious age effects that such transitions would necessarily imply. The questions about the effects timing of such transitions on work-family balance, the effects of employer work-family benefits on satisfaction with work-family balance, and the effects of more egalitarian family roles on satisfaction with work-family balance await the attention of future research.

REFERENCES

Aldous, J. 1978 Family Careers: Developmental Change in Families. New York: Wiley.

Bolger, N., DeLongis, A., Kessler, R. and Wethington, E. 1989 "The contagion of stress across multiple roles." Journal of Marriage and the Family, 51: 175–183.

Coltranc, S. and Ishii-Kuntz, M. 1992 "Men's housework: A life course perspective." *Journal of Marriage and the Family*, 54: 43–57.

Ferree, M. 1990 "Beyond separate spheres: Feminism and family research." Journal of Marriage and the Family, 52: 866–884.

Hanson, S. and Ooms, T. 1991 "The economic costs and rewards of two-earner, two-parent families." Journal of Marriage and the Family, 53: 622–634.

Hill, R. and Rodgers, R. 1964 "The developmental approach." Pp. 171–211 in H. T. Christensen (Ed.), Handbook of Marriage and the Family. Chicago: Rand McNally.

Hogan, D. P. 1978 "The variable order of events in the life course." American Sociological Review, 43: 573–586.

———. 1981 Transitions and Social Change: The Early Lives of American Men. New York: Academic Press.

Marks, S. R. 1977 "Multiple roles and role strain," American Sociological Review, 42: 921–936.

Mattessich, P. and Hill, R. 1987 "Life cycle and family development." Pp. 437–469 in M.B. Sussman & S. Steinmetz (Eds.), Handbook of Marriage and the Family, New York: Penguin.

Menaghan, E. and Parcel, T. 1990 "Parental employment and family life: Research in the 1980's," Journal of Marriage and the Family, 52: 1079–1098.

Menaghan, E. 1989 "Role changes and psychological well-being: Variations in effects by gender and role repertoire." Social Forces, 67: 693–714.

Pleck, J. 1984 "The work-family role system." Pp. 8–19 in P. Voydanoff (Ed.), Work and Family: Changing Roles of Men and Women. Palo Alto, CA: Sage.

Morgan, S. and Riridfuss, R. 1985 "Marital disruption: Structural and temporal dimensions" American Journal of Sociology, 90: 1055–1077.

Rodgers, R. 1973 Family Interaction and Transaction: The Developmental Approach. Englewood Cliffs, NJ: Prentice-Hall.

Rodgers, R. H. and White, J. M. 1993 Family development theory" Pp. 225–254 in P. Boss, W. Doherty, R. LaRossa, & W. Schumm (Eds.), Sourcebook of Family Theories and Methods. New York: Plenum.

Thoits, P. 1983 "Multiple identities and psychological well-being: A reformulation and test of the social isolation hypothesis." American Sociological Review, 48: 174–187.

Tiedje, L., Wortman, C., Downey, G., Emmons, C., Biernat, M. and Lang, E. 1990 "Women with multiple roles: Role-compatibility perceptions, satisfaction, and mental health. Journal of Marriage and the Family, 52: 63–72.

Voydanoff, P. 1987 Work and Family Life. Newbury Park, CA: Sage.

———. 1988 "Work role characteristics, family structure demands, and work/family conflict," Journal of Marriage and the Family, 50: 749–761.

Voydanoff, P. and Donnelly, B. 1989 "Work and family roles and psychological distress." Journal of Marriage and the Family, 51: 923–932.

White, J. M. 1987 "Researching developmental careers: The Career Conformity Scale." Journal of Family Issues, 8: 306–318.

———. 1991 Dynamics of Family Development: A Theoretical Perspective. New York: Guilford.

Voydanoff (1987) actually states that symmetrical role allocation is a way of adapting the traditional simultaneous sequencing to the two career family.

4

Family Stress Theory

―――――――――

Marsha and Sean Peabody have been married for five years; this is the second marriage for both. While Sean has a child from his previous marriage (eight-year-old Billy) who spends every other week, holidays, and one month during the summer with them, they have wanted to have an "ours" baby for some time. After trying to become pregnant for several years they started infertility treatment—which worked! Marsha, a corporate manager at a large software company, had to leave work six weeks early because of a difficult pregnancy—she's having twins! Sean, a salesman at a television station, spent three weeks running back and forth between work and the hospital. Finally, Alicia and Barry were born, but five weeks prematurely, which led to health complications for both but especially for little Barry. Although Alicia was able to come home after just two weeks, Barry was in the hospital for one month. Thus, Marsha and Sean spent a lot of time running back and forth between work, home, and the hospital. This also impacted Billy's visitation schedule, which left him feeling unwanted and angry.

Marsha was not able to return to work because of the health needs of the twins and the fact that child care for two would consume most of her paycheck. Sean kept his job but was able to take off only one week once the twins were born. Needless to say, life has been stressful for the Peabody family!

The twins are now three months old and are getting stronger by the day. They still wake up every three hours needing to be fed, and each is taking different medications that must be administered at different times. Marsha's parents live nearby and are taking turns spending the night and helping with the feedings. Other friends and family members are coming over during the day to help Marsha take care of the twins. Both parents are still exhausted and constantly worry about the health of the twins. They often turn to prayer when they feel overwhelmed and find that it comforts them. They are also both very optimistic people and take it all in stride. They were so desperate to be parents that the lack of sleep and complete loss of any activity outside of taking care of the twins seems like no big deal in comparison to the joy Alicia and Barry bring them. Now if they could just convince Billy how wonderful it is to be a big half brother!

HISTORY

Whereas families have experienced stress since time began, the scientific study of how families deal with stress is a relatively recent phenomenon. The Depression of the 1930s was the impetus for this research as Angell (1936) and Cavan and Ranck (1938) sought to discover how families were dealing with the loss of household income and the stress associated with unemployment. Angell discovered that a family's reaction to the sudden loss of income during the Depression was based on two things: integration and adaptability. Integration means how close or unified a family feels and how economically interdependent they are whereas adaptability means how flexible families are in talking about problems, making decisions as a group, and modifying existing patterns, roles, and rules. Angell found that families who are both integrated and easily able to adapt their family roles to meet the needs of the situation are most capable of dealing with stress such as that caused by job loss during the Depression. Similarly, Cavan and Ranck studied families both before and after the Depression and found that those who were organized and cohesive prior to the Depression were best able to deal with economic losses, whereas disorganized families faced further breakdown.

Koos (1946) also researched how families deal with economic loss, building upon Hill's (1949) "roller-coaster profile of adjustment to crisis" (14). According to Hill's model (see fig. 4.1), families go through four stages when faced with a stressful situation: crisis, disorganization, recovery, and reorganization. The crisis phase is obviously the stress-provoking event that sent the family into crisis. This can be anything from the birth of a new child to the death of a family member. Once the family is faced with a crisis, a period of disorganization follows as family members attempt to cope with the situation. For example, new parents attempt to develop a schedule of feeding and/or waking up with the child at night so that each parent is able to get some sleep. They also must attempt to cope with little sleep, meeting the needs of the infant, and changing how they view each other now that they are parents as well as spouses.

As families figure out how to handle the situation, they enter the stage of recovery, which can be either fairly quick or long term. According to Hill (1949), families will eventually reach a new level of organization; for some it will be the same as the previous level of organization, for others it will be better than it was before; but for still others things become stable but not as good as they were prior to the stressful event.

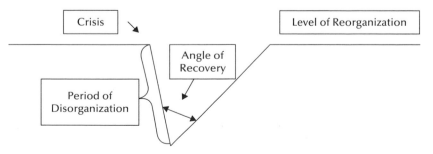

FIGURE 4.1 Roller-coaster profile of adjustment.

Source: Hill, R. 1949. Roller-Coaster Profile of Adjustment. In *Families Under Stress*, 138. New York: Harper & Brothers.

Thus, some new parents eventually find a schedule that fits all of their needs and are able to continue much as they did prior to the birth of their child. Other first-time parents become closer and find that their marital relationship is better because they have bonded over the birth of their child. This may also lead to better communication skills as a result of figuring out how to manage a newborn. Unfortunately, some parents find having an infant in the home overwhelming and never really learn to adjust. In these families, lines of communication break down, resentment and jealousy form, and often divorces occur as the couple is not able to return to a satisfactory level of interaction.

The roller-coaster model of adjustment to crisis was the predecessor to Reuben Hill's (1949) ABC-X model of family stress, which is the foundation of family stress theory. His early research on how families attempt to adjust to the crisis caused by separation and reunion during wartime led to the development of a theory that has remained virtually unchanged over the last five decades. Although other scholars have added to (McCubbin and Patterson 1982), attempted to simplify (Burr and Klein 1994), or built on (Lazarus and Folkman 1984) this theory, the basics as Hill wrote them have remained primarily unchanged. The rest of this chapter will discuss Hill's ABC-X model.

BASIC ASSUMPTIONS

The basic assumptions of family stress theory revolve around the central components of the model. Thus, this section will focus on the theory itself, and then we will focus more specifically on defining each of those components. As was previously stated, stress theory is based on the ABC-X model, with A being the stressor event, B the family resources or strengths, and C the family's perception of the event, or how they define or attribute meaning to the event. If the event or stressor is such that the family cannot immediately figure out how to solve the problem, this will lead to crisis, the X component of the model (Hill 1949). Because of the nature of this theory, the format will be a little different for this chapter.

Stressor Events (A)

Now we'll look at each component of the model a little more closely, beginning with the stressor. It's critical to realize that the stressor event itself is neither positive nor negative because events or situations are neutral prior to our interpretation of them. It is also important to remember that both positive and negative events can cause stress. For example, while it is obvious that events such as loss of a family member are stressful, the birth of a much-wanted child or winning the lottery can also cause stress even though both are events that cause celebration.

Lipman-Bluman (1975) has come up with ten criteria that affect the degree to which a stressor will impact a family, eight of which are commonly used in stress theory and will be addressed here.

1. The first criterion is whether the stressor is internal or external to the family. An example of this would be whether a mother chooses to return to work after

the birth of a child versus the mother who loses her job following the birth of her child. In the first case, the mother makes the choice to quit her job to take care of her child, so this is a decision made internally. In the second case, however, her boss fires her because she is always late to work and is falling asleep on the job; thus, external circumstances control the decision.

2. Whether a stressor is focused on one member of the family, or all members of the family, can make a difference. For example, is a stressful workplace causing one family member to come home unhappy, which might then disrupt the family, or has a recession caused both spouses to lose their jobs, causing the entire family to deal with a loss of income?

3. Suddenness versus gradual onset revolves around how much time a family has to anticipate the stressors' arrival. Whereas an unexpected illness might cause immediate crisis, pregnancy gives couples time to adjust to the idea of being parents.

4. The severity of a stressor can also make a difference. Are you dealing with the death of a child or the purchase of a new home, for example?

5. How long families have to adjust to a stressor can affect how they cope. Whereas the first day of kindergarten happens only once, learning how to care for a spouse with cancer is a long-term stressor event.

6. Whether the stressor is expected or not can also make a difference. We can expect to have difficult times while our children are adolescents, but we do not expect to be the victim of a road-rage crime.

7. The seventh criterion is whether the stressor is natural or artificial/human made. For example, are you trying to deal with the damage left behind by Hurricane Katrina, or are you dealing with the loss of a job because of increased technological advantages at your canning plant?

8. Finally, the family's perception of whether or not they are able to solve the crisis situation can determine how they react to the stressor. It is much easier to respond to something such as being a member of a blended family than it is to deal with a terrorist attack, over which we have little control. Thus, when looking at the A component of ABC-X model, use these eight criteria to determine how to define and describe the stressor event in a determination of how it will affect the family.

Resources (B)

Once a stressor has affected a family, the family must figure out how to deal with the event or situation. One way of doing this is by accessing resources, the B component of this model. Recall the work of Angell (1936), who described the ideas of family integration and adaptability. The ability to pull together as a family and to be flexible based on the circumstances are both resources. These two resources were further developed into a more complex model by Olson and McCubbin (1982), but the premise remains the same: Family members must learn to balance being cohesive and being individuals while also finding ways to retain their boundaries as a family, unless doing so brings harm to the family. In other words, family members stick together as a cohesive unit when facing a crisis and pull together to help one another, but they also learn when they need to go outside the family and seek help.

McCubbin and Patterson (1985) stated that we should think of resources as falling within three categories: individual, family, and community. For example, one way to deal with the loss of a job is to figure out what you can do to solve the problem or find another job. In this case, individual resources would be level of education, job experience, perseverance, and work ethic. One can also use family resources to deal with unemployment by being supportive and encouraging to one another, making contacts with those you know in the job market, helping your spouse with a résumé, and sharing household responsibilities to allow more time for a job search. Finally, one can also turn to the community for such help as job relocation services, headhunters, having people at church help you make contacts and keep you in their prayers, and having other friends help with some of your current tasks to allow you more time to search for a job. The more resources you have available, the better you are able to cope. Thus, the best response to stress is to use a variety of resources.

According to McKenry and Price (2000), social support is one of the most important resources we can access. This can be provided by families instrumentally (i.e., with household chores or writing a résumé), emotionally, and through the building of increased social networks. Being supported also has the added benefit of building one's self-esteem because our feelings of self-worth increase when others are willing to help us—it is seen as a sign of love and support. We can also receive social support from community resources such as increased networking, help with problem-solving skills, and providing assistance in accessing valuable resources.

The role of social support is so strong that Kotchick, Dorsey, and Heller (2005) suggested that it can act as a buffer for single African American mothers living in low-income environmentally hazardous conditions with their children. In their family stress model, the neighborhood is the stressor which decreases mom's psychological functioning which in turn leads to impaired parenting. However, having good social support from friends, neighbors, and family can lead to more positive parenting practices and can minimize the effects of environmental stress.

Definition of the Situation (C)

Lazarus and Launier (1978) suggested that what individuals think about or how they interpret the stressor is as important as accessing resources when determining how a family will react to a crisis. This is often assessed in research concerning coping with a chronic illness such as cancer. Cognitive appraisal and coping processes are thought of as mediators of individual psychological responses to stressors such as being diagnosed and living with cancer (Folkman 1999; Lazarus and Folkman 1984). Optimism, or the belief that more good things will happen than bad, helps a person to view a stressor as more challenging than threatening, which has been associated with more positive outcomes in breast cancer patients (Carver et al. 1993; Epping-Jordan et al. 1999). The appraisal process in turn influences the thoughts and behaviors used to manage stress—coping. Thus, individuals with cancer who are optimistic about their chances of survival are better able to deal with their diagnosis than those who see it as an insurmountable problem (Smith and Soliday 2001).

The self-fulfilling prophecy, which is "a prediction of behavior which biases people to act as though the prediction were already true" (Papalia and Olds 1996, 487), also influences our perceptions of stressors. Burr (1982) related this to stress theory by saying that individuals and families who believe that a stressor cannot be solved are dooming themselves to failure. By contrast, those who can cognitively reframe the problem as being something they can handle are better able to manage the stressor. For example, if a student convinces herself she cannot pass an exam, she is likely to study less than she would otherwise, which may lead to her actually failing the exam. By contrast, if she had confidence that she could pass the exam, or her perception was that she was able to pass the exam, she would probably study more, which would most probably lead to success.

An important part of this process is how the stressor is broken down into manageable tasks. For example, rather than looking at the problem in its entirety, such as moving to a new town to take a new job, make a list of things that have to be done in each location. That way you're focusing on only one item at a time rather than being overwhelmed with all that has to be done. Cognitive reappraisal is a part of this process as well; we attempt to decrease the intensity of the emotions surrounding the situation as much as possible. Rather than viewing the move as tearing you away from a place you love, focus on the endless adventures that await you in a new town and a new work environment. This changes the emotional energy from negative to more positive. Finally, family members should encourage each other to maintain their normal lives rather than allow the problem to consume them. In this example, that would mean spending time with friends you care about and doing things in your community as a family while still working toward completing the tasks necessary to make the big move.

Stress and Crisis (X)

Whether or not a family will enter a state of crisis is determined by the previously discussed components of the ABC-X model. A crisis is reached when the family is no longer able to maintain its usual balance because of the stressor event. It is important to note that not all stressors will lead to crisis. In addition, just because a family faces a crisis does not mean the family will be broken apart because of it. In fact, families often function better and are more cohesive after a crisis than they were before, as was shown previously, when the roller-coaster model of adjustment to crisis (Hill 1949) was discussed in the example of how differently couples adjust to having a newborn.

PRIMARY TERMS AND CONCEPTS

Stressors

Now that we know the basics of the theory, it is important to define a few of the concepts in more detail, which will be done following the ABC-X model. Olson, Lavee, and McCubbin (1988) defined stressors as "discrete life events or transitions that have an impact upon the family unit and produce, or have the potential to produce, change in the family system" (19). Notice that this definition uses the word *discrete*, which implies that stressors are singular. In other words, in this model, we deal with one stress-producing event at a time. It is also important to note that stressors are neither positive nor negative by themselves but become one or the other based on how we define the situation. Thus, what is negative for one person might be a positive event for another. Becoming pregnant may be perceived differently by a fifteen-year-old with plans to attend medical school versus Marsha and Sean discussed at the beginning of this chapter, who have taken extraordinary measures in an attempt to become pregnant. Both families are faced with the same event, pregnancy, but what is a painful and difficult predicament for the teenager is a cause for celebration for the Peabody family.

Your sample reading for this chapter is based on ambiguous loss as a potential stressor for families (Betz and Thorngren 2006). This refers to types of losses, physical or psychological, which are not as commonly understood or accepted as something like the death of a spouse. It includes losses such as a missing family member (i.e., due to war or child abduction), a miscarriage, or having a parent who is suffering from dementia and no longer able to recognize you. Falicov (2007) described transnational migration as a similar type of loss as the length of time away from family, ability to survive in the new country, and challenges faced during the migration itself are examples of the multitude of potential stressors.

Normative Event

Similarly, while stressors can be both positive and negative, they can also be normative or nonnormative. A normative event has three primary components: It is something that occurs in all families, you can anticipate its occurrence, and it is short-term rather than chronic (McCubbin and Patterson 1983). Examples of normative stressors would be the birth of a child, learning how to deal with a teenager, buying your first home, and facing retirement. We are better able to deal with those stressors that are normative because we have had some time to think about how we will handle the situation or what resources we can access. Nonnormative stressors such as losing an infant to sudden infant death syndrome or the separation of family members due to war are not anticipated and, thus, are more likely to lead to a crisis.

Resources

The *B* component of the model—resources—are characteristics, traits, or abilities of individuals, families, or communities, as was discussed earlier (McCubbin and Patterson 1985). One resource not already mentioned is that of *coping*, which is what we do in an attempt to deal with a stressor. Coping is really an interaction of our resources and our perceptions as we choose those resources we draw upon based on our perceptions of what will work and what won't. For example, if a student has a big paper due on Monday, and it's now Sunday night, and he is sick but hasn't started the paper yet, there is a problem. One way for him to cope with that problem is to simply admit that the paper won't be his best work but that he can still get it done if he locks himself in his room with his reference materials and his computer. In this case, he has defined the problem as solvable and used the resources at his disposal—his work ethic, self-confidence, and creativity—to write the paper. If, on the other hand, he decides that he just can't get it done and will explain it to his professor tomorrow, he might cope by going to bed, which in turn is likely to result in a failing grade on his paper.

Lazarus and Folkman (1984), among others, believe there are three primary ways to define how families cope: using direct actions, intrapsychically, or by controlling the emotions associated with the stressor itself. *Direct actions* mean actually doing something, such as searching the community for resources, writing a new résumé, or seeking counseling to help deal with a problem. *Intrapsychic coping* refers to cognitively reframing the problem so that it does not seem so overwhelming or insurmountable. Finally, while some people "control the emotions" caused by the stressor in positive ways such as talking with a friend or going to a religious service, others use more destructive means, such as turning to alcohol or drugs in an attempt to dull the pain or alleviate the emotions. Regardless of how a family copes, the ultimate goal is to return the family to its previous state of functioning—in other words, trying to solve the problem so things can return to normal.

Crisis

Here it is important to make a distinction between stress and crisis. Whereas *family stress* is something experienced by families that causes a change in the family or upsets their sense of normalcy, *crisis* is a state or period of disorganization that rocks the foundation of the family. One should also bear in mind that whereas families can experience different degrees of stress, one is either in crisis or not in crisis. When does stress become crisis? Families encounter crisis when it can no longer maintain the status quo using their existing resources, or when it is so overwhelmed as to be incapacitated (Boss 1988).

Adaptation

The level of family adaptation is usually thought to fall somewhere between *bonadaptation*, a positive result to the crisis, and *maladaptation*, an unhealthy or dysfunctional resolution of the crisis. For example, whereas some families deal with the job loss of one spouse by pulling together and pooling resources until a new job is found (bonadaptation), other families fall apart in this situation, fighting with each other, and turning to alcohol to cope with the loss (maladaptation).

COMMON AREAS OF RESEARCH AND APPLICATION

In their review of the use of family stress theory during the 1970s, McCubbin et al. (1980) pointed out that while much research has taken place to provide support of Hill's (1949) original theory, there was also a good deal of research on normative life events such as the transition to parenthood, adjusting to widowhood, relocation and institutionalization, and adapting to retirement. Interestingly, similar research is still taking place using stress theory as a basis for analysis and discussion.

Informal Family Care

For example, Fredrikson and Scharlach (1999) noted that this theory has been used extensively in the study of informal types of care. Their research focuses on the outcomes of working and caregiving at the same time and the stressor pileup that can result from having multiple, conflicting roles. They suggest that stressors such as caring for disabled family members or finding alternative sick child care can be dealt with using resources such as social support and professional caregivers. It was also found that the greater the intensity of the stressor—job demands, degree of child or parent disability, or accessibility to caregiving resources—the higher the level of stress and greater the potential for crisis.

Work and Family

Bernas and Major (2000) also studied a variation of this topic as they looked at the stress associated with work and family conflict and resources that can alleviate this stress, or at least prevent it from leading to crisis. They focused on social resources such as friends, family members, and coworkers as well as personal resources such as hardiness (i.e., being committed to each role, having a sense of control over roles, and the ability to positively frame stressors as challenges rather than unsurmountable obstacles). They found that both types of resources positively impact a parent's, particularly a mother's, ability to balance work and family roles.

Adolescent Coping

Another normative stressor currently being researched using stress theory is the work of Plunkett and Henry (1999), who studied how adolescents' level of stress, and the type of coping resources they access to deal with these stressors, affect adolescent family life satisfaction. One thing that led to lower levels of adaptation for adolescents was their perceptions of parental overt conflict (hostility, mocking, insulting, screaming, or threatening). They also found that "adolescents who perceived increased stress due to the pileup of life event stressors reported decreased family life satisfaction" (616). In addition, the use of detrimental coping strategies such as drugs or alcohol to escape stress also resulted in lower family satisfaction, whereas those who used social support to cope with stress had more positive views of family life. Thus, one must recognize the multitude of things that cause stress for adolescents, analyze how they perceive each of these stressors, and encourage the use of positive coping strategies to keep adolescents from entering a crisis state, which may lead to problems.

Nonnormative Stressors

Many nonnormative stressors are also being assessed using family stress theory. Although the process of divorce is becoming more normative in its existence, it is still considered a nonnormative event, because couples do not enter a marriage expecting to divorce. Wang and Amato (2000) studied how families adjust to divorce based on divorce stressors (loss of income, loss of friends, moving), perceptions (positive versus negative views), and resources (supportive friends and family, education, employment, and income). While their research, by contrast to past research in this area, found only minimal support for stress theory, they did determine the importance of obtaining a participant's subjective assessment of whether or not the divorce was a positive or negative event. In other words, perhaps one of the most important parts of the model for this topic is the individual's perception of the divorce itself: Having a more positive attitude toward the divorce and available social resources leads to better postdivorce adjustment.

Nonnormative Caregiving

Whereas we discussed some of the caregiving literature focused around normative events, there can also be unexpected situations, such as mental or physical illness, that require a caregiver as well. Provencher et al. (2000) reviewed measures using a family stress theory framework that is available to assess how caregivers of individuals with schizophrenia cope. Primary emphasis was placed on the fact that although much of the literature in this area identifies how caregivers respond to the stress of caring for the behavioral needs of individuals with schizophrenia, there is little study of how caregivers perceive their roles or how they cope with caring for the individual. It seems obvious that each of these components would influence the behaviors of caregivers as discussed in the ABC-X model.

With 10 percent of American grandparents today raising their grandchildren, this is another caregiving situation that is increasing in prevalence (Heywood 1999). Stressors for this population include financial problems, health problems, returning to employment after retirement, and a decreased social life due to returning to childcare activities. Because of this, access to resources such as child and medical care, counseling, and social support is important. Because many of these grandparents are putting their "golden years" on hold to become full-time parents once again, it is also important that they make the choice willingly or perceive the event as being positive. The incredible amount of stress experienced by this population has led to a good deal of research using family stress theory (Sands and Goldberg-Glen 2000).

Similarly, Hardesty et al. (2008) studied caregivers (primarily grandparents) who were caring for children following the violent death of their mothers at the hands of their intimate partners. In addition to the stressors mentioned earlier for grandparents raising grandchildren, you now have children who were typically exposed to domestic violence prior to the homicide, many of whom saw the murders take place or were there for the aftermath, and children who then watched the family members of the victims and perpetrators fight over what should be done with them. The ABC-X model was an excellent tool in this study for understanding the experiences of both the children and their caregivers.

Finally, one more area of nonnormative caregiving is taking care of someone with, or living with, a chronic illness. As was stated earlier, much of the research in the area of chronic illness uses a stress theory approach to determine how individuals and families cope with the diagnosis of a chronic illness such as cancer. This is especially difficult when the form of cancer is extremely rare, as in the case of carcinoid cancer (Soliday et al. 2004). Much of the stress for these patients comes from uncertainty about the disease itself as well as the knowledge that there is currently no cure. It was found that the perception of the diagnosis as either a death sentence or something that can be coped with by living life to the fullest affects patient levels of depression. In addition, coping strategies differed widely from one individual to the next, again supporting the need to address both individual and family reactions to stressors as well as to make inferences to large populations only with extreme caution (Smith and Soliday 2001).

Family Ambiguity

As you will soon read, family systems theory states that families have boundaries which determine who is or is not a part of the family system, and/or what roles people play within the family. When those positions or roles are unclear, family boundary ambiguity exists (Boss and Greenberg 1984). Researchers have integrated this concept into family systems theory as being either the cause of stress (the *A* component) or as being defined by the perceptions of the individual family members (the *C* component). So, for example, integrating a stepparent into the home may cause family members to have to share resources, change rituals, or reevaluate their boundaries, and so could all be potential stressors. How they perceive this person, however, will also influence the level of boundary ambiguity. Family stress research and therapeutic practices have benefited from the integration of boundary ambiguity into the ABC-X model of family stress in areas such as missing-in-action family members, death of a family member, divorce, remarriage, stepfamilies, family health care issues, and research on clergy families (Carroll, Olsen, and Buckmiller 2007).

Thus, if there is one thing we can conclude from this review of current literature based on family stress theory, it is that the theory is as relevant today as it was in its inception in the 1930s. One would predict that as people face more and more stressors in their lives, and society becomes increasingly complex, the use of this theory will remain stable. Perhaps the most common approach will be a combined theoretical orientation as authors discuss issues, such as those in the previous paragraph, using this theory in addition to other theoretical approaches more specific to their topic of study.

CRITIQUE

Despite the fact that this theory has been widely used since its introduction in the 1930s, many have identified problems in the theory. Perhaps the most well-established problem is the fact that this is a linear model trying to explain complex families and situations. In other words, it is often not one single event that causes a family to become stressed to the point of crisis but rather an accumulation of events. To address this problem, McCubbin and Patterson (1982) developed the Double ABC-X model (see fig. 4.2), based on their research on families who had a member either captured or unaccounted for after the war. The model begins with the traditional ABC-X model and treats this as the precipitating event. However, it adds the postcrisis period of adjustment, which takes into consideration the fact that families must respond not just to the initial crisis itself but to the events that precede and follow that event as well. With that in mind, the Double ABC-X model uses the traditional model as its base and then replicates this model with a different interpretation to represent postcrisis adjustment.

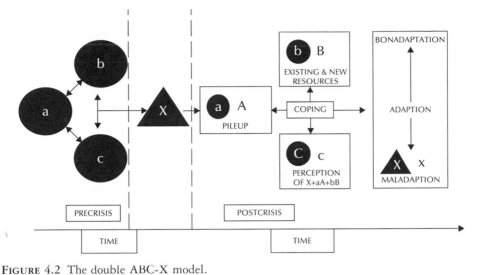

FIGURE 4.2 The double ABC-X model.

Source: McCubbin, H. I., A. E. Carble, and J. M. Patterson. 1982. *Family Stress Coping and Social Support,* 46. New York: Brunner/Mazel.

The Double A Factor: Stress and Change

There are three components to the double A factor: the initial stressor, changes in the family, and stressors resulting from attempting to cope with the initial stressor. Therefore, if you're attempting to deal with the loss of a job, the initial stressor event, you often have other things that happen at the same time that compound the stress. Perhaps, the family has to change roles to accommodate the husband now being at home while the wife is the only parent working. In this case, the father will now take on housework and childcare responsibilities, which can be stressful for him as he learns to balance those duties while also searching for employment. It is also possible that the resources you access to help you deal with the loss of a job, such as having an in-law come and help out with the kids because you can no longer afford childcare, are in and of themselves a source of stress. Having multiple stressors at one time is called stressor pileup.

The Double B Factor: Family Resources

While the initial stressor caused the family to access those resources that were immediately available, often those resources are not enough to keep the family from entering a crisis state. When those resources fail, families must turn to new sources, learn new skills, or strengthen old skills in order to cope. Thus, the double B factor takes into account the fact that sometimes those resources on which we rely cannot help us solve the problem, in which case we must seek out new opportunities.

The Double C Factor: Family Perception

The double C factor component is concerned not only with the family's response to or beliefs about the initial stressor but also with how they interpret their previous responses to the crisis situation itself. For example, a family faced with the death of a child will assess how they interpret the death of the child and then how they assess their ability to cope with that loss. How a family perceives its ability to respond to situations such as this can determine how they will continue to cope with the ramifications of this event.

The Double X Factor: Family Crisis and Adaptation

In the double X factor, the postcrisis adaptation hinges on how the family has adapted to the initial crisis as well as how it has adapted to the new level of family functioning. In other words, does the situation break the family apart or build the family up? This time, however, we are referring to the entire family system rather than just how the family responded to one event or situation.

Mundane Extreme Environmental Stress Model

It was thought by Peters and Massey (1983) that family stress theory does not truly represent the experiences of those who experience oppression on a continual basis as, for example, African American family members do. In fact, these researchers thought that racism and discrimination were so much a part of their daily lives that they were not an additional stressor as implied by Hill's (1949) model but instead were a part of everyday life. Thus, they developed the mundane extreme environmental stress (MEES) model, which adds three components to the original ABC-X model. The first addition is an A factor, which represents constant exposure to racial discrimination, most of which is both chronic and unpredictable. In this case, it's not another stressor but simply a piece of the puzzle that must be examined when studying African American family stress. The second addition is the D factor, which is the pervasive environmental stress associated with being of minority status in the United States. This is more anticipated because it is a part of daily living. Finally, the Y factor is the lens through which crisis situations must be viewed for African American families because their experiences are different from those of majority status. Thus, this model simply builds upon the traditional family stress theory by adding the need to take racial discrimination into account when studying African American families.

Family Adjustment and Adaptation Response (FAAR) Model

A final extension of family stress theory, which addresses critics who say that this is only an individual theory focusing on one specific topic, is Patterson's (1988) FAAR model, which basically expands the previous theory to be more inclusive of family systems. In this framework, families attempt to balance the demands they face with their capacity to deal with them, as influenced by the family meaning or definition/interpretation of the situation. When these demands are beyond the family's ability to deal with them, the family experiences crisis. Thus, the model looks at the processes families use in an attempt to restore balance while also including what is added by individual family members, the family unit itself, and the community.

This model has been further tested in the field of family resiliency (Patterson 2002). Resiliency means thriving or succeeding despite adverse circumstances.

The focus here is on why some families do well while others are torn apart by stressful or high-risk situations. It is hoped that by determining the process that allows those families to thrive, we can help those families that are unable to balance their demands on their own.

Another common criticism of family stress theory is that it focuses on only one issue: stress. Because of this, the theory will perhaps never be considered a grand theory or a theory that one can apply to any discipline or situation. However, this should not overshadow the primary strength of this theory, which is its applicability to real-life situations. There is a great deal of literature using this theory as a basis for therapy. For example, you can help a couple deal with their lack of communication by having them analyze each component of the ABC-X model in an attempt to keep them from entering crisis, or if they're already in crisis to help them adapt positively. Similarly, this theory is helpful when studying any topic that produces stress that has the potential to lead to crisis for an individual or a family. In addition, this is one of the few theories reviewed that has shown continual development, as is illustrated in this critique. Although it may not have reached the status some would like in order for it to be included in a textbook on family theory, it is a great example of an evolving theory with more and more application to family situations in modern times. Thus, while the scope of the theory is perhaps limited to dealing with stress, its applicability is far reaching.

APPLICATION

1. Think about the story of the Peabody family at the beginning of this chapter. How does the ABC-X model apply to their lives? What are the family's stressor(s), resources, and definition of the situation? How are they coping? Would one of the other models covered be more useful here? If so, why?

2. Name three things that are causing you stress right now in your life. How would you use the ABC-X model to analyze each situation and figure out how to keep those stressors from leading to crisis?

3. Look at your list of stressors again. Which of these would be better explained by using the Double ABC-X model? Analyze the situation again using this model.

4. Early family stress research was focused on the Depression and the effects of war on families. What are some events in society today that could benefit from research using this theory? Outline the basic components of the model as they apply to current situations.

5. What do you think the ABC-X model is missing? How do current models address or fail to address these issues? How would you further modify the model?

6. Entering college exposes you to many potential stressors (Darling et al. 2007). A freshman has come to you because he is dealing with some of these stressors. How would you use the ABC-X model to help him deal with these issues?

7. Think about the eight criteria Lipman-Bluman (1975) developed to determine how much a stressor will impact a family. Pick a form of ambiguous loss as described in your sample reading and see how each of these eight criteria apply to it. How will these factors affect the family's ability to cope?

REFERENCES

Angell, R. C. 1936. *The family encounters the depression*. New York: Charles Scribner.

Bernas, K. H., and D. A. Major. 2000. Contributors to stress resistance: Testing a model of women's work-family conflict. *Psychology of Women Quarterly* 24(2): 170–178.

Betz, G., and J. M. Thorngren. 2006. Ambiguous loss and the family grieving process. *The Family Journal* 14(4): 359–365.

Boss, P. 1988. *Family stress management*. Newbury Park, CA: Sage.

Boss, P., and J. Greenberg. 1984. Family boundary ambiguity: A new variable in family stress theory. *Family Process* 23: 535–546.

Burr, W. R. 1982. Families under stress. In *Family stress, coping, and social support*, ed. H. I. McCubbin, A. E. Cauble, and J. M. Patterson, 5–25. Springfield, IL: Charles C. Thomas.

Burr, W. R., and S. R. Klein. 1994. *Reexamining family stress: New theory and research*. Thousand Oaks, CA: Sage.

Carroll, J. S., C. D. Olson, and N. Buckmiller. 2007. Family boundary ambiguity: A 30-year review of theory, research, and measurement. *Family Relations* 56(2): 210–230.

Carver, C. S., C. Pozo, S. D. Harris, V. Noriega, M. F. Scheier, D. S. Robinson, A. S. Ketcham, F. L. Moffat, and K. C. Clark. 1993. How coping mediates the effect of optimism on distress: A study of women with early stage breast cancer. *Journal of Personality and Social Psychology* 64: 375–390.

Cavan, R. S., and K. H. Ranck. 1938. *The family and the depression*. Chicago: Univ. of Chicago Press.

Darling, C. A., L. M. McWey, S. N. Howard, and S. B. Olmstead. 2007. College student stress: The influence of interpersonal relationships on sense of coherence. *Stress and Health* 23: 215–229.

Epping-Jordan, J. E., B. E. Compas, D. M. Osowiecki, G. Oppedisano, C. Gerhardt, K. Primo, and D. N. Krag. 1999. Psychological adjustment in breast cancer: Processes of emotional distress. *Health Psychology* 18: 315–326.

Falicov, C. J. 2007. Working with transnational immigrants: Expanding meanings of family, community, and culture. *Family Process* 46(2): 157–171.

Folkman, S. 1999. Thoughts about psychological factors, PNI, and cancer. *Advances in Mind-Body Medicine* 15: 236–259.

Fredrikson, K. I., and A. E. Scharlach. 1999. Employee family care responsibilities. *Family Relations* 48(2): 189–196.

Hardesty, J. L., J. C. Campbell, J. M. McFarlane, and L. A. Lewandowski. 2008. How children and their caregivers adjust after intimate partner femicide. *Journal of Family Issues* 24(1): 100–124.

Heywood, E. M. 1999. Custodial grandparents and their grandchildren. *Family Journal* 7(4): 367–372.

Hill, R. 1949. *Families under stress: Adjustment to the crisis of war separation and reunion*. New York: Harper and Brothers.

Koos, E. L. 1946. *Families in trouble*. New York: Kings Crown Press.

Kotchick, B. A., S. Dorsey, and L. Heller. 2005. Predictors of parenting among African American single mothers: Personal and contextual factors. *Journal of Marriage and Family* 67(2): 448–460.

Lazarus, R. S., and S. Folkman. 1984. *Stress, appraisal, and coping*. New York: Springer.

Lazarus, R. S., and R. Launier, R. 1978. Stress-related transactions between person and environment. In *Perspectives in interactional psychology*, ed. L. A. Pervia and M. Lewis, 360–392. New York: Plenum.

Lipman-Bluman, J. 1975. A crisis framework applied to macrosociological family changes: Marriage, divorce, and occupational trends associated with World War II. *Journal of Marriage and the Family* 3: 889–902.

McCubbin, H. I., C. B. Joy, A. E. Cauble, J. K. Comeau, J. M. Patterson, and R. H. Needle. 1980. Family stress and coping: A decade review. *Journal of Marriage and the Family* 42: 855–871.

McCubbin, H. I., and J. M. Patterson. 1982. Family adaptation to crisis. In *Family stress, coping, and social support*, ed. H. I. McCubbin, A. E. Cauble, and J. M. Patterson, 26–47. Springfield, IL: Charles C. Thomas.

———. 1983. Family transitions: Adaptation to stress. In *Stress and the family: Coping with normative transitions*, ed. H. I. McCubbin and C. R. Figley. Vol. 1, 2–25. New York: Brunner/Mazel.

———. 1985. Adolescent stress, coping, and adaptation: A normative family perspective. In *Adolescents in families*, ed. G. K. Leigh and G. W. Peterson, 256–276. Cincinnati, OH: Southwestern.

McKenry, P. C., and S. J. Price. 2000. Families coping with problems and change: A conceptual overview. In *Families and change: Coping with stressful events and transitions*, ed. P. C. McKenry and S. J. Price, 1–21. Thousand Oaks, CA: Sage.

Olson, D. H., and H. I. McCubbin. 1982. Circumplex model of marital and family systems V: Application to family stress and crisis intervention. In *Family stress, coping, and social support*, ed. H. I. McCubbin, A. E. Cauble, and J. M. Patterson, 48–72. Springfield, IL: Charles C. Thomas.

Olson, D. H., Y. Lavee, and H. I. McCubbin. 1988. Types of families and family response to stress across the family life cycle. In *Social stress and family development*, ed. D. M. Klein and J. Aldous, 16–43. New York: Guilford.

Papalia, D. E., and S. W. Olds. 1996. *A child's world: Infancy through adolescence.* 7th ed. New York: McGraw-Hill.

Patterson, J. 1988. Families experiencing stress: The family adjustment and adaptation response model. *Family Systems Medicine* 5(2): 202–237.

Patterson, J. M. 2002. Integrating family resiliency and family stress theory. *Journal of Marriage and the Family* 64(2): 349–360.

Peters, M. F., and G. Massey. 1983. Chronic vs. mundane stress in family stress theories: The case of black families in white America. *Marriage and Family Review* 6: 193–218.

Plunkett, S. W., and C. S. Henry. 1999. Adolescent perceptions of interparental conflict, stressors, and coping as predictors of adolescent family life satisfaction. *Sociological Inquiry* 69(4):599–620.

Provencher, H. L., J. P. Fournier, M. Perreault, and J. Vezina. 2000. The caregiver's perception of behavioral disturbance in relatives with schizophrenia: A stress-coping approach. *Community Mental Health Journal* 36(3): 293–306.

Sands, R. G., and R. S. Goldberg-Glen. 2000. Factors associated with stress among grandparents raising their grandchildren. *Family Relations* 49: –105.

Smith, S. R., and E. Soliday. 2001. The effects of parental chronic kidney disease on the family. *Family Relations* 50(2): 171–177.

Soliday, E., J. P. Garofalo, S. R. Smith, and R. R. P. Warner. 2004. Psychosocial functioning of carcinoid cancer patients: Test of a stress and coping medicated model. *Journal of Applied Biobehavioral Research* 9(3): 156–171.

Wang, H., and P. R. Amato. 2000. Predictors of divorce and adjustment: Stressors, resources, and definitions. *Journal of Marriage and the Family* 62(3): 655–668.

SAMPLE READING

Betz, G., and J. M. Thorngren. 2006. Ambiguous loss and the family grieving process. *The Family Journal* 14(4): 359–365.

This article uses the ABC-X model as a therapeutic tool to help families who are dealing with an ambiguous loss. An ambiguous loss is one not typically socially recognized, such as a family member whose whereabouts are not known or having a spouse with Alzheimer's disease who no longer knows who you are despite the fact that you are providing care on a daily basis.

SAMPLE READING

AMBIGUOUS LOSS AND THE FAMILY GRIEVING PROCESS

Gabrielle Betz
Jill M. Thorngren
Montana State University

Ambiguous losses are physical or psychological experiences of families that are not as concrete or identifiable as traditional losses such as death. Ambiguous loss could include anything from miscarriage to losing one's spouse to Alzheimer's disease while he or she is still living. Ambiguous loss may include not knowing whether or not a loved one is living or dead, such as cases of child abduction or military personnel who are missing in action. Ambiguous loss is inherently characterized by lack of closure or clear understanding. This article defines types of ambiguous losses and details some of their characteristics. A model for counseling families who are experiencing ambiguous loss is described. Specifically, the model combines family stress theory with narrative therapy techniques to help families define their losses, assess their resources, and develop meaningful narratives about the loss.

Keywords: ambiguous loss; grief; family stress; narrative therapy

CHARACTERISTICS OF AMBIGUOUS LOSS

When Grandmother dies, it is a clear and recognizable form of loss. Although it is terribly painful to lose a loved one, the passing of an elderly person is viewed as a natural part of life. There are prescribed rituals such as the receipt of the death certificate, the reading of a written will that allocates finances and possessions to certain

Authors' Note: Correspondence concerning this article should be addressed to Jill Thorngren, College of Education, Health and Human Development, Montana State University, Bozeman, MT 59717; e-mail: jillt@montana.edu.

THE FAMILY JOURNAL: COUNSELING AND THERAPY FOR COUPLES AND FAMILIES, Vol. 14 No. 4, October 2006 359–365
DOI: 10.1177/1066480706290052
© 2006 Sage Publications

individuals, and an obituary in the newspaper, and there is typically a funeral where friends and family members gather to lay the deceased to rest. It is often unquestionable that family will take time off from work, and they will receive condolences, cards, and flowers from sympathizers. Many find comfort in their religion and hope to be reunited with their loved one after death. These cultural practices and social support systems help to facilitate the grieving process. Because their loss is publicly recognized and legitimized, family members are more likely to receive support from the community.

There are numerous losses families experience on a daily or ongoing basis that are not recognized or legitimized by society. Many losses are not as clearly definable as death. It may not even be certain as to what was lost. Loss may involve a person, an object, an experience, or an event. Such ambiguous losses may include divorce or the ending of a relationship, infertility, miscarriage, abortion, unemployment, migration, sexual abuse, chronic illness or disability, adult children leaving home, or mental illness (Boss, 1999; Knauer, 2002; Rycroft & Perlesz, 2001). Boss (1999) identifies two types of ambiguous loss. The first is when a person is physically absent yet psychologically present. A child who is given up for adoption, a soldier who is listed as missing in action, or a divorced father who is no longer living with his children are all examples. Family members may not know if the person is still alive or the state of his or her wellbeing. Although the person is not physically present, he or she is still very much a part of the psychological family and continuously in family members' thoughts. The second kind of ambiguous loss involves someone being physically present but psychologically absent. A mother who is slowly deteriorating because of Alzheimer's disease, a brother whose life is consumed by alcoholism, or a husband who is preoccupied with his career and spends little time with his family are examples. Psychological absence is confusing because the emotional bond appears to be missing or gradually slipping away. As with Alzheimer's, the sufferer may no longer recognize loved ones or resemble the person he or she used to be. Family members may question whether the person who is psychologically absent is even a part of the family anymore. This may bring up further questions regarding role shifts in the family.

For the family who experiences ambiguous loss, the situation is stressful and oftentimes cruel in its unending torment. Because the loss is intangible or uncertain, the mourning process for family members becomes complicated. Ambiguous loss is characterized by factors that inherently impede the grieving process (Boss, 1999, 2002). For example, it is cognitively difficult to understand what has happened or why. The family of a child who has been kidnapped may endure for years not knowing if that missing child will ever return. The natural progression of their lives stops the day the child is abducted. Parents may berate themselves for not having protected their child and jump at every phone call hoping that it may be news of their child's whereabouts. A surviving child may harbor guilt for fighting with his or her sibling, wondering if he or she is to blame or if he or she may be abducted as well. The family may be terrified of betraying their missing member by considering the child dead when they should be out searching. The typical stages and rituals related to grieving no longer apply.

When faced with ambiguous loss, family members may get stuck in the same roles or no longer know what their roles entail. For the mother who has given up her child for adoption, she is uncertain how to answer the question when posed as to how many children she has. She may feel confused as to whether or not she is a mother at all if she is not raising her child. A family whose member is physically absent but psychologically present may go on with daily life as if the person is still with them. They may set a place for the missing person at the dinner table or buy gifts for the holidays. Family members may feel on edge, afraid to talk about what is happening or how they really feel. They become trapped in their helpless roles. Other losses such as divorce, infertility, chronic illness, and disability can cause one to view the self as less than ideal, a failure as a man or woman (Tshudin, 1997).

Loss is a reminder that life is not always kind or fair (Boss, 1999). Tragic circumstances can strike the happiest and healthiest of families. The family is put in a no-win situation, and their questions may never be resolved. Ambiguous loss leaves people feeling powerless in their lives and insecure in their future. For example, a woman who suffers a miscarriage may wonder if she did something wrong. Others may not understand or recognize the depth of her loss—the death of a child, the ending of a dream and future, and the unfilled expectation of being a mother (Werner-Lin & Moro, 2004). Comments such as "you can always have another one" or "it was meant to be" invalidate the experience as an important loss. Perhaps if she miscarried early in the first trimester, she may not have told others yet about the pregnancy and subsequent miscarriage. She can become isolated in her grief. Loss forces the individual to recognize that there are some things that cannot be controlled.

Grieving often involves an examination of one's values and beliefs and calls into question who one truly is. Losing a job may prompt the unemployed person to consider his or her self-worth if he or she is not contributing or supporting his or her family financially. He or she may feel incapable, helpless, angry, ashamed, rejected, betrayed, and useless (Tshudin, 1997). It is customary in American culture to define oneself by a person's career. When people ask, "What do you do?" they are really asking, "Who are you?" Job loss affects a person's identity and role in society. When people lose their previous state of health because of illness or injury, they may no longer be able to do the things most important to them such as traveling, recreating, or socializing. They lose their identity and way of being in the world. They may question if life is even worth living. The recently deceased Christopher Reeve expressed his desire to die after he was paralyzed in a horseback riding accident. It was only through a painful grieving process that he redefined himself and became a passionate advocate for stem cell research. Losses such as death can trigger associated ambiguous losses. The death of an elderly mother may cause the adult daughter to grieve for her own lost youth and realize her own mortality (Tshudin, 1997). She mourns the loss of her role as daughter or caretaker and a connection to her past. She may feel that her relationship was not what she had hoped and sense the loss of the opportunity to resolve past differences or issues. She may regret that her children no longer have a grandmother.

If not dealt with, ambiguous loss can exacerbate family stress tremendously. Although stress in all families is inevitable and the stress related to ambiguous loss can be particularly depleting, family stress theory contends that the family's response to stress determines the degree of its impact (Madden-Derdich & Herzog, 2005). Utilizing Hill's (1958) ABC-X model of family stress is one method for helping families who are experiencing ambiguous loss recognize their grief and harness the resources they have for coping with such loss. Although Hill's original work is somewhat dated, adaptations of the model are still very much used in working with contemporary family issues (McKenry & Price, 2005). The ABC-X model of family stress contends that the intensity or severity of stress is comprised of three components. The actual stress (A), plus the available resources for coping with the stress (B), plus the perceptions of each family member about the stress (C) equals the actual degrees of stress (X).

Because of the inherent nature of ambiguous loss, there is no one-size-fits-all model for helping families cope with its multifaceted stressors. One must cope differently when still caring for a spouse with Alzheimer's than one would cope with the ambiguous loss that accompanies losing a spouse through divorce. Rituals surrounding a terminally ill child are probably different than those related to coping with a child who is missing. The first step, therefore, in applying this model to ambiguous loss would entail determining what the actual stress is or defining the loss. Is the loss physical or psychological? What or who exactly is lost or missing? How does the loss redefine relationships, roles, and responsibilities? For some family members, simply defining their experience as loss and worthy of grief may be comforting. Because their loss is not typical, it may be that they have not allowed themselves the same empathy that they would allow for an actual death or more readily identifiable loss.

In conjunction with identifying the loss, an exploration of available resources must also be conducted. Social support may be difficult for the family to find (Boss, 1999). People are afraid to face their own fears about loss and do not have the language to discuss ambiguous loss. Caretaking of a chronically ill person may go on for years, so friends and neighbors may not have the stamina or desire to make such a long-term commitment. Most often, people do not understand the trauma of loss—especially when that loss is unclear and uncertain (Rycroft & Perlesz, 2001). When the loss is not acknowledged socially, family members may be denied their right to grieve (Werner-Lin & Moro, 2004). This is especially true if the loss is socially stigmatized, such as if a loved one suffered from AIDS. Lesbian, gay, bisexual, and transgendered people may not have their losses validated because they are a marginalized group. The loss of a relationship or death of a partner may not be recognized if the couple had not been open about their relationship or did not receive public recognition as a married couple. Often the surviving partner has few, if any, legal rights and may lose his or her home, possessions, and children. When mourners are socially isolated, they tend to believe that they do not have a right to their feelings (Rycroft & Perlesz, 2001). Such invalidation prevents people from understanding their loss and asking for help (Werner-Lin & Moro, 2004).

Although resources may be limited when dealing with ambiguous loss, counselors still need to explore what family members are already doing to cope with the loss. The assumption is that in his or her own way, each family member is doing things to help him or her function in the face of loss. This exploration is important for two reasons. First, as family members hear what each is doing, they may develop new ideas about how to better support one another and gain new respect or understanding for what others around them are experiencing. Acting out or misbehavior may make more sense in this light. Second, the family counselor can develop an awareness of both the strengths and weaknesses in the coping strategies. Healthy behaviors such as seeking out friends or journaling can be encouraged, whereas less healthy behaviors such as turning to substances or ignoring feelings can be empathized with and then a search for more healthy coping skills can begin. In addition to assessing what resources are already being used, counselors will also want to assess what or who could be a resource that the family is not utilizing. Perhaps family members have not thought to tap potential resources, or perhaps there are negative beliefs in the family about seeking help. Accessing resources, in sum, involves looking at the behaviors related to the ambiguous loss. What are members doing or not doing, and what could be done differently in terms of coping are questions to ask.

Exploring the family's beliefs about seeking help is related to Hill's (1958) third component of stress: beliefs or perceptions family members have about the stressor. Here it is important to explore each member's thoughts and feelings about the loss. Some family members may believe that they are responsible for the loss. Others may only be expressing a limited amount of emotion regarding the loss because they are not sure what feelings they are entitled to have regarding it.

Contributing to the perceptions and emotions family members have about their loss is the fact that for most ambiguous losses, there are no rituals for mourning (Boss, 1999; Rycroft & Perlesz, 2001). A child of divorced parents is expected to adjust to his or her parents' new lifestyles. He or she desperately misses his or her old life when his or her family was all together. For the woman who has an abortion or a miscarriage, there is no body to bury or a funeral to attend (Werner-Lin & Moro, 2004). The father who experiences "empty nest syndrome" may regret not spending more time with his child and does not have a ritual to help him release the past and embrace the future (Boss, 1999). With the absence of ritual or social support, family members believe that they are unjustified in their emotions. They may try to suppress their grief and move on as they are socially expected without giving themselves permission to mourn their loss.

Counselors can help each family member tell the story of his or her loss from his or her perspective and each should be allowed an opportunity to express a wide range of feelings applicable to the loss. From this exploration of the family's stories about their losses can arise new rituals that honor the past yet also embrace the future and present. For example, the child who is experiencing the loss of his or her parent's marriage can be encouraged to mourn what he or she misses about the past and having his or her parents together and also to develop new rituals in each of his or her new homes or for staying in contact with the parent he or she less frequently sees. The woman who gives up her baby for adoption can share the mixed feelings she has regarding this decision and decide to do something that honors that child regardless of where the child now lives.

A never-ending rollercoaster, ambiguous loss takes its toll on family members physically, cognitively, behaviorally, and emotionally (Boss, 1999; Weiner, 1999). Physically they may experience fatigue, sleep disruption, headaches, or stomachaches. Cognitively they may experience a preoccupation with the loss, forgetfulness, dreaming about the loss, or worrying. Behaviorally they may experience talkativeness, quietness, crying, hyperactivity, inactivity, sighing, support seeking, withdrawal, dependence, or avoidance. Emotionally they may experience loneliness, yearning, anxiety, depression, fear, anger, irritability, apathy, or relief (Weiner, 1999). For years, they may go through cycles of hope only to be disappointed once again. The unpredictable nature of an uncertain future leaves family members in a reactive position. The family may feel tremendous guilt and may be unable to make decisions, fearing that the wrong choice will be made. Family members experience an onslaught of conflicting emotions—love and hate, hope and despair, joy and sadness, anger and frustration. Something is wrong, and the family does not know how to fix it. Family members likely differ in their views and emotions. They may withdraw from one another furthering their sense of isolation. Their grief can be exhausting.

Although working with families who are experiencing ambiguous loss is similar to working with those who are struggling with more typical grief scenarios, the biggest differences lie in defining the losses and creating meaningful narratives about the loss. Losses are more readily identifiable in traditional grief work. Those who are experiencing ambiguous loss may need additional help with defining their loss. They may also struggle with understanding that although their losses are ambiguous in nature, this makes them no less real than more tangible losses.

Although it is clear that ambiguous loss is a complex phenomenon that presents many different scenarios to which families can and do react very differently, family stress theory (Hill, 1958; McKenry & Price, 2005) provides counselors with some useful parameters within which their work can be loosely structured. In sum, these guidelines include defining the loss, assessing resources, and exploring the perceptions or meanings members have about the loss.

EFFECTS ON FAMILIES

In spite of the 2-month allotment for bereavement of the *Diagnostic and Statistical Manual of Mental Disorders* (American Psychiatric Association, 2000), mourning is a natural and lifelong experience. Grief does not disappear after one has accepted the loss. Mourning a loss is a unique and complicated experience for the individual and the family. Grieving is a physical, emotional, intellectual, spiritual, and social event (Tshudin, 1997). Rycroft and Perlesz (2001) stated that grief is misunderstood within the counseling field. Grief counseling is considered a specialization; yet all counselors deal with grief and loss at some level with their clients. The grieving process in American culture is constricted and denied, viewed as something to avoid or to get through quickly. The language used surrounding loss often implies judgment and societal expectations. For example, when someone asks if the loss was expected, it often implies that an expected loss should be easier to deal with than an unexpected loss (Hedtke, 2002).

The ABC-X model of family stress (Hill, 1958; McKenry & Price, 2005) is an example of a broad systemic approach that is appropriate for counselors to take when working with grieving families. It allows room for consideration of cultural and religious practices and beliefs, the family support system, the environment, and multigenerational relationships and issues. Counseling should focus on the family's strengths and coping strategies that have already been working for them (Shapiro, 1994). When working with families from diverse backgrounds, it is important to consider their culture or family history. Cultures vary greatly in their perceptions, beliefs, and rituals about death and other types of losses (Weiner, 1999). Entire nations and groups of people can be seriously affected by ambiguous loss (Boss, 1999). Jews who survived the Holocaust, Native Americans whose cultures have become decimated by disease and Anglo American oppression, or African Americans who were slaves and separated from their families of origin are examples. The residual effects of ambiguous loss—grief surrounding the loss of a way of life and cultural identity—are passed down through the generations.

People are expected to move on with their lives after a loss. With ambiguous loss, the family simply cannot just move on. Their immobility or inability to deal effectively with the situation is not the result of the family's failure; it is the impossibility of the situation that may leave them powerless (Boss, 1999). Especially early in the counseling process, family members may need to tell their stories over and over. It is through telling stories that meaning is made. "People make meaning; meaning is not made for us" (Drewery & Winslade, 1997, p. 33). If we make meaning through talking and language, then meaning can also be changed through talking and language (Drewery & Winslade, 1997). By telling their story over and over, family members can create new meanings about their losses and discern what they need to heal (Tshudin, 1997).

The counselor needs to help the family identify the ambiguous loss and label it as such. The counselor can help to normalize the family members' experiences even if the situation is not typical. Family members may hesitate to share their grief with others because of shame, fearing judgment, or believing that they should just get over it (Shapiro, 1994). Feelings are not inherently good or bad; it is the clients' perception that labels them such. When the counselor assures the family that no matter how they have responded to the loss, their feelings and behaviors are understandable given the situation. The family is less likely to be resistant in therapy if they feel validated by the counselor. The counselor should help family members accept and explore their wide range of emotions. By practicing mindfulness, the clients may learn to observe their thoughts and emotions passively without judgment, censorship, or action (Tshudin, 1997).

Death or loss interferes with the family's natural developmental process. The family is thrust into crisis and seeks stability (Shapiro, 1994). With ambiguous loss, the crisis is ongoing and the family may be unable to adjust on some levels. According to Shapiro (1994), "Grief is a crisis of both attachment and identity, disrupting family stability in the interrelated domains of emotions, interactions, social roles, and meanings" (p. 17). The grief process includes an adjustment and redefining of identity and roles. Families want to derive meaning from the loss to restructure and define their roles. The therapist can help facilitate the process of reorganizing the family structure and adjusting roles (Rycroft & Perlesz, 2001).

In counseling, the family may not be able to resolve the situation but can create ways to deal with the stress so that the loss does not devastate the family (Boss, 1999). The therapist provides a safe holding environment for the family to discuss their issues and air emotions that may have become suppressed (Rycroft & Perlesz, 2001). All family members need to have the time to express their views, what they believe is happening, and what the loss means to them personally. By pointing out similarities, the therapist can help family members find common ground when there is conflict and disagreement. However, the family does not need to agree to improve intimacy. The therapist should encourage family members to validate one another, listening and drawing closer, even when they disagree. The therapist's task is to help the family members reduce isolation within the family. By giving the loss a name, family members have the opportunity to change relationships, roles, and interactions. Family members can learn to compromise with each other about those changes. Boss

(1999) states that "overcoming the solitude of ambiguous loss is the first step on the road to healthy change" (p. 103).

Grief is a complicated emotion. It surfaces as sadness, shock, anger, confusion, apathy, and guilt. It is common for individuals to experience a variety of conflicting feelings such as love and hate or joy and despair (Tshudin, 1997). For individuals who are depressed, unresolved grief may be at the root of their symptoms, and loss may have been unrecognized by health care professionals (Boss, 1999; Knauer, 2002). It can be helpful for the therapist to point out to the clients that their mixed and strong emotions are a part of grief. Grief is multidimensional and not just limited to sadness. If the counselor can help normalize those feelings, the client may learn to embrace and accept the full spectrum of emotions (Tshudin, 1997).

Families are faced with many important decisions. When there is uncertainty about how to proceed, the family resists change while waiting for some kind of resolution. Boss (1999) calls it the family gamble when the family makes an educated guess about the most likely outcome of a situation and creates a plan. It is risky because the family may make the wrong decision or may never know if they have gone in the right direction. The family may fear that a wrong decision will finalize the loss. Part of the healing process is for the family to give up the idea of perfection and absolute truth. They may have to make some difficult decisions based on very little information. At some point, the family must be willing to live with their decisions. Although the family may have to come together to make decisions, each individual should consider for themselves what will work for them and how to personally deal with the loss.

Family members may enter counseling blaming themselves or each other for their situation. Boss (1999) believes that blame is toxic and only interferes with the grieving process. Family members must learn to forgive themselves and each other. Ambiguous loss leaves the family struggling to understand the causes of their pain. Searching for meaning despite a lack of answers is important to the family's grieving process (Boss, 1999). Discussions do not need to always focus on the negative aspects of the loss. The family should be encouraged to share individual memories and experiences. Clients need to tell their family stories—traditions, how they celebrate holidays, rituals, relationships, and roles. Through storytelling, family members can begin to piece together their lives and figure out what place the loss should take (Rycroft & Perlesz, 2001).

NARRATIVE THERAPY AND AMBIGUOUS LOSS

When working with families who are experiencing ambiguous loss, it is suggested that counselors use a broad, systemic approach such as the ABC-X model of family stress (Hill, 1958; McKenry & Price, 2005). This model encourages counselors to help families define all aspects of their loss, assess what resources they are currently using and what other resources they could use to cope with their losses, and provide families with ways to share their perceptions and beliefs about their losses. This last piece, sharing perceptions about loss, lends itself to further therapeutic work in the form of helping families redefine or create new meanings and rituals surrounding their losses.

From an early age, children learn family rules such as those concerning what can and cannot be openly discussed, what emotions are acceptable, and what roles family members play. This becomes part of their family story. When family stories do not provide for adequate means to grieve or cope with stressors related to ambiguous losses, the family may function in less than healthy ways. Often there are triangles created in grieving families in an effort to protect themselves and manage anxiety. Loss can become debilitating in families whose anxiety is high and differentiation is low. Symptoms such as behavioral disorders, compulsions, marital conflicts, or mental illness may reflect the family's inability to adjust to loss (McGoldrick, 2004). If families can share their current stories related to their loss and have the experience of being heard, in a nonjudgmental and accepting manner, they may also be able to tell their stories again in new ways that capture different nuances of their experiences. This does not change the facts of the experience or loss, but it can change the meanings that family members assign to their losses and to their part of the loss.

Narrative therapy (Freedman & Combs, 1996; White, 1989; White & Epston, 1990) provides a way for clients to be heard and validated and also to explore alternate meanings around their experience of ambiguous loss. Narrative therapy assumes that each individual is the author of his or her life. Within each life is a multitude of stories that could be told about our experiences. Some stories are more meaningful and useful than others. For example, stories told about loss could have plots of blame or guilt or plots of hope and good memories.

Using elements of narrative therapy in conjunction with the ABC-X model of family stress (Hill, 1958; McKenry & Price, 2005) allows counselors to help family members articulate and define their losses, explore current and potential resources, and therapeutically define and redefine the meaning assigned to losses.

Identifying the stressor can be accomplished by asking each family member to tell his or her story of what he or she has lost. Perhaps it is something or someone tangible; perhaps it is a feeling or part of a relationship. Each client should be encouraged to recall the memories of who or what he or she has lost, including positive and negatives. He or she can then be encouraged to name the loss or the stressors associated with the loss. Perhaps the name is something like "missing grandma" or "readjusting to life without him." When problems or stressors are named, they can be externalized (White, 1988/1989), which means that although they are still part of the person's life, they are not the person. This allows clients to be able to step outside of their losses and stressors and look at them more objectively with less blaming of themselves.

In writing about illness narratives, Weingarten (2001) borrows from Frank's (1995) classification system to describe three types of stories that can be told in relation to illness. Restitution narratives are told from the perspective of diagnosis and treatment. Modern medicine and science are the key players in this plot. Chaos narratives are told from the perspective of the patient who is experiencing the turbulence of conflicting emotions, thoughts, and physical experiences. Quest narratives are those that allow for fate to be turned into experience and meaning to be extrapolated from the turbulence. Restitution, chaos, and quest narratives could all be articulated in relation to ambiguous loss.

As stories about illness or other ambiguous losses are told, it may be helpful to introduce two of Weingarten's (2001) and Frank's (1995) classifications of narratives. Is the story being told from a factual (restitution) perspective of what actually happened and what is being done to alleviate the loss? Perhaps a narrative of chaos more clearly depicts the range of emotions and thoughts that are occurring. Weingarten notes that chaos narratives are the most difficult to hear because of their rawness and poignancy. These may be the most important stories to hear as they encapsulate the myriad of feelings and beliefs associated with ambiguous loss.

In addition to naming and describing the problem, the narrative technique of mapping the problem (White 1988/1989) can also be used in relation to the loss. Here, clients are asked to describe all the ways in which the loss affects them. Included may be school and employment issues, changes in relationships with friends and other family members, changes in family rules and routines, and so on. This exercise is conducted to help normalize the experiences that family members are having that they may not connect to the loss they are experiencing. It is helpful for families to become aware of how they are being affected and how their experiences are affecting one another. Empathy is typically engendered when members begin to understand how others are feeling and what is influencing their behaviors.

As the losses are named and mapped, it is then important to begin assessing the resources available for coping. White (1988/1989) uses "exception" questions to ferret out when people are able to cope healthily despite their feelings of grief. For example, "When was the last time you allowed yourself to rest despite your ongoing worry?" is an exception question that points out that family members are coping and allowing themselves to do healthy activities despite their grief. Another strategy is to discuss what the person who is physically or emotionally absent might name as strengths of the family if he or she were present. As families create maps of their loss and the influences of the loss, members can be encouraged to notice who else is feeling similarly to them and to ascertain ways in which the members can help one another. No potential resource, however small, should be overlooked.

Finally, an assessment of the perceptions that each family member has about the loss should be conducted. This includes an exploration of not only what is being experienced by each person but what each is telling himself or herself about the loss. Previous activities focused more on the present and past. Here is an opportunity to discuss the future. The quest (Frank, 1995; Weingarten, 2001) category of narrative may be used to extrapolate issues such as, "What will the loss mean to the family?" How will it affect their future goals and plans? How can they continue to function in a healthy manner while still honoring the loss? Now is the time to gently lay to rest the guilt and blame that family members may be experiencing and help them construct a new meaning system that incorporates what they have learned about themselves and each other. To paraphrase Weingarten, "How can fate be turned into experience?" It is important to help family members develop rituals that allow each to move on developmentally but still provide for remembrance and celebration of his or her loved one.

The assessment of the family's stressors, resources, and perceptions thus also becomes a treatment strategy. Through exploring ambiguous loss using narrative techniques, counselors can become more aware of the intensity and context of the stressors, and family members can become more aware of their resources and potential ways to reframe their perceptions. This model can be used flexibly, of course. The primary premises include letting family members share their stories, empathizing with their feelings, and encouraging them to take authorship of new and more meaningful stories about their losses.

CONCLUSION

Ambiguous loss can complicate the grieving process. Rycroft and Perlesz (2001) state that counseling can help the family "to find a balance between grieving and living, between the past and the future, and between despair and hope" (pp. 63–64). Even when a family member is lost either psychologically or physically, remembering that person and maintaining a connection is important to the family. The loved one does not have to be forgotten to move forward in life. Family members should be encouraged to share individual memories or stories about their loved one (Hedtke, 2002). Storytelling can transform grief into a growth process rather than leaving the family stuck. Whether the loss involves a person, event, object, or experience, the same principles of expression, exploration, and connection apply. Change becomes possible when families are willing to let go of the need to be in control (Boss, 1999). Mourning does not have to unfold in neat stages. Family members may need to revisit their ambiguous loss many times through the years and continue to grieve. The biggest risk for the family is to move forward even when they are unsure of the way.

REFERENCES

American Psychiatric Association. (2000). *Diagnostic and statistical manual of mental disorders* (4th ed). Washington, DC: Author.

Boss, P. G. (1999). *Ambiguous loss: Learning to live with unresolved grief.* Cambridge, MA: Harvard University Press.

Boss, P. G. (2002). Working with families of the missing. *Family Process, 41,* 14–17.

Drewery, W., & Winslade, J. (1997). The theoretical story of narrative therapy. In G. Monk, J. Winslade, K Crockett, & D. Epston (Eds.), *Narrative therapy in practice: The archaeology of hope* (pp. 32–52). San Francisco: Jossey-Bass.

Frank, A. W. (1995). *The wounded storyteller: Body, illness and ethics.* Chicago: University of Chicago Press.

Freedman, J., & Combs, G. (1996). *Narrative therapy: The social construction of preferred realities.* New York: Norton.

Hedtke, L. (2002). Reconstructing the language of death and grief. *Illness, Crisis, and Loss, 10,* 285–293.

Hill, R. (1958). Social stress on the family: Genetic features of families under stress. *Social Casework, 39,* 139–150.

Knauer, S. (2002). *Recovering from sexual abuse, addictions, and compulsive behaviors: "Numb" survivors.* New York: Hawthorne.

Madden-Derdich, D. A., & Herzog, M. J. (2005). Families, stress, and intervention. In P. C. McKenry & S. J. Price (Eds.), *Families & change: Coping with stressful events and transitions* (3rd ed., pp. 403–425). Thousand Oaks, CA: Sage.

McGoldrick, M. (2004). Echoes from the past: Helping families deal with their ghosts. In F. Walsh & M. McGoldrick (Eds.), *Living beyond loss* (2nd ed., pp. 310–339). New York: Norton.

McKenry, P. C., & Price, S. J. (2005). *Families & change: Coping with stressful events and transitions.* Thousand Oaks, CA: Sage.

Rycroft, P., & Perlesz, A. (2001). Speaking the unspeakable: Reclaiming grief and loss in family life. *The Australian and New Zealand Journal of Family Therapy, 22*(2), 57–65.

Shapiro, E. (1994). *Grief as a family process.* New York: Guilford.

Tshudin, V. (1997). *Counselling for loss and bereavement*. Philadelphia: Bailliere Tindall.

Weiner, I. (1999). *Coping with loss*. Mahwah, NJ: Lawrence Erlbaum.

Werner-Lin, A., & Moro, T. (2004). Unacknowledged and stigmatized losses. In F. Walsh & M. McGoldrick (Eds.), *Living beyond loss* (2nd ed., pp. 247–271). New York: Norton.

White, M. (1988/1989, Summer). The externalizing of the problem and the re-authoring of lives and relationships. *Dulwich Centre Newsletter*, 3–20.

White, M. (1989). *Selected papers*. Adelaide, Australia: Dulwich Centre.

White, M., & Epston, D. (1990). *Narrative means to therapeutic ends*. New York: Norton.

Weingarten, K. (2001). *Working with the stories of women's lives*. Adelaide, Australia: Dulwich Centre.

Gabrielle Betz is a recent graduate of the marriage and family counseling program at Montana State University.

Jill M. Thorngren, College of Education, Health and Human Development, is an associate professor and assistant dean at Montana State University. She serves as program leader of the marriage and family counseling program.

5

FAMILY SYSTEMS THEORY

Fred and Cassie have been married for three years. For the most part, they do not have any serious disagreements, or at least any that they can really put their finger on. But sometimes Fred says or does something that offends Cassie. He then feels somewhat guilty for what he has done, but he does not feel that it is totally his fault, and doesn't like the superior attitude she sometimes has when he does apologize. Therefore, he acts defensively instead, giving the impression that he is now responding to a revengeful reaction on her part, even though she has not (at least yet) given one. Cassie can't understand why Fred was mean to her and is angry but doesn't want to show it, so she acts indifferently. Fred notices the indifference and wonders if it is feigned or deliberate. He is afraid to apologize because it would be embarrassing and even more hurtful if the apology were rejected or taken advantage of. Besides, it wasn't like she hadn't done something to him earlier that precipitated his offense. Meanwhile, Cassie wants to hear an apology but isn't sure that it will be enough. She would like restitution but isn't sure that she can demand it. So, neither one apologizes or forgives, and the relationship spirals downhill. They eventually stop talking to each other without really understanding why and are urged by their friends to seek marriage counseling.

This continuous circular interaction, where each is responding to his or her perception of the other, is at the heart of family systems theory and illustrates its complexity.

HISTORY

It is generally believed that family systems theory emerged primarily in the 1960s. However, the basic concepts that would eventually lead to a coherent theory were being discussed a long time before that. For example, in 1926, Ernest Burgess made a presentation to the American Sociological Association that became a landmark publication. He referred to the family as "a unity of interacting personalities." He explained that this means that the family is much more than its formal or legal definition; instead, it is a living, growing superpersonality that has as its essence the interaction of its members.

Burgess (1926) went on to describe two basic family types: the highly integrated and the unintegrated family. The first is characterized by rituals, discipline, and interdependence; and the second, by a lack of those features. He discussed the importance of the roles played by each family member, how problems result when they conflict, and how one member can be identified as the "family problem."

These insights are all elaborated on in Chapter 2 of Waller's (1938) classic textbook on the family. This chapter, titled "The Family as an Arena of Interacting Personalities," begins by discussing how the family is basically a closed system of social interaction. It also discusses how the family is the greatest source of influence on a child and that the child's personality also affects the parents. And perhaps most important, Waller explores the idea that family experiences are repetitive and are based on patterns of interaction.

During the late 1920s, biologist Ludwig von Bertalanffy (1969) was beginning to develop the basic ideas of general systems theory. However, for the most part, systems theory as it relates to families remained hidden as a part of structural functionalism until after World War II. At that point, family therapists (Bateson et al. 1956) began to seek explanations for the transactions between family members that seemed to be at the heart of the dysfunctions with which they were dealing rather than focusing on the faults or qualities of individual family members. The therapeutic application of general systems theory is also referred to as family process theory (Broderick 1993). In general, family systems theory has its greatest utility in communication and clinical applications. During the 1980s, there was a plethora of activity using systems' theory in addressing a variety of family issues in both family scholarship and family therapy.

Bronfenbrenner (1989), most well known for his ecological theory of human development, uses systems concepts in his theory. He focuses on the role of different environments, such as home, school, and the community, and how they interact with an active child. We see that not only are children being influenced by parents, the school, and the neighborhood, but also that the child impacts those environments and helps to shape them as well.

There are four basic systems that make up our ecological environment. The first is the *microsystem*. This represents the immediate environment of the child, such as the family and school or day care center, church, peers, and so forth. The environment itself interacts with the age, health, sex, and other aspects of the individual. Because of this a child's behavior will vary, based on the microsystem or the environment. The second level is the *mesosystem*, which recognizes that those various components of the child's environment are not independent. Instead, they interact with each other and with the components of the next systems as well. Thus, a child may learn something at school that will make the home environment better.

The *exosystem* is those institutions that are beyond the child's immediate environment but impact upon his or her development in less direct ways. Examples include friends, neighbors, and extended kin, the parent's place of work, social service agencies, and the media. So, if a parent has a bad day at work, even though the child never entered that place or environment, he may be affected by the short temper of the parent once the parent gets home. Beyond that is the *macrosystem*, which includes the customs, attitudes, values, and laws of the culture in which the child lives. Each of our lives is affected on a daily basis by laws such as speed limits, over which we have no control.

All of these systems must be understood and taken into account if one is to have a full understanding of a child's development. In addition, it should be within the context of a *chronosystem*. This refers to changes in the environment across time (Gardiner and Kosmitzki 2002).

BASIC ASSUMPTIONS

The whole is greater than the sum of the parts. A family is much more than a collection of individuals who live together and are related to each other; it has a holistic quality. As a natural social system, it possesses its own characteristics, rules, roles, communication patterns, and power structure. It represents an integration of parts such that individual members can only be understood within the context of the whole.

A common analogy to illustrate wholeness can be depicted by a cake. While the individual ingredients (e.g., flour, sugar, cocoa, oil, baking soda) are the component parts, what is removed from the oven (i.e., the cake) is of a very different quality; it is more than each of the individual elements. An insignificant member (e.g., small amount of baking soda) has the potential to impact the whole by influencing whether the cake rises or is flat.

The locus of pathology is not within the person but is a system dysfunction. Systems theory requires a *paradigm shift* in the way we think about the world. Most social science theories have taken what we call an intrapsychic viewpoint. Here, the individual is the unit of study, and problems are presumed to be "in the head" of that person. However, with systems theory, the *locus of pathology*, or the location of the problem, is not within the person. Rather than saying that an individual has a disease, we say that the system of which he or she is a part is *dysfunctional*. That is, problems are seen as being a function of a struggle between persons. Think of a family as being represented by a circle for each member, with lines connecting them. The lines represent the communication patterns—the ways they speak to and act toward each other—between the members. Systems theorists believe that the problems are in the lines rather than in the circles. This applies, of course, to normative or functional behaviors as well, even though clinical applications tend to focus on difficulties. Another way of thinking about it is to compare a system to a child's mobile hanging over a crib. A number of interesting objects are connected by strings or wires. Whenever one is hit, it causes the others to move. Similarly, if you remove one of the objects, the entire system becomes unbalanced.

This interpersonal rather than intrapsychic perspective considers all behavior to be a part of ongoing, interactive, and recurring events, with no real beginning or end points. Therefore, a person who manifests some symptomatic behavior is seen as representing a dysfunctional system. Some are disturbed by this, taking it to mean that individuals are not responsible for their behavior and that they can, therefore, blame their problems on their family or society. Actually, according to systems theory, time is not wasted on blaming because the beginning points of a conflict typically cannot be found. We are then free to focus on how to resolve the problem rather than being distracted by trying to find someone to punish for it. It is recognized that individuals are ultimately responsible for their own behavior but that no behavior can be understood in isolation. One's behaviors, emotions, and interactions make sense only within the context of their social world or the environment in which they occur.

As an example, let us say that there is a teen with an eating disorder, which may have resulted in part from her mother's tendency to control her behavior. So is the teen's behavior the mother's fault? Before we answer, let us further assume that the mother became controlling in part because of living with an abusive father, who himself grew up under similarly abusive conditions, which is where he learned that pattern of interaction. Pretty soon, we are back in time to where the family ancestors who may have started the behavioral patterns to begin with are all deceased. So, rather than attempt to trace the behavior to its roots in order to place blame, a family therapist can focus on looking for ways to break the present chains of interaction that are maintaining the symptoms.

This paradigm, which is more than a therapeutic approach but actually a new way of conceptualizing human problems and understanding behavior, requires its own *epistemology*. This term refers to the way that knowledge is gained and how conclusions are made. The relationship outlook shifts the attention from content to process, or from the behavior itself, to how it is maintained.

Circular causality guides behavior. With *linear causality* the focus is on content. If you believe that one event causes the next in straight-line stimulus response fashion, the observer will be distracted by what a couple is arguing about and how it got started. By contrast, *circular causality* is the idea that with human social interaction there are a number of forces moving in many directions simultaneously. It is all about process. That is, it doesn't matter if the couple is fighting about money or child rearing—it is the repetitive pattern of interaction that is of interest. The focus is on *how* they interact, regardless of the topic, and what can be done to change that pattern into a more functional one (i.e., one that leads to happiness rather than unhappiness or relationship satisfaction versus dissatisfaction).

Take as an example a young, recently married couple. Desiring to be autonomous, they resent and avoid their parents and in-laws for calling and visiting too often and giving unwanted advice. From their viewpoint, they are running away from the parents because the parents are running after them. However, the parents see it differently—they would not have to call and counsel so often if the adult children would just see them occasionally. Each sees themselves as reacting to the other and believes that the other one "started it." Are the children avoiding because the parents are intrusive, or are the parents intrusive because the children are avoiding? We think linearly, but the behaviors are circular. Reciprocal causality exists in that the exchange occurs within a context of mutual influence.

Rules result from the redundancy principle and are critical in defining a family. Couples begin to create the rules of their relationship as soon as they meet. Families cannot have an infinite reservoir of possible behavioral responses for every situation, so a few are selected and used over and over. This is the *redundancy principle*, which results in family rules. These repetitive patterns of interaction are the rules that a family lives by. Some rules are dysfunctional (such as husband withdraws every time his wife wants to discuss their money management problems), but once established, they tend to remain. Positive change is made in a family by helping them to change their dysfunctional rules.

A few rules are clear and overt—that is, you can ask family members what the rules are and they can consciously identify them and agree on them. They might include a curfew for the teenagers and not talking back to mom or dad. Many rules are implicit, outside conscious awareness. Examples of unspoken rules might include where everyone sits at the dinner table or that dad gets to control the TV remote. The most powerful rules are the ones that are covert and unstated. They might include such possibilities as the fact that mom can get mad but dad may not; brother can get away with poor school performance but not sister; or that in an argument, one person blusters while the other ignores it.

A family's rules differentiate it from other family systems and delineate its boundaries. A family's rules, which insist that its members observe certain religious practices, enact certain gender roles, maintain a certain standard of job performance, reserve Saturday afternoons for family functions, and treat one another with respect, distinguish it from another family whose rules may be different.

So, how do these ideas work in therapy? An example will further explain the basic ideas. A couple comes for counseling because of a problem with domestic battery. The husband is defensive and blames his wife for forcing him to be mean to her because she won't do as she is told. She responds apologetically that if she were just a better house-wife, the marriage would be OK. Putting the specific content or presenting behavioral problem aside for the moment, the therapist determines the following repetitive sequence of events: (1) The husband has strict expectations about what his wife should be or when she should have things ready for him; (2) He has been drinking; (3) She fails to meet an expectation, such as arriving late from work when he has been waiting to pick her up; (4) He becomes angry and berates her; (5) She withdraws—becomes quiet and makes no eye contact in the hope that it will blow over; (6) This makes him more upset, so he escalates his abusive behavior to force a reaction from her; and (7) She finally responds, either with an apology or anger. Either way, this ends the sequence and all is well until it starts again.

Think of these behaviors as circular. They represent some of their family rules that are repeated over and over again. The therapist would choose to intervene at the point where it appears the couple would be most likely to be able to make changes. It could be with the husband's attitudes or drinking behavior, or it could be with the wife's tendency to withdraw before responding. Regardless, it is the process that must be dealt with, not just the physical abuse.

Feedback loops guide behavior. A family system corrects itself or tries to regain homeostasis through the use of feedback loops. *Negative feedback* occurs when a family member begins to move outside the accepted limits of family behavior and others enact corrective measures to get that member back in line. The family tries to restore the member to the proper way of acting. For instance, when a teen sasses, a parent offers negative feedback by grounding the teen or by giving "the look." The same would occur when breaking a dysfunctional rule, so "negative" does not refer to good or bad but suggests that no change in behavior is permitted.

Positive feedback is a rewarding response for the deviation. In this case, the person is encouraged to break out of the homeostatic balance. Therapists will often give positive feedback for attempts to replace dysfunctional rules with functional ones. Also, family members receive positive feedback for behaviors that stay within the rules, whether they are functional or not. Thus, the focus of systems theory is on the quality of communication among family members.

Pathological communication contributes to relationship problems. Emotional illnesses have generally been considered to be "in the head" of the patient, although we now understand the important role of genetics in these disturbances. Early family therapists, however, discovered some important family connections. For example, a young person would be hospitalized for schizophrenia and receive behavioral and psychoanalytic therapy. As a reward for getting better, his family would be allowed to visit him, but then he would relapse. They initially thought that it had to do with having interactions once again with a cold, rejecting mother and coined the term *schizophrenogenic mother* to describe this situation. This, in combination with a passive, ineffectual father, was believed to result in sons, particularly who could become confused and feel inadequate, and thus become schizophrenic.

As the communication theorists refined their work, it became clear that the primary source of dysfunctions such as schizophrenia was communication patterns rather than these gender and parental behavior issues. *Pathological communication* refers to the various kinds of unclear and confusing ways of relating, which can cause problems in a relationship. One is mystification, in which the speaker denies the reality of a situation by perhaps saying that nothing is wrong when there clearly is. Another is the indirect communication of beating around the bush instead of coming out and clearly stating one's desires. Volumes have been written about these and other difficulties in communication.

One of the most prominent concepts in systems work is the *double bind*. It is a special form of contradictory communication. Whenever someone speaks, he or she sends two messages: the verbal and the nonverbal. In other words, there is what you say and how you say it. When someone says "I love you" in the proper tone of voice and in an appropriate circumstance, then he or she "affirms" the communication. That is, when the two parts of the message are congruent, the message is clear and more believable This is functional because a person sends the message he or she intended to send, and it is received appropriately. However, levels of messages sometimes contradict each other, leaving the recipient to decide what the truth is and how to respond. This is particularly difficult for children, who can be stressed into dysfunctional behaviors as a result. It also predictably leads to conflict in adult relationships.

When the two contradicting messages are commands, a double bind occurs. That is, the individual is told to do two things but cannot do one without disobeying the other. Either way, he or she will be punished—the classic "damned if you do, damned if you don't" situation. The person feels compelled to respond, and the family rules are such that one may not comment on the contradiction or leave the situation. It is like the classic joke where the child is given two shirts for his birthday and puts one on. His mother then responds: "What's the matter, you didn't like the other one?" No matter which shirt he does or does not put on, he is in trouble.

Let's return to the case described in Goldenberg and Goldenberg (2000), a schizophrenic son who is visited by his mother. Happy to see her, he goes up and gives her a hug. In response, she stiffens, so he withdraws, to which she responds by asking why he doesn't love her anymore. He can hug her and be rejected or not hug her and still be rejected. If he points out what she is doing, she will deny it. Instead, he can choose the "schizophrenic way" and withdraw from reality so as not to be responsible for making any decisions. In other words, "crazy" behavior is the logical way to respond to a system with dysfunctional rules. Therefore, we see that the identified patient is often the person in the family who is the healthiest, in the sense of not wanting to endure dysfunctional rules. Even though it is well known now that most serious emotional disturbances have a genetic base, just like any other illness, it is also true that such disorders are most evident in the families with the highest levels of communication deviance. That is, pathological communication patterns are stressful and make things worse, whereas healthy rules result in a calmer family life and, therefore, fewer symptoms in its members.

Systems clinicians such as Virginia Satir also see a loop between self-esteem and ability to communicate. Dysfunctional communication patterns between family members results in low self-esteem. People tend to defend themselves from threats to their esteem by using defensive and dysfunctional communication styles. Therefore, one leads to the other in a downward spiral. Satir (1964) goes back to the family-of-origin causes and helps the clients to "reframe" (i.e., consider less negative motivations for the behaviors of others) their childhood experiences into more positive and generally truthful memories and then teaches congruent and value-building communication styles that raise self-esteem. As self-esteem rises, so does a person's ability to communicate in a functional manner (Satir 1964).

All family members take on roles. Family roles are defined as "recurring patterns of behavior developed through interaction that family members use to fulfill family functions" (Galvin, Bylund, and Brommel 2004, 169). Through dialogue and interactions with one another, families create shared meanings or expectations about how various roles should be played. While children might be given explicit instruction about how to enact the role of daughter or son, adults might utilize their observation of roles in their family of origin as starting points in role negotiation (Galvin et al. 2004). The fact that we all tend to play out certain roles is part of the redundancy principle. In addition to being a parent, child, student, or athlete, there are common psychological roles that family members take on. Refusing to play one's role can upset the family equilibrium and result in negative feedback.

In their classic work, Kantor and Lehr (1975) identified "four player parts" in the family. The *mover* initiates action. The *opposer* disapproves of the mover's action and tries to block it. The *follower* approves of the mover's action, or the opposer's reaction, thus empowering the side with whom he or she allies. The *bystander* witnesses the action of the mover but is passive about overtly aligning with mover or the opposer. Instead, the bystander remains on the periphery of family functioning.

Dysfunctional families, particularly alcoholic families, reveal certain roles that are found to some degree in most families (Winton 1995). The parent with the chemical dependency (in this example, the father) plays the role of the *dependent* person. His job is to bring grief to the family while blaming others for his abuses. For example, if you did what he asked then he wouldn't have to drink. He denies his problems and manipulates others in order to perpetuate them. His wife is the *enabler* (also referred to as the *codependent*), who helps him to avoid the consequences of his behavior. She may call in sick to work for him or encourage the children to stay away from him when he "gets like that." Perhaps there were alcoholics in her family of origin, and her husband was drawn to her because of her traits of covering for others. She often has psychosomatic symptoms due to her repressed feelings of anger and guilt.

The firstborn child is often the *hero*. He or she is the ideal student and caretaker who seems to have it all together. This is a stressful role but one that is difficult to give up because it has many rewards. The second child is the *delinquent*. This is the scapegoated child, who does poorly in school or manifests other acting-out behaviors. It is a negative approach to getting dad to change because the hope is that by turning attention to the child it will alleviate the need of the father to drink. The next child is the *invisible child*, who just keeps a low profile in the hope that it will help lessen family tensions. This child, who basically stays out of the way and thus never deals with emotions, is the most likely to suffer from an emotional illness. The last child is the *clown*, who attempts to use humor in dealing with the family problems.

For any one person to change, the entire system must be changed. Instead of focusing on why the father became an alcoholic and how bad that is, a therapist would help some of the others, particularly the enabling spouse, to give up their supportive roles. All this occurs at more subtle levels in families with less serious problems. For example, a young woman might marry into an extended family at whose reunions she is expected to babysit all the children while the other adults socialize. No one knows how this happened, or would even admit to it being the case, but trouble ensues if she refuses to play her role. Another might be selected as the family rebel, or star, and be the focus of the same family reunion.

Family types are based on the rigidity of family boundaries. Some researchers (Kantor and Lehr 1975) have identified three basic family types, based on the rigidity of family boundaries and rules. *Open families* are basically democratic, and the rights of individuals are protected and interactions with outsiders are permitted. There is also consensus and flexibility, and family members are bound together by love and respect. This is often called mutuality, and healthy children and patterns of interaction are common in these families.

The second type is the *random family*. Here there are almost no boundaries; few rules exist about defending the "family's territory." The members are seen as *disengaged*, and their commitments to and investments in the family are *transitory*. Children often see this level of freedom as a sign of a lack of love and concern from their parents, and social problems are common. In fact, as adolescents, they often yearn for the rules imposed on their peers by their parents because they see the rules as an indication of love, care, and concern. The final type is the *closed family*. In this one, family members are *enmeshed* or overly involved in each others' lives. Individual identities are not allowed, and family boundaries close off much of the outside world. Such families might value privacy, even secretiveness, and limit exposure to media or other external influences. Emotional illnesses can result from this family configuration because individuals cannot think or function on their own behalf.

A family's response to their children's friends might offer a simplified illustration of these family types. A closed family is likely to discourage children from inviting their friends to the family's home at all, while an open family might help their children to discriminate between "good" and "bad" friends. Only friends with desirable traits that are in line with the family's values and rules are invited to the family's home. In a random family, any of a child's peers can exit and enter the family's home indiscriminately.

PRIMARY TERMS AND CONCEPTS

Broderick and Smith (1979) provided us with explanations for the key concepts of systems theory. An updated version is found in White and Klein (2002). For our discussion, the following terms are most relevant to systems theory.

System

A system is essentially any set of objects, with their attributes, which relate to each other in a way that creates a new superentity. The family is a social system (Winton 1995). It is a boundary-maintained unit composed of interrelated and interdependent parts such that an alteration in one part affects all components of the system. Family systems are typically composed of one or more subsystems, smaller units (e.g., parental, spousal) which serve various functions within the family system.

Boundaries

Boundaries are lines of demarcation which distinguish a system from its environment and impact the flow of information and energy between the two (Broderick and Smith, 1979; White and Klein, 2002). A family maintains its boundaries by filtering out any external elements that seem hostile to the goals and policies of the family while at the same time incorporating those that are deemed beneficial. Kantor and Lehr (1975) identified this process as "bounding." This is similar to the role of the placenta during pregnancy. In addition to the boundaries for the overall household kin group, boundaries exist between family subgroups or subsystems, such as those between parents and children. Family boundaries typically can be classified as falling between two extremes on a continuum from open (highly interactive with outside environment) to closed (extremely private with little external interchange), depending on how permeable or flexible the boundaries are. More recently Pauline Boss (2002) introduced the concept of *boundary ambiguity*, the inability to determine who is in and out of the family. It typically occurs when there is incongruence between *physical presence* (person is bodily present in the home) and *psychological presence* (physically absent person is emotionally present in a family member's mind). For instance, a family whose father/husband is MIA (missing in action) may experience boundary ambiguity in that while he is physically absent, he is still very much on their minds and in their hearts.

Entropy

Entropy is the natural tendency of a system to move from order to disorder. Without attention, a marriage or family system will move toward disorganization or disrepair. Energy—new information or input—is the lifeblood of systems. A family must be able and willing to incorporate energy into its system in order to thrive. Open and permeable boundaries make the flow of energy into a system more likely. Interchange with the environment is critical for the viability of a system.

Family Rules

Family rules are the repetitive behavioral patterns, based on the *redundancy principle*, that regulate family functioning by offering guidelines for future family interactions (Goldenberg and Goldenberg 2000). Rules help families know how to deal with input and change. Rules can be *explicit*, clearly articulated, and acknowledged by the family; or implicit, invisible, and not discussed (Satir 1972). If families do not have rules in place, which allow them to respond appropriately to new situations, they may either adjust or simply break down. The typical response is to fall back on an already existing rule, even when it is insufficient to solve the problem. However, families do have *metarules*—rules about the rules—which dictate how families might interpret, enforce, change, or create new rules.

Feedback

Feedback refers to the response a family member makes to the behavior of another person, particularly when it deviates from existing patterns of interaction. It may be *positive* or deviation amplifying in that it encourages more of the stimulus or input from the other or *negative* in that it discourages change and is deviation dampening. Positive feedback encourages further change while negative feedback tries to restore the system to a steady state. There are continuous "feedback loops" as each member speaks to, and impacts upon, the behaviors of the others.

Equilibrium

There is a tendency for a system to seek a balance between stability and change in the variety of its behaviors and its rules. This natural inclination to maintain the status quo and resist change is usually referred to as *homeostasis*, which means the system has equilibrium.

Clinical Concepts. There are additional concepts that must be understood when applying the theory, particularly in therapy. These are important for understanding how family members affect the emotional lives of each other (Goldenberg and Goldenberg 2000).

Circular Causality Versus Linear Causality

Humans tend to "punctuate" behavior sequences in order to make sense of interactions, assigning "cause and blame to individuals instead of focusing on the problematic pattern" (Galvin et al. 2004, 61) between family members. A wife might say she nags because her husband withdraws, while the husband reports that he withdraws because his wife nags. Each is suggesting that one event causes the next in unidirectional stimulus-response fashion or linear causality. Systems theory, however, recognizes the futility of trying to assign cause and effect because many forces impact the relationship system simultaneously. There is a continuous series of circular feedback loops in which everyone influences everyone else in the family without any clear beginning or ending points. Because of this you cannot identify a specific beginning cause or event. Instead, emphasis is upon the reciprocity and shared responsibility of *what is transpiring*, not *why* it is occurring (Becvar and Becvar 2006).

Identified Patient

Often one person may manifest more symptoms, or is believed by the others to be the major cause of family problems and is, therefore, sent for counseling. We call this individual the identified patient. In actuality, that individual is simply the symptom bearer in a dysfunctional family, or the one who carries much of the family burden. In family therapy, then, the entire family is the focus of attention rather than a particular individual member. The key to understanding a family is to refrain from paying attention to the individual members, but instead, to focus on their behavioral exchanges.

Double Bind

A double bind is a kind of pathological communication in which a person is given two commands that contradict each other and, given that the contradiction is concealed and denied, is not allowed to comment on the existence of incongruent messages. If you obey one request, then you are in trouble for disobeying the other. This confusion leads to emotional or mental distress. Such would be the case when an adult child tells an aging parent "We will help you to remain independent. If you refuse our help (by not following all our advice and directives) this will be a sign to us that you are unable to continue living independently" (Herr and Weakland 1979, 147).

Family Cohesion

Family cohesion is the degree of closeness or emotional bonding family members have for one another. According to Olson (2000), there are four levels of family cohesion. At one extreme is disengagement, when family members are insufficiently involved in each other's lives and members hold a high degree of individuality and little sense of togetherness. Enmeshment, represented by extreme togetherness and high dependence, exists at the opposite end of the continuum. Enmeshment can be characteristic of a closed family, and it often results in psychosomatic symptoms due to the lack of personal autonomy.

Family Flexibility

A family's adaptability to new and/or stressful situations represents a family's flexibility. Like cohesion, Olson (2000) identifies four levels of flexibility. At one end of the continuum are rigid families, those that are characterized by little or no ability to change their roles, rules or relationship patterns. At the other extreme are chaotic families. Such families evidence little or no constancy to the point that family members have a difficult time knowing what to expect. Given the external and developmental changes that occur within individuals and families, some degree of flexibility is essential for healthy family functioning.

Mutuality

Mutuality is found in open families in which all are accepted and loved, even with differences of opinion. The opposite is *pseudomutuality* in which a family gives the surface impression that it is open and understanding when, in fact, it is not.

COMMON AREAS OF RESEARCH AND APPLICATION

The two areas of greatest research productivity and application of systems theory concepts are family communication and family therapy. These actually overlap a great deal because therapy often focuses on the communication patterns in families.

Communication and Family Typologies

Whitchurch and Dickson (1999) provide an excellent summary of what we presently know about family communication from a systems perspective. David Olson (2000) for one, has developed what is probably the most well-known use of science with therapy in his circumplex model of marital and family systems. The model includes three dimensions: family cohesion, flexibility, and communication. It assumes that very high or very low levels of cohesion and/or flexibility are problematic for couples and families. Moderate or balanced levels of these two factors are the ideal, promoting healthy family functioning. Communication, the third dimension of the model, serves a facilitating role in that it helps families move around on the other two dimensions. By using communication skills such as active listening, respect, and clarity, families are better able to achieve balanced levels of cohesion and flexibility. In addition to Olson and his colleagues, several researchers have utilized the circumplex model for examining various types of families (e.g., families with head trauma; Kosciulek 1996). Using FACES and the clinical rating scale, the model is also useful in couple and family therapy. Therapists use the information to help couples and families move to a balance between the two traits, which is characteristic of well-functioning families.

Broderick and Pulliam-Krager (1979) did an excellent job of linking the three basic family types to childhood outcomes. They begin by reviewing the various aspects of pathological communication, which they term *paradoxical pressure*. This is then connected to open, closed, and random families. Using a flowchart model, they show how boundary maintenance can result in varying childhood problems. We begin by asking if paradoxical pressure exists in a family—that is, are there double binds or any other type of crazy-making communication patterns? The assumption is that few families can totally escape communication problems, but for the few who do, the result is a child who is an "unchallenged normal." Lacking such pressures, the child will grow up in the normal range but have no motivation to understand those who do have psychological problems. They make good accountants but not great therapists, for instance.

If the answer to the question about dysfunctional communication is "yes," then we move to the next choice point and ask whether the family "screened out the deviant perspective." That is, do the parents protect their children from antisocial elements such as gangs, adult media, drug use, and so forth. If the answer to that question is "no," then we see that this is a random, disengaged family. The likely childhood outcome is delinquency; the children are not emotionally ill, but they rebel against both a family and society that does not seem to care about them.

However, if the answer had been "yes," meaning that the deviant perspective is screened out, then we go to the next choice point and ask whether the family "screened out the normative perspective." In other words, are children also kept from prosocial aspects of society such as school, church, and good friends? If the answer is "no," then we have an open family. Here, the boundaries keep out the bad elements but, recognizing that they are not perfect, let in good ones. This way, the children can compare and gain an understanding of their own families' craziness and avoid it in their own lives. We call these individuals achieved normals.

If the answer to the last question is "yes," then we have a closed, enmeshed family. Here, the rigid boundaries keep out all outside forces, either pro- or anti-normative. So, all the children have is their own family craziness. Without a meta-perspective (the ability to compare their worldview with that of others), the outcome for these children is some form of neurotic or psychotic behavior. Therefore, one of the great insights of systems theory is that enmeshment leads to emotional problems. The other families provide an escape from their pathological communication, but in a closed family, developing a symptom is just about the only way to deal with double binds.

Haley (1959) explained that families with an emotionally ill member continuously engage in contradictory and double-binding communication. They not only disqualify whatever anyone else says but also disqualify their own communications as well. This dysfunctional protection, which keeps them from ever being held responsible for their behaviors, is based on the need for love and the fear that if you let people act freely, they may choose not to love you. This exaggerated concern comes from family-of-origin difficulties.

The greatest concern about family rules turns out not to be what the particular rules are but rather who makes the rules. Everyone wants life to go his or her own way, so ultimately marriage relations become a struggle for power. Emotional fights are about who should make the rules rather than what they should be. People usually do not recognize this consciously and thus cannot understand why their spouse will not agree to some simple request. This is complicated by the different levels of messages that we communicate.

For instance, a wife wants her husband to pick up his own dirty clothes, indicating that they should have an equal relationship. But if he does so, then he is doing what she says, and the relationship is not equal after all. This may cause him to erupt in indignation without understanding why, and she will be dismayed that he will not do this one little thing. In another example, a wife may want her husband to be the leader in the family and make the big decisions but it is impossible for that to happen if she tells him to do so because then he would just be doing her bidding. Human communication in all settings is incredibly complex. This becomes especially true in emotional settings like the family. Systems theory may be the approach that can best deal with the levels of complexity and intimacy that are so central to human interaction.

Couples and Family Therapy

Family systems theory and its related concepts are useful within therapeutic contexts. For instance, Bettinger (2005) examined how a family systems approach is helpful when working with open gay male couples. He asserts that systems concepts like boundaries, homeostasis, rules, and roles are critical in understanding and accepting gay male sexuality, including the practice of "polyamory," defined as "responsible non-monogamy" (151) which frequently occurs among gay male couples. So, too, altering interaction patterns, establishing new roles, and reworking family structures are critical objectives in treating families with chemical dependency (Curtis 1999). Mercado (2000) examined how systems concepts are helpful in providing therapeutic intervention with Asian American substance abusers and their families.

CRITIQUE

There are some legitimate criticisms of systems theory. White and Klein (2002) summarized three principal concerns. The first is the belief that systems theory is more of a model or flowchart for conceptualizing, but it does not qualify as a true theory. The major concepts seem to be too vague for true testing and do not predict in the sense of deducing from propositions. This is a valid criticism if you are coming from the dominant epistemology of science, which is the hypothetical-deductive model of empirical testing. However, systems advocates counter that the worldview most appropriate for this theory is the *constructivist* position in which different models may be useful for different purposes.

The second criticism is that systems theory is too global and abstract, and therefore, is virtually meaningless. In other words, it is too "general" to pick up important distinctions that would make it worthwhile. The defense here is that the world is very diverse and that systems can make connections between the natural and social world that discipline-specific theories are not capable of doing.

Finally, some critics claim that the family process theorists in particular make the mistake of reifying the idea of system. That is, instead of remembering that it is just a model for understanding, they slip into considering the system to be reality. They confuse the "model" with the "thing." The response from systems apologists is that all theories have their naive claims and that systems theory is no less prone to reification than any other theory.

One finds validity in these criticisms due to the relative lack of useful mathematical models and predictive propositions that have emerged over the years from this approach. It may be that the kinds of interactions attended to by systems theory are simply too complex for the traditional scientific method to deal with in an understandable fashion. As a result, the theory has been most useful in the areas of family communication and family therapy. Broderick and Smith (1979) list the following as the most productive types of issues for examination by systems theorists:

1. *Sequential patterns of interaction.* Other disciplines, such as economics, have benefited for many years by utilizing such concepts as feedback loops, escalation, and dampening in the context of temporal patterns of everyday life. Systems theory can use the same conceptual tools to understand family interactions.

2. *Communication and control.* Traditional family literature tends to see communication as a variable that ranges in amount and satisfaction, but little else. The family process therapists have accumulated considerable evidence that controlling behavior is the most important aspect of communication.

3. *Goal orientation.* The dynamics of system goal achievement and its relationship to control and family rules appears to be a topic unique to systems theory literature.

4. *Boundary maintenance.* The importance of maintaining systems boundaries is more important to systems theory than it is to any other. There is considerable evidence now that whether a family boundary is relatively open or closed is crucial to its effectiveness.

5. *Complex relationships.* Finally, most other theoretical approaches utilize causal models that are linear, avoid too many interaction effects, and tend to average outputs into mean results. Systems theory recognizes that life is nonlinear, with multiple causal paths and outcomes. Therefore, its models emphasize branching, rather than averaging.

APPLICATION

1. Answer these questions based on the scenario at the beginning of the chapter:
   a. Consider Fred and Cassie's communication exchange from a linear perspective (punctuation) versus a circular perspective. Why does it make a difference?
   b. How might this couple employ positive feedback to alter this unfruitful pattern of interaction?

2. One of the best ways to understand systems concepts is to apply them to your own family life. The following are some good exercises adapted from Goldenberg and Goldenberg (2000):
   a. List the roles that you currently play in their order of importance. How many are family (family versus career or other) roles? Which of all the roles is the most integral to your sense of self?
   b. What homeostatic or corrective feedback do you engage in when dealing with conflict with a loved one? How do they respond to it?
   c. List some behaviors of friends or family members that irritate you. Now, try to reframe the motivations into more positive possibilities. Does this change your feelings toward the person?
   d. Most communications between people have a "command" aspect as well as the content of the message. For instance, asking where the salt is at dinner implies a command to go get it. List some common comments in your family that have implicit commands in them.
   e. Identify multiple rules that your family enforces. Are the rules implicit or explicit? What rule has someone most recently attempted to change and how has the family responded (feedback)?
   f. In reference to the situation given at the beginning of this chapter, list examples of circular causality from your own family. What are some examples of endless arguments in which each person blames the other for "starting it"?

3. The article by Bacallao and Smokowski (2007) under Sample Reading shows that Mexican immigrant families lose contact with extended family because of geographic separations and, therefore, find a variety of ways to cope. What do you think are some of the long-term effects of these coping mechanisms on the family system? What are other ways in which the families attempted to restore family equilibrium?

REFERENCES

Bateson, G., D. Jackson, J. Haley, and J. Weakland. 1956. Toward a theory of schizophrenia. *Behavioral Science* 1: 251–264.

Becvar, D. S., and R. J. Becvar. 2006. *Family therapy: A systemic integration.* 6th ed. Boston: Pearson Education.

Bertalanffy, L. 1969. *General systems theory: Essays in its foundation and development.* New York: Braziller.

Bettinger, M. 2005. A family systems approach to working with sexually open gay male couples. *Journal of Couple and Relationship Therapy* 4: 149–160.

Boss, P. 2002. *Family stress management: A contextual approach.* 2nd ed. Thousand Oaks, CA: Sage.

Broderick, C. 1993. *Understanding family process.* Newbury Park, CA: Sage.

Broderick, C., and H. Pulliam-Krager. 1979. Family process and child outcomes. In *Contemporary theories about the family*, ed. W. R. Burr, R. Hill, F. I. Nye, and I. L. Reiss. Vol. 2, 604–614. New York: Free Press.

Broderick, C., and J. Smith. 1979. The general systems approach to the family. In *Contemporary theories about the family*, ed. W. R. Burr, R. Hill, F. I. Nye, and I. L. Reiss. Vol. 1, 112–129. New York: Free Press.

Bronfenbrenner, U. 1989. Ecological systems theory. In *Six theories of child development*, ed. R. Vasta. Vol. 6, 187–250. Greenwich, CT: JAI Press.

Burgess, E. 1926. The family as a unity of interacting personalities. *The Family* 7: 3–9.

Curtis, O. 1999. *Chemical dependency: A family affair.* Pacific Grove, CA: Brooks/Cole.

Galvin, K. M., C. L. Bylund, and B. J. Brommel. 2004. *Family communication: Cohesion and change.* 6th ed. Boston: Pearson Education.

Gardiner, H., and C. Kosmitzki. 2002. *Lives across cultures: Cross-cultural human development.* Boston: Allyn and Bacon.

Goldenberg, I., and H. Goldenberg. 2000. *Family therapy: An overview.* Belmont, CA: Brooks/Cole.

Haley, J. 1959. The family of the schizophrenic: A model system. *Journal of Nervous and Mental Disease* 123: 357–374.

Herr, J. J., and J. H. Weakland. 1979. Communications within systems: Growing older within and with the double bind. In *Aging parents*, ed. P. K. Ragan, 144–153. Los Angeles: Simon & Schuster Adult Publishing Group.

Hill, R. 1972. Modern systems theory and the family: A confrontation. *Social Science Information* 10: 7–26.

Kantor, D., and W. Lehr. 1975. *Inside the family.* San Francisco: Jossey-Bass.

Kosciulek, J. F. 1996. The circumplex model and head injury family types: A test of the balanced versus extreme hypotheses. *Journal of Rehabilitation* 62: 49–55.

Mercado, M. M. 2000. The invisible family: Counseling Asian American substance abusers and their families. *The Family Journal: Counseling and Therapy for Couples and Families* 8: 267–272.

Olson, D. H. 2000. Circumplex model of marital and family systems. *Journal of Family Therapy* 22: 144–167.

Satir, V. 1964. *Conjoint family therapy.* Palo Alto, CA: Science and Behavior Books.

Satir, V. 1972. *Peoplemaking*. Palo Alto, CA: Science and Behavior Books.

Waller, W. 1938. *The family: A dynamic interpretation*. R. Hill, rev., 1951. New York: Holt, Rinehart and Winston.

Whitchurch, G., and F. Dickson. 1999. Family communication. In *Handbook of marriage and the family*, ed. M. Sussman, S. Steinmetz, and G. Peterson. 2nd ed., 687–704. New York: Plenum.

White, J., and D. Klein. 2002. *Family theories*. 2nd ed. Thousand Oaks, CA: Sage.

Winton, C. 1995. *Frameworks for studying families*. Guilford, CT: Duskin Publishing Group.

SAMPLE READING

Bacallao, M. L., and P. R. Smokowski. 2007. The costs of getting ahead: Mexican family system changes after immigration. *Family Relations* 56: 52–66.

Based on qualitative interviews with fourteen parents and twelve teenagers from ten undocumented Mexican immigrant families, the authors explore the impact of immigration on family dynamics, with particular attention to parent–adolescent relationships. Grounded theory methods helped to explain the many adjustments that these Mexican families had to make to their family systems.

SAMPLE READING

THE COSTS OF GETTING AHEAD: MEXICAN FAMILY SYSTEM CHANGES AFTER IMMIGRATION*

Martica L. Bacallao
*Paul R. Smokowski***

This study explored how immigration influenced Mexican family relationships. Qualitative interviews were conducted with 12 adolescents and 14 parents from 10 undocumented Mexican families. Participants immigrated to North Carolina within the past 7 years. A conceptual model derived from the data using grounded theory methods suggested that, after immigration, parents had less time to spend with children because of demanding new jobs and mothers entering the work force. Decreased time as a family was associated with adolescents' loneliness, isolation, and risk-taking behavior. In response to perceived environmental threats, Mexican parents became authoritarian, precipitating parent-adolescent conflict. Parent-adolescent acculturation gaps were viewed as an asset as adolescents helped parents navigate within the new cultural system. Families coped with postimmigration changes by maintaining high levels of familism and enacting cultural traditions.

Key Words: acculturation, familism, family systems, Latinos, migration.

*The authors wish to thank the Latino families who participated in this study. This study was supported by grants from the Center for Disease Control's National Injury Prevention Center (R49/CCR42172-02) and from the Centers for Disease Control's Office of the Director (1K01 CE000496-01).
** Martica L. Bacallao is an Assistant Professor in the Department of Social Work at the University of North Carolina—Greensboro, P.O. Box 26170, Greensboro, NC 27402-6170 (m.bacallao@ uncg.edu). Paul R. Smokowski is an Associate Professor in the School of Social Work at the University of North Carolina at Chapel Hill, 301 Pittsboro Street, CB # 3550, Chapel Hill, NC 27599-3550 (smokowsk@email.unc.edu).

Family Relations, 56 (January 2007), 52–66. Blackwell Publishing.
Copyright 2007 by the National Council on Family Relations.

Mexico, lindo y querido, si muero lejos de ti, por siempre te extranare. Para siempre.
{Mexico, beautiful and beloved, if I die far away from you, know that I will always
miss you. Always.}—

Yariela, Mexican female adolescent, age 12,
living in United States for 1 year

Researchers from the Pew Hispanic Center estimate that 11 million undocumented individuals currently live in the United States; a 30% increase from the 8.4 million estimated in 2000. Six million of these undocumented individuals are Mexican. The same researchers estimate that one sixth of this population, or 1.7 million people, are younger than 18 years (Passel, 2005). Although there is clearly a large group of undocumented Mexicans living in the United States, we know little about these families and how they function. It is important to learn more about the unique challenges faced by undocumented families who, compared to legal immigrants or refugees, live in fear of deportation and cannot easily travel back and forth to Mexico.

Most of the research on Latino immigration, acculturation, and adjustment has been conducted with adults, leaving us with scant information on adolescents and even less on family relationships (García Coll & Magnuson, 2001). Little attention has been given to the *1.5 generation*, that is, children and adolescents who were born and socialized in a foreign country and subsequently immigrated to the United States (Hirschman, 1994; Portes & Rumbaut, 2001). Notwithstanding the emphasis that acculturation research has placed on comparisons between different generations within immigrant families (e.g., U.S.-born children vs. their immigrant parents), these 1.5 generation children arguably experience the most upheaval of the family system and are most likely to either become bicultural or get caught between cultural systems (García Coll & Magnuson; Hirschman).

This study focused on understanding family system dynamics in undocumented Mexican families and the changes that parents and adolescents experience after immigration. We contribute to the body of knowledge on Latino immigrant families by exploring three fundamental questions that have not received adequate attention in the previous research on undocumented Mexican immigrant families: (a) how do undocumented Mexican families change after immigration, (b) how do these changes affect family members and their interactions, and (c) what factors explain postimmigration family system adjustment in undocumented families?

The immigration experience and stressors that arise therein such as learning a new language, finding jobs, and coping with discrimination can lead to both acculturation stress and familial stress. Depending upon the reasons for relocation, as well as the exiting and entering environments, immigrant families often experience significant upheaval during migration, shifts in socioeconomic status, loss of social networks, and disorienting cultural changes in the new land (Hernandez & McGoldrick, 1999). We sought to delineate how these challenges influence undocumented Mexican family system functioning and family relationships.

Past research suggests that after immigration (a) acculturation differences (i.e., gaps) between parents and adolescent children precipitate family stress (Hernandez & McGoldrick, 1999; Szapocznik & Kurtines, 1980) and (b) the strong sense of family cohesion (i.e., familism) many Mexican families arrive with erodes over time (Cortes, 1995; Rogler & Cooney, 1984). These changes may be considered what we currently

know about the "costs" of getting ahead in the United States. However, few studies have used qualitative data to examine the processes behind these family system
dynamics. The following sections describe sensitizing concepts—acculturation gaps
and the erosion of familism—that provided a foundation for the present study.

Acculturation Gaps

Normative conflicts between parents and adolescents can be exacerbated by acculturation stress, creating intercultural as well as intergenerational difficulties between
family members (Coatsworth, Pantin, & Szapocznik, 2002). Children commonly
acculturate faster than adults, creating an acculturation gap between generations that
precipitates family stress (Hernandez & McGoldrick, 1999; Szapocznik & Kurtines,
1980). Because of this cultural clash, Latino families' external boundaries often become
rigid to preserve culture of origin beliefs and norms (Hernandez & McGoldrick). This
conflict can fuel adolescent rebellion, alienate parents and adolescents, and contribute to the development of adolescent behavioral problems (Coatsworth et al., 2002;
Szapocznik, Santisteban, Kurtines, Perez-Vidal, & Hervis 1986).

Familism

Familism involves a deeply ingrained sense of the individual being inextricably rooted
in the family. The term encompasses attitudes, behaviors, and family structures within
an extended family system and is believed to be one of the most important factors influencing the lives of Latinos (Cooley, 2001; Parra-Cardona, Bulock, Imig, Villarruel, &
Gold, 2006). This strong sense of family orientation, obligation, and cohesion has noteworthy protective effects. For example, Cooley found familism to be an important factor associated with less child maltreatment in both Latino and non-Latino families.
Gil, Wagner, and Vega (2000) reported familism to have a highly significant, negative
association with acculturation stress, though this relationship was stronger for immigrant
Latino adolescents than it was for U.S.-born Latino adolescents.

Familism is thought to decrease as acculturation progresses. Cortes (1995) found
levels of familism decreased with higher levels of education and were higher for children and adolescents who were older when they arrived in the United States. Rogler
and Cooney (1984) found that second generation adult children were less familistic
than their first generation parents.

To summarize, current research on Latino families suggests that acculturation
gaps between family members contribute to intergenerational stress, and familism
tends to erode over time spent in the United States. These sensitizing concepts further
underscore the need for the present study.

METHOD

Participants and Procedure

Participants. The first author conducted in-depth, semistructured interviews with
10 undocumented Mexican immigrant families. Families were recruited from Latino
communities in North Carolina as a part of a large mixed-methods study (Bacallao &

Smokowski, 2005). Recruitment was conducted through churches, English as a Second Language programs, and at Latino community events. The 10 participating families consisted of undocumented Mexican immigrants with adolescents who were born in Mexico and had come to the United States in late childhood or adolescence. Within these 10 families, one adolescent and one parent were interviewed. In two of the families, two adolescent siblings were interviewed. Both parents were interviewed in four of the families, fathers only in three, and mothers only in the remaining three. Interviews provided qualitative data on 12 adolescents and 14 parents. Interviews were conducted with seven mothers and seven fathers, lasted 4–5 hr, and were conducted in the participants' homes in Spanish, the participants' preferred language. Participants' names were changed to protect confidentiality.

On average, adolescents were 14 years of age and had been in the United States for an average of 4 years when interviews were conducted in 2004. Forty percent (4 of 10) of the undocumented families had mothers and fathers who obtained only an elementary school education in Mexico, although 30% (3 of 10) of the families had at least one parent who had attended some high school in Mexico. The remaining 30% of families had at least one mother or father who had graduated from high school in Mexico. All of the families had two parents and lived in trailer parks or crowded apartment buildings. The average annual family income was $21,000.

Interview protocol and analyses. The semistructured interview protocol contained open-ended questions. To prompt participants to discuss acculturation, family members were asked the following questions: "In what ways are you Mexican? In what ways are you American?" To solicit information on coping and adaptation, family members were asked: "What have you overcome? What has it been like for you to adjust to life in the U.S.?" The following questions were asked to prompt participants to discuss personal and interpersonal relationship changes: "What is your relationship like with your parents (for parents: with your adolescent child) since you've been here? How have you (for parents: has your child) changed since coming to the U.S.?" These semistructured interview questions often generated lengthy narratives that were the focus of our analyses.

Parents were interviewed first, enabling them to hear the questions that their child would be asked. In every participating family, parents allowed the first author to privately interview their adolescent child. Consequently, all interviews occurred separately so that parents and adolescents did not influence one another's answers. All interviews were conducted in Spanish and translated into English during transcription by the first author.

This study used grounded theory methods (GTM) for the analyses of interview data (Charmaz, 2000). We specifically sought to explain undocumented Mexican family system adjustment after immigration, using GTM to build a conceptual model from "concepts" and "indicators" that emerged from the data (LaRossa, 2005). We used Atlas/ti version 4.1 for Windows to code text files. Following the stages of analyses in ground theory, we used open, axial, and selective coding to derive the concepts and indicators in the conceptual model (LaRossa).

During open coding, the authors broke the text down into discrete parts or units of analyses called concepts. In vivo coding was carried out similarly when participants' own words were used as a code or concept. For example, an adolescent saying "I just can't stop thinking about how my life was in Mexico" was coded "thinking about the past after immigration" during open coding; whereas a mother saying "family separations made us do things differently" initiated an in vivo code called "family separations." Open and in vivo codes were clustered into more abstract categories or variables with multiple indicators theoretically saturating each category (LaRossa, 2005). Our sensitizing concepts, familism and acculturation gaps, surfaced as open codes and categories.

Axial coding followed open and in vivo coding by examining relationships between and among categories or variables (Charmaz, 2000). Using the constant comparison method, we compared codes, concepts, and categories from different adolescents, parents, and families to examine their universality and to identify cases where they did not fit. Code notes, theory notes, and process notes were kept in memos attached to the data files to record the potential relationships between codes and categories (Parra-Cardona et al., 2006). Finally, selective coding was used to craft the story line (LaRossa, 2005). In our case, the story line emerged as articulating the costs of getting ahead and how undocumented Mexican families coped with these costs. A conceptual model was finalized to describe postimmigration adjustment in undocumented Mexican families, and exemplars were identified to illustrate the concepts and indicators in the final model.

Trustworthiness of the analysis. Qualitative researchers emphasize rigor in their studies by examining trustworthiness of the results. Triangulation of methods, sources, analysts, and perspectives are strategies for enhancing credibility in qualitative research (Patton, 2002). In this study, we used all of these triangulation methods. We triangulated information from multiple sources in the interviews with adolescents and their parents. Informal discussions with participating families after the interviews confirmed what was included in the formal interviews. With 7 of 10 families, the first author talked with both parents when the interviews were completed, gaining multiple perspectives from the same family. She also spoke with five siblings. These conversations were documented in field notes, providing multiple perspectives from which we could view the data.

In addition, as part of a large mixed-methods study, the authors discussed themes from the qualitative analyses with research staff who conducted quantitative assessments to confirm themes and integrate feedback. We shared our conceptual model with consultants and audiences at local, state, and national conferences to gain insights from other professionals working with undocumented Mexican families.

Positionality. Qualitative researchers believe that it is critical to understand and make overt the positionality, or personal beliefs and biases, brought to the research endeavor (Patton, 2002). The first author, who conducted the interviews and led the analyses, is a bicultural mental health social worker with an emphasis on the importance of family and social support, qualities that influenced her positionality. In every interview except for one, she went beyond the interview protocol to provide guidance, information, and links to local resources. We believe that this positionality enhanced the study by encouraging families to provide detailed information about their experiences.

RESULTS

Figure 1 shows the conceptual model generated in the GTM analyses. The bold titles within each box are abstract concepts underpinned by the indicators shown in each bulleted list. These concepts and indicators were salient for all of the families for both adolescent and parent data. Each concept and indicators cluster captured at least 20 single-spaced pages of thick description text from the families; the overall model characterizes over 200 pages of thick description. All of the concept and indicators clusters were associated with overall adjustment in the undocumented Mexican families. This conceptual model of postimmigration undocumented Mexican family adjustment guides the presentation of findings. We use exemplars from adolescents and parents to illustrate each element in the model. As stated above, pseudonyms are used in quotations.

THE CONTEXT OF GETTING AHEAD

Relocation as a Means to "Grow Toward the Light"

The Mexican families interviewed for this study immigrated to the United States for two primary reasons. First, all of the families thought better job opportunities existed in the United States to support their family members who immigrated and those who stayed in Mexico. Four families wanted to save enough money to return to Mexico to start businesses. All of the families discussed escaping chronic poverty in Mexico and considered the most basic living conditions in the United States a marked improvement. The second reason for relocation was to seek a better future for their children, to try to "get our children ahead." Getting children ahead meant educating them in the United States and having them learn English to enhance future opportunities. This was an organizing theme for all of the parents, making immigration-related difficulties worthwhile. Future dreams for children provided inspiration during stressful times. One mother offered this metaphor:

> Diocelina (mother): I did not come here [to the U.S.] to become rich. I didn't even come here to be happy, no. I came here to get my children ahead. I tell my children that we came here for them, and to become better persons. We work like burros here. This is not a happier life. My father told me when I was seven that everything grows towards the light. We are here to grow towards the light even when we think that darkness surrounds us. In this family, under these circumstances, we are seeds in the soil trying to grow towards the light.

THE COSTS OF GETTING AHEAD

There were significant costs associated with the possibility for getting ahead. Immigration brought serious family system changes along with economic opportunities in the United States and enhanced prospects for children's futures.

Family Separations

Life without "a boss": Sequential immigration and shifting family roles. Having family members immigrate at different times (i.e., sequential immigration) was a common experience that disrupted family functioning. Eight fathers relocated first in order to find work and lay the groundwork for bringing other family members. The fathers contributed as much as they could to the family in Mexico by sending money home. At the same time, family homeostasis or equilibrium, members' roles, and patterns of functioning were influenced by the father's absence.

The severity of separation problems appeared to depend upon the length of the separation. When the separation was short, 6 months to a year, families said they were able to cope with the stress. In the father's absence, mothers and children typically lived with and received support from extended family members. Although families originally believed that the separation from the father would last only a year, in six of eight families the separation lasted considerably longer (3 years or more). Fathers did not return to visit the family because of their undocumented legal status, the inherent risk in being smuggled across the border, and the high cost of the travel—reported to be $4,000 for one undocumented person. Family members said that long separations brought significant changes in family roles and patterns of functioning, contributing to family stress.

In the father's absence, the family left behind restructured itself and established new patterns of functioning. In three families, both parents immigrated, leaving their children with grandparents, aunts, or uncles. The loss of key parent relationships sometimes allowed adolescents, especially young males, to drift into high-risk situations, such as getting involved with antisocial peers or in illegal activities. Adolescents said these separations prompted the family to reconfigure itself around the single parent or surrogate parents that remained—a dynamic that was helpful for coping with the absence, but one that commonly created difficulties when the family was reunited. One adolescent male, Manuel, reported that he became strongly attached to his resilient mother during his father's absence. Manuel described his mother as the greatest influence in his life. His relationship with his father after separation was never the same.

> Manuel (male adolescent): My mom probably influenced me the most. I got really close to her when my dad wasn't with me. She was like the head of the family, and somehow, even though my dad's with us now, that's never been restored. She's still the head of this family. Nothing against him, it's just the way she is as a figure head. We grew up with her for six years while Dad was here [in the U.S.]. She takes charge.

Another adolescent male experienced the same intense bonding with his mother. His parents divorced after immigrating. The father returned to Mexico to get the boy when he heard that his son stopped going to school and was associating with delinquent peers. Father, son, and the father's second wife began to live together for the first time in 8 years. The son explained the difficulties he experienced in the situation.

> Jaime (male adolescent): We were separated seven or eight years. When I was . . . six, he [the father] left [for the U.S.]. And he returned to get me when I was 13. I had little memory of him when he came back. Even though it's been 3 years that I'm here with him, it's still difficult for me to adapt to him, his way of being. Now I finally know how to control things better. Back there [in Mexico], there was no boss. My older brother was here. My stepfather was living in Chicago. There was no boss. It was difficult adjusting to a boss in this house. He told me when

I got here that he was the boss. He didn't talk. But he would tell me to talk to my brother. Call my mother [in Chicago]. Talk to my sister. With my mother, I had a lot of trust. My father was more closed. I couldn't talk with him like I do with my mother. Well, he would tell me one thing: Use condoms.... That would be the only thing he'd tell me. My mother would explain everything to me.... I haven't developed that sense of trust with anyone else.... I'm still getting to know my father.

Once families were reunited after immigration, they described an adjustment period in which structural changes created new configurations of roles, boundaries, and communication processes, as well as a stormy period after reuniting. In three families,

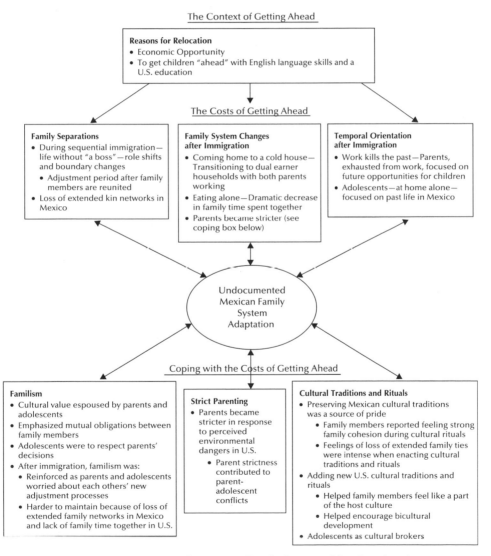

FIGURE 1. Getting Ahead: Mexican Family Systems After Immigration.

the father would argue with his wife, yell, and use foul language when speaking with the children. Family members, especially mothers, said that it took at least 1 year to readjust to living with each other. Others, like Jaime, said they were still struggling to readjust to family changes.

The loss of extended kin in Mexico. In addition to family separations during sequential immigration, there were also separations between family members who immigrated and extended kin who remained in Mexico. Given the importance many Mexicans place on familism, adolescents and parents said that the loss of close relationships with extended family members (e.g., grandparents, aunts, uncles, cousins) was hard to bear. Parents missed the companionship, support, and help extended family members provided. They also worried about aging relatives in Mexico and were limited in their ability to go back to visit. One father said that he felt closer to his daughter because they had only their nuclear family in this country; this was an uncommon contrasting view. All the other parents and adolescents said they missed the extensive family support that characterized their lives in Mexico. Adolescents reported missing family members in Mexico as much as or more than their parents. For adolescents, the family members remaining in Mexico were strongly linked to memories of childhood in Mexico, especially if the relatives had served as surrogate parents during sequential immigration family separations. During the difficulties of adjusting to life in the United States, most adolescents thought of happy times with family members in Mexico. This focus on the past made adolescents feel ambivalent about their new lives in America.

> Elena (female adolescent): The United States. I think of it with many dollars but the people are sad. You have everything, but you don't have your family. It's not like in Mexico where you visit with your grandparents and your other relatives. In Mexico, you don't have money but you're much better because you're with your family. I know that my parents do this for our well-being, so we're here. But I think all the people in Mexico are happy because they are with their family. You see, here, it is mostly sadness. I feel like crying instead of feeling good. We used to always be with my family, that's who I miss.

Thinking about loved ones left behind saddened adolescents, making some adolescents yearn to return to Mexico. Nostalgic memories were particularly enticing when adolescents felt lonely, isolated, and friendless. These memories and attachments sustained one adolescent during the difficult adjustment to life in America when she was depressed and suicidal. The interviewer asked if she was thinking of hurting herself.

> Teresa (female adolescent): Sometimes—I've felt that way when I feel shut in, when there are problems, when I've just had a fight with my mom or dad, things like that. The only thing I do is I get into my room and I make myself think. I just try to let it pass. I used to be a happy person. So, I just try to let this thing pass. [She started to cry.] I think about my grandparents, my uncles, my friends [back in Mexico]. I haven't seen my uncles and grandparents for so long that I feel like I hardly know them. But I think about them and how they would suffer if this happened to me [if she hurt herself attempting suicide]. So, no, I can't let them down. They would suffer so much.

Memories of her family in Mexico fueled this adolescent's sense of family loyalty and prevented her from hurting herself. Yet, feelings of loss associated with separation from family in Mexico also contributed to adolescents' depression. This young girl's experience of shifting from being "a happy person" to being depressed provides a bridge to broaden our discussion of family separations to postimmigration family system stress.

Mexican Family System Changes After Immigration

Coming home to a cold house: The transformation into dual-earner households.
Fathers played the role of family provider in Mexico, maintaining low-paying employment and shouldering financial responsibilities for the family. Mothers managed the home and took primary responsibility for raising children. Parents and adolescents described traditional gender roles reinforced by Mexican cultural norms, prompting mothers to be at home with their children spending time together and fathers to feel proud of their role as sole providers for their families.

After immigrating, Mexican families reconfigured themselves into dual-earner households. In 7 of 10 families, both parents worked. Financial stress and the higher U.S. cost of living prompted five of seven mothers to enter the labor force for the first time. This change helped family finances but was a difficult adjustment for family members. Mexican men who were invested in traditional gender roles said they found it particularly distressing because it was now publicly displayed that the father, as head of the household, could not solely provide for his family. Women found jobs in factories, cafeterias, restaurants, or hotel housekeeping services. According to both parents and adolescents, the amount of time the family now had to spend together decreased dramatically. All families reported that this change took a toll on both the marital relationship and parent-child relationships. In addition, adolescents were commonly left with much more unsupervised time on their own. One father described his difficulty with the changes.

> Carmelo (father): In Mexico, I would come home with my little briefcase, and my kids would come greet me when I came home. They'd say, "Dad! Dad! What do you bring?" I have this or I have that.... Now, no, I come home to an empty and cold house. Empty and cold, because there's no one here. We only share our time together for a little while. We miss out on some conversation, something we may need to say to one another. In Mexico, I had my worries from work, but as soon as I go home, my bad mood would be gone. The aggravations from work would go away because people are waiting for you. My wife would tell me, "Look, I just made you your favorite dish," or simply, "I made you your cup of coffee how you like it." In the U.S., we both come home from work with the same bad mood.

How work kills the past: Parents' stress from demanding jobs. Dual-earner families described being overloaded and having little flexibility to absorb additional stressors. In the quotation below, one mother described the conflict she felt having to work, while she worried about her adolescent children and her ailing mother, who lived nearby. Her work demands did not allow her the time to support her family members in the ways she would have liked.

Alicia (mother): I would like my daughter to talk to someone. She doesn't have papers, but she needs to talk to someone...like a psychologist. I'm not home to be with her. I had to work. The jobs here are tiring, very tiring. But we must keep our eyes on our children, and get them ahead. My husband and I have three teenagers, and one married daughter.... We have to sacrifice so many things to get the family ahead. There are so many more worries about our children here. I just want to sit here and cry, but my children, they lift me.

Family stress seemed to be worsened by the nature of the parents' work, which was physically exhausting and emotionally stressful. This may be one reason that parents did not seem to mourn family separations with extended kin in Mexico as much as adolescents did. Exhausted parents had little time to reminisce. They focused on the multiple tasks of daily life, struggling to support both their families in Mexico and in the United States. One parent described what it was like to be consumed by work.

Miguel (father): Work kills all your concentration on what used to be. By working, you don't realize anything but what is in front of you, the job ahead of you. I concentrate so much on myself and on my job. That's how I adapted. You learn about the ways here at your job.

In addition to the demanding physical labor, parents found that their work skills did not translate to work settings in America, requiring quick acquisition of new skills, often without the benefit of adequate communication with supervisors. The language barrier made this occupational adjustment particularly difficult. Four men described having to learn complicated skills, such as furniture assembly or using new machinery, after watching it done only once or twice. All fathers and four of the working mothers described being frustrated and unable to advance themselves at work because of their limited English language skills. This frustration was compounded by daily experiences of discrimination, such as being told to go back to Mexico. However, parents said they did not measure their success by their work. Work, and the stress inherent in their jobs, was a sacrifice made to provide for their families. Success for parents meant helping their children get ahead.

Eating alone: Family relationships and the decrease in shared family time. Parents' stress from work in dual-earner households influenced parent-adolescent relationships, family dynamics, and communication processes. Seven parents worked 12-hr days, 6 days per week. Two adolescents had jobs at fast food restaurants to help their parents with finances. Family members said that these work schedules, along with both parents working, reduced the amount of time family members could spend with one another. Four parents said they would not see their adolescents for 1–3 days because of conflicting work and school schedules. There was markedly less shared family time in the United States than in Mexico. Parents often worked for hourly pay; more hours worked meant more financial gain for the family. A female adolescent commented on the impact of work on family life.

Nohemi (female adolescent): My relationship with my parents has changed because, in Mexico, mom was always at home while we were at school. She would do the housework...ironing. When I came home from school, everything was ready, the food would be prepared, the clothes were washed and ironed and all that, you know? I would sit down with mom and dad to eat. And in the U.S., sometimes I don't see my dad for three days. Living in the same house, you know? For example, I go to school, then I go to work and sometimes, I get home late at night, and he's already sleeping when I come home. And the next day, it's the same thing. I don't get to see him until the third day. That's changed our relationship when you don't eat with each other every day.

Less time spent together meant adolescents had to handle problems on their own. This increase in the time they spent alone may have contributed to adolescents missing the close relationships they had in Mexico. Five female and two male adolescents described feeling isolated, lonely, and depressed in their homes. Feelings of sadness seemed to stem from grieving the loss of time spent with their parents and family in Mexico reflected in the words of a female adolescent:

Reyna (female adolescent): I just stay in my room. I like to draw.... Sometimes, I'll sleep. There's no one in the house. I don't go out of my bedroom for anything except to brush my teeth and wash myself. My mother is always working or going to church. My mother and sister are gone, so, here is where I pass the time. Alone. Always alone.

The amount of unsupervised time also allowed adolescents the opportunity to get into trouble. One immigrant father described the difficulties he had with his son who habitually skipped school after coming to the United States. On one occasion, the police escorted the adolescent home after he was found in an abandoned house partying with his Mexican gang associates. After a great deal of effort and structure from his father, this adolescent began to attend school regularly. The father commented:

Victor (father): He's changed 100%. When he lived in Mexico, he did not go to school. I decided I had to go to Mexico and bring him here. He is relatively intelligent, and had to get out of that situation in Mexico...Since he's been here, he has been told that he has to go to school, and if he doesn't go to school, he will get me in trouble. And if he doesn't obey me, he will get both of us in trouble, in trouble with the law. His behavior can either protect us, or can get us into problems. Also, he doesn't have his mother near him since he left Mexico. That has been difficult for him. He's had to adapt to being more on his own in the house. When I come home from work, I have to pay more attention to where he's going, what he did that day, if the homework is done. It's difficult because I work all day, and then, this at home.

Both parents and adolescents seemed greatly affected by the loss of maternal supervision, decreased family time together, fatigue from physically demanding jobs, and relationship changes because of sequential immigration and the loss of extended kin in Mexico. These new family system stressors had different psychological impacts on parents and adolescents. One of the differences was the temporal orientation after immigration.

Temporal orientation after relocation. Although all family members understood the reasons for relocation, parents and adolescents had dramatically different temporal orientations in the postimmigration adjustment process. Parents focused on the future, on getting their children educated, and anticipated the enhanced opportunities they perceived that their children would have with bilingual skills and a U.S. education. In contrast, adolescents focused on the past, mourning the loss of the lifestyle, family, and friends they left in Mexico. The following quote captures one adolescent's ambivalence.

> Juana (female adolescent): I feel sad because I had to leave a place that I loved very much for something that's better, better in that, if we were to go back [to Mexico], I'd have more opportunities because I'd know another language, and maybe we'd be able to get better jobs. But, I miss my family, my cousins [in Mexico].

If the metaphor for family relocation was indeed Diocelina's "plant growing toward the light," it seemed adolescents' thoughts centered on the roots under the soil that they could no longer see, whereas parents' dreamt of the future buds they hoped would bloom. These contrasting temporal orientations were one important way in which parents and adolescents went through different processes in their postimmigration adjustment to life in the United States. This provides a helpful bridge to shift our focus onto how parents and adolescents coped with these costs of getting ahead.

COPING WITH THE COSTS OF GETTING AHEAD

Parental Strictness as a Means to Counter Americanization

Both parents and adolescents reported that parents tended to become stricter with their children after immigrating to the United States. This was both an important change in parent-adolescent dynamics and a strategy for coping with new family stressors. Parents had little time to spend with their children and were worried about dangers they perceived in the environment (e.g., drug use, pulling away from the family, having too much freedom). In this new context for parenting and without the network of support from extended family members, parents did not allow their adolescents many opportunities to explore their new environment. Parents also reported feeling vulnerable to the effects of their adolescents' behavior. Families in the United States without legal papers were especially worried about being involved with the police, which may be one of the reasons parents restricted their adolescents' freedom outside the home. Participation in school-affiliated activities was uncommon. Parents and adolescents said that rules were stricter for daughters than sons, permitting daughters little latitude to recreate outside of the home. Sons generally had more freedom than daughters but were more frequently told to obey the law and keep out of legal trouble. A female adolescent commented on her understanding of the strict parenting:

> Eva (female adolescent): I think for us Latinos there are more restrictions at home because our parents do not exactly know how it is out there, and how other [American] people are...They feel better if we stay home. Maybe because they do not want us to behave like [Americans] that we are [Mexicans] in other words that we don't become so liberal but rather that we remain like we were before we left Mexico. So we do not change our way of being. When you are too liberal many things can happen to you. One of them is using drugs, or having trouble with your studies. Those are things the parents fear that will happen here. They do not want that to happen, so they do not want you to go out.

Adolescents said that parental strictness caused the most parent-child conflict. Seven adolescents disagreed with the restrictions but acquiesced to their parents' decisions. It was difficult for adolescents to question their parents' decisions because these Mexican family systems strongly valued familism and respect for parents (respeto). This left the adolescents quietly simmering with conflict against parents who set the restrictive rules. Several parents reported that having their children question their decisions brought home to them the extent to which the adolescents were becoming "Americanized." One mother commented on her daughter's Americanized attitude:

> Zunilda (mother): Eva will say to me... "Well, why is that not good?" And I'll repeat, "Why is that not good?" At her age, I wouldn't dare question my parents. I wouldn't even think of it. She's questioning her parent [facial expression widened with disbelief]. I say these kids are Americanized in those ways. But I will tell her "I don't have to answer that question because I am your mother. You don't ask me to explain 'why.'" I think that correction is needed because our customs are this way.

Cultural Assets and Family Strengths After Immigration

Familism: Connection makes me Mexican. Immediate family members relied on family cohesion, trust, and mutual support to cope with stressors in the new cultural system. The concept of familism refers to a strong sense of family orientation, obligation, loyalty, and cohesion (Parra-Cardona et al., 2006). One adolescent captured the concept of familism when he expressed his devotion to his family.

> Juan (male adolescent): I think it's being close to my family. That's always a really big part of the Hispanic population, being close to the family, and the family being a priority all the time. My friends, they've always got time for school sports, being at school after school. For me, it's my family. And it's not strange. I have people say, "Why do you want to go to a party where your family's at? Don't you want to get away from them?" You know, I don't really get tired of them. I've always been really close to them. That connection to my parents, that trust that you can talk to them, that makes me Mexican.

Familism was an important cultural asset for the Mexican adolescents. Adolescents said they recreated and relaxed physically and emotionally with family members unlike with anyone else. There was a pervasive sense that the families supported the adolescents, especially during difficult times. At the same time, there were important obligations to be met. Parents said they expected respect and obedience from their children. There was a clear hierarchical structure in which parents were responsible for making decisions that adolescents were required to obey. There was a shared sense of success and failure. Parents believed their success and accomplishments were for their children. Conversely, parents would feel like they had failed if their children did not succeed. At the same time, adolescents said that their own failure becomes their parents' failure.

Both parents and adolescents said that familism provided initiative for at least some family members to become bilingual and bicultural in order to help other family members interact with the host culture. Adolescents were proud that they could help their parents navigate the new cultural system. Parents were proud of their adolescents' new cultural skills, seeing these skills as a sign their children were getting ahead. However, parents worried about how their adolescent's biculturalism would affect the family in the future. Parents were highly invested in keeping their family together and worried that the family might end up living in two different countries. One mother remarked:

> Adriana (mother): Now, if the children want to stay here, and the parents have finished educating their children and want to return to their land, that is difficult because the family doesn't stay together after all this.... we come here to grab...economic security for our children, and then the family separates in two countries?...That is worrisome. And it happens at the end, when the obstacles have been overcome.

All of the parents and adolescents described familism as a core value in Mexican family life both before and after immigration. However, during the postimmigration period, familism became complex and reflected a dialectic. On the one hand, familism appeared to be strengthened after immigration because adolescents were worried about their parents' vulnerability in the new cultural system and strived to acquire new cultural skills to help their families. At the same time, family ties were more difficult to maintain because of new family circumstances with both parents working multiple jobs, distance from family left in Mexico, and uncertainty over where adolescents would live after they adjusted to life in the United States. Familism was at the heart of this ongoing dialectical tension described by both parents and adolescents.

Cultural traditions and rituals. Mexican cultural traditions and rituals were important to both parents and adolescents because they intensified the families' collective pride and identity. Adolescents said that they felt Mexican because of the traditions that they practiced. Parents said that they would never let go of their traditions and rituals that helped to build family identity and unity. Traditions and rituals centered on religious holidays. Some holidays, like Christmas, were the same religious holidays practiced in the United States, but they were celebrated differently in Mexico. There were also Mexican holidays, such as *Dia de los Muertos* [Day of the Dead] to honor deceased ancestors, and *Posadas*, which were typically not celebrated in the United States. Families tried to replicate their Mexican traditions in their homes and sometimes in their churches. The holidays did not feel quite the same without their family members who remained in Mexico. One mother shared her insights about the importance of family traditions:

> Graciela (mother): Customs and traditions have changed, yes, in the sense that I don't have my whole family here. We do celebrate Christmas, but it is not the same. Still, I wouldn't let go of my Mexican traditions. Now I must think of my family as my husband and my children. When there is a celebration where traditional foods are made, we really enjoy ourselves. There is much happiness. The traditions that I've brought from Mexico, how we celebrate holidays is very different. There is no Christmas here like there was in my town. We would begin Christmas festivities the 16th of December and continue them until January.

Maintaining cultural rituals and traditions was one way that families described staying close to their Mexican culture. Adolescents said that practicing these traditions and rituals helped them preserve their Mexican cultural identities, their history, sense of familism, and ethnic pride even as they experienced stress and pressure to assimilate from social systems outside of their homes. At the same time, the postimmigration adjustment process prompted families to adopt new traditions and rituals. Adopting and adapting U.S. cultural traditions and rituals helped the Mexican families take part in the host culture. One adolescent explained how learning celebrations and traditions was a key aspect of feeling one is a part of the host culture and was a sign of growing bicultural competencies.

> Eva (female adolescent): I like to learn about the things that the [U.S.] culture likes to celebrate, its traditions. Halloween, St. Patrick's Day, Mother's Day, all of those. These holidays are different and that is why you learn and feel a part of them, even if you are not too much a part, but you feel a part of this culture. You learn your culture and you learn other cultures, and you mix the cultures, and you can make something new out of one and the other, or you can pick the way that you like how things are done.

A mother from a different family expressed the same sentiment, explaining how her family adapts new cultural customs to participate in the host culture.

> Adriana (mother): My daughter is learning a little more English, and we can start grabbing some of their [American] customs. Like here, the first year we heard, "No work tomorrow. It's Thanksgiving." And we say among ourselves, "What's Thanksgiving?" Then the second year, we started knowing a little more of what Thanksgiving is. Little by little, we learn the customs. We know that we give thanks to God on Thanksgiving. We said, "We can do that here at home." We start grabbing a little of their customs because we live here. I think we must learn their [American] customs, and celebrate what we can of them.

Adolescents as cultural brokers. Parent-adolescent cultural differences (e.g., acculturation gaps) did not just contribute to conflicts in some of the families. All of the parents said they welcomed some aspects of acculturation in their adolescents because this helped the family meet daily needs. Adolescents paid bills, provided translation for their parents, and advised their younger siblings when their parents did not. Adolescents' growing knowledge of English placed them in a highly valued position in the family. One male adolescent commented on his new family role:

> Manuel (male adolescent): My parents didn't really have to adapt because of us [pointed to himself]. We are there as their mediator between the two cultures, and when they need some-thing, they'll say, "Can you help us out?" We don't tell them that we need this or that. We go to the bank, the doctor, the store. We [children] help them. Like at the bank, they'll say, "Say this for us." They didn't need to adapt too much. They live their way here, and when they want something from the outside, they come to us, and that's just how it is. We help them out.

Adolescents said that along with this new power came the responsibility inherent in using new cultural knowledge and language skills to assist parents. Nearly all of the adolescents said they worried about their parents being vulnerable in the new cultural system. The majority of these adolescents used this new role as cultural brokers to take a step toward maturity.

DISCUSSION

This study sought to explore three major questions: (a) how do undocumented Mexican families change after immigration, (b) how do these changes affect family members and their interactions, and (c) what factors explain postimmigration family system adjustment in undocumented families? A conceptual model explaining undocumented Mexican family adjustment was created using GTM. Past research on Latino immigrant families contends that acculturation gaps precipitate parent-adolescent relationship stress and that familism decreases with time spent in the United States (Coatsworth et al., 2002; Cortes, 1995; Szapocznik & Kurtines, 1980). If these dynamics were indeed occurring, we wanted to illuminate why they were taking place and what underlying processes were fueling these changes in parent-adolescent relationships and the family system as a whole using the conceptual model that emerged from the data.

The conceptual model shown in Figure 1 delineated three major domains related to postimmigration adjustment of Mexican families—the context of getting ahead, the costs of getting ahead, and coping with the costs of getting ahead. In the "context for getting ahead," all of the participating parents and adolescents said they had relocated to the United States for work opportunities and to get their children ahead by providing them with English language skills and a U.S. education. Families in this study also described a number of costs or challenges associated with getting ahead. Adolescents and mothers said that family relationships, especially relationships with fathers, were often strained and roles needed to be redefined because of lengthy separations during sequential immigration. After immigration, parents lamented having less time to spend with their children because of demanding new jobs and mothers entering the work force. Parents endured these new challenges by focusing on the future and on how their children would get ahead. In contrast, adolescents reported that decreased family time together, coupled with the loss of relationships with family members left in Mexico, left them focused on the past, feeling lonely, and mourning the losses they had experienced. The costs of getting ahead influenced Mexican family system adjustment.

Families compensated by developing strategies to cope with the costs of getting ahead. After immigration, a complex dialectic surfaced around familism. All parents and adolescents said familism continued to be of utmost importance and was even reinforced after immigration because of the new challenges to family unity. Adolescents expressed worries about their parents' vulnerability in the new cultural system, whereas parents made major sacrifices to get their children ahead. Although parents and adolescents were highly invested in familism, maintaining strong family cohesion seemed increasingly difficult while facing the challenging costs of getting ahead.

Our conceptual model helps to explain why past researchers have found familism to erode over time spent in the United States (Cortes, 1995; Rogler & Cooney, 1984) and posits new theoretical propositions for future research. Geographic separations cut family members off from the extensive network of family relationships they enjoyed in Mexico. Parents reported reluctantly having to redefine their notion of the family to emphasize relationships with immediate, nuclear members. Parents coped by focusing on the future of their children. Adolescents spent time mourning their losses but had to adjust to the new living circumstances. Their new lives in the United States consisted of nuclear family members juggling multiple jobs with far less external social support and little time to devote to one another. Despite dynamics that made it particularly difficult to maintain high levels of familism, parents and adolescents continued to stress the importance of this cultural value in their new environment. Our model suggests that family system changes (e.g., family separations, becoming a dual-earner household, spending less time together) are more strongly connected to postimmigration changes in familism than adoption of American cultural norms. Future research should examine this new proposition as an alternative to traditional assimilation hypotheses (Hirschman, 1994).

Our conceptual model also proposes that parent-adolescent acculturation gaps are more complex than previously hypothesized. Hernandez and McGoldrick (1999) reported that parent-adolescent conflicts arose from parents' insistence on maintaining culture of origin traditions in the face of their children's acculturation to the host culture—that is, from the acculturation gap (see also Szapocznik & Kurtines, 1980; Szapocznik et al., 1986). Coatsworth et al. (2002, p. 118) also asserted that parent-adolescent conflict because of acculturation gaps contributed to Latino parents having low investment in their children. In contrast, we found parent-adolescent acculturation gaps to be less problematic and no evidence to link these gaps with low parental investment. All of the parents and adolescents in this study said they wanted to maintain their Mexican traditions and reported little conflict directly because of acculturation. Instead, conflicts revolved around parents' fears of the dangers they perceived in the U.S. environment. In these families, conflicts arose when adolescents requested—and were consistently denied—permission to recreate with their Latino friends outside the home. From the adolescents' perspective, these conflicts with parents were complex because they wanted to recreate in the U.S. environment with Latino friends who shared similar cultural ways. Adolescents were not necessarily rapidly adopting U.S. cultural behaviors. Nine of 10 of the adolescents maintained high levels of involvement with their Mexican cultural norms, values, and traditions. This dynamic makes the acculturation gap between parents and adolescents more complex than if adolescents were eagerly assimilating. We propose that postimmigration parent-adolescent conflict is due more to increasingly restrictive parenting styles adopted in response to perceived dangers in the families' new environments than to acculturation gaps caused by the rapid assimilation of children.

Although the literature on parent-adolescent acculturation gaps has focused on how these gaps precipitate family stress, we found that acculturation gaps may also serve an adaptive purpose. In our interviews, all of the parents wanted their adolescents to become bicultural. Adolescents who learned English were called upon to help other family members navigate the host culture, creating a valuable new role in the family. Theoretically, we posit that adolescent development of new bicultural skills in the host culture (e.g., becoming cultural brokers) is encouraged by the family as one way to foster family system adjustment and cope with the costs of getting ahead. Future research should examine the relative contributions of these competing explanations, examining how acculturation gaps are connected to both stress and adaptation in Mexican immigrant families.

Limitations

We relied on interview data from multiple family members for this study. Family interactions were chronicled in field notes before, during, and after the interviews. Using constant comparison methods, we took great care to triangulate the data from multiple informants. Even so, there are alternative qualitative methods, such as conducting family observations, which would have yielded helpful data. Including multiple data types, such as journals and school records, would further have strengthened this study's design and should be included in future studies.

Implications for Clinical Practice and Policy for Mexican Families

Our findings support the need for the development of prevention and intervention programs for Mexican immigrant families. These programs should work to decrease acculturation stress, help families cope with postimmigration changes (e.g., becoming dual-earner households, maximizing the little time spent together), and promote cultural assets such as familism and ethnic traditions. Programs for Latino immigrant families have been developed and show promising results (see Bacallao & Smokowski, 2005, for a review; see also Coatsworth et al., 2002; Szapocznik et al., 1986) but require dissemination and further testing. Two programs in particular, Familias Unidas developed by Szapocznik et al. (Coatsworth et al.) and Entre Dos Mundos developed by Bacallao and Smokowski, adopt a family focus to address parent-adolescent cultural conflicts and enhance coping skills for handling acculturation stressors. Clinicians facilitating these programs should pay special attention to the accumulation of losses and the grieving process family members experience in being separated from family in Mexico. Clinicians should help family members address relationship issues that develop during sequential immigration and aid in creating adaptive new roles to meet postimmigration challenges.

Finally, social policymakers should consider initiatives, like guest worker programs, that would decrease acculturation stress by allowing undocumented families to come out of hiding. Many proposals for reforming immigration policies focus on border enforcement, making safe travel back and forth from Mexico increasingly difficult and dangerous. Our findings suggest that this approach increases the stress of family separations, contributing to difficulties in the postimmigration period.

CONCLUSIONS

This study delineated the ways in which the costs of getting ahead influenced the postimmigration adjustment in undocumented Mexican families who immigrated to North Carolina. Parents chose to relocate to the United States for their families' economic security and to get their children ahead with bilingual skills and a U.S. education. Immigration was a difficult and protracted event that disturbed the family's homeostasis, often requiring profound changes in the Mexican family system to reestablish equilibrium. After immigration, these families mourned the loss of family connections and familial support both in Mexico and in the United States. Families also had to adjust to becoming dual-earner households, juggling multiple jobs and stressful work conditions, which left little time for family relationships. Parents became more authoritarian in order to shield their adolescents from perceived dangers in the U.S. environment. Without extended family support that protected children in Mexico, parents were reluctant to let their adolescents recreate in the new U.S. environment with Latino friends, and this generated conflict in parent-adolescent relationships.

The families' sense of familism and maintenance of cultural traditions helped buffer families coping with the costs of getting ahead. Although familism became more difficult to maintain after immigration, this cultural value provided families with a sense of mutual obligation that delineated roles and responsibilities in meeting the challenges in their new living situations. Cultural traditions and rituals also helped families preserve their ethnic pride and develop bicultural competencies.

Because the number of undocumented immigrants continues to rise, we need to learn more about how undocumented families function. Having a deeper understanding of undocumented family processes will guide efforts to help individuals and families like these who are trying to "get ahead" and will aid in fashioning programs and policies for reducing the costs of getting ahead.

REFERENCES

Bacallao, M. L., & Smokowski, P. R. (2005). Entre Dos Mundos: Bicultural skills training with Latino immigrant families. *Journal of Primary Prevention, 26*, 485–509.

Charmaz, K. (2000). Grounded theory: Objectivist and constructivist methods. In N. K. Denzin & Y. S. Lincoln (Eds.), *Handbook of qualitative research* (2nd ed., pp. 509–535). Thousand Oaks, CA: Sage.

Coatsworth, J. D., Pantin, H., & Szapocznik, J. (2002). Familias Unidas: A family-centered ecodevelopmental intervention to reduce risk for problem behavior among Hispanic adolescents. *Clinical Child and Family Psychology Review, 5*(2), 113–132.

Cooley, C. (2001). The relationship between familism and child maltreatment in Latino and Anglo families. *Child Maltreatment, 6*(2), 130–142.

Cortes, D. E. (1995). Variations in familism in two generations of Puerto Ricans. *Hispanic Journal of Behavioral Sciences, 17*, 249–256.

García Coll, C., & Magnuson, K. (2001). The psychological experience of immigration: A developmental perspective. In M. M. Suarez-Orozco, C. Suarez-Orozco, & D. Quin Hilliard (Eds.), *Interdisciplinary perspectives on the new immigration: Vol. 4. The new immigrant and the American family* (pp. 69–110). New York: Routledge.

Gil, A., Wagner, E., & Vega, W. (2000). Acculturation, familism, and alcohol use among Latino adolescent males: Longitudinal relations. *Journal of Community Psychology, 28*, 443–458.

Hernandez, M., & McGoldrick, M. (1999). Migration and the family life cycle. In B. Carter & M. McGoldrick (Eds.), *The expanded family life cycle: Individual, family, and social perspectives* (3rd ed., pp. 169–184). Needham Heights, MA: Allyn & Bacon.

Hirschman, C. (1994). Problems and prospects of studying immigrant adaptation from the 1990 population census: From generational comparisons to the process of "becoming American." *International Migration Review, 28*, 690–711.

LaRossa, R. (2005). Grounded theory methods and qualitative family research. *Journal of Marriage and Family, 67*, 837–857.

Parra-Cardona, J. R., Bulock, L. A., Imig, D. R., Villarruel, F. A., & Gold, S. J. (2006). "Trabajando duro todos los dias": Learning from the experiences of Mexican-origin migrant families. *Family Relations, 55*, 361–375.

Passel, J. S. (2005). Estimates of the size and characteristics of the undocumented population. Retrieved March 3, 2006, http://pewhispanic.org/files/reports/44.pdf

Patton, M. (2002). *Qualitative research and evaluation methods* (3rd ed.). Thousand Oaks, CA: Sage.

Portes, A., & Rumbaut, R. G. (2001). *Legacies: The story of the immigrant second generation*. Berkeley: University of California Press.

Rogler, L. H., & Cooney, R. S. (1984). *Puerto Rican families in New York City: Intergenerational processes*. Maplewood, NJ: Waterfront.

Szapocznik, J., & Kurtines, W. M. (1980). *Acculturation, biculturalism and adjustment among Cuban Americans*. In A. Padilla (Ed.), Acculturation: Theory, models, and some new findings (pp. 139–159). Boulder, CO: Praeger.

Szapocznik, J., Santisteban, D., Kurtines, W. M., Perez-Vidal, A., & Hervis, O. (1986). Bicultural effectiveness training (BET): An experimental test of an intervention modality for families experiencing intergenerational/intercultural conflict. *Hispanic Journal of Behavioral Sciences*, *8*, 303–330.

6

Conflict Theory

Deborah and Jackie live together with their mother and children in Chicago. Deborah, the older sister, works as a licensed practical nurse on the evening shift at a hospital downtown. Her two boys stay with their grandmother when they get home from school. They do not see their father. Jackie, the younger sister, works the day shift at the local bakery and occasionally picks up an extra shift on the weekends. Her daughter goes to the day care center down the street from her house and spends the weekends with her father.

Deborah and Jackie are out shopping. They want to buy some new clothes for their children for Christmas but do not have the money to shop at the fanciest clothing shops in the mall. In fact, they drive forty miles out of town to an outlet mall to find some bargain shops. As Jackie drives, she laments their financial state.

> Jackie: I wish that, for once, I could just go to the mall and tell all those snooty salespeople to wrap up anything I want for the kids and us. I know that the kids feel badly because they don't have the "coolest" clothes. And I'd love to buy Mom a cashmere sweater. Just think—I could tell them to wrap it up and deliver it! Wouldn't that be great?

> Deborah replies: Yeah, Sis, it would be, but you know it isn't ever going to happen. We were born poor and we're always going to be poor. All we can hope for is that our children will go to college somehow and maybe get good jobs and not have to always worry about money.

Deborah and Jackie have a fun afternoon shopping together, but having stayed too late, they are driving home too fast. A police officer pulls them over for speeding, and despite their pleas, they receive a ticket for $150. On the drive home, Jackie and Deborah begin to argue with each other.

> Jackie laments: We went all that way to save money and look what happened! We don't have the money to pay for this! Why does this stuff always happen to us? Now we're going to have to work overtime just to pay for this speeding ticket.

Deborah replies: What do you mean we? You were the one who was driving! How can you be so irresponsible? You should have been watching the speed more carefully! Jack continues: I wasn't driving that fast. Did you see that Mercedes pass us? He was doing eighty-five miles per hour and he didn't get pulled over. I bet if we'd been driving a BMW, we wouldn't have been stopped either! You know I can't afford to pay this ticket. How am I supposed to get overtime when they are laying off people? I thought I could count on you to help cover this—after all, you were in the car with me!

Deborah cries: This is just the kind of thing you always do. You get your-self in over your head and you always expect me to bail you out. I'm tired of it. This was clearly your fault, and this time you are on your own!

Jackie shouts: You are the worst sister in the world!

By this time, both sisters are emotionally overwrought and drive home the rest of the way in silence.

HISTORY

Conflict theory is rooted in sociology where it is used to explain differences between classes within society and the competition for scarce resources, including economic wealth, political power, and social status. In some earlier (as well as some current) societies, people were born into their roles in society as defined by their social class (such as slave, serf, working class, or aristocracy), and remained there for life. Some social theorists believed that, if conditions were right, eventually those who were in the lower classes could move into the higher classes, but this would happen only as the result of conflict.

The famous social philosopher Karl Marx (1818–1883) is sometimes referred to as the father of conflict theory. His thinking was profoundly influenced by an earlier German philosopher, Georg Wihelm Friedrich Hegel (1770–1831). Hegel's theory about the evolution of ideas, known as the Hegelian dialectic, postulated that an accepted idea (the thesis) would eventually be challenged by its opposite (the antith-esis) until a stable middle ground was reached that combined aspects of both extremes (the synthesis). The synthesis would then become the new thesis, and the whole pendulum process would begin again (Russell 1945/1972).

Whereas Hegel's philosophy focused on the conflict of ideas, Marx focused on much more pragmatic issues—the economic well-being of individuals in society. Marx took Hegel's approach and applied it to a theory of social and economic change. He studied social change throughout history and proposed that such change followed a dialectical form. He maintained that ruling classes in a society (the ones control-ling the economic wealth and the political power) were always overthrown by the oppressed classes through conflict, after which they in turn became the ruling classes, which were likewise eventually overthrown by those classes that they had oppressed (Russell 1945/1972; Turner 1998).

Marx envisioned a time when the laborers (the oppressed and exploited proletariat) would unite their forces and overthrow the capitalist landowners and industrialists (the oppressive and exploitative bourgeoisie) and create a world where everyone had equal access to resources. This was the basic idea in his now famous *Communist Manifesto* (1848). But before a communistic society could prevail, there had to be many years of class conflict in which the focus was on how the distribution of scarce resources played out and on who ultimately maintained the power in those communities.

Whereas Marx was a major proponent of conflict theory, his focus was primarily on the economic impact of the theory. Later sociologists focused on its interpersonal uses, most notably Max Weber, Georg Simmel, and Lewis Coser. Simmel (translated 1998) added interpersonal dimensions of love, ownership, valuing, and jealousy to the perspective of conflict in families, noting that we seem to move from one extreme to the other in interpersonal relationships but find a synthesis in our need for loving. Human interaction has, within its structure, components of inequality (Sprey 1999). Coser said that conflict can solidify and unify a group as well as promote cohesion and adaptability within groups. This is because dealing with conflict brings flexibility to the system's structure and increases its capacity to change (Turner 1998).

Although these sociologists were important in helping us understand the uses of conflict in society at large, one theorist has been most important in helping define the need for understanding conflict in families—Jetse Sprey. Sprey (1969, 1979, 1999) wrote that conflict was a part of every relationship, including those in families. He outlined how conflict may be understood in families by specifying the components of the theory, by helping researchers to generate ways in which to classify conflict in families, and by distinguishing conflict in families as unique from other types of conflict.

BASIC ASSUMPTIONS

Conflict theory focuses on the explanation of orderly as well as disorderly societal processes. In the context of marriage and family studies, it explains "how and why stability and instability occur, and under what conditions harmonious interpersonal bonds are possible" (Sprey 1979, 130). All humans engage in conflict situations, and understanding the management of conflict will lead to an understanding of stability and instability in marriage and family.

The nature of humans is that they are self-oriented. Conflict theorists make certain assumptions about human nature. They assume that the individual is self-oriented or focused on self-interests. They believe that individuals are symbol-producing, which means that they are able to ascribe value to things (such as a corner office, shares of a piece of cake, or praise from parents). This ability sets up the system of scarce resources for which individuals are in competition. Conflict theorists also believe that humans have unlimited potential to hope, which means they have unlimited potential to desire power, prestige, and privilege, thereby setting up relationships with other humans as real or potential competitors (Farrington and Chertok 1993; Sprey 1979).

Societies operate under a perpetual scarcity of resources. Conflict theorists also make certain assumptions about the nature of society. Societies represent organized systems for species survival. They operate under a perpetual scarcity of resources, and this leads to perpetual confrontations. According to conflict theorists, such confrontations keep societies in a state of flux and lead to upheaval, social change, and growth.

Like structural functional theorists, conflict theorists recognize that inequality is an inevitable aspect of most relationships; unlike other theorists, conflict theorists try to manage the inequality rather than resolve it.

Group dynamics are different in families than in other groups. When applying conflict theory, one must recognize the differences between groups and families. The demand for resources varies between groups and families because some crises can drain family resources. For example, an illness in a family can cause a family to stress its resources to the maximum, whereas an illness in a group will generally not. Membership in a group is voluntary, whereas membership in a family is generally involuntary. If membership in a voluntary group becomes too intense or too competitive, a member may choose to leave. However, it is more difficult to leave a family than it is to leave a group. Relationships in a family are by definition more intense because they are closer in proximity and generally have a longer history. Also, dissolution of a family is more threatening than having a group dissolve. It takes two to form a group but only one to break it up. Thus, the person with the least interest has the most power. The ability to dissolve a family group is great power indeed, so families generally tolerate a higher degree of conflict than groups (Sprey 1979).

The power differentials are also different in voluntary groups. Groups often consist of just one sex, so there is more equality of status. Also, group power remains rather static for the life of the group, but power changes over the life cycle of the family. As children age, they gain more power; as adults age, they lose power. These changes keep the family dynamics of power continuously fluid (Farrington and Chertok 1993).

Conflict is a confrontation over control of scarce resources. Conflict is categorized as either internal or external. Internal conflict is conflict originating from inside the social system (be it between individuals, families, or societies). In closely knit groups, members may suppress conflict. Negative emotions may accumulate and intensify, a phenomenon which social psychologists refer to as "gunny-sacking." When the conflict finally boils over, it is intensified. Not only is the conflict a problem but it is also compounded and magnified by the expression of conflict. Thus, one outcome of conflict theory is the study of conflict management.

External conflict is conflict originating from outside the social system. One cannot deal with internal conflict while also using energy to fight external conflict. An example might be the conflict between political parties over tax policies (an internal conflict with respect to the country). But if war is declared on a foreign aggressor, the parties put aside their differences to concentrate on dealing with a war against another country (an external conflict). Likewise, a couple may be going through a difficult time and feeling as though their marriage is "on the rocks." Then they learn that their young child has a life-threatening illness. They bond together for the sake of the child to fight the aggressor—in this case, the disease.

One of the advantages of conflict is that, in the context of discussions, arguments, negotiations, and management, people come to new understandings of one another. This is often the case in families when couples or parents and their children learn about each other in the course of an argument. Thus, conflict can produce new or different values and revitalize existing norms. For example, in a disagreement with her fourteen-year-old daughter, a mother might learn that the curfew of 9 p.m. every night was too early to allow her to see even the early movie with her boyfriend. The mother, while still maintaining strict control over her adolescent daughter's dating habits, might be willing to negotiate a 10 p.m. curfew for weekends while maintaining the 9 p.m. deadline for all other nights. The negotiation maintains social structure in that the mother maintains the power, although neither mother nor daughter is truly satisfied with the outcome (The mother probably doesn't want her daughter to date at all; the daughter probably doesn't want a curfew at all), but the social order is maintained. Furthermore, the conflict allows for growth to occur in the relationship between the daughter and mother as they both learn something about power, negotiation, family relationships, growing up, letting go, and communication skills.

Conflict can be classified. There are two major ways of classifying conflict in families—from a macrosocial perspective and from a microsocial perspective. Depending on one's educational orientation (more sociological or more developmental), the questions and focus (and related research) are different. Conflict theory is one of the few theories that can be used in both ways, although it does make the theory a bit more complex to fully understand.

As noted above, the conflict perspective allows us to see society as a place that generates and perpetuates inequality, which leads to conflict and change. Unlike structure functionalists, who see society as basically finding its own equilibrium, conflict theorists see that, as a society, we ascribe meaning and value, and stratify people into unequal roles, with varying levels of power and access to resources (Farrington and Chertok 1993). When we apply the theory to families, we analyze how families are classified based on their access to scarce resources and determine who has the power to maintain those value structures. For example, conflict theorists analyze the unequal distribution of power and social status based on social class, gender, race, ethnicity, and education.

From the macrosocial perspective, conflict theorists look at issues of conflict between classes of people who have privilege or dominance and those who are disadvantaged—the "haves" versus the "have nots"—(e.g., men versus women, rich versus poor, Whites versus Blacks, those with access to health care versus those without, employed versus unemployed, heterosexuals versus gays and lesbians, adults versus children, married versus single, married versus divorced). This is not to imply that any one individual has more or less than another but rather that a group as a whole has more privilege than another group, and those privileges impact the families and their opportunities and choices. Conflict theorists are concerned with how people manage the discrimination and stigma they face, how they negotiate their inequality in the face of unyielding privilege, and how society creates a shared value about what people "deserve" (Seccombe 1999, 2000).

A conflict theorist who studies families from this perspective might, for example, study how adoption placements are made. Consider the various levels of privilege and disadvantage of the following five potential parents for an adoption placement: a White, married, upper-income heterosexual couple; a White, middle-class lesbian couple; a Hispanic, single, upper-class gay man; a single, upper-class Black woman; and a White, previously divorced, lower-class married couple. If you were the adoption caseworker, how would you rank order the placement, if all other factors were equal? What aspects of stratification enter into that decision? Generally, it is not the case that families fit neatly into stereotypical distinctions and, at times, values about certain families are based on myths rooted in class consciousness.

From a macrosocial perspective, conflict theorists help to deconstruct and analyze the ways in which our society ascribes values and how this leads to inequality in the family. They focus on broad social issues such as economic inequities between men's and women's salaries, differing societal expectations of men's and women's responsibilities for child-rearing, and the acceptance of violence toward women and children. Family conflict theorists make the link between these broad social issues and family dynamics. In this way, feminist family theory and conflict theory share common goals.

From the microsocial perspective, conflict theorists look within the family system at the elements that can bring about conflict. Two major structural distinctions in families are gender and age. These structural differences bring about a distinct asymmetry in member resources and authority (Farrington and Chertok 1993). Regardless of the intent of the family members, society gives them access to resources in different ways. Adults have access to resources that children do not have (e.g., money, freedom, and power); males frequently have access to resources that females do not have (e.g., physical power, higher salaries, and opportunity). In addition, children have an involuntary membership in families. In most other societal groups, membership is voluntary or is the result of one's behavior. But children join families without any consultation. Thus, despite their perspective on membership, they must stay within the group and be governed by those in authority within the group.

The family life cycle also affects the long-term balance of resources within the family. Resource utilization and contribution may be different at various stages of the life cycle. In the earlier stages of the life cycle, parents have the power while children have little power. But in the later stages of the life cycle, the children typically gain power while the parents often lose power. This power shift may create conflict.

The interplay between the various macrosocial influences on intrafamily dynamics can be seen in the example of how power shifts over the life course. In our culture, power tends to decrease as one approaches old age. People are valued by their ability to contribute financially, and older adults are often thought of as being "past their prime" in this regard. In some other cultures, power tends to increase as one approaches old age. The wisdom and experience acquired over the years is regarded as a valuable resource, and so older adults are held in high esteem, even if their physical abilities are not what they once were.

Marital conflict is the most dramatic form of conflict in families in many ways. First, whereas it takes two to make a relationship, it takes only one to end it. So, as in exchange theory, the person with the least interest in maintaining the relationship has the most power in the relationship. Secondly, marital conflict can be intense simply because it is dyadic. By definition, in a conflict there are differences, and in a dyad there are no other allies. Third, marital conflict can also be intense because the marital relationship can come to an end. In contrast, other family relationships are for life. Whenever the stakes are high, the level of conflict can easily escalate.

The outcomes in marital conflict can be assessed in two ways. The first method is to determine the patterns of "winning" and "losing"—that is, "keeping score." The idea of keeping score includes calculating the importance of the battles won and lost as well as the numbers of battles won and lost. The second method is to answer the question, "What are the consequences for the relationship after conflict?" Conflict in a relationship ends either constructively or destructively. Marital dissolution affects the family as a whole but does not end it. At any given point, families are seen in the midst of their life course, at different points of conflict, growth, and change along the way (Sprey 1999).

Conflict has positive aspects. Conflict theorists believe that, ultimately, conflict is good, which is to say that the aftermath (the result) of conflict is beneficial. They argue that conflict is actually at the root of progress and change. (This is the legacy of Marx.) Conflict brings about the process of assimilation and compromise. It brings solidity and unity within groups and challenges the values and power we ascribe to those in other groups.

We learn as we change and grow in families, and the process of learning to negotiate, communicate, and manage conflict is a positive aspect of development in families. Indeed, in close relationships, it is less important that there are conflicts than how the conflicts are handled (Mace and Mace 1980). Facing conflict can bring relationships to new levels of intimacy, relieve tension and resentment, help to identify problems, increase understanding, and bring about a renewed appreciation for the relationship (Farrington and Chertok 1993; Stinnett, Walters, and Stinnett 1991). Macrosocial conflict theorists believe that conflict theory promotes change by identifying the inequities in society and in families and by promoting a reflection and critique of the structures and values that perpetuate oppression.

PRIMARY TERMS AND CONCEPTS

Competition

Sprey (1979) defined conflict as the "state of negative interdependence between the elements of a social system" (134). When one member of the family or group gains, others lose. Groups that exist over time, such as families, have highly honed abilities to function within a system of competitiveness and to recognize their interdependence. They realize that they can take turns winning and losing and make decisions whereby members jointly win or lose, depending on their willingness to negotiate, cooperate, and seek compromise.

Conflict

Conflict is the direct confrontation between individuals or groups over scarce resources. It occurs when people use controversial means to obtain their goals or when they have incompatible goals, or some combination of these. Conflict implies a direct confrontation between opponents, whereas competition is more indirect and less personal. Conflict behavior can include physical force and litigation or the use of other external powers to achieve one's goals. Conflict can end only when both parties reach a mutually recognized agreement (e.g., one party gives up, a settlement is negotiated, or a peace treaty is signed). This does not, however, eliminate the underlying competitive basis.

Conflict Management

Conflict management involves dealing with the conflict while acknowledging the continued existence of the underlying competitive structure. It requires recognizing that (1) there are at least two competing perspectives, (2) there are scarce resources, and (3) each side should have an opportunity for access to those resources. Through negotiation and bargaining, conflict management can help competitors decide whether they wish to participate in a reciprocal sequence of access to resources (win–lose now, but lose–win later), a compromise in which both lose some resources, or a win–win option in which both sides jointly win. Conflict management does not negate the conflict, but it seeks ways to keep it from escalating.

Conflict Resolution

Conflict resolution refers to both the end state of conflict and the process of a given conflict's ending. Conflict resolution is different from conflict management, in which the conflict is maintained but negotiated into a stable state. In conflict resolution, the parties no longer see the issue as competition for scarce resources; there is no more conflict (on a particular matter), and resolution is the outcome. This may require redefining the situation so that conflict is no longer perceived as present.

Let's consider the difference between conflict management and conflict resolution by examining a rather common conflict in new relationships: money. A young couple begins their relationship with two separate bank accounts. Each pays half of the bills for housing, food, and other shared expenses; they spend the rest of their income on whatever they choose. But conflicts arise as their relationship begins to change and they want to buy a house, invest in expensive furniture, and save for their future. Who should be responsible for giving up their "fun" money for clothes, CDs, or going out? A conflict-managed solution might be for the couple to continue to pay one-half of the bills and for each to put some percentage of their extra funds into shared funds for future expenses (e.g., a down payment for a house, furniture, and other items) and continue to maintain control of the rest of their money. A conflict resolution would have occurred, if this couple decided to combine their incomes into a joint checking account and then set up saving funds for their long-term goals. All the bills are paid, but now they are jointly focusing on their goals together rather than seeing themselves as competitors. Because of a shift in their perspectives, money is no longer seen as an individual resource to be hoarded but rather as a resource that has shared value for them as a couple.

Consensus

Consensus refers to a stable state in which society, groups, or families exist, sharing common awareness or knowledge of given issues, values, and norms. Consensus is reached when all parties "see things the same way." Unanimity, reached during decision making and negotiation, is a special case of consensus that occurs when all parties agree to a given course of action or perception of a situation. Conflict management seeks consensus of the involved parties.

Negotiation and Bargaining

According to Sprey (1979), much conflict behavior is actually focused on negotiation and bargaining rather than fighting per se. These terms refer to the exchange process designed to reach a collective agreement on a disputed issue. Although the exchange may be heated or passionate as individuals and groups explain their positions, the underlying position is that they are trying to maintain access to their share of scarce resources and must, at least for the purposes of this exchange, perceive those "on the other side" as adversaries who seek to take scarce resources away from them. At times, negotiation and bargaining can be associated with hostility, but that is not always the case.

Power

Power refers to the ability to control the direction or course of action of others. It may apply to individuals or groups. It is a particularly salient concept in the analysis of families because structures in families give authority to parents over children, and society has historically and culturally given power to men over women and boys over girls. Power can also be a function of personality and temperament because some people tend to be more able to be persuasive (or overpowering interpersonally, regardless of age, gender, or status). Conflict theory looks at the degree to which interpersonal uses of power enter into the reciprocal interactions, identifying ways in which power can be used either positively, as a resource (e.g., authority or privilege), or negatively (e.g., to unduly control others).

Assertion and Aggression

Assertion is acting in a way that affirms one's rights and positions but does not necessarily do so at the expense of others. This is in contrast to aggression, which is a behavioral use of power to get others to behave to suit one's own advantage, even at the expense of others. Whereas assertion is most typically used in verbal statements, aggression can escalate to psychological and physical overpowering of others.

Threats and Promises

Threats are messages, not behaviors, that communicate the delivery of punishment if demands are not met at some point in the future; promises are messages, not behaviors, which communicate the delivery of something positive or rewarding if demands are met at some point in the future. These messages, verbal or otherwise, require shared understandings of symbols and meanings, making them sometimes more meaningful to groups and families who have had similar shared experiences and less meaningful to outsiders who do not see their inherent power. For example, a wife may threaten to ruin her husband's reputation if he leaves her, or a husband may threaten to leave his wife poor and destitute if she leaves him. Both of these constitute threats, are coercive, and have a negative impact on the relationship by maintaining power, although no physical aggression is necessary.

COMMON AREAS OF RESEARCH AND APPLICATION

Conflict Management

For those studying conflict theory, it is often difficult to separate the difference between having a conflict with someone from seeing the relationship in the context of conflict. We all know that being in conflict with someone is draining, frustrating, and often disheartening. In intimate relationships, it is difficult to figure out that there are winners or losers—both partners lose when conflict is destructive. Although it seems intuitive that conflicts need to be resolved for relationships to be stable, conflict theorists believe that growth and change are necessary to achieve true stability. Thus, conflict theorists reject the notion that conflict between partners should focus on resolution and instead believe that the focus should be on conflict management (Alberts 1990; Cahn 1990; Sprey 1979). The focus then turns to how couples and families communicate their needs and manage their individual desires as a group.

Power in the marital dyad has been studied extensively. Blood and Wolfe (1960) used the concept of power to understand decision making between husbands and wives. Goode (1964) defined a negative authority as someone who could prevent someone else from doing something and indicated that this hidden power was often found in the husband's role. Cromwell and Olson (1975) defined three types of power in intimate relationships: power bases, power processes, and power outcomes. *Power bases* are what we bring into the relationship, or our personal assets such as knowledge or skills, that might serve as a reward for the other partner. *Power processes* refer to the techniques we use to gain control in relationships. These might include our abilities to be assertive, persuade, problem solve, or coerce. *Power outcomes* refer to the final decision that is made. These elements of power have been used to evaluate many components of family dynamics and decision making.

Although other factors, such as money, education, and employment, contribute to the balance of power in social conflict, communication seems to be one of the key factors in interpersonal conflict (Richmond, McCroskey, and Roach 1997). One of the best-known researchers in the past twenty years in the field of couples' communication is John Gottman. Research by Gottman and his associates (Gotman 1979; Gotman et al. 1976; Gottman and Notarius 2000) has demonstrated the differences between the ways distressed and nondistressed couples communicate, illustrating that those who have negative communication patterns also have higher degrees of marital dissatisfaction and conflict. Furthermore, even highly distressed couples who reported high levels of conflict could be taught to manage their conflict in more positive and satisfactory ways, leading to more positive outcomes and higher marital satisfaction. Conflict management, then, is not a static skill but rather one that improves over time (Gottman 1979; Mackey and O'Brien 1998). The Gottman team's research was so precise that they could predict the outcome of a disagreement 96 percent of the time by the amount of criticism and negative emotion apparent at the beginning of the conflict (Gottman and Notarius 2000). Further, they found that the single most important predictor of divorce is that negative emotion escalates in a disagreement (e.g., anger is met with contempt).

When coupled with the concept of power, negative communication takes on additional meaning. For example, some people have a higher tolerance for conflict than others and can use that power to escalate a conflict. Those partners would be classified as *demanders*, and their partners are often *avoiders*. Researchers used to see those labels simply, with the demanders having more power in the relationship than the avoiders. But more careful analysis of communication and power clarified several points. First, couples who avoided conflict entirely were less satisfied with their relationships than those who confronted one another (Gottman and Krokoff 1989). Second, avoidance was not always found to be a negative or deficient element in a relationship; it was found to be a beneficial skill used by couples to postpone discussions until they had the time and energy to discuss issues (Alberts 1990). Combining power dimensions with communication also is one of the emerging avenues of research on domestic violence and power discrepancies (Babcock et al. 1993).

Gender is also an important variable in the assessment of power in relationships. In fact, conflict theory forms the basis of some aspects of feminist theory because it underscores the inevitability of conflict between men and women who have unequal access to resources in our society, which is often reflected in the power relationships of intimate relationships. This is discussed in much more detail in the chapter on feminist theory.

Divorce

Obviously not all conflicts can be managed, and divorce is the result when marital conflicts cannot be resolved. Researchers studying divorce have identified various processes that correspond to the divorce experience, including the emotional, economic, and societal divorce (Shehan and Kammeyer 1997). These processes represent resources that impact the couple differentially and will impact the divorce experience for each partner differently. For example, if one partner has more emotional power by having more emotional closeness to the children, then custody arrangements might be of most importance for that member in the divorce proceedings. If the couple has vast economic holdings and no children, then perhaps the economic settlement may be the most important. If the couple lives in a small community, then perhaps the social aspect of the divorce will carry the most weight. In the worst-case scenarios, these resource issues collide as one partner spreads rumors of drug use or child molestation in order to ensure child custody, or another partner declares bankruptcy in order not to have to pay child support to retaliate for the ex-spouse winning child custody. Obviously, in these conflict-habituated relationships, conflict did not lend itself to the positive growth and change that the theorists envisioned but still demonstrated the use of competition, power, and attempts to access scarce resources.

Developmental Changes

Of particular interest to developmental family scholars is how family dynamics change over the life course and how power differentials change as individuals age. For example, parents and adolescents are generally expected to have more conflict than parents and children because adolescents are seeking to gain power as individuals (Smetana and Gaines 1999; Steinberg 1989). Before their children reach adolescence, parents have all the power, but as adolescents age, they have increased power, through increased access to social and financial networks and, particularly for males, increased physical power. Yet, for most families, the conflicts are generally about minor things, for example, daily activities such as chores, keeping rooms clean, and choice of foods and snacks (Dacey and Kenny 1997). The research on parent–adolescent conflict also reflects, though, that the frequency and magnitude of conflict in parent–adolescent relationships depend on whom one asks. When adolescents were surveyed, they reported that adolescence was not particularly conflicted (Gecas and Seff 1990), but parents reported adolescence as more turbulent (Pasley and Gecas 1984). Despite this difference in perspective, it is important to remember that conflict can serve to teach adolescents how to appropriately manage and negotiate conflict as they age and leave home.

The interplay between developmental issues and macrolevel social issues can be seen in families as they struggle to negotiate the myriad of pressures that adolescents face. One level of conflict is found in the internal conflicts within emerging adolescents as they enter formal operational thought. For example, their cognitive ability to consider the real versus the ideal enables them to imagine idealized versions of themselves, their families, and their society. A second level of conflict exists as the adolescent seeks to individuate from the family while still maintaining some connection to the family. A third level of conflict exists as the adolescent seeks to connect with society at large but may not have the resources to do so. A fourth level of conflict exists if the adolescent can, in fact, connect with society but must "leave the family behind" to do so.

More recently Fouts, Hewlett, and Lamb (2005) identified weaning as a point of conflict in family life. In their ethnographic study of Bofi farmers and foragers of Central Africa, they employed parent–offspring conflict theory to examine conflicts surrounding weaning of children. From a conflict perspective, mothers might desire to wean their children so that they can prepare for the birth of a new child or be more productive in their farming or foraging work. Children, on the other hand, might resist weaning by throwing temper tantrums and using other "psychological weapons" (30) in an effort to preserve maternal investment in them. Results revealed that Bofi farmer children were markedly more distressed with the cessation of breast feeding than were the Bofi forager children. Farmer mothers weaned their children much earlier (between eighteen and twenty-seven months versus between thirty-six and fifty-three months) and within a few days or a week, employed more frightening techniques (e.g., painting their nipples with red nail polish), and held their weaned children significantly less, contributing to their children's expression of distress. On the other hand, Bofi forager mothers did not interrupt or discourage their children from breast feeding, allowing them to stop nursing when they are ready to do so on their own accord. Lower weaning distress expressed by forager children may be the result of more gradual shifts in breast feeding, enhanced involvement of other adults as mothers became less attentive, and less fear-invoking weaning practices. This article demonstrates how conflict theory is best employed when embedded within cultural and social contexts.

Abuse

Conflict theory has frequently been used in family studies to clarify issues in family violence and abuse. The clear dynamics of conflict and power are a part of abusive relationships, and family scholars have analyzed these relationships to determine how and why abuse occurs, what the predetermining factors are, why people stay in abusive relationships, and what motivates people to leave such abusive relationships.

Typically, when we consider couple violence, we often consider physical strength as the power in the relationship, but conflict theorists broaden our perspective. The 1950s picture of domestic violence was of a strong man telling "his woman" what to do, and forcing her, if necessary, to bend to his will. The twenty-first century picture of domestic violence must take into account dating and courtship violence, cohabiting violence, violence perpetrated on men by women, same-sex relationship violence, and our increasing knowledge of the many forms of abuse (Johnson and Ferraro 2000; Miller and Knudsen 1999). *Wife abuse* is no longer a term sufficient to include the types of abuse found in intimate relationships today. Even such labels as partner abuse, child abuse, and elder abuse are not sufficient. Within couples we must now distinguish between common couple violence, intimate terrorism, and violent resistance (Johnson and Ferraro 2000). Conflict theorists have helped us to analyze the complexity of the many forms of violence perpetrated in families.

One of the most important predictors of domestic violence is inequity in power (Sagrestano, Heavey, and Christensen 1999). Couples with more egalitarian distributions of power in their relationships are less likely to report violence than those with unequal power (Coleman and Straus 1986). Further, the severity of the abuse toward a female is dependent on the abuser's perception of her power (Claes and Rosenthal 1990). Power differentials can be seen in communication patterns because verbal coercion can be a form of emotional abuse and a precursor to physical abuse (Babcock et al. 1993). Ironically, despite the hope that women would be empowered by educational and occupational achievement, violence against women is greater in couples when the woman's economic, educational, or occupational status is higher than the man's (Claes and Rosenthal 1990; Sagrestano, Heavey, and Christensen 1999).

Siblings can also resort to the use of violence in order to resolve conflicts resulting from such things as sibling jealousy or competition for parental attention, distribution of household chores, and the need to share space and possessions. Recognizing that most family violence occurs between siblings, Hoffman, Kiecolt, and Edwards (2005) used conflict, feminist, and social-learning theories to ask 651 first-year college students about their experience with physical violence with siblings. As might be expected from a conflict theoretical perspective, sibling violence, particularly among males, was more prevalent when parents elevated one child as a standard for other children. Such resentments exacerbated sibling arguments and also made it more difficult for siblings to share property.

CRITIQUE

One of the criticisms of conflict theory is that it analyzes families in destructive, negative terms—that is, conflict, power, and competition. Many family theorists prefer to focus on constructive and positive terms—cooperation, equity, and compassion. In other words, it simply does not fit our ideal of what relationships "ought" to be, and therefore, provides a less positive model for study.

Another criticism is that conflict theory, once it has described relationships in terms of its components of competition, power, and access to resources, does not propose how families can improve. Other theories focus on order and being able to make predictions about families. Conflict theory, by definition, does not engender a static view of families but rather an always changing perspective. Thus, conflict theory does not lend itself to research or application outcomes that are immediately transferable to skill building. One exception is the work by Gottman, but his focus has been on conflicts at the interpersonal level and not at the social level.

Despite some scholars wishing that families were safe and happy places, conflict theory does, in fact, describe situations where families are not. Conflict theory raises our awareness of situations that families face regarding inequities in health care, income, access to education, and equal opportunity (both legally and subtly). It encourages us to see families in their complex social systems. In addition, conflict theory takes into account the ever-changing elements brought into families by development, social events, social pressures, and by internal and external forces.

APPLICATION

1. Using the scenario at the beginning of the chapter, answer the following questions:
   a. How is Deborah and Jackie's socioeconomic status illustrated by the case study? What elements of class conflict are apparent in their situation?
   b. How might the elements of class conflict that are expressed by Deborah and Jackie earlier in the day be a part of the interpersonal conflict experienced between the sisters later in the day?
   c. Find an example of each basic assumption in the case study.
   d. There were examples of both conflict and competition in this case study. Identify some of them and discuss how socioeconomic, educational, gender, or power components combine to make the situations more complex.
   e. Discuss your perspective on the conflict between Jackie and Deborah. Was it positive or negative? Was it good or bad for the relationship? How? In what ways?
   f. Discuss some of the consequences of the conflict between the sisters on the family as a whole. What if the children were present during the argument? Would that have made a difference? What other ways, aside from observing parents arguing, do children learn how to manage conflicts in their lives?
   g. In this family, there are three generations living together. What additional issues of power and conflict management does this family face because of the extended family system?

2. Over what resources has your own family experienced competition and/or conflict? How has your family managed the conflict? Are there any issues around which conflict was resolved? Consider how, and under what circumstances, your family has sought consensus, exhibited power, and employed the use of negotiating/bargaining, assertion and aggression, and threats and promises.

3. Answer the following questions based on Secombe's (1999) work provided as Sample Reading:
   a. Is the conflict represented a macrolevel or microlevel conflict? Can the level of conflict at one level (either macro or micro) create conflict at the other level for women in these circumstances? Give some examples.
   b. Discuss some of the societal restrictions that inhibit full access to resources for women who are on welfare. What are the negative consequences of continued scarcity of resources from a conflict perspective? Are there any positive consequences?

REFERENCES

Alberts, J. K. 1990. The use of humor in managing couples' conflict interactions. In *Intimates in conflict*, ed. D. D. Cahn, 105–120. Hillsdale, NJ: Lawrence Erlbaum.

Babcock, J. C., J. Waltz, N. S. Jacobson, and J. M. Gottman. 1993. Power and violence: The relations between communication patterns, power discrepancies, and domestic violence. *Journal of Consulting and Clinical Psychology* 61: 40–50.

Blood, R. O., and D. M. Wolfe. 1960. *Husbands and wives, the dynamics of married living*. New York: Free Press.

Cahn, D. 1990. *Intimates in conflict: A communication perspective*. Hillsdale, NJ: Lawrence Erlbaum.

Claes, J. A., and D. M. Rosenthal. 1990. Men who batter women: A study in power. *Journal of Family Violence* 5: 215–224.

Coleman, D. H., and M. A. Straus. 1986. Marital power, conflict, and violence in a nationally representative sample of American couples. *Violence and Victims* 1: 141–157.

Cromwell, R. E., and D. H. Olson. 1975. *Power in families*. New York: Wiley.

Dacey, J., and M. Kenny. 1997. *Adolescent development*. 2nd ed. Madison, WI: Brown and Benchmark.

Farrington, K., and E. Chertok. 1993. Social conflict theories of the family. In *Sourcebook of family theories and methods: A contextual approach*, ed. P. G. Boss, W. J. Doherty, R. LaRossa, W. R. Schumm, and S. K. Steinmetz, 357–381. New York: Plenum.

Fouts, H. N., R. S. Hewlett, and M. E. Lamb. 2005. Parent offspring weaning conflicts among the Bofi farmers and foragers of Central Africa. *Current Anthropology* 46: 29–50.

Gecas, V., and M. A. Seff. 1990. Families and adolescents: A review of the 1980's. *Journal of Marriage and the Family* 52: 941–958.

Goode, W. 1964. *The family*. Englewood Cliffs, NJ: Prentice Hall.

Gottman, J. M. 1979. *Marital interaction: Experimental investigations*. New York: Academic Press.

Gottman, J. M., and L. J. Krokoff. 1989. Marital interaction and satisfaction: A longitudinal view. *Journal of Consulting and Clinical Psychology* 57: 47–52.

Gottman, J. M., and C. I. Notarius. 2000. Decade review: Observing marital interaction. *Journal of Marriage and the Family* 62: 927–947.

Gottman, J., C. Notarius, J. Gonso, and H. Markman. 1976. *A couple's guide to communication*. Champaign, IL: Research Press.

Hoffman, K. L., K. J. Kiecolt, and J. N. Edwards. 2005. Physical violence between siblings: A theoretical and empirical analysis. *Journal of Family Issues* 26: 1103–1130.

Johnson, M. P., and K. J. Ferraro. 2000. Research on domestic violence in the 1990's: Making distinctions. *Journal of Marriage and the Family* 62: 948–963.

Mace, D., and V. Mace. 1980. Enriching marriages: The foundation of family strength. In *Family strengths: Positive models for family life*, ed. N. Stinnett, B. Chesser, J. DeFrain, and P. Knaub, 89–110. Lincoln: University of Nebraska.

Mackey, R. A., and B. A. O'Brien. 1998. Marital conflict management: Gender and ethnic differences. *Social Work* 43: 128–141.

Miller, J. L., and D. D. Knudsen. 1999. Family abuse and violence. In *Handbook of marriage and the family*, ed. M. Sussman, S. K. Steinmetz, and G. W. Peterson. 2nd ed., 705–741. New York: Plenum.

Pasley, K., and V. Gecas. 1984. Stresses and satisfactions of the parental role. *Personnel and Guidance Journal* 2: 400–404.

Richmond, V. P., J. C. McCroskey, and K. D. Roach. 1997. Communication and decision-making styles, power base usage, and satisfaction in marital dyads. *Communication Quarterly* 45: 410–426.

Russell, B. 1945/1972. *A history of Western philosophy*. New York: Simon and Schuster.

Sagrestano, L. M., C. L. Heavey, and A. Christensen. 1999. Perceived power and physical violence in marital conflict. *Journal of Social Issues* 55: 65–79.

Seccombe, K. 1999. *"So you think I drive a Cadillac?" Welfare recipients' perspectives on the system and its reform*. Boston: Allyn and Bacon.

———. 2000. Families in poverty in the 1990s: Trends, causes, consequences, and lessons learned. *Journal of Marriage and the Family* 62: 1094–1113.

Shehan, C. L., and K. C. W. Kammeyer. 1997. *Marriages and families: Reflections of a gendered society*. Boston: Allyn and Bacon.

Simmel, G. (trans. Mark Ritter and David Frisby). 1998. On the sociology of the family. *Theory, Culture and Society* 15(3–4): 283–293.

Smetana, J., and C. Gaines. 1999. Adolescent–parent conflict in middle-class African American families. *Child Development* 70: 1447–1463.

Sprey, J. 1969. The family as a system in conflict. *Journal of Marriage and the Family* 31: 699–706.

———. 1979. Conflict theory and the study of marriage and the family. In *Contemporary theories about the family*. Vol. 2 of *General theories/theoretical orientations*, ed. W. R. Burr, R. Hill, F. I. Nye, and I. L. Reiss, 130–159. New York: Free Press.

———. 1999. Family dynamics: An essay on conflict and power. In *Handbook of marriage and the family*, ed. M. Sussman, S. K. Steinmetz, and G. W. Peterson. 2nd ed., 667–685. New York: Plenum.

Steinberg, L. 1989. *Adolescence*. 2nd ed. New York: Knopf.

Stinnett, N., J. Walters, and N. Stinnett. 1991. *Relationships in marriage and the family*. New York: Macmillan.

Turner, J. H. 1998. *The structure of sociological theory*. 6th ed. Belmont, CA: Wadsworth.

SAMPLE READING

Seccombe, K. 1999. Why Welfare? In *So you think I drive a Cadillac? Welfare recipients' perspectives on the system and its reform*. Boston: Allyn and Bacon.

This chapter reveals some of the many reasons why women are on welfare, despite the stigma and negative perceptions of being on welfare. Drawing from interviews of forty-nine women, Seccombe analyzes their stories, outlining the social stratification and conflict issues in society and exhibiting how scarce resources are distributed in the United States.

SAMPLE READING

WHY WELFARE?

Karen Seccombe

Why do women use welfare? Given the stigma that surrounds welfare use, and the negative perception of welfare mothers, why would women choose to receive welfare? Laziness? Lack of motivation? Desperation?

Women on welfare often disassociate themselves from other welfare recipients. They tend to attribute their own welfare use to circumstances that are largely beyond their control. They need welfare, they told me, because "there are no jobs"; "how can I take care of all my kids and work too?"; "I would be fine if he would just pay child support"; "I was raped"; "I was beaten and abused"; "he deserted us, and I'm trying to get my feet on the ground"; "I'm trying to better myself"; "the welfare system penalizes me if I get a job." In the lives of women, these are not small or trivial reasons.

Rhonda, like most women interviewed, believes that she has little in common with other welfare recipients. She says that she knows many other women who receive welfare for their families whom they raise alone: her friends, her neighbors, and her son's father's family. She perceives that they "enjoy" being on welfare and "...getting everything handed to them." But what about herself and her son? Why is she on welfare? Her situation is entirely different, she told me. She elaborated on the circumstances that brought her to welfare: Can't find a permanent job; her son's father pays no child support; her son has a chronic medical condition. Exactly how is her situation different? Despite her belief that her circumstances are highly unusual, her story has a familiar ring to it.

Rhonda is a 28-year-old white woman, with a five-year-old son named Bobby, who is in kindergarten. She has been off and on welfare for five years since her son was born. Rhonda remains in contact with Bobby's father who lives out of state; he is a truck driver and visits his son regularly once each month. During that visit he will take Bobby out, buy him clothes, and take him to dinner at McDonalds. He, however, does not pay child support. Rhonda and Bobby's father remain cordial, and she appreciates the monthly visits, clothing, and dinners for her son. She expects little else from Bobby's father, financially or otherwise, and receives little else.

Rhonda and her son's father never married. They were romantically involved, but the relationship ended shortly before Bobby was born. After the birth of her son, she lived with her mother briefly. But it was difficult having two families under one small roof. Rhonda wanted to be on her own, so she applied for welfare.

When I interviewed Rhonda, she and Bobby had recently moved from a trailer to an apartment within a subsidized housing project. They had lived there for six months, and she detested it. Neither she nor her son socialize with neighbors; they were abusive to her son, she told me. She also believes they are criminals, dependent on the system, and have no interest in "bettering themselves."

The apartment in which Rhonda and Bobby live is cramped, dingy, and run down. There is no carpeting, just dark brown linoleum that is peeling in many places. Two chairs, one end table, and a television are about all that fit in her tiny living room. She stays in the projects because, after losing her job, the eleven-dollar monthly rent is all she can afford. A sizable chunk of her $241 welfare check goes for utilities, which cost approximately $140 a month, because her apartment is poorly insulated. Heat and air conditioning (nearly a requirement in Florida's sweltering six-month summers) escapes through the windows and door cracks. After paying for car insurance, which runs $22 a month; for cleaning supplies, laundry soap, and other miscellaneous expenses, Rhonda has little money left over. When her budget permits, she buys clothes for her son who is growing rapidly, often from the Salvation Army or Goodwill.

Rhonda does not see herself as dependent on the welfare system. During the five years she has been off and on welfare, she has held a variety of jobs. She has worked in the housekeeping department of a hospital, as a cashier, at a warehouse where she sorted lids for a printing company, and she recently ran a daycare center out of her home. She took great pride in her daycare center, and claimed it is her ideal job, and one that she would like to try again someday. She enjoys young children. Having children around the house taught her son Bobby responsibility, and her job did not take her away from Bobby for eight or nine hours a day. Like other women who were interviewed, and consistent with the views of women with greater financial means, an ideal job was seen as one that interfered as little as possible with her responsibilities as a single parent. Unfortunately, Rhonda was forced to close her daycare because many of her clients were considerably delinquent in paying their childcare bills. Unable to force them to pay the money they owed her, Rhonda wasn't able to keep up with her own bills. She had to close her daycare.

Rhonda told me that she "hates welfare." Then why is she receiving it? She, like so many others before and after her, told of having a very difficult time finding a permanent job that pays well enough for her to take care of her family. She had an easier time securing employment when she lived in Maryland. She moved to Florida to be near her sister and father, but has had a difficult time finding a full-time permanent job in a university town. Moreover, her job options are limited; Rhonda quit school in the 10th grade, eventually earning her GED after Bobby was born. She says she actively looks for work, but usually can only turn up temporary jobs that expire after a period of several months. Rhonda told me that she desperately wants to work because she sees it as a ticket to a better life for her and Bobby. Since he's now enrolled in school she will not have to shell out the $200 a month for daycare like she used to do. A job, she believes, holds promise for a better life. She enthusiastically told me about a job lead she had from her sister. A nearby factory may be hiring over twenty new people, and she is hopeful that she will be one of them. She submitted her application last week. She knows that by securing a job, her rent will go up, her welfare check will be eliminated, and her food stamps will likely be significantly reduced. She acknowledges that these are "disadvantages" but she insists that she prefers "to be out working, meeting people, you know. Making it better for me and my son."

But Rhonda is concerned about losing her medical benefits. As a welfare recipient she receives virtually free medical care for herself and Bobby. Finding a job that would provide medical benefits poses a challenge. But given Bobby's condition, medical benefits are of paramount importance. Bobby suffers from lead-paint poisoning. As a baby he ingested paint peeling off a wall in a house they rented. Lead-paint poisoning is a serious and common problem in old, dilapidated structures that the poor often inhabit. An estimated three million poor children may be at risk of impaired physical and mental development related to ingesting lead-based paint flaking off the walls of older homes (Needleman, Schell, Bellinger, Leviton, & Allred, 1990). Low income preschoolers are three times more likely than children living in moderate income families to have lead levels in their bloodstream of at least 10 micrograms of lead per deciliter of blood, a level at which harmful effects have been noted. Lead exposure damages the brain and central nervous system. Consequently, one study reported that second grade children with high levels of lead in their bloodstream were six times more likely to have a reading disability, had significantly lower IQ rates, and lower scores on vocabulary tests. When researchers followed these children over time, they noted that the children were seven times more likely to drop out of high school (Children's Defense Fund, 1994). Bobby continues to suffer serious bouts from the poisoning several years after ingesting it. He endures frequent pain, and during these episodes is lethargic and without an appetite. His flare-ups occur every few months, and physicians closely monitor him. He continues to be in and out of the hospital with regularity.

Despite what Rhonda may think, her situation is fairly typical. She receives no child support from her son's father. She has difficulty finding permanent work with pay sufficient to pull her above the level she would be at if she stayed home and received welfare. Moreover, a job necessitates that she will lose most of her welfare benefits, including Medicaid. Given the health problems in her family, losing medical benefits is a steep price to pay for a minimum wage job. Despite her insistence that she will be off of welfare very shortly, would we be surprised to find that she later returned to the system?

The truth is that Rhonda is on welfare because of structural problems more so than personal shortcomings. She is not particularly lacking in personal drive or initiative. Since having a baby on her own she has earned a GED and has opened her own business—fair accomplishments for someone who is the sole parent to a young child; a child with a serious illness. She describes one of her personal strengths as being "responsible." Rhonda ingeniously sought to combine work and motherhood so that she could excel at both, and neither would suffer. She struggled as a small business owner, as do many small business owners, until she was forced to close her business due to clients who refused to pay their bills. Rhonda is hardworking and is motivated to improve her circumstances in life. In these ways, she is quite typical of many women I met who receive welfare. Despite her thinking to the contrary, she was not the exceptional case.

Women on welfare, including Rhonda, largely point to two general explanations to explain their own use of welfare: They cite the problems inherent in our social structure, and they cite fate. Neither perspective focuses on the individual as much as to external forces largely outside of her control. A structural perspective attributes poverty and welfare use to economic or social imbalances that restrict opportunities for some people. Fatalism assumes that poverty and welfare use can be traced to bad luck, unpredictable quirks of human nature, or simply to chance. These explanations generally are not accorded to other welfare recipients. They are, however, used routinely by recipients to elucidate why they themselves receive aide.

THE INFLUENCE OF SOCIAL STRUCTURE

Women on welfare commonly attributed their reliance on welfare to problems and concerns related to the way our social structure is organized. Their concerns, they told me, primarily revolved around (1) a lack of jobs paying a living wage; (2) lack of good quality and affordable daycare; (3) lack of father involvement and child support enforcement; (4) inadequate transportation systems; (5) broader problems in our social structure, such as racism or sexism; and (6) a welfare system that penalizes women for initiative and eliminates their welfare benefits prematurely.

Employment

Many women talked about the difficulty of finding employment, particularly a job that pays a living wage. Although the unemployment rate in the nation is a low 5.2 percent, many women told me of submitting application after application, to no avail. "You can't make someone hire you," they said.

One woman, Cassandra, told me of her frustration after applying for job after job, with no luck at landing one. Her responsibilities related to taking care of her home and her children are not considered legitimate work experience, even for service sector occupations. She described her frustration after applying for a job as a custodian.

> I even applied for custodial work at the University, and I know I'm qualified to sweep floors. And the lady even told me at the desk that I'd be competing with people who already have experience in this area. Now, I know I'm qualified to sweep floors. If I'm going to do it at home for free, I might as well get paid to do it.

Sarah, a white 30-year-old divorced mother who, after an extended job search, finally landed a part-time job at a fast food franchise while also attending college in pursuit of an A.A. degree. She commented on her difficulty in finding even minimum wage work. She has many years of experience, including as a manager in the fast food industry. She wondered if her difficulty in finding work was due to the fact that she has been on Workman's Compensation, and therefore was viewed as a high risk by potential employers. But too many others voiced similar complaints for her case to be an isolated incident.

> It is very hard to find a job. Because people are picky and some of these places, you'll only get a job if you know someone. I spent a year looking for a job, and Colonel Sanders was the first place to hire me. I've gone places, because when you

are on Workman's Comp you have to fill out a list every month, and how many jobs you've applied in. I've applied for 20 to 100 a month. And this was the first place that even contacted me in a year. It's not that I'm not qualified. I've had 6 years of management.

Moreover, when women do find work, most are employed in service sector jobs, such as the fast food industry, which generally pay minimum wage and offer no fringe benefits. Fast food franchises such as Wendy's, McDonalds, Burger King, Hardees, and several others offer the most recurrent avenues of employment to women on welfare. They generally do not require a high school diploma nor extensive experience. Yet, despite their possibilities, these jobs do not pay enough to support a family or even pull them above the poverty line. At $5.50 an hour, working 40 hours per week yields approximately $900 a month before taxes. Working 52 weeks a year, an employee would earn approximately $11,800 per year. Taxes take a sizable chunk out of these earnings. For even the smallest families who have only one child, living and surviving on minimum wage poses a challenge.

Yet, many women were eager to take on this challenge. They told me that they want to work, and enthusiastically told me about leads or tips that they had heard regarding which businesses were hiring, and at how much pay. Although most women did not shun minimum wage jobs, jobs that paid eight dollars an hour or more were highly sought after. Women felt confident that they could live on the nearly $16,000 a year that such jobs would provide. Several women told me that they heard the postal service might be hiring—the postal service is notorious for paying "good money." Three other women told me about jobs in the nearby jails or prisons which also offer wages substantially higher than minimum wage.

They are hiring and so I want to submit my application for this corrections job. They pay $5 an hour to start out with the training. Then, when you get past the correctional course, then you go to the prison and you start working. But they don't pay $5 an hour for being a correctional officer. They pay more than that. They pay you about nine or ten dollars an hour! Plus benefits. See, I'm looking for where the money is at!

It is easy to reduce the number of people on welfare; simply make them ineligible for benefits after two or three years, as many states have done. In this sleight of hand, statistics can be pulled out and dangled to the public showing that welfare use, thus poverty itself, has declined. This, however, is incorrect. The true extent of poverty will not decline until the poor are paid higher wages for the work that they do.

Childcare

The question of who will care for children is one of the most pressing and perplexing questions of our time. If we expect poor single mothers to be employed, who then, will care for, socialize, nurture, discipline, play with, teach, and love their children? And, how much will this cost, both financially, and socially?

Concern over the lack of safe and affordable childcare emerged as a common structural reason why women turned to, or remained on welfare. They know that children need more than custodial care in large and crowded day care centers in order to thrive.

Yet, for most poor and working class families, childcare is often patched together in a fashion that leaves mothers anxious. Some told me that they did not feel comfortable leaving their children with strangers. They preferred to depend on other family members, but acknowledged that their mothers, sisters, or other female relatives cannot always be counted on. They have their own family responsibilities and obligations, and cannot always provide day care when needed. Living in high density and high crime areas, they worried about the safety of their children. "I'm not going to leave him with someone I don't know until he's old enough to tell me what happened." And they worried about the psychological effects of inadequate care—crowded, dirty, or impersonal conditions—upon their children.

Moreover, mothers worried about the cost of daycare. Unless a program within the welfare office subsidized childcare, costs for childcare within the interview area approximated $300 to $500 a month, depending on the type of care provided. The size of an AFDC grant for a mother and one child in the region is $241 a month, obviously making full-time childcare an impossibility, prompting many women to comment, "I had to quit—the money went to the baby-sitter." Childcare costs vary dramatically across the country, with costs in many communities in Florida being well below averages costs in other communities, yet still beyond the reach of most poor and low income families. A recent study which compared childcare costs in six communities around the nation found that average costs for care of a two-year-old ranged from $3,100 a year in Birmingham Alabama, to almost $8,100 in Boulder Colorado (Clark & Long, 1995). Not surprising, then, a study sponsored by Wellesley College found that more than 15 percent of low-income parents reported that their 4 to 7-year-old children regularly spent time all by themselves or in the care of a sibling under the age of 12 (Alter, 1998). Their parents cannot afford the costs of childcare.

Moreover, Rhonda, who has a GED, reminded us that jobs that welfare recipients take are often in the service sector, and they are therefore required to work evenings and weekends when childcare might not be available. Her son Bobby is only five years old, far too young to remain at home alone at night while she works.

> My hardest problem is—I can find a job—it's trying to work around my son. On weekends I ain't got nobody on weekends to watch him. Like my sister, she's busy with her own kids. And my dad, he's kind of a senior citizen, you know. And that's the only problem I have. It's like they always want nights and weekends. See I can do days while he's in school, you know. It's hard.

Childcare is not simply an issue for mothers of young children. Mothers with older, school-age children also face considerable dilemmas about how to juggle employment and parental responsibilities. Low-income children are less likely to live in neighborhoods that have Before and After-School programs. In 1993, only 33 percent of schools in low-income neighborhoods had these school programs, compared to over 50 percent of schools in more affluent neighborhoods (U.S. Department of Education, 1994). Yet these programs have been shown to help low-income students perform better academically, and they help improve student conduct and study habits (Posner & Vandell, 1994).

Some mothers interviewed suggested that parenting is more time consuming and labor intensive as children become teenagers. Peer pressure is strong, including pressure to act out and behave in destructible ways. They feared that their children would get into trouble with the law; that they might use, abuse, or sell drugs; that they may get pregnant; or that they may drop out of school. Mothers here, as well as those responding to nationwide studies, clamored for more organized activities for their school-aged children (Center for Research on Women, 1996; Meyers & Kyle, 1996). Moreover, because they are the sole parent to their children, they have no one to share the burden and responsibilities of childcare. They do not have a spouse, and generally they cannot rely upon the father of their children for assistance or relief from their duties.

Women on welfare juggle their employment and parental responsibilities in a variety of ways, but one aspect was very clear: Their children are more important than any specific job. Their jobs were seen as "work;" they were not careers, with the degree of commitment that careers entail. While "work" was considered important psychologically and financially, under no circumstances should it interfere significantly with family responsibilities. Their first and foremost responsibility was perceived as being a "good mother" to their children. So, how do women on welfare reconcile being good mothers with working? Many women did not want to work before their children were in preschool. Some women refused work that entailed weekends. Others preferred to work the night shift so that they could be home in the afternoons to help their children with their homework after school. Others wanted to work in the afternoons so that they could get their children up and off to school. Others insisted that they could only work part-time so that they could be available to their children in the morning and at night. And finally other women pursued or dreamed of work that allowed them to stay at home, such as Rhonda's childcare center, or several other women's stated desire to be cosmetologists working out of their home. The structure of the desired workday or setting may differ significantly, but the underlying theme is that work should be built around their family schedule and important family events, rather than vice versa. This, however, is not easily accomplished.

One woman, Cassie, revealed a strong preference for working the night shift, leaving her children home alone at night despite the fact that they are only twelve, nine, eight, and six years of age. Although some people might abhor the thought of leaving children this age alone at night, she saw it as the best possible alternative because it allowed her to spend her days with them. She further explained that her oldest daughter has experience getting the kids up and ready for school. All her children chip in with chores and are very responsible, she elaborated.

> I'd rather work at night. I could be home with my kids when they get home from school. Yeah, I'd have the whole afternoon to be with them. It's from 12 midnight to eight. And at midnight I'd be gone to work, I'd come home at eight and get me some sleep. And when they come home I'll be fresh and ready to go again....My daughter was getting them up when I worked at XXX food franchise, and she was not but nine. Eight or nine. I had to be at work at six o'clock in the morning, so I would call home and she would be up, and everybody would be up and ready to go to school. I taught her to help me, and that's what she's been doing.

Father's Involvement

A third structural problem cited was the lack of involvement on the part of the children's fathers. Fathers' participation in the emotional or financial upbringing of their children was noticeably absent in the vast majority of cases we examined. Absentee fathers represent a growing and alarming national trend. Less than half of fathers who are court ordered to provide child support payments pay the full amount regularly (U.S. Bureau of the Census 1997b, Table 609, p. 389).

The women I interviewed were required to report the name and whereabouts of the fathers of their children, if known, when they signed up for welfare. When the children's fathers did pay child support, the money went to the welfare agency, and mothers were given an additional fifty dollars per month in their check. This fifty dollars is designed to serve as an incentive to provide information on the children's fathers to the welfare agency, just in case women are reluctant to do so. Yet, despite the mandatory ruling that fathers be identified, the apparent eagerness of women to comply with this ruling, and the welfare agency's supposed vigorous search for the fathers, the majority of the women interviewed continued to received no, or very sporadic, child support. Some women resented this. They resented the freedom that their children's fathers have, while they themselves are stigmatized for receiving welfare. A divorced African American mother who received welfare for her two children responded typically to our question as to whether she received child support.

> No, I don't. And with my ex-husband, he was court ordered to pay child support. He works. But I don't get child support from him. They have money—they can go out and buy themselves cars and they can save money in the bank, but they're not supporting their kids. And I don't like it. I don't think the government should have to take care of a man's kids, especially if he can take care of his own kids. I don't understand it. They are so hard on us, but where is my child support? My kids deserve that money.

She and many others acknowledged that mothers on welfare are stigmatized for caring for their children, whereas fathers are rarely stigmatized for their failure to support their children. Pearl summarized the sentiment of many when she expressed that their fathers' resistance to paying child support has cheated her children. She is a 48-year-old African American woman who is divorced. Pearl has born eight children, three of whom still reside in the home and receive welfare. They live in the housing projects, where she has lived for 25 years. Pearl's life has been hard. She only finished school to the 8th grade, quitting so that she could work as a farm laborer and help support her siblings. She's been married twice, divorced because of her husbands' continual infidelity. She has worked on and off for most of her life—hard jobs, such as farm laborer and housecleaner. Now alone, she dreams about taking her younger children out of the projects to live in the country where she envisions a safer life for them, free from the pressures of drugs and dropping out of school. The likelihood of her dream materializing is extremely slim. She complained of health problems, and has not held a job in many years. The father of her oldest children is in prison, as are her two oldest sons. The father of the youngest children previously contributed to their support, but quit paying child support a few years prior to this interview. He remarried, "he figured he got a new wife and shouldn't have to pay," she told me. Pearl continued:

> All my kids' daddies owe child support. I used to talk to their daddies about that. I said, well, if you would have been willing to help take care of your kids, they would have had a living and wouldn't have had to been on welfare.

Until the dismal trends in child support are altered through stricter enforcement and through changing norms of greater paternal involvement, it will be very difficult for women to fully support their children on their own.

Transportation

It also became clear in the interviews that transportation was a major structural barrier to women getting or keeping jobs. Women on welfare cannot afford to buy reliable automobiles. Those few women who owned newer models likely received them as gifts from family members or boyfriends. Often they did not put the car in their name, hiding it from the welfare office even if they were the sole driver, because it would jeopardize their welfare benefits. The personal asset value of an automobile (value minus debt) must be less than $1,500; otherwise it disqualifies one for welfare. This poses a dilemma for a rational person—how can I find and maintain a respectable job, if I am not allowed to have reliable (e.g., more expensive) transportation? Most women who had cars, even those exceeding the maximum asset level, owned older models that were in a constant state of disrepair. Many cars guzzled gas. Car maintenance is expensive. One woman explained that her car, although a necessity in many respects, also assisted in keeping her poor.

"It's either your tires, or extra gas, or a part tearing up on your car. No, I can never really get caught up." Obviously, women on welfare are not driving Cadillacs.

Public transportation, and walking, are the primary alternatives to the private automobile. While public transportation is available in the largest community in the county, women complained that it was expensive (one dollar, plus an additional 25 cents per transfer) and inconvenient. Moreover, public transportation, even with all its logistical problems, was completely unavailable in some of the smaller communities within the county.

Communities built since the 1950's are often spread out, not geared toward pedestrians or public transportation systems, but geared instead toward private automobile ownership. A strong, central, vibrant downtown area for work, shopping, and entertainment are memories of a bygone era in most communities. Instead, numerous "strip malls" are spread throughout the city limits and fringe areas. Sidewalks may not exist, traffic whizzes by at 45 miles per hour, and without a central core, walking, bicycling, or relying on public transportation becomes difficult and inconvenient. While offhand it is easy to say, "you can walk to work," reality may dictate something else. In many communities walking to work can be more than just inconvenient, it can be dangerous or impractical. Walking through high crime neighborhoods or crossing highways, especially at night, poses special dangers. Walking can add an hour or two to childcare bills, and may necessitate being away from one's children for 9, 10, or 11 hours a day instead of the usual eight. Moreover, in inclement weather, such as heavy rains or snow, it is impractical to expect women to walk for miles and still appear freshly groomed and ready for work. Life without a car is difficult in most cities and towns in the United States. Even with the best intentions, it is not surprising that women without cars find it difficult to maintain steady work.

Several women revealed to us elaborate transportation logistics that allowed them to work or go to school, including commutes of an hour to an hour and a half each way. One African American mother, Dee, who is studying to become an accountant, lives five miles from campus and described her transportation ordeal using the city bus:

> I leave here by 6:45 to get to school at 8:00. So that's an hour and 15 minutes. I leave school at 2:00 to get home by 4:00, so that's 2 hours. So that's 3 hours and 15 minutes I spend. I could leave here at 7:30 and be there by 8:00. And then I have 3-hour breaks in between so I could be home relaxing or doing something.

Transportation problems prevent many women from seeking work altogether, and they inhibit other women from staying at their job. Several women told me that they quit otherwise "good" jobs because of inadequate transportation schemes. When they worked at night, after the buses stopped running, they were forced to rely on friends, family, or a taxi service for rides home after work. Friends and family, although well meaning, were sometimes unreliable. Taxis were expensive. Consequently, the risk of job failure increases, often becoming an eventuality. Many might ask, why try?

> I just had a job in September where I worked six days. But I had to quit my job because I had to pay transportation. And transportation was costing me, like $40 a week. Sometimes at night it was difficult because the shift that I was working was three to twelve—three in the afternoon to twelve at night. And a lot of people don't want to get up and come get you. So, I had to quit the job because of the transportation costs that I had to pay.

In this instance, and several others like it, a recipient sought work despite the obstacles, explored alternative transportation with some optimism, and finally quit due to rational personal economics. People who have always had reliable personal automobiles often overlook the magnitude of this issue for many would-be workers. Growing urban sprawl increases the likelihood of distance to the workplace, and therefore reduces the likelihood of regularly getting to a job without a personal automobile.

Racism and Sexism

Racism and sexism are unpleasant realities in our polarized society. The famous tennis star, Arthur Ashe, before he died of AIDS in 1993, disagreed with a reporter who assumed that AIDS must be the heaviest burden he has ever had to bear. "No, it isn't," Ashe told the reporter. "Being black is the greatest burden I've had to bear. Having to live as a minority in America...because of what we as a people have experienced historically in America, and what we as individuals experience each and every day" (Ashe & Rampersad, 1994: 139–141). Likewise the social construction of gender permeates all aspects of life, and people continually distinguish between males and females and evaluate them differently.

Racism and sexism generally have three components: (1) negative attitudes toward minority group members and toward women; (2) stereotypical beliefs that reinforce, complement, or justify the prejudice; and (3) discrimination—acts that exclude, distance, or segregate minorities and women (Lott, 1994). They can be blatant or more subtle. Blatant racism and sexism can take the form of not being hired in the first place, being passed over for a job promotion or a pay raise, or being fired prematurely. A few African American women told us directly that racism had hindered their ability to get, or keep, a good paying job. One woman spoke of her neighbor in the housing project who "has a problem with, excuse my language, white people. They did her real bad."

Racism and sexism can also be more subtle, and this form is sometimes referred to as "institutional" racism or sexism. Patterns of inequality may be woven into the fabric of society, so that it becomes institutionalized, or normative. It may be imbedded in our culture or our social policy. It often goes unnoticed. And, when pointed out, sometimes people will fail to grasp its significance. For example, job opportunities for women are limited in ways that men's generally are not, in part due to the ways women are socialized. Women may not seek training in the higher paying skilled trades, for example, because they have been taught that these are "unfeminine" occupations.

Stephanie, a 26-year-old mother who is in the nursing program at the university, explicitly acknowledged that sexism, as well as racism was likely to limit opportunities for social mobility. She is the mother of one young daughter, and is attuned to issues of social inequality. Like many of the women I interviewed, she was married when she had her daughter, and assumed that her marriage would last forever. Instead, after a painful divorce, her husband has never once paid child support or contacted his daughter.

> Why are people on welfare? There have to be at least a thousand reasons why people are on welfare. Like I tell my daughter, life isn't fair. Things happen. And you have to do the best you can. There are lots of socioeconomic groups in this country, races, blacks, Hispanics, women who don't really have the same opportunities that most people consider normal opportunities. I mean, for myself, look who got stuck taking care of the child?

The Welfare System Breeds "Dependence" on the System

Finally, a reoccurring theme throughout most narratives was that the welfare system itself is responsible for their reliance on welfare. A few respondents felt that the welfare system can indeed make people get lazy, and lose their motivation to work, as some social conservatives have argued. A 29-year-old African American woman with 3 children who has been on and off the system repeatedly said:

> Sometimes I think people get a little too satisfied with it and stay on it a little longer than they should. Once you start getting this check [the] way we do, you get a little lazy sometimes.

However, the majority of women who expressed concerns with the welfare system said *it wasn't that it made recipients lazy per se, but rather that the welfare system had built-in disincentives or penalties for work.* Working, especially at minimum wage jobs which usually lack health insurance and other critical benefits, would not achieve their goals of self-sufficiency, and in fact would jeopardize the health and well being of their children because they would lose critically needed benefits. Moreover, as good mothers, they said, they would never want to jeopardize their children's well being. From these interviews, it became clear that without continued assistance with (a) health insurance; (b) childcare; (c) transportation; (d) food stamps; and (e) subsidized housing, working becomes not only prohibitive, but sometimes was seen as downright dangerous. Many women claimed that they want to work, or that they could find a job, or even that they had a job previously, but felt compelled to quit because working, and the automatic reduction in their welfare benefits, actually lowered their standard of living or jeopardized their children's health. They expressed frustration that the welfare system, as currently structured, actually discourages them from working by raising their rent, eliminating Medicaid, and cutting them off of needed social services before they had a chance to establish themselves. Jo, a mother of two young children claimed:

> I've had a job before, and I know I can get a job. It's just really hard. It's like, I got a job at Hardee's (fast food franchise) and I had a friend take me back and forth. I was paying her 20 dollars a week for gas. I got off the system. I was honest about it and told them I had a job. They took my assistance away, and they raised my rent 200 dollars. And they said they weren't going to give me any Medicaid for them either, and I didn't have any health insurance. I had a baby at the time, and she was only a year old. She had to go the periodic appointments and stuff, and I was like, "okay, well I'm going to try to do it." And I had to work there six months to a year to get health insurance. I was really scared, like, what am I going to do? But I'm gonna do it. So I started doing it, and then I started realizing that, you know, that after about 2 months, was under the welfare level. I mean, by making minimum wage I couldn't keep my bills up, and I could never afford to take her to the doctor. It wasn't getting me ahead. I was being penalized for trying to get off the system, and it's happened to all my friends that are on welfare. It's like a trap, and they don't help.

Jo did what our society expects of welfare mothers—she found a job. But with that job, her financial picture became even more bleak. She told me it caused her to be "under the welfare level." Jo's situation was not an isolated case. Therefore, without considerable change, what hope is there for her, and for other mothers trying to get off welfare?

Concern about losing Medicaid was commonly expressed. Medicaid is a program designed to pay the health care costs of the poor. Not all poor are eligible for Medicaid, however. Like other welfare benefits, Medicaid has specific eligibility requirements, some of which are established at the state level. Today, less than 50 percent of the poor are covered by Medicaid, down from 71 percent in 1975 (Lewin, 1991). Each state is required to extend Medicaid to recipients of AFDC, and now TANF, and to recipients of Supplemental Security Income (SSI), which covers the impoverished elderly and the disabled. However, it is up to state discretion whether to cover others who are impoverished, such as the homeless, or the working poor. Medicaid benefits are a primary reason why women stayed on welfare as long as they have. If they leave welfare, they risk joining the ranks of the uninsured. More than 37 million Americans, or 18 percent of the population have no health insurance from any source whatsoever (U.S. Department of Health and Human Services, 1997). Nearly three-quarters of these individuals are employed or are the dependents of an employed adult, usually working at a low wage, part-time, or temporary position. Over ten million of the uninsured are children under age of fifteen. Another 25 to 48 million people are "underinsured"—meaning that their insurance is inadequate to meet the needs of their family because of extraordinarily high deductibles or co-payments, or because certain procedures are not included, or specific family members are not covered.

It is well documented that persons without health insurance or with inadequate insurance use the health care system less frequently than do others, resulting in a variety of negative health outcomes (Cornwell, Berne, Belzberg, Velmahos, Murray, & Demetriades, 1996; Seccombe, 1995; U.S. Congress, Office of Technology Assessment, 1992). The uninsured are more likely than both privately and publicly insured individuals to lack a usual source of care; to have fewer episodes of inpatient hospital care and lack preventative services; and to report delays in receiving health care. They typically seek care at hospital emergency rooms, which are increasingly turning people away and transferring the most serious cases to public hospitals (Cornwell, Berne, Belzberg, Velmahos, & Demetriades, 1996). Consequently, without health insurance, adults and children, are more likely to experience unnecessary pain, suffering, disability, and even death. Women on welfare know this. They fear joining the ranks of the uninsured or underinsured if they were to take a job. Stephanie, in school to become a Registered Nurse, echoed this concern with losing Medicaid. Her daughter has several specific health problems:

> We gripe and we gripe about the fact that we are paying all this money for people who don't seem to be doing very much for themselves, but if you looked at the system from an insider's point of view, you would see that there are actually penalties built into the system for a person with initiative, going out to get a job, or doing something to try to better themselves. As soon as you earn a buck, they take it away from you. You are penalized if you have any kind of asset whatsoever. You have to be so damn poor that it's not even funny.... Next summer in nursing school there are no classes. Yet I can't work. And I will tell you why. I would like to work as a nurses aide, and that is something I can do with my training that I have had. But I can't afford to lose my benefits, specifically my medical benefits. Because if I went to work, they would cut me off. Even though I would not be making enough to pay my bills, I would be cut off from Medicaid. And I can't afford that, you know? It's part-time, usually a nurses aide gets $5–6 an hour, which is not that much above minimum wage. And you know, you work 20 or 30 hours a week. No health benefits, no nothing. So I can't work. It's not that I don't want to work. I'd love to work. But I can't.

An African American mother of two, who works part-time as a nurses-aide, but continues to receive a partial welfare benefit, explains how her benefits were reduced when she began to work:

> The thing that gets me, being a single parent, once my income exceeds a certain amount, I'm in a Project, and my rent goes up. It has been close to $300 for this [she laughs and sweeps her arms around the room]. And then I have to end up paying expensive childcare, and the Medicaid stops for me and my children. You know, most jobs the health insurance is so expensive you can't afford it. Then, you pretty much be where you started from. You end up with nothing.

These interviews, which are grounded in the real-world receipt of welfare, suggest that the presumed link between social programs and welfare dependency touted by social conservatives is flawed. Yes, on a cursory glance, the welfare system does appear to "reduce" one's incentive to work, but a more thorough examination from an *insider's perspective* reveals that welfare programs do not encourage laziness or dependency. Both white and African American women talked about desperately wanting to work, but felt that employment reduced their already meager standard of living and often placed their children at risk because it eliminated or reduced their eligibility for critical medical and social services. They repeatedly pleaded that the welfare system be changed so as to not penalize them by cutting them off of critically needed services, at least temporarily, while they "pull themselves up by their bootstraps." Rather than being lazy or dependent on the system, they are making the most rational, intelligent choice they can, given their circumstances.

In summary, these women frequently cited concerns related to the social structure when explaining their welfare use. Problems with finding inexpensive or reliable childcare; a scarcity of jobs, particularly those which pay a livable wage; lack of father involvement with their children, and ineffective child support policies; inadequate public transportation systems; racism and sexism; and a welfare system that prematurely reduces income and benefits, were recognized as factors which inhibited their upward social mobility.

Fatalism

Bad luck, unfortunate circumstances, and soured relationships—these events come under a heading that others have coined "fatalism," which many women alluded to in their responses. They need welfare for personal reasons that are not their fault. They felt that they simply couldn't help it; they turned to welfare as a way out of a desperate, unplanned, and unfortunate situation.

Bad Luck

For example, many discussed their bad luck at becoming pregnant. Several, who were unmarried teenage girls when they had their first child, told me that they were surprised at becoming pregnant—they didn't know that sexual activity caused pregnancy, or they didn't know that they could get pregnant the first time they had sexual intercourse. They were confused and unknowledgeable about sex. Many disclosed that they had intercourse as a way to please a boyfriend, or because of peer pressure from their girlfriends at school or in their neighborhoods. They rarely used birth control. Either they didn't know it was necessary, or their partner complained about wearing a condom and they acquiesced to his wishes. When they discovered they were pregnant, they were surprised. How did this happen? Abortion was rarely a consideration among the women interviewed. Instead, these young girls accepted that they somehow got "caught," and had their babies.

Terri Lynn, the young mother previously introduced who works at the bowling alley to support herself and her six-year-old son, told me of her surprise at becoming pregnant. She did well in high school, and never suspected that it would "happen" to her.

> Sure, I don't want to be on AFDC, but I don't have a choice. You know, I didn't plan to get pregnant with him, but it just happened. You know? I don't want to be on AFDC. I'm going to get off it as soon as I put him in school.

An African American woman with four children commented on the bad luck that young women have in their encounters with young men. Her attitude indicated that teenage pregnancies are unfortunate, but that not much can be done about it. It's acceptable, or at least unavoidable. Her greater concern is with women who have multiple births out of wedlock, but having one child "just happens":

> I know a first baby is a mistake. You know what I'm saying? It happens. You go out there, you young, you have sex. It's a mistake. I mean, they got birth control methods, but guys are so persuasive about sex these days. Girls don't think about rubbers or birth control. They just think about impressing him, so they have sex. So they get pregnant. If they keep having babies then they should get a job and help support the rest of those kids, but not the first child.

As both women allude to, peer pressure to have sex is powerful, and difficult to avoid. One recent study involving 1,000 girls in Atlanta found that 82 percent said the subject they wanted to learn most about in their sex education class was "How to say no without hurting the other person's feelings" (reported in Besharov, 1993).

National data indicate that over 20 percent of 14-year-olds have had sexual intercourse, and this increases to 30 percent by age 15, 42 percent by age 16, and up to 59 percent by age 17. Approximately half of women aged 15 to 19 have had sexual intercourse regardless of race, income, religion, or residential location. Nearly one-quarter of teenage women never use contraceptives. Others use contraceptives sporadically. The United States' rate of premarital pregnancy, at 97 pregnancies per 1,000 women under the age of 19, is more than double that of most of western European nations and Canada, nearly three times that of Scandinavian nations, and nearly ten times that of Japan. Although nearly half of teen pregnancies in the United States are aborted, our birth rate among teens is among the highest in industrialized nations (Forrest & Singh, 1990; Sonenstein, Pleck, & Ku, 1989).

Poor Health

For other women, health concerns interfered with their ability to look for, or keep a job, and thus they continued to rely on welfare. Nearly one-third of women interviewed complained of health problems, including asthma, depression, high blood pressure, or back pain.

Many other women told us that their children were sickly, or had emotional problems, and consequently they did not feel comfortable leaving their children with baby-sitters.

Poor children are more likely to suffer a wide array of ailments, both chronic and acute, than are more affluent children (Children's Defense Fund, 1994). For example they are more than three times as likely to be iron deficient; 1.5 times more likely to have frequent diarrhea or colitis; two times more likely to suffer from severe asthma; and 1.5 times more likely to suffer from partial or complete blindness or deafness. These are due to a variety of prenatal and postnatal factors. One important culprit is that poor children are more often born with a lower birthweight than are other children, due to the mother's poor nutrition, lack of prenatal care, stress, youth, insufficient weight gain, or smoking or other drug use. Moreover, poor children are also more likely to die. According to the Children's Defense Fund, "poor children are about three times more likely to die during childhood as their non-poor peers," (Children's Defense Fund, 1994). Thus, the effects of poverty on the health and well being of children, and adults, is not exaggerated. They are significant, long-term, and can cause considerable heartache, consternation and chaos in the lives of families.

Mothers expressed worry that their children would not get the attention, physically and emotionally, that they might need. Jasmine, for example, has a history of working full-time, often at several different jobs in order to make ends meet. She is divorced, and has a ten-year-old daughter who lives with her ex-husband's sister, and a five-year-old daughter and an infant to care for. Doctor's appointments are routine for Jasmine and her two young children, but they are stressful nonetheless. Both of her children have severe cases of asthma. She's been on welfare for four years, because of "the sickness of the children," she told me. She gives them breathing treatments on and off, as needed. For Jasmine, as was the case with many other women we interviewed, being a "good mother" means being there physically to care for her sick or needy children. Women routinely told us that they did not feel comfortable leaving their sick children in day care, with a baby-sitter, or even with family members for extended hours. They see, first and foremost, that their job is to provide the direct care that they believe their child needs. Among the more affluent, these "family values" would be applauded. Returning to more traditional "family values" is a popular theme espoused by Democrats as well as conservative Republicans. However, among poor women who receive welfare, such values are not applauded, they are, instead, suspect.

The Termination of Relationships

A primary reason that women turned to welfare was that a relationship which ended, and they could not support their family on their own. When married or living together, a spouse or partner may have provided an important source of income for the family. When a relationship ends, that income is abruptly halted. Some women find that they are unable to secure a job providing wages above the poverty line. Or they may have no experience working, and do not know how to go about finding a job to support the family. The termination of a relationship was a primary reason that women turned to welfare. As a 35-year-old divorced African American woman told me,

> What made me get on was, I guess, my broken marriage. Because when I was married, I wasn't on AFDC. My husband was employed, and I was working.

The United States has the highest rate of divorce of any country in the world. Our divorce rate rose dramatically in the 1960's, and has since then stabilized to approximately 19.8 divorces per 1,000 married women over the age of 15 (Singh, 1995). Divorce is more prevalent among lower socioeconomic classes, despite the economic hardships it creates. One national study of men and women between the ages of 25 and 34 found that people who had only high school diplomas were significantly more likely to divorce than were people who had bachelor's degrees (Glick, 1984). This is due to a variety of reasons, including younger age at marriage; greater likelihood of premarital pregnancy and childbirth; and greater stress, crises, and disruptions in their lives related to economic vulnerability. When people marry young, for example, they are less prepared for marital responsibilities. They are more unhappy about their partners in terms of love, affection, sex, wage earning, companionship, and faithfulness.

They also are more likely than their older counterparts to complain that their spouses are moody, jealous, spend money foolishly, or get in trouble with the law (Booth & Edwards, 1985; Teti, Lamb, & Elster, 1987).

African Americans are nearly twice as likely to divorce as are whites (Saluter, 1994). This is due to many factors, including that African Americans are disproportionately poor or have low incomes, and therefore face many poverty-related stresses. Moreover, they are more likely to marry earlier, have a premarital pregnancy, and have a child born out of wedlock. These factors increase their odds of divorce.

Lillian Rubin, in her book, *Families on the Fault Line* (1994), re-interviewed 32 working-class families 20 years after their original interviews, and found that 56 percent of them had divorced sometime during this period. All but one of the men had remarried, and the lone exception was already in a serious relationship after being separated for only a few months. In contrast, Rubin found that divorced women fared differently. They remained single for a longer period of time after a divorce, and over half needed either welfare or food stamps during this financially difficult period. Over one-third of the women had not remarried. For most of these women, life continued to be a series of economic struggles.

Although both men and women go through financial adjustments after divorce, women's income declines more dramatically than does men's.

Most women have little experience being the "primary" breadwinner in relationships. When they are forced to do so, while taking care of the children as well, it can be overwhelming. Many women reported that receiving welfare was perceived as a method of regaining control over their lives. It allowed them the opportunity to take stock of their situation, to regroup, to assess their options, or to attend school or find a job. Some women reported that they were deserted by their partners, and left alone to care for their children. One such case was Dee, an African American woman with three small children under the age of five. Dee served five years in the Army, a career that she enjoyed. But her husband pressured her to quit, saying that her job was too hard on the family. She quit, and became a housewife at her ex-husband's insistence. Then, when she was dependent on him for financial support, he left her without warning.

> My husband left us with no food. The rent was due. You know, when he left he just split. It was like he was never there, no clothes, nothing.

Stephanie, the nursing student at the University, spoke about the shock of having to raise her child alone. Since the divorce, her husband has never once paid child support, nor visited or contacted their daughter. She, like all women, thought that their marriage would last forever, and that he would support both her and their child. She made a wrong choice, but she had no way of knowing it was wrong at the time. It was a choice that any woman could make. She never imagined that she would be on welfare.

> I gave birth thinking—he begged me to keep the child when I found out I was pregnant—thinking that we would be a couple, that we would always be together, and he would always want her. And now, it's four years later, and I am by myself, and I am doing this by myself. Even the best-laid plans sometimes go down the drain.

Both Dee and Stephanie, and many others that we interviewed, saw welfare as a critical, but temporary form of assistance, which enabled them to take care of their children immediately after a husband or partner disappeared, or when the marriage or relationship ended. Welfare made it possible for them to pursue further training so that they could be the sole support of a family, or it provided some base level of financial support while they reassessed their life options. They did not see themselves as being irresponsible. Instead, the temporary receipt of welfare was viewed more positively. It allowed them to take control of their lives and provide a better home environment for their children until they could provide it themselves.

Violence

Some detrimental relationships involved violence and abuse. Violence, or its threat, is a part of every woman's reality. No woman is really exempt from this threat. A rape, for example, is reported in the United States every five minutes (U.S. Federal Bureau of Investigation, 1995), and most rapes remain unreported. Two women interviewed told us that they bore children as a result of rapes. They credit welfare with giving them the opportunity to bear and raise their children, rather than forcing them to have abortions or give up the child for adoption.

Although no direct question about violence was asked, many other women volunteered that they were fleeing abusive relationships or had left an abusive relationship in the past. Violence in the home has reached staggering levels. It is a critical social problem affecting the lives of millions, poor or rich. The true rate of domestic violence can perhaps never be known, as it often occurs, "behind closed doors," where a "man's home is his castle." Groundbreaking research by Straus and Gelles, referred to as the national Family Violence Surveys, was conducted in 1975 and 1985 with a national probability sample of 8,145 husbands, wives, and cohabiting couples. They define violence as "an act carried out with the intention, or perceived intention, of causing physical pain to another person," synonymous with the legal definition of assault. The respondents of these surveys were asked about their involvement in violent acts such as: throwing something at the other; pushing; grabbing; shoving; slapping; kicking; biting; hitting with fists; hitting with an object; beatings; burning, scalding, or choking; threatening with a knife or gun; and using a knife or gun. Together, the two surveys found that in 16 percent of the couples, at least one of the partners had engaged in a violent act against the other during the previous year. In other words, these data reveal that, every year in the United States, approximately one out of every six couples have at least one act of violence in their relationship. Moreover, Straus and Gelles found that, over the course of the entire marriage, 28 percent of the relationships, or nearly one out of three couples, contained violence (Straus & Gelles, 1986, 1988). The true rate may be even higher (Straus, 1991).

Other data from the National Crime Survey by the United States Justice Department estimates that over 600,000 cases of violence between intimates occurs each year—murders, rapes, or assaults committed by spouses, ex-spouses, boyfriends, or girlfriends, or former lovers. This represents more than 13 percent of violent crimes committed within these categories each year (U.S. Department of Justice, 1994). As many as three thousand women are killed by their husbands or boyfriends each year.

Although domestic violence occurs in all social classes, the preponderance of data indicate an inverse relationship between social class and likelihood of violence. That is, women who have lower incomes and lower levels of education are more likely to be victimized than are more affluent or well educated women. Some of this difference may be due to social class differences in the likelihood of reporting violence. Nonetheless, a 1996 Justice report, for example, stated that women living in households with annual incomes below $10,000 are four times more likely to be violently attacked than are other women, usually by their intimate partners. When income and educational levels are taken into account, white, African-American, and Hispanic women have equivalent rates of domestic violence being committed against them.

One battered woman who fled violence, Molly, turned to welfare for support after escaping while her husband was asleep. She has three young sons, the oldest of whom was four at the time she fled. They lived in a rural mountainous area, thirty miles from the nearest town. Her husband deliberately kept her isolated from family and friends, and put a block on the telephone. He was abusive to both her and the children:

> I left my husband when he was asleep. I stayed in a shelter. I grabbed some clothes for the kids and left. My mom came up and got us. I had no car, no nothing. No furniture. Zero. That was August of '92. So I had to start completely over from scratch. I got a few of my things back, but basically I lost everything that I had.

Molly has been on welfare for three years, continuously, since leaving her husband. During that time she had nearly completed an AA degree at a community college, and intends to transfer to the University to work on her Bachelor's Degree. At the same time, she cares for her three young children, the oldest of whom is now seven years of age. Two of her children have been diagnosed with Attention Deficit Disorder (ADD), a disruptive and challenging learning disability. They had difficulty in school until they were correctly diagnosed, and began to take appropriate medication. Working through these issues by herself, she cannot imagine what her life would be like without the help she received from welfare. She receives no child support, and doubts that her ex-husband will ever pay the tens of thousands of dollars that he currently owes.

The belief that poverty and welfare use are something that is not one's fault and is beyond one's control, something that was forced upon them, was commonly used to explain their own use of welfare. Because of bad luck with relationships, or being raped or victimized in abusive relationships, many women felt that they had no other choice but to turn to welfare to help them out of an unplanned, but potentially desperate situation. Many women implied that turning to welfare was the *responsible* and *rational* thing to do for their children, and for themselves. They indicated that they were not to blame, and in fact, for many, welfare was a source of empowerment. It allowed them to be independent of an abusive spouse, retain custody of their children, or to take care of their family when a husband or lover deserted them. These are laudable goals, ones that our society would support, at least in theory. Who would really suggest that a woman remains in an abusive situation, lose custody of her children simply because of money, or move her family to a homeless shelter? The women interviewed were likely to see welfare as a short-term phenomenon, a temporary helping hand while they planned the next step in their lives. Each woman interviewed, with the exception of two, was confident that she would be off welfare within five years. Women were less optimistic about the lives of other women who receive assistance.

Why the Inconsistency Between Explanations of Their Own and Others' Use of Welfare?

These interviews revealed an important contradiction: Women perceived that their own use of welfare was due to structural factors, or fate, or to the idiosyncrasies of the welfare system itself; but welfare use by other women, in contrast, was often attributed to laziness, personal shortcomings or other inadequacies. This was the case for both the African American and the white women interviewed. They perceived the economic hierarchy in the United States as essentially fair, and that one's placement in the hierarchy tends to reflect work effort and motivation. They generally believed the popular constructions of the "welfare mother," but evaluated their own situation as distinctly different from the norm. They tended to segregate themselves from other recipients, and saw structural constraints as applying uniquely to themselves. "I'm sure people look at me and say the same thing, but I really do have a legitimate excuse;" or "my situation is different because I injured my back," they told me.

Janie, who has been on welfare since being ganged raped and giving birth to her daughter two years ago, denied being on welfare altogether:

> I'm not on welfare. I don't even know exactly what welfare is. I'm just receiving AFDC, and that might be considered welfare, I'm not sure. As it stands, most of them get on it because they don't want to work, they don't want to take care of their kids. I've seen more people on welfare lose their kids because of it, rather than to take care of themselves. Why they do that is beyond me.

Given the strong negative messages about welfare and welfare recipients, perhaps it is not surprising that both white and African American women who receive welfare also subscribe to Individual or Cultural of Poverty blaming perspectives. Critical theorists, such as Foucault (1980), suggest that our social structures produce cultural ideologies of truth and knowledge that are disadvantageous to the less powerful. These cultural ideologies camouflage the self-serving interests of the powerful by making them appear as though they are natural, normal, and serving the interests of everyone. Likewise, Gramsci's (1971) notion of "ideological hegemony" refers to the process by which consensus is obtained between dominant and subordinate groups, such as the rich and the poor. Social arrangements, which are in the best interest of the dominant group, are presented as being in everyone's best interests. Subordinates come to accept these interests as their own, and the contradictions inherent in the interests of the dominant and subordinate groups are ignored. Thus, the ideology becomes "common-sense" and normative, and cohesion is created where there would otherwise be conflict. The ideologies reflect the interests and perspectives of the elite, but the poor, who fail to see the shared political nature of their problems, also internalize them. Instead, poverty and welfare use is relegated to the realm of a personal problem, rather than a social problem (Mills, 1956). Consequently, like others who are more affluent, women on welfare essentially deem that the popular construction of the "welfare mother" is just. They accept the dominant ideology that stigmatizes welfare recipients.

However, it is important to note that these women infused Structural and Fatalistic perspectives in their worldviews as well, constructed out of their own experiences. They suggested, at least in so far as their own experiences were concerned, that their needs for welfare were due to circumstances over which they had little control.

This research is not alone in these findings. A classic study by Briar (1966), using a sample from 92 African American, white, and Mexican American families receiving AFDC, also found that the respondents almost never referred to welfare recipients as "we" but instead used the word "they." The tendency to view oneself as an atypical recipient, disassociating oneself from other recipients was identified as a coping mechanism for dealing with stigma. More recently, interviewing 16 women in focus groups, Davis and Hagen (1996) also found that welfare recipients had the tendency to view themselves as atypical recipients. For example, while they were quick to condemn others for being welfare frauds, they did not see their own actions as fraudulent. Instead, they were merely "beating the system" by working to get extra money to pay for necessary items that their checks could not pay for.

What then, may explain why many women do not see the commonalties of their experience? One explanation may be found in attribution theory, which proposes that people have a tendency to overestimate the degree to which other people's behavior is caused by individual traits or dispositions, and underestimate the degree to which it is caused by structural factors. And, in contrast, although we tend to attribute other people's actions to their own personal traits or dispositions, we are more likely to attribute our own behaviors to the social structure or situational factors over which we have little control (Jones & Nisbett, 1972).

Consistent with attribution theory, our respondents assigned individual traits or dispositions to other women to explain their use of welfare, ones that are well touted in the media and within the larger cultural milieu. Recipients were accused of laziness, of lacking sufficient motivation to improve their condition, of having deficiencies in human capital such as low education or few job skills, of having little desire to "better themselves," and of living in cultural surroundings that encourage welfare use. It appears that welfare recipients, just like the more affluent, overestimate the degree to which individualistic notions of very negative personality traits or dispositions shape welfare use behavior. Yet, when it comes to explaining the causes of their own welfare use behavior, also consistent with attribution theory, they tend to blame it on structural or situational causes that are beyond their control. They assess little personal blame; it is simply not their fault. "There are no jobs"; "How can I take care of all my kids and work too?"; "I would be fine if he would just pay child support"; "I was raped"; "I was beaten and abused"; "He deserted us, and I'm trying to get my feet on the ground"; "I'm trying to better myself"; "the welfare system penalizes me if I get a job," were frequently voiced. While all of these factors may be justifiable reasons why a woman would turn to welfare, they are reasons that can apply to all women, and indeed, they did apply to the majority of women interviewed. Women assumed they were exceptions to general trends, however these "exceptions" were common and widespread. They were grounded in their experiences as women in a patriarchal society. Few women were nonchalant about welfare. Instead, most were embarrassed, pained, appreciative, or resigned, and applied for welfare as a last resort. As Rhonda bluntly told me,

It's not what I want for me and my son. It's just that there are a lot of disadvantages to it. I just don't want to be on it. I'd rather be out working, meeting people. Making it better for me and my son.

REFERENCES

Acs, G., & Loprest, P. (1995). The effects of disabilities on exits from AFDC. Paper presented at the 17th Annual Research Conference of the Association for Public Policy Analysis and Management, November 2–4.

Alter, J. (1998). It's 4:00 p.m. Do you know where your children are? *Newsweek*, April 27, 29–33.

Ashe, A., & Rampersad, A. (1994). *Days of grace: A memoir.* New York: Ballantine.

Bernstein, A. (1997). Off welfare—and worse off. *Business Week.* December 22, p. 38.

Booth, A., & Edwards, J. N. (1985). Age at marriage and marital instability. *Journal of Marriage and the Family*, 47, 67–75.

Bourdieu, P. (1977). *Outline of a theory of practice.* New York: Cambridge University Press.

Briar, S. (1966). Welfare from below: Recipients' views of the public welfare system. *California Law Review*, 54, 370–385.

Burns, J., Ballew, M., Hsiao-Ye Yi, & Mountford, M. (October 1996). *Child care usage among low-income and AFDC families.* Washington, DC: Institute for Women's Policy Research.

Center for Research on Women. (1996). *School-age child care project—"I wish the kids didn't watch so much TV": Out-of-school time in three low income communities.* Wellesley, MA: Wellesley College: Center for Research on Women.

Chandler, D. (1998). Workshop calls for challenge to welfare. *The Gainesville Sun.* Pp. 1B, 3B.

Children's Defense Fund. (1998). *The state of America's children yearbook 1998.* Washington, DC: Children's Defense Fund.

———. (July 1994). *Wasting America's Future.* Washington DC: Children's Defense Fund.

Clark, A. L., & Long, A. F. (1995). *Child care prices: A profile of six communities—Final report.* Washington, DC: The Urban Institute. p. 54.

Cornwell, E. E., Berne, T. V., Belzberg, J. A., Velmahos, J. M., & Demetriades, D. (1996). Health care crisis from a trauma care perspective. *Journal of the American Medical Association*, 276, 940–947.

Dahrendorf, R. (1959). *Class and class conflict in industrial society.* Stanford: Stanford University.

Davis, L., & Hagen, J. (1996). Stereotypes and stigma: What's changed for welfare mothers. *Affilia*, 11, 319–337.

Della Face, R. L. (1980). The meek shall not inherit the earth: Self-evaluation and the legitimacy of stratification. *American Sociological Review*, 45, 955–971.

Enda, J. (1998). Proposal expands child care. *The Gainesville Sun.* January 8, Pp. 1A, 7A.

Forrest, J. D., & Singh, S. (1990). The sexual and reproductive behavior of American women, 1982–1988. *Family Planning Perspective*, 22, 206–214.

Foucault, M. (1980). In Collin Gordon (Ed.), *Power/Knowledge: Selected Interviews and Other Writings, 1972–1977.* New York: Pantheon.

Glick, P. C. (1984). Marriage, divorce, and living arrangements: Prospective changes. *Journal of Family Issues*, 5, 7–26.

Gramsci, A. (1971). *Selections from the prison notebooks of Antonio Gramsci.* Edited and translated by Quintin Hoare and Geoffrey Nowell Smith. New York: International.

Habermas, J. (1973). *Legitimation crisis.* Boston, MA: Beacon.

Herbert, B. (November 20, 1997). The game is rigged. *The New York Times.* [Online]. Available: *http://www.nytimes.com/1997/11/20/oped*

Jones, E. E., & Nisbett, R. E. (1972). The actor and the observer: Divergent perceptions of the causes of behavior. In Edward E. Jones, David Kanouse, Harold Kelley, Stuart Valins, and Bernard Weiner (Eds.), *Attribution: Perceiving the causes of behavior.* New York: General Learning.

Kaplan, A. (1998). *Transportation and welfare reform.* [Online]. Available: *http://www.welfareinfo. org/transita.htm*

Lewin, T. (April 28, 1991). The ailing health care system: A question of access. *The New York Times*. Pp. 1, 28.

Loprest, P., & Acs, G. (1996). *Profile of disability among families on AFDC*. Washington, DC: Urban Institute report to the Henry J. Kaiser Family Foundation.

Lott, B. (1994). *Women's lives: Themes and variations in gender learning* (2nd ed.). Pacific Grove, CA: Brooks/Cole.

Marx, K., & Engels, F. (1959). Manifesto of the communist party. In L. S. Feuer (Ed.), *Marx and Engels: Basic Writings on Politics and Philosophy*. Garden City: Doubleday.

McElroy, S. W., & Moore, K. A. (1997). Trends over time in teenage pregnancy and child-bearing: The critical changes. In R. A. Maynard (Ed.), *Kids having kids: Economic costs and social consequences of teen pregnancy*. New York: Urban Institute.

Meyers, J., & Kyle, J. E. (1996, March). *Critical needs, critical choices: A survey on children and families in America's cities*. Washington, DC: National League of Cities.

Meyers, M. K., Lukemeyer, A., & Smeeding, T. M. (1996). Work, welfare, and the burden of disability: Caring for special needs children in poor families. Syracuse, NY: Center for Policy Research, Maxwell School of Citizenship and Public Affairs, Syracuse University, Income Security Policy Series, Paper No. 12.

Mills, C. W. (1956). *The power elite*. New York: Oxford University.

Needleman, H. L., Schell, A., Bellinger, D., Leviton, A., & Allred, E. N. (1990). The long-term effects of exposure to low doses of lead in childhood. *New England Journal of Medicine*, 322, 83–88.

Pavett, L., & Duke, A. E. (1995). *Increasing participation in work and work related activities: Lessons from five welfare reform demonstration projects*. Report prepared for the Office of the Assistant Secretary for Planning and Evaluation, U.S. Department of Health and Human Services. Washington, DC: The Urban Institute.

Peterson, R. R. (1996). A re-evaluation of the economic consequences of divorce. *American Sociological Review*, 61, 528–536.

Posner, J., & Vandell, D. L. (1994). Low-income children's after-school care: Are there beneficial effects of after-school programs? *Child Development*, 65, 440–456.

Presser, H. B., & Cox, A. G. (1997). The work schedules of low-educated American women and welfare reform. *Monthly Labor Review*, April, 25–33.

Rubin, L. B. (1994). *Families on the fault line*. New York: Harper Collins.

Saluter, Arlene F. (1989). *Singleness in America*. U.S. Bureau of the Census, Current Population Reports, Special Studies, Series P-23, no. 162. Washington, DC: U.S. Government Printing Office.

Seccombe, Karen. (1995). Health insurance coverage and use of services among low-income elders: Does residence influence the relationship? *The Journal of Rural Health*, 11, 86–97.

Sonenstein, F. L., Pleck, J. H., & Ku, L. C. (1989). Sexual activity, condom use, and AIDS awareness among adolescent males. *Family Planning Perspectives*, 21, 152–158.

Straus, M. A. (1991). Physical violence in American families: Incidence, rates, causes, and trends. In Dean D. Knudsen and Jo Ann L. Miller (Eds.), *Abused and battered: Social and legal responses to family violence* (pp. 14–36). New York: Aldine de Gruyter.

Straus, M. A., & Gelles, R. (1988). How violent are American families? Estimates from the National Family Violence resurvey and other studies. In Gerald T. Hotaling, David Finkelhor, John T. Kirkpatrick, and Murray A. Straus (Eds.), *Family abuse and its consequences: New directions in research* (pp. 14–36). Newbury Park: Sage.

——. (1986). Societal change and change in family violence from 1975 to 1985 as revealed by two national surveys. *Journal of Marriage and the Family*, 48, 465–479.

Teti, D. M., Lamb, M. E., & Elster, A. B. (1987). Long-range socioeconomic and marital consequences of adolescent marriage in three cohorts of adult males. *Journal of Marriage and the Family*, 49, 499–506.

U.S. Bureau of the Census. (1997). *Statistical abstract of the United States* (117th ed.). Washington, DC: U. S. Government Printing Office.

U.S. Congress, Office of Technology Assessment. (1992). *Does health insurance make a difference?— Background Paper*. (OTA-BP-H-99) Washington, DC: U.S. Government Printing Office.

U.S. Department of Education. (1994). *The condition of education: 1993*. Washington, DC: National Center for Education Statistics.

U.S. Department of Justice. (1994). Violence between intimates. *Bureau of Justice statistics selected findings: Domestic violence*. Nov. No. NCJ-149259. Washington, DC: U.S. Department of Justice, Office of Justice Programs.

U.S. Federal Bureau of Investigation. (1995). *Crime in the United States 1994*. Washington, DC: U.S. Government Printing Office.

Weitzman, L. (1985). *The divorce revolution: The unexpected social and economic consequences for women and children in America*. New York: Free Press.

Reprinted from: Karen Seccombe, "Why Welfare?" In *"So You Think I Drive a Cadillac?"* pp. 74–99. Published by Allyn and Bacon, Boston, MA. Copyright © 1999 by Pearson Education. Reprinted by permission of the publisher.

7

SOCIAL EXCHANGE THEORY

Nicholas and Alyssa have been dating for about a year—exclusively for the last eight months or so. They are both juniors in college and have been thinking about whether or not they should get married. Alyssa frequently discusses the possibility with her roommates, and they debate the pros and cons. "He is so handsome and nice to me, and we are totally in love," says Alyssa. However, she wishes that he were majoring in something more substantial than history—business or law, perhaps. And she knows that he will want them to move back to his rural hometown in the West, which bothers her because she is a city girl. On the other hand, her friends point out, he is nice to children and (they have been told) is a great kisser. But is she really ready to give up dating and settle down?

For Nicholas it is a more private process, but he is also trying to decide. He loves Alyssa and wants to be with her all the time. Their physical relationship is wonderful, and he enjoys her intellect. He is afraid he might not be good enough for her, and that if she knew what he is really like, she might figure she can do better. He has no solid job or income to offer and needs to be in school for at least two more years. She gets upset when he doesn't want to talk about his feelings, and he worries about having to endure that pressure forever. And with the divorce rate as high as it is, is marriage even worth the effort?

Both of them are trying to be logical about this most important life decision, but it is hard to do. Feelings of love and hormonal urges get in the way. Isn't it too calculating to weigh the pros and cons of the relationship? Won't that just kill the romance? Can they even know what the most important considerations are in advance of living the actual relationship?

HISTORY

Philosophers have been discussing the ideas relevant to modern social exchange theory for the last two centuries. The basic concept is that human social relationships can be understood as revolving around the exchange of resources valued by the participants.

201

Utilitarian writers such as Adam Smith taught that people tend to act rationally in ways designed to maximize their profit economically. In the early twentieth century, anthropologists such as Bronislaw Malinowski and Claude Lévi-Strauss demonstrated how many cultures engage in the exchange of various goods and services as a central aspect of their social life. The latter took the collectivist position that one's behavior in social relationships tends to be a function of the social system of which one is a part (Ekeh 1974).

These early anthropologists explored the relationship between social norms and individual behavior. Frazer (1919) concluded that many social structures result from the economic needs of the individuals within the system. He was investigating the tendency of Australian aborigines to marry cross rather than parallel cousins and concluded that because the men were too poor to provide a bride price, they would trade a sister or other female relative for their bride.

Sociologists began to seriously consider the exchange model in the context of human societies and families with the groundbreaking writings of Thibaut and Kelley (1959), Homans (1961/1974), and Blau (1964). These writers took us beyond the concepts of economic exchanges and into the more complex world of the social marketplace where individuals negotiated to maximize their profits. In addition to trading such things as food, money, and other services, humans in relationships make exchanges that are harder to quantify, such as status, attractiveness, and love. Even though each had a somewhat different emphasis, they all agreed that what people want and need can be obtained only through exchanges with others and that we will try to get those things at the lowest possible cost to ourselves (Turner 1991).

George Homans is probably the most influential scholar in bringing social exchange theory to general sociology. Essentially adapting the principles of behaviorism, he held that reinforcement and punishment were the driving forces in human behavior and that sociology should pay more attention to how individuals choose to act within social situations. In his own study of cross-cousin marriages (Homans and Schneider 1955), he rejected the collectivist orientation of Lévi-Strauss. He took the position that societal norms result from the needs of the individuals rather than that society regulates interpersonal behavior.

Richard Emerson (1976) made important contributions to the application of social exchange theory for family studies by proposing that the unit of analysis in the theory is not the individual but the relationship between people. His concepts of "dependence, power, and balance" are not individual properties; instead, they are relational properties that help us focus on interpersonal processes (Sabatelli and Shehan 1993).

Finally, Ivan Nye (1978, 1979) summarized the concepts of the exchange model, showed how they could be applied to a large number of research questions in family science, and offered a series of theoretical propositions and testable hypotheses. His work completed the evolution of exchange from economic to sociological to family science theory. It has been a widely used framework in analyzing family issues since the publication of his chapter in *Contemporary Theories about the Family* (1979).

BASIC ASSUMPTIONS

We will now examine the basic assumptions that undergird social exchange theory. We will draw from the writings of Sabatelli and Shehan (1993) as well as Klein and White (1996) for this section. Although social exchange theory is built upon the principles of behaviorism and economics, it goes beyond just explaining individual behavior. Its focus is on the dynamics of relationships and how they are formed, maintained, and dissolved. As a result, there are assumptions about the nature of both individuals and relationships that are embedded in the framework.

People are motivated by self-interest. The first assumption is that people are motivated by self-interest. This means that we seek those things and relationships that are beneficial to ourselves. Another way of saying this is that we seek rewards and avoid punishments or costs. Thus, we are most likely to engage in interactions we find rewarding while avoiding those we do not like.

Individuals are constrained by their choices. The second assumption is that individuals are constrained by their choices, and it is within that range of possible choices that we strive to understand one's motivations. Nye (1979), in fact, concluded that the theory is more about choice than exchange. Social structure leads us to conclude that family life is rewarding to most individuals because this is a choice most people make.

In interacting with others, individuals will seek to maximize their profits while minimizing costs. Since the actual outcome of an interaction cannot always be known, humans will use their expectations in making their decisions. This means we enter into situations we believe will be rewarding, based on our past experiences.

Humans are rational beings. Another important assumption is that humans are rational beings. This means that we have the analytical ability to calculate the ratio of rewards to costs. We consider the alternatives before acting and choose the outcome that carries the least cost. Exchange theorists also accept the fact that how rewards and costs are evaluated varies from one person to another as well as across time. Thus, what Nicholas finds rewarding may not be rewarding to Alyssa. Similarly, what Nicholas finds rewarding in his relationship with Alyssa today may not be the same as what he considers rewarding in his relationship with her ten years from now.

Social relationships are also characterized by interdependence and reciprocity. This means that, in order to gain a profit in an exchange, we must provide the other person with rewards as well. All parties must expect some rewards in order to continue the relationship or interaction. And finally, social exchanges are regulated by the expectations or norms of reciprocity and fairness. Thus, we expect others to meet our needs if we attempt to meet their needs, and to do so based on what is right or fair.

PRIMARY TERMS AND CONCEPTS

The principal concepts used in social exchange theory are listed by Nye (1979), who draws heavily from Thibaut and Kelley (1959).

Rewards

All of the things in a person's physical, social, and psychological world that are experienced as pleasurable are considered rewards. A reward can be any satisfaction or gratification, status or relationship that one enjoys, and therefore, would like to experience with greater frequency (Thibaut and Kelley 1959). It includes anything that the individual would choose in the absence of added costs. What is rewarding will vary from one person to the next. Rewards positively reinforce behavior.

Blau (1964) identified six commodities that are capable of rewarding another during interpersonal exchanges: personal attraction, social acceptance, social approval, instrumental services, respect/prestige, and compliance/power. Foa and Foa (1980) added six more: love, status, services, goods, information, and money. Nye (1979) contributed autonomy, security, value and opinion agreement, and equality.

Costs

In contrast, any status, relationship, or feeling that the individual does not like is considered a cost. A cost is a factor that would deter an activity, and it can be classi-fied into three categories (Blau 1964). Investment costs are time and energy that an individual will expend in order to gain a new skill that can be used to reward another. Opportunity costs consist of those rewarding feelings or positions that must be given up when selecting some competing alternative. Finally, direct costs are resources that are used up in an exchange. This could be giving up money for a good or service, such as a weekly housekeeper, or marrying an intelligent person who isn't all that attractive.

Profit

Profit refers to the outcome in terms of rewards and costs. People strive to gain the most rewards with the fewest costs. When they do so, they have profited. We all try to maximize profits and minimize costs in our relationships and interactions. Generally, most rewarding outcomes have some costs attached to them which must, therefore, be weighed and considered.

Comparison Level

The evaluation of the profitability of our relationships against what we feel we deserve is our comparison level (Thibaut and Kelley 1959)—that is, we compare the rewards and costs we are experiencing in a relationship and judge our feelings about them based on our ideas of what should be the fair outcome for us. We might also look at how well we think others in similar positions, such as other newly married or nice people, are doing in comparison to what we are experiencing. We expect our rewards to be similar to those of others in comparable situations. The notion of comparison level affects one's satisfaction in a relationship.

Comparison Level of Alternatives

Thibaut and Kelley (1959) also note that individuals will compare their outcomes in a particular relationship with alternative relationships that may be out there. For instance, Nicholas, fifteen years from now, may meet another woman who is more physically attractive and exciting than his wife Alyssa. Because he determines that divorce, having to share custody of his children, and changing locations and families involves considerable expense, Nicholas may decide that leaving his marriage to Alyssa to be with the beautiful new woman is not worth the cost after all. It is assumed that a new relationship is sufficiently superior to compensate for any costs incurred in moving from one relationship to another. The comparison level of alternatives, then is "the lowest level of outcomes a member will accept in the light of alternative opportunities" (Thibaut and Kelley 1959, 21); it determines the stability of a relationship.

Norm of Reciprocity

A cornerstone of social exchange theory, the norm of reciprocity is the social expectation or rule that dictates that people should help those who have helped them, and that they should not injure those who have helped them (Blau 1964). This is an important norm because an effective ongoing society cannot function without it. For social interactions, including but not limited to those found in family life, to take place and continue, they must be rewarding to all of the individuals involved. Others will typically not allow us to reward ourselves at their expense; so, to gain rewards we must give rewards to others. As the saying goes, "You scratch my back and I'll scratch yours."

Rule of Distributive Justice, Norm of Fairness, and Equity

Homans (1961/1974) and Blau (1964) worked with concepts similar to reciprocity and other social norms that offered guidelines about exchange behavior. These relate to the idea that a relationship between two people needs to be roughly equal. If one person is receiving most of the rewards while the other pays the costs, then the latter individual will feel angry or used and may try to end the exchange. While who gives the most may alternate back and forth between partners across time, both partners must feel that overall the balance of give-and-take is equal for exchange relationships to be successful. Relationships are sustained, and trust develops as partners reciprocate obligations and rewards.

COMMON AREAS OF RESEARCH AND APPLICATION

Social exchange has been especially useful in analyzing the mate selection process, divorce, and a few other family dynamics. The concept of the *"marriage market,"* which is used commonly in regular conversation today, comes from exchange thinking. It is the idea that people are making choices for a companion based on what that other person has to offer them that will lead to their happiness. It also implies that the first person must have some things to offer as well. Therefore, single people list what rewards they want from a relationship, what costs they are willing to incur, and what they have to offer a possible mate.

Romantic Issues

Winton (1995) explained how exchange thinking is used in a number of related areas. First, romantic love is seen as resulting when one feels that he or she is getting a high ratio of rewards with little cost. That is, the reward/cost ratio affects how we feel about other people. We come to like or love those whose interactions with us are rewarding. Being in love itself is a very rewarding state of being that can even have addictive qualities (Brown 1990). Similarly, we fall out of love with those who cost us too much of ourselves.

Mate selection is another topic studied using exchange principles. It assumes Nicholas comes to the marriage market with a certain value, which is the sum of what he has to offer in terms of family status, physical appearance, intelligence, and other factors. He will seek someone who is similar to him because he would lose interest in someone of lesser value and fear being rejected by someone of greater value. Over the years, considerable research has been conducted attempting to identify and rank the various traits that are important to couple formation. There is an implication that partners, like material objects, will tend to be discarded when they are no longer of sufficient value to the individual. Cross-cultural research (Ingoldsby, Schvaneveldt, and Uribe 2003) indicates that there are many apparent universals. Women tend to prefer a man who is older, taller, and with good income potential, whereas men value youth and beauty in a mate. Everyone desires positive traits, such as kindness and intelligence, and seeks to avoid ending up with a partner who is violent or has drug addictions.

Why married people take the risks of being involved in extramarital sex is also studied using an exchange perspective. The theory accounts for affairs by making the assumption that the short-term rewards are seen as more powerful than the potential long-term costs of the activity. This may not turn out to be the case, of course, but decisions are based on perception rather than the actual ultimate outcome. Perhaps if people could anticipate all the possible negative outcomes, or costs, there would be fewer affairs.

Relationship Issues

Filial relationships are impacted by social exchange norms. Many societies assume that parents will make up for the costs of bearing and rearing children (time, money, worry, and other costs) when they are elderly and that their children take care of them. If adult children do not fulfill their filial obligations, elderly parents may feel that justice has been violated, and their morale may suffer. Similarly, when adult caregiving daughters experience reciprocity in their relationship with their aging parent receiving care, their stress and burden are reduced (Dwyer, Lee, and Jankowski 1994).

Another family issue frequently studied using an exchange perspective is spousal abuse. Here we would look at the rewards the abuser receives, such as power over the partner and the emotional rush that may come from the behavior. Typically, the costs are found to be minimal for the abuser and would need to be increased in order to provide an escape for the abused spouse (Gelles and Straus 1988). If the abused partner stays with or returns to the abuser, then we would look for what it is that he or she is getting out of the relationship that makes it worth while to remain. Possible rewards include economic security, shelter, and perceived love.

As time goes by in a marriage, many couples reduce the number of reward-ing exchanges that were typical during courtship. Behaviors that they had not paid attention to in the beginning become irritating; therefore, the costs of being in the relationship increase. As a spouse compares profits relative to other marriages, he or she may come to feel deprived. Should the level of satisfaction get low enough, a decision to separate or divorce could be made. However, many very unhappy couples stay together, especially as the length of the marriage increases. This would be explained by the many costs that are related to divorce: alimony, child support, social disapproval, role loss, loss of custody, religious concerns, and so on (White and Booth 1991).

Gender Differences in Sexual Behavior

Klein and White (1996) draw on the work of Nye (1979) to argue the case that males are more likely to exchange rewards (money and marriage in particular) for sexual access. Assuming that the biological drive is equal for the two genders, the theory would posit that sex is more profitable for males than it is for females. This is because pregnancy is more costly for women than it is for men, and males achieve orgasm more consistently than do females. As a result, males must make sexual relations more profitable for females by offering them additional rewards. Baumeister and Vohs (2004) afford a thorough examination of how sex has exchange value for women and not men in the heterosexual marketplace. Van de Rijt and Macy (2006) used social exchange to examine "labors of love" and discovered that sexual effort received and attachment to partner were critical predictors of sexual effort.

Nye (1979), in his seminal summary of the theory, formulates 120 propositions that he feels follow from the research within the context of the theory. They are in the areas of maternal employment, marital timing and parenthood, sexual behavior, communication, marital dissolution, social networks, intergenerational relations, men's work, family violence, social class, and parental behavior. Many of his hypotheses have yet to be adequately tested.

Decision Making

One final area of utility for the theory is decision making (see Kieren, Henton, and Marotz 1975). The social exchange perspective can make the logic of the process followed in important family-related decisions explicit. Using an organized approach that highlights the pros and cons of each alternative should increase the likelihood of coming to a rational conclusion with greater final profit. Hunts and Marotz-Baden (2004) have developed the flow chart in fig. 7.1 for this process.

In their example, a young woman is trying to decide whether or not to accept a marriage proposal. She loves the young man but is concerned because he does not approve of her career decision. With the help of concerned classmates, she goes through the steps of considering each alternative. What would it be like to be married to him and give up her career? Can she talk him into changing his mind? What would it be like to discontinue the relationship? At certain stages, activities are tried and then evaluated. Sometimes, it may be realized that the particular situation is hopeless without new resources, and at other times the goals are reached.

By recognizing that life is about social exchanges, with their resultant rewards and costs, one can take the time to carefully and clearly evaluate one's logic and decision making. In this way, the theory goes beyond just analyzing what we do and helps us to make good decisions. Any time you have made a list, either physically or

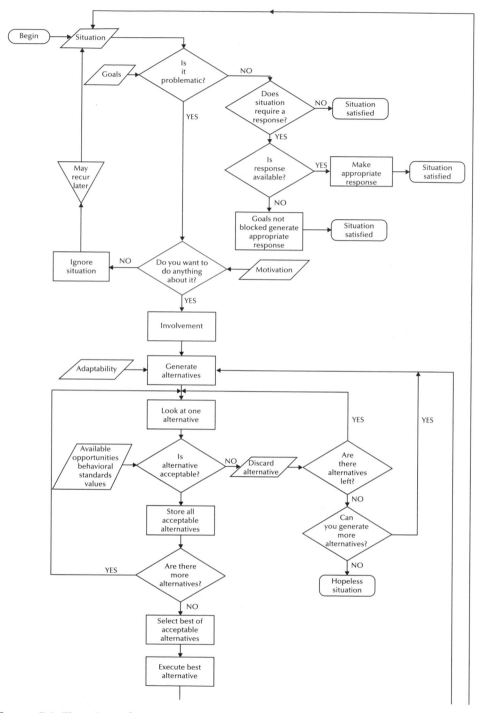

Figure 7.1 Flow chart of the problem-solving process.

Source: Hunts, H., and R. Marotz-Baden. 2004. The GO Model: A new way of teaching problem solving in context. *Journal of Teaching in Marriage and Family* 4: 27–58.

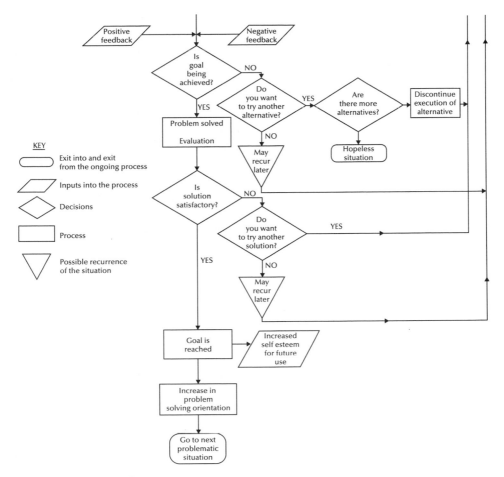

FIGURE 7.1 Continued.

mentally, of the pros and cons of a decision, you have utilized the principles of social exchange theory.

CRITIQUE

The social exchange model does an impressive job of providing a context for predicting and explaining a great deal of human behavior in social contexts. It is just one way of looking at families, but it has a straightforward methodology that is appealing to many scholars. It is clear and relatively easy to "get a handle on," compared with some of the other approaches. Much of its power comes from its emergence from behaviorism; however, the individualistic focus also results in certain limitations.

The assumption that the family is just a collection of individuals is too simplistic for many theorists. For some, the family has too many unique and long-lasting aspects to be reduced basically to an economic system with interchangeable characters (Klein and White 1996).

In addition, the key assumption that humans act rationally in decision making is criticized by many. Hamon (1999) argued that this and other key assumptions are problematic from a Christian faith perspective. Since Freud's time, practitioners and other scholars have made the case that humans are emotional beings who rarely act in ways that could be classified as truly rational and objective. Family life, in particular, is an emotional world where many decisions do not seem to make sense rationally. The case can be made (Beutler, Burr, and Bahr 1989) that the rational focus of the theory makes it impossible for it to deal with love and the other emotional elements that make up family life. Nye (1979) responded to this criticism by stating that people act in accordance with the best information available to them. Because such information is often lacking, they may appear to be less rational than they actually are.

It is also said that social exchange theory, like some other theories, suffers from a tautology in which terms are defined by each other and thus make it impossible to scientifically disprove conclusions. For example, we cannot find a situation in which one's behavior is not a function of rewards because the definition of a reward is the behaviors that one chooses (Turner 1991).

Feminist theorists also point out a masculine bias in social exchange theory, which seems to assume a "separate" rather than a "connected" self. As a result, the theory is less capable of understanding behaviors that support the group over the individual. The assumption of maximizing profit ignores altruistic behavior, for instance. It elevates the traditionally masculine and modern Western notion that autonomy and independence are more functional than caring and sharing (England 1989). Exchange theorists respond that individuals do engage in group supportive behaviors because the social approval is rewarding.

Social exchange theory has been used considerably by family scholars over the last quarter century. Researchers, however, have perhaps been slow to move beyond the basics of reward and cost. Future work would benefit from a focus on the importance of interdependence in families—that is, the model could be used to better clarify joint, rather than individual, profit.

APPLICATION

1. In a small group, play out the roles of Nicholas and Alyssa with the situation at the beginning of the chapter. Weigh the pros and cons of the relationship and decide if the two should get married, and why. What important ways of viewing the relationship are missed by just focusing on the rational aspects?

2. Analyze a relationship within your own immediate family with which you are at least somewhat uncomfortable. What are the rewards you are exchanging? Remember that this includes such intangibles as kindness and humor, in addition to goods (buying clothes) and services (fixing dinner). Now, what does it cost you to be in this relationship? After you make this list of costs associated with relating to the other person, can you identify the costs that he or she must endure to be with you? Now, are there ways that the relationship could be made more equitable, and therefore more rewarding for both of you?

3. Divide into small groups within your class and use the problem-solving model found in the chapter. Take a real problem from one of the members and use the process to see if a solution to the relationship difficulty can be reached.

4. Have you ever been in a romantic relationship where you felt exploited? Or were you the exploiter? Use social exchange theory concepts to write up an understanding of the dynamics of that relationship and what could have been done to make it fair. What aspects of the relationship are ignored by just looking at it through the lens of social exchange theory?

5. After reading the Van de Rijt and Macy's (2006) article provided under Sample Reading, evaluate the basic exchange theory assumptions outlined in this chapter in light of 'their conclusion that sexual effort is determined by effort received.

REFERENCES

Baumeister, R. F., and K. D. Vohs. 2004. Sexual economics: Sex as female resource for social exchange in heterosexual interactions. *Personality and Social Psychology Review* 8: 339–363.

Beutler, I., W. Burr, and K. Bahr. 1989. The family realm: Theoretical contributions for understanding its uniqueness. *Journal of Marriage and the Family* 51: 805–816.

Blau, P. 1964. *Exchange and power in social life*. New York: John Wiley.

Brown, E. 1990. *Patterns of infidelity and their treatment*. New York: Brunner/Mazel.

Dwyer, J. W., G. R. Lee, and T. B. Jankowski. 1994. Reciprocity, elder satisfaction, and caregiver stress and burden: The exchange of aid in the family caregiver relationship. *Journal of Marriage and the Family* 56: 35–43.

Ekeh, P. 1974. *Social exchange: The two traditions*. Cambridge, MA: Harvard University Press.

Emerson, R. 1976. Social exchange theory. In *Annual review of sociology*, ed. A. Inkeles, J. Coleman, and N. Smelser. Vol. 2, 335–362. Palo Alto, CA: Annual Reviews.

England, P. 1989. A feminist critique of rational choice theories: Implications for sociology. *The American Sociologist* 20: 14–28.

Foa, E. B., and U. G. Foa. 1980. Resource theory: Interpersonal behavior as exchange. In *Social exchange: Advances in theory and research*, ed. K. J. Gergen, M. S. Greenberg, and R. H. Willis, 77–94. New York: Plenum.

Frazer, J. 1919. *Folklore of the old testament*. New York: Macmillan.

Gelles, R., and M. Straus. 1988. *Intimate violence*. New York: Simon and Schuster.

Hamon, R. R. 1999. Social exchange and the Christian faith: Is a satisfactory marriage possible? *Journal of Psychology and Christianity* 18: 19–27.

Homans, G. 1961/1974. *Social behavior: Its elementary forms*. New York: Harcourt, Brace & Jovanovich.

Homans, G., and D. Schneider. 1955. *Marriage, authority, and final causes: A study of unilateral cross-cousin marriage*. New York: Free Press.

Hunts, H., and R. Marotz-Baden. 2004. The GO Model: A new way of teaching problem solving in context. *Journal of Teaching in Marriage and Family* 4: 27–58.

Ingoldsby, B., P. Schvaneveldt, and C. Uribe. 2003. Perceptions of acceptable mate attributes in Ecuador. *Journal of Comparative Family Studies* 34: 171–186.

Kieren, D., J. Henton, and R. Marotz. 1975. *Hers and his: A problem-solving approach to marriage*. Hinsdale, IL: Dryden.

Klein, D., and J. White. 1996. *Family theories: An introduction*. Thousand Oaks, CA: Sage.

Nye, I. 1978. Is choice and exchange theory the key? *Journal of Marriage and the Family* 40: 219–233.

————. 1979. Choice, exchange, and the family. In *Contemporary theories about the family*, ed. W. R. Burr, R. Hill, F. I. Nye, and I. L. Reiss. Vol. 2, 1–41. New York: Free Press.

Sabatelli, R., and C. Shehan. 1993. Exchange and resource theories. In *Sourcebook of family theories and methods: A contextual approach*, ed. P. G. Boss, W. J. Doherty, R. LaRossa, W. R. Schumm, and S. K. Steinmetz, 385–417. New York: Plenum.

Thibaut, J., and H. Kelley. 1959. *The social psychology of groups*. New York: Wiley.

Turner, J. 1991. *The structure of sociological theory*. 5th ed. Belmont, CA: Wadsworth.

Van de Rijt, A., and M. W. Macy. 2006. Power and dependence in intimate relationships. *Social Forces* 84: 1455–1470.

White, L., and A. Booth. 1991. Divorce over the life course: The role of marital happiness. *Journal of Family Issues* 12: 5–21.

Winton, C. 1995. *Frameworks for studying families*. Guilford, CT: Duskin.

SAMPLE READING

Van de Rijt, A., and M. W. Macy. 2006. Power and dependence in intimate exchanges. *Social Forces* 84: 1455–1470.

Using data from the Chicago Health and Social Life Survey, Van de Rit and Macy examine the exchange of sexual favors. Results revealed that intimate exchanges are governed by reciprocity: effort expended in offering sexual gratification, is reciprocated by partners who are equally sexually generous.

SAMPLE READING

POWER AND DEPENDENCE IN INTIMATE EXCHANGE

Arnout van de Rijt and
Michael W. Mucy
Cornell University

A division of labor is mediated by exchange of valued goods and services. We use social exchange theory to extend this principal to "labors of love." Sexual activity in a close personal relationship seems outside the domain of bargaining and exchange. Nevertheless, we explore the possibility that this most intimate of human relations is influenced by exchange mechanisms. We derive exchange-theoretic predictions about the level of sexual effort and test these using U.S. survey data on sexual behavior. Results provide modest support for the predictions. Sexual favors are reciprocated, and individuals offer greater sexual gratification to partners who are themselves more sexually generous and less emotionally attached. Evidence is inconclusive for the effects of relative income, physical attractiveness and household chores.

THE THEORY OF SOCIAL EXCHANGE

The social division of labor is mediated by exchange, the terms of which reflect relative power. Social exchange theory (Blau 1964; Emerson 1976; Homans 1958) models power in an ongoing relationship as a bargaining process that reflects the relative dependence of the partners. The theory has received widespread empirical support in several domains, including marriage. Although there are numerous exchange-theoretic studies of marital relations, researchers have been understandably reluctant to extend the theory to intimate relations that seem outside the sphere of bargaining and exchange. As Blau (1964:88) warned, "People do things for fear of other men [sic] or for fear of God or for fear of their conscience, and nothing is gained by trying to force such action into a conceptual framework of exchange." Yet Blau did not regard intimate relations

Power and Dependence in Intimate Exchange
Arnout van de Rijt; Michael W Macy
Social Forces; Mar 2006; 84, 3; Research Library pg. 1455

as outside this framework. "Social exchange can be observed everywhere once we are sensitized by this conception to it, not only in market relations but also in friendship and even in love..." (1964:88) We explore the possibility that this most intimate of human relations is governed by the same exchange mechanisms identified by Blau and elaborated by Emerson.

We begin by briefly outlining the theory of social exchange and reviewing applications of the theory to marital relations. We then propose an exchange-theoretic model of sexual labor, derive predictions about exchange outcomes, and test these hypotheses using survey data. The model predicts greater sexual effort toward partners who are themselves more sexually generous, and who are more desirable, less dependent and who contribute more to the household.

Social exchange differs from economic exchange in three important ways. First, the articles of exchange are not commodities but gifts. No money is involved, nor credit, nor contract. Giving a gift could be seen as a "selfish act of generosity" in that it creates in the recipient the need to reciprocate with something that is desired by the giver Both parties to the exchange "are prone to supply more of their own services to provide Incentives for the other to Increase his supply" (Blau 1964:89) Simply put, in social exchange theory, a gift is not an expression of altruism, it is a way to exercise power over another.

Second, the terms of exchange are unspecified.[1] One side offers something the other values without knowing how or when the partner will return the favor.

Third, the exchange is not instrumentally calculated. Without a quid pro quo and in the absence of explicit bargaining, one cannot know if the gift is optimal in a given transaction. Instead, optimization takes place on the fly through incremental adjustments to behavior in response to experience. These need not be conscious adjustments but could be experienced merely as feelings of satisfaction or dissatisfaction with the relationship, such that the terms of exchange emerge as a byproduct of a learning process. Each partner evaluates the outcomes from the exchange relative to a comparison level corresponding to what the actor expects to receive from his or her best alternative relationship. When the value falls below this standard, the individual is dissatisfied and seeks alternative partners whose offers are perceived as superior (Thibaut and Kelley 1959). On the other hand, "if the outcomes they are receiving from their current relationship are better than what they expect to receive from their best alternative(s), they will feel dependent on the relationship and become committed to it." (Sprecher 1998:34).

These differences with economic exchange make SET applicable to emotionally-charged behaviors where instrumental manipulation of the partner would ruin the experience for both. Social exchanges can be experienced as acts of generosity toward those we trust. Trust is necessary because of the unspecified terms of exchange. It increases when the generosity is satisfactorily reciprocated and decreases when it is not (Blau 1964:93).

Although social exchange lacks explicit terms of trade, enforceable contracts or a monetary medium, it nevertheless follows a basic principle of economic bargaining over the price of commodities, the "principle of least interest." (Waller 1937; Waller and Hill 1951) This principle predicts that the lower the dependence on the relationship, the greater will be the power "The party who is receiving the least comparative benefit from a trade has the greater bargaining power to improve upon that trade. If that power is used, as we assume above, then the terms of the trade will shift until power is balanced." (Cook and Emerson 1978:724).

FROM SOCIAL TO INTIMATE EXCHANGE

SET applies to the balancing of power in exchanges between workers, neighbors, friends and business associates. It has also been applied to exchanges between intimate partners. "Whether it is two lovers who share a warm and mutual affection or two corporations who pool resources to generate a new product, the basic form of interaction remains the same," note Lawler and Thye (1999:217). "Two or more actors, each of whom has something of value to the other, decide whether to exchange and in what amounts."

There is a large and growing research literature that has found consistent support for SET predictions for exchange outcomes in intimate relations. Sprecher (1998:32), one of the key contributors to this field, surveys applications of SET to research on "mate selection, relationship formation, and the prediction of relationship dissolution." A central hypothesis is the matching hypothesis (Hatfield et al. 1985; Sprecher and Hatfield 1996; Walster et al. 1966), which states that the more socially desirable a person is, the more socially desirable will (s)he expect a partner to be (Sprecher 1998:35).

In the realm of mate selection, South (1991:928) summarizes a number of studies that demonstrate strong tendencies toward homogamy—the tendency to marry persons close in status (Kalmijn 1998)—based on age (Atkinson and Glass 1985), race and ethnicity (Labov and Jacobs 1986; Tucker and Mitchell-Kerman 1990), religion (Glenn 1982), education (Rockwell 1976; Schoen and Wooldredge 1989), and occupational status (Morgan 1981). Homophily (Buss 1985; Byrne 1971; Byrne and Nelson 1965; Hoffnnan and Maier 1966; Rubin 1973)—the principle that "likes attract," also known as the "law of attraction"—provides a straightforward explanation. A related explanation focuses on the greater opportunities for interaction with those who are less culturally or socially distant (Blau and Schwartz 1984; Kalmijn and Flap 2001). The matching hypothesis suggests an alternative possibility. Homogamy may reflect not a taste for similarity but rather constraints on the ability to attract a partner who has more valued resources. From an exchange-theoretic perspective, romantic relationships are formed through an assortative matching process in which women and men look for the best "catch" (Shibazaki and Brennan 1998).

However, the matching hypothesis does not require a like-kind exchange. Becker's (1973, 1981) specialization hypothesis, that it is difference rather than similarity in human capital that makes marriage worthwhile, is perfectly compatible with SET Two complementary resources are exchanged. Using data from the National Survey of Families and Households, South confirms the popular impression that "men place higher value than do women on physical attractiveness and youth, while women are less willing than men to marry someone with low earnings or unstable employment." (South 1991:928) Sprecher (1998:928) also cites several other studies that indicate that "women's physical attractiveness is often exchanged for a man's wealth or social standing (e.g., Elder 1969; Stevens, Owens and Schaefer 1990; Taylor and Glenn 1976; Udry 1977; Udry and Eckland 1984)." However, as women's socio-economic standing has improved during the second half of the 20th century, SET predicts more symmetrical exchanges in current relationships. This trend toward greater symmetry has been noted in a number of studies, both theoretically (Bergstrom and Bagnoli 1993; Oppenheimer 1988; Schoeni 1996) and empirically (Blackwell 1988; Kalmijn 1991; Mare 1991; Sweeney and Cancian 2004).

Although exchange theorists have focused mainly on mate selection, recently attention has shifted to the problem of marital stability, satisfaction and duration (McDonald 1981). Equity theory (Walster [Hatfield] et al. 1978), a variant of SET suggests the hypothesis that the more equitable the exchange of resources in a relationship, the more stable, satisfying and durable the relationship will be. Various studies document support for the equity hypothesis (Walster [Hatfield], Walster and Traupman 1978; Schaefer and Keith 1980; Traupman et al. 1981; Cate et al. 1982; Davidson 1984; Michaels, Edwards and Acock 1984). While Sprecher finds the predicted effects of equity in three separate studies (1986,1988, 1992), she notes (1998:34) that the theory overlooks the importance of the comparison level. Comparisons with prospective others are particularly important among young, relatively uncommitted partners. The rewards from the exchange are compared not only to those given to the partner, but also to those that one might receive in an alternative relationship. Relationships are predicted to be stable, satisfactory and durable if rewards in the current relationship are above the ones that one would expect to get in another relationship. According to Sprecher (1998:35), "most researchers examining the degree to which equity forecasts relationship stability have not found it to be a good predictor...On the other hand, absolute reward level, investments, and poor alternatives have been good predictors of relationship longevity." (e.g., Felmlee et al. 1990; Rusbult 1983) Sprecher (2001) reproduces this result for dating couples. Effects of rewards, investments and alternatives on satisfaction and commitment were in the expected direction and generally significant, while results for the effects of inequity were less convincing (Sprecher 2001:606).

SET has also been applied to the exercise of power in the family. The principle of least interest predicts a positive effect of relative socioeconomic position on conjugal power in decision-making (Heer 1963; Rank 1982). For example, Sprecher and Felmlee (1997) report that women with high-paying jobs are less dependent on their husbands and thus have more power in marital exchange than do women without such jobs. Similarly "being the less emotionally involved partner in the relationship was associated with greater power." (Sprecher and Felmlee 1997:361)

Sprecher (1998) overviews evidence for the operation of exchange mechanisms at three stages of the sexual relationship: the negotiation of the onset of sex, evaluation of sexual satisfaction and decisions about extra-dyadic sex. Walster [Hatfield], Walster and Traupmann (1978) found that undergraduates who had relationships that were perceived as more equitable were more likely to engage in premarital sex. Lawrance and Byers (1992) note that a model of sexual satisfaction "needs to take into account the interpersonal context in which sexual activity occurs...exchange theories offer such an approach." (p. 268) They found sexual satisfaction to be independently related to both *absolute* and *comparative* reward and cost levels and equality in reward.

Sprecher also reports support for SET in studies of extra-dyadic sex (1998:38). She speculates that "extra-dyadic behavior may be one way in which a partner in an inequitable relationship restores equity to his or her relationship." Both Hatfield et al. (1979) and Prins, Buunk and Van Yperen (1993) find a positive relationship between inequity and desired and actual extra-dyadic involvement, the latter only for women. Rusbult, Drigotas and Verette (1993) find that a constructive response to extra-dyadic sex (i.e., trying to save the relationship) is more likely in the case of greater satisfaction, commitment, investments and poorer alternatives.

Intimate Exchange

Although support has been found for exchange theory hypotheses about the formation, duration and satisfaction of sexual relationships, one area of intimate exchange that has been largely ignored by SET is the exercise of power in the bedroom. The important exception is Sprecher, who believes "this framework is useful for understanding... which partner has more influence on what sexual activities they do together" (1998:32) And "because most dyadic sex occurs within the context of an emotional relationship in which partners are interdependent at many levels," she continues, "an exchange approach is particularly applicable to the *study of sexual phenomena in close relationships*." (1998:40, emphasis in original)

SET predicts that the exchange of sexual favors will be direct reciprocity or "for other resources in the relationship such as intimacy, love, favors and money." (Sprecher 1998:32) Based on the least-interest principle, "the partner who is more reluctant to have sex has a valued resource—his or her consent to sexual activity. At some point he or she may agree to have sex, and although there may never be any discussion of a 'trade' or an 'exchange,' one or both partners may treat the act as having exchange value. Gifts or special favors may be presented by the person who wants sex more, either before sex occurs (to create a sense of obligation) or after sex begins (as a form of reciprocation)." (Sprecher 1998:36) Sprecher offers an example of a working-class woman interviewed by Lillian Rubin, who appreciated the exchange value of oral sex: "He gets different treats at different times, depending on what he deserves. Sometimes I let him do that oral stuff you're talking about to me. Sometimes when he's very good, I do it to him." (Rubin 1976:207)

More precisely, SET predicts that, all else being equal, sexual effort (defined as the acts aimed at the physical gratification of one's partner) increases with the gratification received from the partner, and with the value of other resources that one's partner brings to the relationship, including contributions to household tasks. Conversely, effort decreases with the value of other resources that one brings to the relationship.

In addition, SET also predicts that sexual effort varies with relative dependence on the partner as a source of valued resources. The greater the relative attraction and attachment to the partner, the greater the partner's power, and thus the greater the sexual effort that must be invested in the partner in order to balance the partner's power.

MEASURES AND METHODS

We tested the SET predictions using data from the Chicago Health and Social Life Survey (CHSLS), a retrospective survey ($N = 2,114$) containing detailed questions about past and current sexual relationships and with unique information on sexual activities.[2] The CHSLS was conducted between 1995 and 1997 using a stratified random sample of the non-institutionalized Chicago population, composed of five sub-samples on two geographical levels. The greater Chicago sub-sample consists of 890 respondents from Cook County, including the inner suburban ring. Another 1,224 respondents were sampled from four ethnically-targeted neighborhoods within the city of Chicago, each characterized by the dominance of a particular ethnic group. Response rates were

71 percent for the city-level sub-sample and ranged from 60 percent to 78 percent for the neighborhood sub-samples. We tested for neighborhood-level heterogeneity by estimating the model separately for each neighborhood but found no significant neighborhood differences. Therefore we report only the results for the pooled sample.

The survey was executed using Computer Assisted Personal Interview (CAPI) techniques, with responses entered directly into laptop computers. Respondents were surveyed in person by experienced interviewers from the National Opinion Research Center (NORC), who matched respondents on various social attributes such as race and ethnicity for an interview averaging 90 minutes. Spanish-speaking interviewers were employed so that recent migrants lacking facility in English could be included.

Respondents answered a series of questions concerning their most recent sexual relationships. Table 1 displays the descriptive statistics of the observed variables that we used in the empirical analysis. Sexual effort refers to the willingness to confer physical and sexual pleasure.[3] Respondents were asked to indicate on a scale of 1 (always) to 5 (never) their own and their partner's participation in six sexual activities: active & passive chest/breast stimulation, active & passive manual sex, and active & passive oral sex. The three responses for respondent R's participation were standardized and added as a composite measure of R's sexual effort ($\alpha = .69$). R's three responses for partner P's participation were standardized and added as a composite measure of Ps sexual effort ($\alpha = .72$).[4]

We also included a measure of R's desire to please P, and R's desire for P to please R. Unfortunately the survey included only a single activity oral sex, using two items that asked R to indicate on a scale of 1 to 4 how appealing they found "performing oral sex on your partner" and "your partner performing oral sex on you."

Attractiveness was measured by responses to the question: "How would you rate your partner in terms of attractiveness compared to other men/women in his/her age group (during the time you were involved with him/her)," on a scale of 1 (very unattractive) to 7 (very attractive). A similar question was asked about R's own attractiveness.

Emotional attachment was measured by responses to two related questions: "On a scale of 1 (not at all) to 5 (deeply), how in love is your partner with you?" and a similar question about R's love for her or his P.

We also use measures for the total personal income of last year for both R and P Respondents picked one out of a series of income categories. We constructed two income variables, transforming the mean income value of each category by taking the natural logarithm. Note that the difference in standard deviation between the two variables in table 1 is a result of a difference in categorization in the questionnaire.

Respondents were also asked to indicate the weekly hours spent by R and P on seven different household tasks: preparing meals, washing dishes, cleaning the house, outdoor tasks, shopping, washing and ironing, and paying bills. Participation in household tasks was asked only if R and P cohabited at the time of the interview.

We included standard demographic controls for age, gender, ethnicity and education (highest degree). Three ethnic compositions of relationships dominate: both Hispanic (431), both white (470), and both African American (436). We created four race/ethnicity dummy variables, one for each of the above and one 'other' category (146), which contains mixed race couples and very small minorities such as Asian and

Table 1. Mean, Standard Deviation, Minimun, Maximum and Number of Cases for Each Observed Variable

Variable	Mean	St. Dev.	Mininum	Maximum	N
Dependent					
R's sexual effort[a]	.597	.239	0	1	1,491
Breast/chest stimulation	2.973	1.183	0	4	1,491
Digital sex	2.722	1.206	0	4	1,491
Oral sex	1.466	1.275	0	4	1,491
Independent					
Male	.419	.493	0	1	1,491
Race/ethnicity					
African American	.293	.455	0	1	1,482
Hispanic	.290	.454	0	1	1,482
White	.317	.465	0	1	1,482
Other	.098	.298	0	1	1,482
R's age	35.299	10.270	18	60	1,491
P's age[b]	35.703	10.799	18	72	1,490
R's education	1.973	1.751	0	6	1,491
P's education	2.026	1.755	0	6	1,481
R's church attendance	4.064	2.101	1	8	1,491
R's attraction to P	5.801	1.261	1	7	1,489
P's attraction to R	5.144	1.290	1	7	1,478
R's attachment to P	4.232	1.088	1	5	1,490
P's attraction to R	4.339	1.011	1	5	1,477
R's income	25,803	38,284	2,500	400,000	1,453
P's income	26,181	36,689	0	400,000	1,367
P's sexual effort	.607	.242	0	1	1,491
Breast/chest stimulation	3.029	1.114	0	4	1,491
Digital sex	2.704	1.221	0	4	1,491
Oral sex	1.557	1.287	0	4	1,491
R desires active P	2.975	1.131	1	4	1,473
R enjoys own effort	2.726	1.081	1	4	1,472

Native American couples. We also included a measure of church attendance because religious norms are likely to influence sexual behavior

This information was available for the two most recent heterosexual[5] relationships that were current at the time of the interview ($N = 1,491$). Our analysis is limited to these observations. The two 'most recent' relationships are those for which the moments of first sexual contact are most recent. A relationship is considered 'current' on the basis of the answer to the question, "Are you still sexually involved with your partner, that is, do you expect to have sex with your partner again?" One hundred fifty-five respondents answered this question affirmatively for *both* their most recent and second most recent sexual relationship. For these respondents, we have two observations.[6] Our estimates are based on the assumption of independence between respondents, but interdependence between multiple observations for a single respondent (Huber 1967). We thus obtained conservative standard errors.

Measurement Validity

Following the publication of "The Social Organization of Sexuality" (Laumann et al. 1994), based on responses to a survey very similar to the one used in our study critics scoffed at the ability to study sexual behavior using survey responses (Lewontin 1995). We acknowledge that survey respondents, at best, "tell us the truth as they see it." (John H. Gagnon in Boxer 2000) For example, Table 1 shows that the people of Chicago, like the children of Lake Wobegon, are "all above average" in attractiveness, indicating that respondents have inflated assessments of themselves and their partners.[7] We also recognize the need to confirm survey-based results with in-depth interviews, ethnographic case studies and laboratory experiments that provide measures whose strengths and weaknesses complement those of the survey methods. Nevertheless, we believe much can be learned from survey responses, despite the discrepancies that undoubtedly exist between what respondents report and what they experience.

We base this view on four considerations. First, the theory we are testing is about the effects of *subjective* beliefs, not objective conditions. If R's assessments of R's and P's attractiveness differs systematically from the consensus of third parties, it is not a problem as long as those inflated reports correspond to what R actually believes. Second, even if respondents intentionally and consciously misrepresent what they believe, these distortions do not necessarily invalidate the results. For example, misrepresentation of attractiveness, sexual effort or emotional attachment does not bias the results if the errors are uncorrelated with the dependent measure, and moreover, the inflated scores impose a ceiling effect that actually makes our estimates conservative. Third, because of the sensitive nature of some of the questions (Laumann et al. 2004:51), special care was taken to ensure response validity, including self-administration of some items and the use of racially matched interviewers. Less than 1 percent of respondents refused to answer the questions about intimate behavior Fourth, the responses in this survey were in line with those of other surveys (Hamilton 2003).

RESULTS

We present the results in three parts. We begin with the effects of the demographic controls. We then address the two principal SET predictors, direct reciprocity and dependence. Finally, we consider secondary SET predictors (e.g., non-sexual contributions).

Table 2[8] reports unstandardized multivariate regression coefficients for three models of R's sexual effort.[9] Models 1 and 2 are nested. Model 1 includes only demographic measures and factors that are not relevant to SET Model 2 then adds the SET predictors, except for household effort (which was only asked of cohabiting couples). Both models are estimated for the full sample. Model 3 adds household effort for a sub-sample of cohabiting couples.

Table 2. Three Regression Models of Respondent's Sexual Effort

Predictor	Model 1		Model 2		Model 3	
	B	S.E.	B	S.E.	B	S.E.
Male	.0699***	.0128	.0818***	.0103	.0856***	.0140
African-American	−.0819***	.0167	−.0160	.0120	.0006	.0141
Hispanic	−.1213***	.0181	−.0225^	.0134	−.0302*	.0151
Other race/ethnicity	.0097	.0178	.0032	.0132	−.0047	.0174
R's age[a]	−.0011	.0011	.0010	.0008	.0003	.0010
P's age[b]	−.0014	.0011	−.0010	.0008	−.0009	.0010
R's education	.0178***	.0045	.0031	.0034	.0066	.0042
P's education	.0087*	.0042	.0039	.0030	−.0001	.0039
R's church attendance	−.0075*	.0030	−.0017	.0022	−.0016	.0024
P's sexual effort			.5691***	.0225	.5765***	.0261
R's attraction to P			.0062	.0039	.0085^	.0045
P's attraction to R			−.0050	.0038	−.0062	.0041
R's attachment to P			.0234***	.0069	.0167	.0109
P's attachment to R			−.0206**	.0073	−.0145	.0114
R's income (log)			.0050	.0049	.0046	.0057
P's income (log)			.0046**	.0014	.0043*	.0017
R enjoys own effort			.0562***	.0070	.0554***	.0086
R desires active P			−.0023	.0071	−.0092	.0084
R's household effort[c]					−.0003	.0002
P's household effort[c]					.0003	.0002
Constant	.6957***	.0294	.0346	.0529	.0070	.0698
R^2	.18		.61		.63	
N	1491		1491		946	

Note: Model 1 and 2 are nested and run on the full sample. Model 1 includes only demographic variables and factors that are not relevant to SET. Model 2 adds the SET variables except household effort. In model 3, measures of household effort are added for a sub-sample o cohabiting couples.
[a] R = Respondent.
[b] P = Partner.
[c] Currently cohabiting couples only.
^$p<.10$ *$p<.05$ **$p<.01$ ***$p<.001$ (based on a two-tailed test).

DEMOGRAPHIC DIFFERENCES IN SEXUAL BEHAVIOR

Model 1 documents demographic differences in sexual behavior, based primarily on gender, ethnicity and education. All else being equal, male respondents report a .07 higher level of sexual effort than females (on a scale of 0, no effort, to 1, maximum effort), while African-Americans (−.08) and Hispanics (−.12) report less sexual effort than do white couples. (See also Laumann et al. 1994.) Sexual effort also increases with R's education (.02) and decreases with religious attendance (−.01). Age negatively affects sexual effort (James 1974; Jasso 1985; Kinsey et al. 1948, 1953; Udry 1979; Udry and Morris 1978; Udry et al. 1982). Due to mild collinearity, the effect of R's age becomes significant when P's age is omitted as predictor.

Except for gender, these demographic differences largely disappear after we take into account the determinants of power as hypothesized by SET. The inability of SET to explain gender differences should not be surprising, given the existence of cultural norms that define gender-appropriate sexual behavior (West and Zimmerman 1987; Ridgeway and Correll 2004). Some of these differences are related to differences in the bargaining power men and women derive from the resources they bring to the relationship.

Core SET Predictions: Reciprocity and Dependence

The core prediction in SET is direct reciprocity, in which effort is rewarded with effort. The results suggest that this principle extends to intimate exchange. The single most important predictor of sexual effort is the effort received (.57, $p < .001$). This means that a 1 point increase in effort by the partner produces a .57 increase in one's own effort.[10] Despite the size and significance of the effect, the evidence is only suggestive. Part of this effect could be spurious for two reasons. First, respondents with inflated or deflated perceptions of the frequencies of P's sexual activities may have similar biases in their self-assessments. Second, respondents may be reluctant to report imbalances in the frequencies of active and passive sexual activities. Future studies could avoid these potential biases by interviewing both partners separately

Along with R's desire for P's effort, we also included a measure of R's enjoyment of R's own effort. Model 3 shows that R's effort increases with R's intrinsic gratification and decreases with R's lack of enjoyment (.06). This is consistent with the exchange-theoretic prediction that resistance to exchange increases with the cost of the expenditure.

Along with direct reciprocity a key prediction in SET is the effect of relative dependence on generosity toward the exchange partner. All else being equal, the greater one's dependence on the partner for a valued resource, the more one is willing to exchange in order to obtain it. Results for Models 2 and 3 (in which the effects are somewhat weaker) provide some support for SET. R's attachment to P increases R's sexual effort in Model 2, while P's attachment to R has the opposite effect. The effects are smaller and statistically insignificant in Model 3, which is limited to a sub-sample of cohabitants. The reason for this difference is that virtually all cohabitants indicate that they love their partner a great deal, and that this love is reciprocated, leaving little variation in these two variables.

The effects of attachment also appear to account for much of the effect of physical attraction on sexual effort. The effects of physical attraction are in the right direction, but are too small to rule out random fluctuation as the default explanation. The effects become significant when measures of attachment are excluded from the model, suggesting the possibility that at least some of the effect of physical attraction on effort may be mediated by increased willingness to commit to the relationship.

Although reciprocity and dependence have the greatest weight in theories of social exchange, other valued resources can also indirectly affect exchange outcomes. In intimate exchange applications, these other resources might include income (which has a long history of exchange for sexual gratification) and other contributions to the house-hold, such as cooking, cleaning and yard work. Results reported in Table 2 show that these secondary factors do have some effect on sexual effort, albeit modest. The effect of P's income is in the predicted direction and strongly significant, while the effect of R's income is in the wrong direction and insignificant. Separate regression models for male and female respondents (not shown in Table 2) reveal that men ($p < .001$) but not women respond to P's income, while women ($p < .01$) but not men respond to P's degree. Neither men's nor women's effort increases with their own income or degree. These findings do not parallel the significant effects of income and education that have been found for the case of household effort as the dependent variable (cf. Bianchi et al. 2000). For the sub-sample of cohabiting couples, these models show a margin-ally significant ($p < .1$) positive effect of women's income on their sexual effort.

We also found that the effects of household effort by respondent and partner were in the expected directions but the effects were not significant for the sub-sample of cohabiting couples. Decomposing the composite measure of household effort does, however, reveal a significant effect ($p < .05$) for preparing meals, while all other chores had insignificant effects. Apparently the way to a lover's heart is through his or her stomach.[11]

DISCUSSION AND CONCLUSION

The division of labor is mediated by exchange of valued resources. This study extends social exchange theory to labors of love. Although this most intimate of human relations seems outside the domain of bargaining and exchange, we find evidence that the most important determinant of sexual effort is effort received, suggesting that intimate exchange is governed by principles of reciprocity similar to those that have been widely observed in kinship, marriage, friendship and work relations.

Social exchange theory also emphasizes the importance of dependence as a deter-minant of exchange outcomes, and that prediction is also partially supported by this data along with nonsexual contributions to the relationship. Regardless of gender, respondents report greater sexual effort if they are more deeply loved and cook. Evidence regarding the effects of income, physical attractiveness, and household work other than cooking, however, is inconclusive.

The positive effect of women's income on their sexual effort constitutes the only direct violation of SET predictions. This effect may be due to self-selection in which women with more assertive attitudes are more successful in their careers and more active in their intimate relations. An alternative explanation is masculine overcom-pensation in reaction to an identity threat (Brines 1994; Bittman et al. 2003; Munsch and Wilier 2005; Wilier 2005).

The support for exchange theoretic predictions should not lead us to downplay the importance of emotional determinants of intimate sexual behavior, just as one would not want to deny the role of emotions in other relations such as work teams. As Thibaut and Kelley (1959) showed, there is no need to assume coldly calculating behavior (although there is also no reason to preclude it). Exchange outcomes can also be obtained through a learning process that converges with the balance point pre-dicted for actors whose choices are strictly governed by instrumental calculation.

Another important determinant of the division of labor in the bedroom is gender. While SET is gender-neutral, some of our effects vary by the gender of the partner Resources that women and men bring to the relationship may be differently valued by women and men, and gender norms of sexuality (cf. Sanchez, Crocker and Boike 2005) may keep exchange partners from obtaining the full sexual rewards for their resources.

Although the results we report are consistent with SET and with intuitions about the non-instrumentality of sexual behavior, we nevertheless urge caution in generalizing from this single study. The more private the behavior, the greater the difficulty in making accurate measurements. New surveys need to be conducted, with items constructed to better gauge the full range of manifestations of sexual effort. We also need to replicate these findings using different data collection methods. For example, the quote from Rubin's (1976:207) qualitative study strongly suggests an exchange-theory interpretation of our quantitative findings rather than an interpretation informed by another theoretical framework. While we caution against reading too much into these results, we do hope this study will encourage other researchers to extend social exchange theory from non-sexual marital relations, where it has been widely employed for several decades, to the bedroom, which has remained off limits.

NOTES

1. "Social exchange differs in important ways from strictly economic exchange. The basic and most crucial distinction is that social exchange entails unspecified obligations." (Blau 1964:91–2)

2. We did not use data from the National Health and Social Life Survey (NHSLS), the predecessor of the CHSLS, because it does not include questions on sexual effort.

3. Respondents privately answered written questions on the frequencies of sexual practices for themselves; no interviewer saw their answers and respondents were guaranteed the information they provided could not be traced back to them. Less than 1 percent of the respondents refused to answer these questions.

4. Principle Component Analysis reveals a single dimension with all measures scoring positively, accounting for 65 percent of the variance. This supports the validity of our composite measure.

5. Although social exchange theory applies equally to homosexual and heterosexual relationships, there were too few cases ($N = 92$) to establish statistical significance for the predicted effects, but the signs of the effects were identical to those for heterosexual relationships.

6. Results are not qualitatively different if these 310 relationships are omitted.

7. We checked self-reports of attractiveness against an interviewer-reported measure. Although the correlation was statistically significant ($p < .001$), the relationship was not strong ($r = .108$), suggesting that beauty is indeed in the eye of the beholder, especially when looking in the mirror. The interviewer-reported measure was not available for partner attractiveness.

8. Byers, Demmons, and Lawrance (1998) use SET to predict sexual satisfaction within dating relationships as a function of many of the same factors we use to predict sexual effort. We therefore estimated parallel models with sexual satisfaction, rather than sexual effort, as the dependent variable. Results were similar to those reported in Table 2.

9. The dependent variable is ordinal and has a lower and upper bound. We therefore replicated the model using ordered logistic regression and linear regression with a transformed dependent variable. Results were robust across these models.

10. Part of this effect could be spurious, due to reporting bias. First, respondents with inflated (or deflated) perceptions of the frequencies of P's sexual activities may have similar biases in their self-assessments. Second, respondents may be reluctant to report imbalances in the frequencies of active and passive sexual activities. Future research could address these limitations by interviewing couples, to allow an independent measure of the partner's behavior.

11. That cooking is more closely linked to intimate exchange than other household tasks may not be too surprising, given the similarities of physical and emotional gratification involved in both activities, compared to, for example, raking the leaves or paying bills. This is consistent with Blau's (1964) distinction between social and economic exchange and his belief that the articles of social exchange are not commodities but gifts, with symbolic meaning to the exchange partners.

REFERENCES

Atkinson, Maxine R., and Beckly L. Glass. 1985. "Marital Age Heterogamy and Homogamy 1900 to 1980." *Journal of Marriage and the Family* 47: 685–91.
Becker, Gary S. 1973. "A Treatise on the Family." *Journal of Political Economy* 81: 813–46.
———. 1981. *A Treatise on the Family.* Harvard University Press.
Bergstrom, Ted C., and Mark Bagnoli. 1993. "Courtship as a Waiting Game." *Journal of Political Economy* 101: 185–203.
Bergstrom, Ted C., and Robert F. Schoeni. 1996. "Income Prospects and Age-at-Marriage." *Journal of Population Economics* 9: 115–30.
Bianchi, Suzanne M., Melissa A. Milkie, Liana C. Sayer and John R. Robinson. 2000. "Is Anyone Doing the Housework? Trends in the Gender Division of Household Labor." *Social Forces* 79: 191–228.
Bittman, Michael, Paula England, Liana Sayer, Nancy Folbre and George Matheson. 2003. "When Does Gender Trump Money? Bargaining and Time in Household Work." *American Journal of Sociology* 109: 186–214.
Blackwell, Debra L. 1998. "Marital Homogamy in the United States: The Influence of Individual and Paternal Education." *Social Science Research* 27: 159–88.
Blau, Peter M. 1964. *Exchange and Power in Social Life.* Wiley.
Blau, Peter M., and Joseph E. Schwartz. 1984. *Cross Cutting Social Circles: Testing a Macrostructural Theory of Intergroup Relations.* Academic Press.
Boxer, Sarah. 2000. "Truth or Lies? In Sex Surveys, You Never Know." *New York Times.* July 22.
Brines, Julie. 1994. "Economic Dependence, Gender, and the Division of Labor at Home." *American Journal of Sociology* 100: 652–88.
Burress, David. 1995. "Sex, Lies, and Sociology" *New York Review of Books* 42: 68–9.
Buss, David M. 1985. "Human Mate Selection." *American Scientist* 73: 47–51.

Byers, E. Sandra, Stephanie Demmons and Kelli-an Lawrance. 1998. "Sexual Satisfaction within Dating Relationships: A Test of the Interpersonal Exchange Model of Sexual Satisfaction." *Journal of Personal and Social Relationships* 15: 257–67.

Byrne, Donn E. 1971. *The Attraction Paradigm.* Academic Press.

Byrne, Donn E., and Don Nelson. 1965. "Attraction as a Linear Function of Proportion of Positive Reinforcements." *Journal of Personality and Social Psychology* 1: 659–63.

Cate, Rodney M., Sally A. Lloyd, June M. Henton and Jeffry H. Larson. 1982. "Fairness and Rewards as Predictors of Relationship Satisfaction." *Social Psychology Quarterly* 45: 177–81.

Cook, Karen S., and Richard M. Emerson. 1978. "Power, Equity and Commitment in Exchange Networks." *American Sociological Review* 43: 721–39.

Davidson, Bernard. 1984. "A Test of Equity Theory for Marital Adjustment." *Social Psychology Quarterly* 47: 36–42.

Elder, Glen H., Jr. 1969. "Appearance and Education in Marriage Mobility." *American Sociological Review* 34: 519–33.

Emerson, Richard M. 1981. "Social Exchange Theory." Pp. 30–65. *Social Psychology: Sociological Perspectives.* Morris Rosenberg and Ralph H. Turner, editors. Basic Books.

Felmlee, Diane, Susan Sprecher and Edward Bassin. 1990. "The Dissolution of Intimate Relationships: A Hazard Model." *Social Psychology Quarterly* 53: 13–30.

Glass, Shirley P., and Thomas L. Wright. 1985. "Sex Differences in Types of Extramarital Involvement and Marital Dissatisfaction." *Sex Roles* 12: 1101–20.

———. 1992. "Justifications for Extramarital Relationships: The Association between Attitudes, Behaviors, and Gender." *Journal of Sex Research* 29: 361–87.

Glenn, Norval D. 1982. "Interreligious Marriage in the United States: Patterns and Recent Trends." *Journal of Marriage and the Family* 44: 555–66.

Gouldner, Alvin W. 1960. "The Norm of Reciprocity: A Preliminary Statement." *American Sociological Review*, 25: 161–79.

Hamilton, Deven T. 2003. "Sexual Histories: Does it Matter Who is Asking?" University of Washington: unpublished manuscript.

Hatfield, Elaine, Mary K. Utne and Jane Traupmann, 1979. "Equity and Extra-Marital Sexuality." *Archives of Sexual Behavior* 7: 127–41.

Hatfield, Elaine, Jane Traupmann, Susan Sprecher, Mary K. Utne and Joel W. Hay 1985. "Equity and Intimate Relations: Recent Research." Pp. 91–117. *Compatible and Incompatible Relationships.* William J. Ickes, editor. Springer.

Heer, David M. 1963. "The Measurement and Bases of Family Power: An Overview" *Journal of Marriage and the Family* 25: 133–9.

Hoffman, Richard L., and Norman R. F. Maier 1966. "An Experimental Re-examination of the Similarity-Attraction Hypothesis." *Journal of Personality and Social Psychology* 3: 145–52.

Homans, George C. 1958. "Social Behavior as Exchange." *American Journal of Sociology* 63: 597–606.

Huber, Peter J. 1967. "The Behavior of Maximum Likelihood Estimates Under Non-Standard Conditions." *Proceedings of the Fifth Berkeley Symposium on Mathematical Statistics and Probability* 1: 221–33.

Jasso, Guillermina. 1985. "Marital Coital Frequency and the Passage of Time: Estimating the Separate Effects of Spouses' Ages and Marital Duration, Birth and Marriage Cohorts, and Period Influences." *American Sociological Review* 50: 224–41.

Kalmijn, Matthijs. 1991. "Shifting Boundaries: Trends in Religious and Educational Homogamy." *American Sociological Review* 56: 786–800.

———. 1998. "Intermarriage and Homogamy: Causes, Patterns, Trends." *Annual Review of Sociology* 24: 395–421.

Kalmijn, Matthijs, and Henk Flap. 2001. "Assortative Meeting and Mating: Unintended Consequences of Organized Settings for Partner Choice." *Social Forces* 79: 1289–312.

Kinsey, Alfred C., Wardell B. Pomeroy and Clyde E. Martin. 1948. *Sexual Behavior in the Human Male*. W. B. Saunders.

Kinsey, Alfred C., and Paul H. Gebhard. 1953. *Sexual Behavior in the Human Female*. W. B. Saunders.

Labov, Teresa, and Jerry A. Jacobs. 1986. "Intermarriage in Hawaii, 1950–1983." *Journal of Marriage and the Family* 48: 79–88.

Laumann, Edward O., John H. Gagnon, Robert T. Michael and Stuart Michaels. 1994. *The Social Organization of Sexuality: Sexual Practices in the United States*. University of Chicago Press.

Laumann, Edward O., Stephen Ellingson, Jenna Mahay Anthony Paik and Yoosik Youm. 2004. *The Sexual Organization of the City*. University of Chicago Press.

Lawler, Edward J., and Shane R. Thye. 1999. "Bringing Emotions into Social Exchange Theory." *Annual Review of Sociology* 25: 217–44.

Lawrance, Kelli-an, and E. Sandra Byers. 1992. "Development of the Interpersonal Exchange Model of Sexual Satisfaction in Long-Term Relationships." *Canadian Journal of Human Sexuality* 1: 123–28.

————. 1995. "Sexual Satisfaction in Long-Term Heterosexual Relationship: The Interpersonal Exchange Model of Sexual Satisfaction." *Personal Relationships* 2: 267–85.

Lewontin, Richard. 1995. "Sex, Lies, and Social Science." *New York Review of Books* 42: 24–9.

Mare, Robert D. 1991. "Five Decades of Educational Assortative Mating." *American Sociological Review* 56: 15–32.

McDonald, Gerald W. 1981. "Structural Exchange and Marital Interaction." *Journal of Marriage and the Family* 43: 825–39.

Michaels, James W., John N. Edwards and Alan C. Acock. 1984. "Satisfaction in Intimate Relationships as a Function of Inequality, Inequity, and Outcomes." *Social Psychology Quarterly* 47: 347–57.

Morgan, Barrie S. 1981. "A Contribution to the Debate on Homogamy Propinquity, and Segregation." *Journal of Marriage and the Family* 43: 909–21.

Munsch, Christin L., and Robb Wilier. 2005. "The Effect of Identity Threat on Tolerance for Violence against Women." Unpublished Manuscript. Cornell University.

Oppenheimer, Valery K. 1988. "A Theory of Marriage Timing." *American Journal of Sociology* 94: 563–91.

Prins, Karin S., Bram P. Buunk and Nico W. van Yperen. 1993. "Equity, Normative Disapproval, and Extra-Marital Relationships." *Journal of Social and Personal Relationships* 10: 39–53.

Rank, Mark R. 1982. "Determinants of Conjugal Influence in Wives Employment Decision Making." *Journal of Marriage and the Family* 44: 591–604.

Ridgeway Cecilia L., and Shelley J. Correll. 2004. "Unpacking the Gender System. A Theoretical Perspective on Gender Beliefs and Social Relations." *Gender & Society* 18: 510–31.

Rockwell, Richard C. 1976. "Historical Trends and Variations in Educational Homogamy." *Journal of Marriage and the Family* 38: 83–95.

Rubin, Zick. 1973. *Liking and Loving: An Invitation to Social Psychology*. Holt, Rinehart and Winston.

Rubin, Lillian B. 1976. *Worlds of Pain: Life in Working-Class Family*. Basic Books.

Rusbult, Caryl E. 1983. "A Longitudinal Test of the Investment Model: The Development (and Deterioration) of Satisfaction and Commitment in Heterosexual Involvements." *Journal of Personality and Social Psychology* 43: 101–17.

Rusbult, Caryl E., Stephen M. Drigotas and Julie Verette. 1991. 'The Investment Model: An Interdependence Analysis of Commitment Processes and Relationship Maintenance Phenomena." Pp. 115–39. *Communication and Relational Maintenance*. D. Canary and L. Stafford, editors. Sage.

Sanchez, Crocker and Boike. 2005. "Doing Gender in the Bedroom: Investing in Gender Norms and the Sexual Experience." *Personality and Social Psychology Bulletin* 31: 1445–55.

Schafer, Robert B., and Patricia M. Keith. 1980. "Equity and Depression Among Married Couples." *Social Psychology Quarterly* 43: 430–435.

Schoen, Robert, and John Wooldredge. 1989. "Marriage Choices in North Carolina and Virginia, 1969–71 and 1979–81." *Journal of Marriage and the Family* 51: 465–81.

Shibazaki, Kozue, and Kelly A. Brennan. 1998. "When Birds of Different Feathers Flock Together: A Preliminary Comparison of Intra-Ethnic and Inter-Ethnic Dating Relationships." *Journal of Social and Personal Relationships* 15: 248–56.

South, Scott J. 1991. "Socio-Demographic Differentials in Mate Selection Preferences." *Journal of Marriage and the Family* 53: 928–40.

Sprecher, Susan. 1986. "The Relation between Inequity and Emotions in Close Relationships." *Social Psychology Quarterly* 49: 309–21.

———. 1988. "Investment Model, Equity, and Social Support Determinants of Relationship Commitment." *Social Psychology Quarterly* 51: 318–28.

———. 1992. "How Men and Women Expect to Feel and Behave in Response to Inequity in Close Relationships." *Social Psychology Quarterly* 55: 57–69.

———. 1998. "Social Exchange Theories and Sexuality." *Journal of Sex Research* 35: 32–43.

Sprecher, Susan, and Elaine Hatfield. 1996. "Premarital Sexual Standards among U.S. College Students: Comparison with Russian and Japanese Students." *Archives of Sexual Behavior* 25: 261–88.

Sprecher Susan, and Kathleen McKinney 1993. *Sexuality.* Sage.

Sprecher, Susan, and Pamela C. Regan. 1996. "College Virgins: How Men and Women Perceive their Sexual Status." *Journal of Sex Research* 33: 3–15.

———. 1998. "Passionate and Companionate Love in Courting and Young Married Couples." *Sociological Inquiry* 68: 63–85.

Sprecher, Susan, and Pepper Schwartz. 1994. "Equity and Balance in the Exchange of Contributions in Close Relationships." Pp. 1141. *Entitlement and the Affectional Bond.* Melvin J. Lerner and Gerold Mikula, editors. Plenum.

Sprecher, Susan, and Diane Felmlee. 1997. "The Balance of Power in Romantic Heterosexual Couples over Time from 'His' and 'Her' Perspectives." *Sex Roles* 37: 361–79.

Stevens, Gillian, Dawn Owens and Eric C. Schaefer 1990. "Education and Attractiveness in Marriage Choices." *Social Psychological Quarterly* 53: 62–70.

Stinchcombe, Arthur L. 1995. "Sex, Lies, and Sociology." *New York Review of Books* 42: 68–9.

Sweeney Megan M., and Maria Cancian. 2004. "The Changing Importance of White Women's Economic Prospects for Assortative Mating." *Journal of Marriage and the Family* 66: 1015–28.

Taylor, Patricia A., and Norval D. Glenn. 1976. "The Utility of Education and Attractiveness for Females' Status Attainment through Marriage." *American Sociological Review* 41: 484–97.

Thibaut, John W., and Harold H. Kelley 1959. *The Social Psychology of Groups.* Wiley.

Traupmann, Jane, R. Petersen, Mary K. Utne and Elaine Hatfield. 1981. "Measuring Equity in Intimate Relations." *Applied Psychological Measurement* 5: 467–480.

Tucker M. Belinda, and Claudia Mitchell-Kernan. 1990. "New Trends in Black American Interracial Marriage: The Social Structural Context." *Journal of Marriage and the Family* 52: 209–18.

Udry, J. Richard. 1977. "The Importance of Being Beautiful: A Re-Examination and Racial Comparisons." *American Journal of Sociology,* 83: 154–60.

Udry, J. Richard, and Bruce K. Eckland. 1984. "The Benefits of Being Attractive: Differential Payoffs for Men and Women." *Psychological Reports* 54: 47–56.

Waller, Willard. 1937. "The Rating and Dating Complex." *American Sociological Review* 2: 727–34.

Waller Willard, and Reuben Hill. 1951. *The Family: A Dynamic Interpretation.* Hold, Rinehart & Wilson.

Walster, Elaine, Vera Aronson, Darcy Abrahams and Leon Rottman. 1966. "The Importance of Physical Attractiveness in Dating Behavior." *Journal of Personality and Social Psychology* 4: 508–16.

Walster Elaine, G. William Walster and Jane Traupmann. 1978. "Equity and Premarital Sex." *Journal of Personality and Social Psychology* 37: 82–92.

Walster, Elaine, G.William Walster and Ellen Berscheid. *1978. Equity: Theory and Research.* Allyn and Bacon.

West, Candace, and Don H. Zimmerman. 1987. "Doing Gender." *Gender & Society* 1: 125–51.

Wilier Robb. 2005. "Overdoing Gender: A Test of the Masculine Overcompensation Thesis." Unpublished Manuscript. Cornell University.

We thank Stephen W. Benard, Douglas D. Heckathorn, Edward O. Laumann and Sarah Thebaud for helpful comments and suggestions on earlier drafts. We also express our appreciation to the National Science Foundation (SES 0241657 and SES 0432917) for support provided to the second author. Direct correspondence to Arnout van de Rijt, Department of Sociology, Cornell University, 323 Uris Hall, Ithaca, NY 14853. E-mail: av85@cornell.edu.

8

FEMINIST FAMILY THEORY

Bob and Alice Stephens were having dinner at a nice restaurant to celebrate their tenth wedding anniversary. Bob said to Alice, "Isn't this relaxing? A dinner alone without the kids. We should treat ourselves to this more often." Alice smiled politely but was unconvinced that it was such a treat. It's true that Bob suggested that they go out to dinner, but Alice had made the reservations. In fact, Alice had picked up Bob's suit from the cleaners on her way home from work. She had arranged for the babysitter, made dinner for the kids before she left, washed the basketball uniform that Bobby Junior needed for tomorrow's gym class, and helped little Alicia study for her spelling test before she drove downtown to Bob's engineering office, where he changed into his suit for dinner. She felt too tired and anxious to relax.

Alice had been feeling a great deal of stress lately. She enjoyed her job as a lawyer but was worried about making partner in her firm. Two men who had joined the firm after her had already achieved partner status. When she asked the senior partners about it, they explained that she was "off track" because of the maternity leave she had taken to have her children. They also indicated that her work with the Legal Aid fund was notable but did not bring in the kind of money to the firm that was expected of a partner. Alice worked with single mothers whose ex-husbands had failed to pay child support. But now she had to find ways to bring in clients who could afford to pay more money. And as much as she loved her husband, children, and her work, what Alice really wished for was an evening at home, soaking in a nice hot bath, and some peace and quiet to read a book.

HISTORY

Feminist family theory, not surprisingly, has its roots in the feminist movement. Feminism can be defined as the search for rights, opportunities, and identities women believe they deserve (Thomas 2000). Feminism in the United States might be said to have begun with the Seneca Falls Convention in 1848. Women—most notably Elizabeth Cady Stanton and Susan B. Anthony—fought for the right to vote;

a battle that was not won until ratification of the Nineteenth Amendment to the U.S. Constitution in 1920.

The modern feminist movement, or the second wave of feminism, began in the 1960s, concurrent with the civil rights movement, the anti–Vietnam War protests, and the general cultural challenge to the established institutional authorities and the "status quo." Leaders in this movement, like Betty Friedan, Gloria Steinem, and the National Organization for Women (NOW), worked toward resolution of issues such as equal pay and job training for women, reproductive choice, maternity leave, subsidized childcare, and an end to sex discrimination (Okin 1997).

The feminist movement of the 1960s and 1970s was characterized by several branches, each with a slightly different emphasis. *Liberal feminists*, like Friedan, spoke out against the subjugation of women, particularly in terms of their career paths. They stressed the importance of challenging laws and customs that restricted women's ability to achieve significant roles in society. *Marxist feminists* focused on the exploitation of women in their reproductive roles and in household labor, which maintained women as "second-class" citizens. *Radical feminists* emphasized male dominance as the problem with society, specifically male power and authority as oppressive to women. Radical feminists proposed that individuals should not be limited by masculine or feminine traits but should strive toward androgyny (a combination of both masculine and feminine traits). Families, as the source for patriarchy (male dominance) and oppression of women, could not be reformed into something positive and should therefore be avoided. *Socialist feminists* focused on women's liberation from the combined aspects of class oppression and patriarchy, particularly as found in families (Okin 1997; Osmond and Thorne 1993). Most feminists in the United States identify themselves primarily with the liberal branch of feminism (Shehan and Kammeyer 1997).

Within every field of study, knowledge is advanced by pioneers who propose cutting-edge ideas. Often we see that several extreme philosophies are presented, and after a time, a middle ground is reached that incorporates elements of each but is not as extreme as any individual original branch. This is also the case in feminism. By the 1980s, the distinctions between the feminist branches melted away. Feminists focused on issues related to women's second-class status in society and in families, reproductive rights, discrimination faced in the workplace, and how a gendered society affects the socialization of women (Okin 1997).

In the 1960s, one of the dominant theories of the family was structural functionalism. Structural functionalists proposed that roles in families should be divided in a "natural" way, generally based on sex. They proposed that families functioned best when men did the instrumental tasks of earning money and caring for basic needs, and women provided the expressive tasks of caretaking for the family members (Baca Zinn 2000). In 1972, sociologist Jessie Bernard wrote *The Future of Marriage* in which she contradicted this male and female perspective on marriage. Bernard found that there were two marriages—his and hers—and that his was better than hers. This finding was in direct opposition to the ideas presented in structural-functional theory.

Based on the work of Bernard and others, feminist family theorists began to consider status in families, causing them to analyze how males may dominate family power, both intentionally and unintentionally. When this happened, males benefited but females did not, thus leading to two types of marriages. Feminist family theorists recognized that male power and dominance were the result of socialization and challenged the concept that male power was natural and inevitable as suggested in structural functionalism. Feminist scholars examined how the family was influenced by social institutions and politics and how it was affected by the wider system of societal norms.

Feminist understanding was furthered in the 1980s by the groundbreaking work of Carol Gilligan, who analyzed the psychological and internal development of women's sense of self as different from that of men's. In her book, *In a Different Voice*, Gilligan (1982) explored how women defined their identity and understood reality through relationships, particularly intimate relationships. Their experiences must be taken into account in the analysis of their development, particularly as they internalized their sense of self and their moral code. She further clarified that, for women, nonviolence and caring for others dominated their views of justice and equality.

In the 1990s, feminist scholars sought to combine both the societal perspective and the individual perspective of oppression, paving the way for a third wave of feminism. This perspective focused on the multiple forms of oppression that might be experienced on an individual basis as a result of societal oppression. A "matrix of domination" (Collins 1998, 2000) could include oppression based on gender, class, race, ethnicity, sexual orientation, religion, or physical ability. For example, although all women experience relatively less status than men, White women experience relatively more status than women of color, middle-class women have more status than poor women, and heterosexual women have more status than lesbians or bisexual women. Multiracial feminism (MRF) is one example of feminism that developed from this third wave of feminism. MRF focuses on the intersection of gender, race, and ethnicity and challenging the assumptions that gender is the only issue that matters. It encourages us to understand "social location" as a more complex social phenomenon (Lorber 1998).

BASIC ASSUMPTIONS

Whereas there have been many different forms of feminism, feminist family theorists generally base their work on the following basic assumptions (Baca Zinn 2000; Osmond and Thorne 1993; Sollie and Leslie 1994):

Women's experiences are central to our understanding of families. Feminist family theorists begin with the question "What is the perspective of women?" Other theories have investigated the structures, the roles, and the resources people bring to their relationships. Feminist family scholars focus on women's perspectives and feelings, how women have been left out of the social and historical dialogue, and how women's issues have been ignored. Gender becomes the organizing concept. For example, the concept of "work" used to mean only paid work, which used to mean only men's work. Adding women's experience to the conceptualization of the term expanded it to include the unpaid labor that women did for families and communities as well.

According to Katherine Ferguson (as cited in Osmond and Thorne 1993), "Feminist theory is not simply about women, although it is that; it is about the world, but from the usually ignored and devalued vantage point of women's experiences" (592–593). Osmond and Thorne go on to add:

"By making women's experiences visible, feminist scholarship reveals gaps and distortions in knowledge that claims to be inclusive but in fact is based on the experiences of Euro-American, class-privileged, heterosexual men. Starting with the life experiences of women, in all their diversity, opens new epistemologies or ways of knowing the world." (593)

Feminist family theorists "analyze gender as a central principle of social organization and as something that all people do in their daily activities in every institution" (Osmond and Thorne 1993, 593). Two related concepts are that people exaggerate differences between men and women and that they use "these distinctions to legitimize and perpetuate power relations between men and women" (Osmond and Thorne 1993, 593).

Feminist family theory also addresses the development of women across the lifespan. Because women have been oppressed, their development has been hindered. The theory investigates how their development might be different if society did not constrain them (Thomas 2000) and asks questions about the experience from a gendered perspective (Gilligan 1982).

Gender is a socially constructed concept. When we talk about gender, we talk about something different from sex. Sex refers to biological assignment; gender refers to "the social meanings of masculinity and femininity that are produced through social processes and interactions that produce 'men' and 'women'" (Rutter and Schwartz 2000, 61).

Feminist family theorists make the point that gender roles are defined by society, not by biology. In the past, fathers went to work; mothers stayed home. Doctors were men; nurses were women. Business executives were men; secretaries were women. Boys were football players; girls were cheerleaders. These were socially constructed roles. In today's society, gender roles are changing, but there is still resistance. Women are members of the U.S. military, but they are not allowed in combat. Women are allowed on aircraft carriers but are not allowed on submarines. Contrast that with the Israeli army, in which women are drafted and fight alongside the men.

Language is an important element in socially constructed gender roles. In French, for example, all nouns have a male or female gender, usually indicated by the article (*le pere*—father, but *la mere*—mother). While English is not so obvious, words still have gender connotations. Usage becomes so natural that the implications of the word are not necessarily recognized. For example, using the term *mankind* instead of *humanity* implicitly excludes women.

A more subtle example is using the word *spinster* to refer to an unmarried, childless female. What word do we use to refer to an unmarried, childless male? There is no comparable word. We might use the word *bachelor*, but it doesn't have the negative connotation that the word *spinster* has. We define spinsters in terms of what they are not—not wives, not mothers (Allen 1994). Feminists pay attention to this kind of language use to ensure that women are not excluded from the social conversation.

Putting behaviors and labels together is termed *categorization*. Behaviors and roles are labeled and categorized according to gender. At a very early age, boys and girls learn what boys do, what girls do, what men do, and what women do. Behaviors by parents or other adults reinforce these categorizations. For instance, if a father were to see his three-year-old son dancing in a tutu, he might yell at the childcare provider, "Don't ever let my son wear that again! I want my son to grow up to be a real man!" Based on these comments, the boy will probably never play with the tutu again. The son's exploration in the fantasy play area of the childcare center had no social meaning until the father ascribed a strict gendered meaning to it.

Stratification is an outcome of categorization. Once tasks for men and women and boys and girls have been divided, people begin attributing value (even unintentionally) to those tasks. The value attributed to male tasks has generally been greater than the value attributed to female tasks. People who are more highly valued have more power in the society. Feminists refer to those with power as *privileged*. People with less value have less power (are less privileged) and can be oppressed because of this. In gender analysis, stratification is most commonly found when women's behaviors and roles are given less value than men's. For example, "women's work" like housework and childcare is unpaid whereas men's work is given greater value and pay in society. Feminists seek to illuminate the status differences so that women can become empowered.

One way to do this is to bring attention to the ways language influences, and perhaps perpetuates, stratification. For example, a man believes himself to be an equal partner and proudly proclaims that he "helps around the house," as if this were an unusual behavior, and therefore, notable. This implies that the woman is still in charge of, and ultimately responsible for, the housework because the man is just "helping out." The old gender roles are still there. Privilege is also evident in race, ethnicity, sexuality, nationality, age, physical ability, and religion (Collins 1998). Recognizing the multiple levels on which privilege is located, and the language that distinguishes status, is a complicated task. Many of the hierarchies we learn are learned in our families (Collins 1998; Walker 1993), and challenging those beliefs can be important but difficult.

Social and historical contexts are important. To understand women and families, we must understand the contexts in which they live. As they define women's roles in families, feminist family theorists look for meaning in both the sociological and the historical contexts. The analytical focus is not just on the individual and interpersonal relationships but also on the larger social forces that influence those relationships (Ferree 1990). Indeed, feminist family theorists contend that one must study the larger contexts to understand the position of women in the family. For example, the idealized concept of the nuclear family is still the norm in family research despite obvious demographic changes. The historical norm no longer applies to the new forms of family (which we will investigate below). But if a researcher does not take into account the larger social changes that are occurring, the nuclear family might remain the norm by which to measure; this could lead to incorrect conclusions.

There are many examples of how society may negatively impact women—politically, economically, religiously, socially—and those ultimately impact the family. Some examples are women being paid less for doing the same job; women's standards of living dropping more significantly after divorce than men's; insurance paying for Viagra but not for birth-control pills (even when they are prescribed for noncontraceptive medical reasons); and the fact that in most states the maximum age limit for adoption is higher for men than women. Many women face additional discrimination in terms of race, class, age, sexual orientation, and religion, which adds burdens to their families.

Investigating the influences of religion on culture, families, and women's experiences provides a good example of taking the sociocultural context into account. In the early Judeo-Christian world, women were considered property and were exchanged from father to husband along with a dowry of land, money, and livestock. Although this practice is not acceptable in the United States, remnants of the subjugation of women are still evident in some religious perspectives. For example, predominant in the discussion of women's roles in certain Christian families is the question of whether the man is the head of the home (as Christ heads the Church). The issue of power, as influenced by religious conventions and beliefs, needs to be considered in this important social context and in how it affects women and girls within families.

Trying to understand the multiple levels of influence on women's experiences is the starting point for feminist family scholars. Analyzing these contexts is the basis for understanding how society developed particular views of what women and men should be. Feminist family scholars refer to the act of analysis as social deconstruction. The reflection on and discussion of that analysis forms the basis of the social discourse of gender roles.

There are many forms of families. Feminist family theorists broaden our view of families. The traditional view of the nuclear family is an inadequate description of families in today's society. Economic forces, divorce, and other social factors have changed the nature of the family in the United States. Today, families include long-term cohabiting couples, single parents and their children, multiethnic families, multigenerational families, same-sex families, stepfamilies, remarried couples, and fictive kin.

Research data indicate that the most successful family relationships are based on loving friendship, models of equality, intimacy, caring, and cooperation. These qualities are applicable to more than simply the traditional nuclear family (Allen and Baber 1992). Limiting families to the traditional nuclear definition restricts women's roles to a subordinate position and discounts the experiences of women in diverse family forms.

Emphasis is placed on social change. One goal of feminist family theory is an activist orientation—that is, challenging the status quo. Feminists seek to empower the disenfranchised or those with less power (Sollie and Leslie 1994). They advocate looking at diverse family forms, challenging sexism, and challenging aspects of our society that act against women and children, including homophobia and male violence, so that we can bring the acceptance of difference and diversity to human interactions. *Feminist praxis* refers to the feminists' struggle to put their beliefs into action.

Not only do feminist family theorists seek to uncover gender biases, they also work to change existing gender relations in society, in the economy, in education, and in families (Allen and Baber 1992; MacDermid and Jurich 1992; Osmond and Thorne 1993). They seek to bring public attention to what had previously been considered private issues, particularly with respect to families. Their slogan is, "The personal is political." In other words, what happens personally to women has political and social impact. Given that much of a woman's experience is located within the family, one might also say that "the family is political" as well. You can see the dynamics of power both in society and in families, but power in families (whether of men having power over women or parents having power over children) has often been seen as "natural," and therefore, less likely to be challenged. Although few in today's society would dispute the fact that family members should not use their power to the extremes of child or wife abuse, feminist family scholars have continued to uncover less obvious forms of power differentials, such as differing amounts of influence in decision making, division of labor in the household, and differences in anticipated costs when leaving a relationship (Okin 1997).

One example of the personal-made-political revolves around the issue of *sexual agency*. Sexual agency refers to the degree of control one has over one's own sexuality and reproductive activity, clearly a personal and a private issue. Early feminists pointed out how power over one's reproductive capacity led to power in one's life, both personally and economically (Baber 1994; Sollie and Leslie 1994; Thompson 1992). Prior to the advent of reliable birth control, women (married or not) who wanted an active sexual life had to be prepared for pregnancy. Until the Pregnancy Discrimination Act of 1975 was passed, women could be fired from their jobs simply because they were pregnant. Years after the federal mandate was passed, young married women were still discriminated against in hiring because employers feared that they would get pregnant and leave their jobs. Jobs, therefore, were more likely to be given to young men or single women. As birth control became more reliable and the women's movement opened the workplace, women who were pregnant and women who were mothers had increased access to economic opportunities, and therefore, more power.

However, in the United States women who are pregnant or have children still suffer economically and socially. Pregnant women are not fired, but the law does not require that they be paid for their time-off to have the child. When they return to work, they often must pay for childcare thereby reducing their resources. Contrast this with several European countries that actually provide one-year paid maternity leave to women after childbirth and subsidize childcare so that all children receive the same quality of care when mothers return to work (Glazer 2006).

A subtler example of the personal-made-political may be seen in how women reflect on their roles. Many women believe that they need to stay at home with their children if they can. For economic reasons, most are unable to do that, and they often report feeling guilty about it. These women, and perhaps their families and society in general, interpret their inability to care for their children and work at the same time as a personal failure (Mahoney 1996). This guilt, generally not expressed by men, is an indication of how subtle and pervasive the social inequality is in our society.

There is no objective, unbiased observation of humans. Our observation is influenced by social realities. This is implied by "the personal-is-political" slogan that we talked about above. Something that is personal is by definition subjective and not objective.

Feminist family scholars have challenged the traditional approach to scientific understanding. Even the questions that we ask are influenced by how we are trained to be scientists (Thompson 1992). Traditional science teaches objectivity and observation free of bias with an emphasis on neutral "fact." Feminist family scholars challenge this perspective by saying that there is no neutral observation of humans. If our social realities are constructed based on a gendered perspective, then our perspective on reality, and therefore, the facts as we know them, are socially constructed. So, the real focus for feminists is not about obtaining objective facts but rather about understanding how people's social reality is constructed by understanding their experience (Sollie and Leslie 1994).

Feminist family scholars believe that families should not be treated as a unitary whole. If they are, the lesser voices in the family are oppressed. For example, if an abuser is asked, "How is your family life?" he might respond, "Fine." His abused spouse probably views the state of the family differently. The question should not be "How is your family life?" but rather "What is your experience of this relationship?" Feminist family scholars seek to uncover the voices in families that have been oppressed or neglected by traditional social science. In order to uncover these voices, feminist researchers are more likely to use case studies, qualitative analyses, and ethnographic studies in addition to traditional survey data.

PRIMARY TERMS AND CONCEPTS

Sex

Sex refers to one's biological assignment as genetically defined at birth—that is, male or female.

Gender

Gender refers to the social meanings and behaviors ascribed to one's sex, particularly with regard to roles and behaviors expected of someone because of one's sex. Gendered behaviors are learned as a result of socialization and are, therefore, the result of one's culture, not genetic predisposition. For example, we often give preschool boys trucks and preschool girls dolls to play with because that is what society, not genetics, deems acceptable.

Categorization

Categorization is the process of applying labels to behaviors and roles according to one's sex. Certain behaviors, roles, words, and symbols are considered "male" (e.g., aggression, playing with trucks, "strong," the color blue) whereas others are considered "female" (e.g., being nice, ballet, "soft," the color pink).

Stratification

Stratification refers to the application of value to different categories. Assigning social value to categories ranks those categories in the social context. For example, is it better to be nice or aggressive? In the first grade of elementary schools, it is probably better to be nice, and girls may be treated more positively than boys by their teachers and their peers in that social context. But in the social context of a Fortune 500 company, it is probably more highly valued to be aggressive than nice, so a woman who has been socialized only to be nice and never encouraged to learn any aggressive skills probably won't ever be hired as a chief executive officer, no matter how well educated she may be.

Privilege

Privilege refers to the social status given to one with more power and value in society. The concept of privilege urges feminists to ask not only who has power but who does not and to ensure that those who have been previously marginalized and oppressed by those who have had power and privilege are now included in the matrix of voices represented.

Social Deconstruction

The first step in the analysis of how views of reality are constructed by social interactions, particularly in light of how gendered meanings are developed, is social deconstruction (see fig. 8.1). It involves the consideration of how society has categorized and assigned values to behaviors and roles according to sex.

Social Discourse

The next step in the analysis, social discourse, brings the analysis of social deconstruction into the "conversation" of gender expectations and behaviors. Social discourse raises awareness of the analysis into the work of social scientists through examining the ways in which we invite people to participate in the dialogue of deconstruction, ensuring that those who do not have privilege are included in the conversations. It challenges us to question how we focus our questions, and how we analyze the data.

Praxis

The step after analysis, in which beliefs and values are put into action, is praxis. For feminist family scholars, this includes advocacy for women, inclusiveness in language and behavior, and reflecting on one's own behavior with intention.

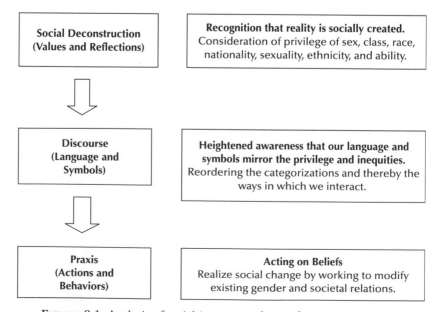

FIGURE 8.1 Analysis of social interaction from a feminist perspective.

COMMON AREAS OF RESEARCH
AND APPLICATION

Division of Labor

One of the major areas of feminist research is division of labor within the family. Labor divisions are often constructed according to gender, including both paid and unpaid labor in our society. The stereotypic family has been the traditional, idealized, nuclear family, in which the father is the breadwinner and the mother stays home to care for the house and children. Although the nuclear family is no longer representative of most families in the United States today, we often still see people reacting to women's labor outside the home as "intrusive" because of our societal expectations that the woman's first responsibility is to home. Further, unpaid work in our society is not considered "real work." The work that is done at home—maintaining the home, paying the bills, raising the children, tutoring the children, ferrying the children back and forth to their activities, nursing, getting up in the middle of the night, cooking, and cleaning—are not considered valuable work in our society because these jobs do not produce an income (Glazer 2006).

Even as women enter the workforce in increasingly higher-status, higher-income professional roles, they are still expected to be "wives" in spite of the outside work. Many high-level corporate jobs are structured according to the assumption that a worker has a partner for support thereby creating what is essentially a two-person career. One partner, typically the male, is expected to work long hours, as if he does not need to worry about the needs of the children and the rest of the family because those needs will be met by the wife. The outcomes of this arrangement oppress both men and women and are perpetuated by social norms that feminist family scholars challenge. Furthermore, analyses of dual-earner couples show that women continue to do the majority of household tasks and childcare in addition to their full-time jobs (Noonan, Estes, and Glass 2007).

This is not a result of income, as it has been shown that even women who are the primary wage earners for their families do more housework and childcare than their husbands. This is a result of upholding societal gender role norms. In the extreme, it has even been shown that men who are financially dependent on their wives do even less housework than other men—this is how they "do gender." They exert their power by reverting to even more traditional gender roles at home because they cannot fulfill their traditional role of breadwinner. Thus, the more money women begin to earn within a relationship, the more threatened gender roles become, and the more traditional gender roles within the household become (Mannino and Deutsch 2007).

In her analysis of this "second shift," Hochschild (1989) found that women in general not only did more housework and childcare but also often believed that it was their responsibility. Feminist family theorists analyze this division of labor from an equity perspective and also deconstruct the reality of why a woman would believe those jobs are her responsibility.

Family Violence

A second application of feminist family study is family violence. According to feminist family scholars, in our attempt to maintain privacy in the family, we have failed in our social obligations to identify injustices in the family (Wood 1998). Families are not always the "havens of love, goodwill, and affection" that we would like to believe exist, and families are not safe places for many women and children.

While some homes are places that foster support for many of us, many other homes are places where "abuse, violence, exploitation, cruelty and persisting inequities fester for far too many citizens in our country" (Wood 1998, 129). By drawing attention to such abuse in families, feminist family scholars have identified facts about families that others have not noticed. For example, a violent act against a woman is perpetrated every twelve to eighteen seconds in the United States, and four women die each day because of family violence (Wood 1998). In some studies of dating violence, as many as 50 percent of college men admitted that they had sexually coerced a woman against her wishes, and one-third admitted that they would commit rape if they could be certain no one would find out (Wood 1998).

Recent research has expanded this discussion outside of the family. Hines (2007) looked at sexual coercion in romantic relationships using a college aged sample and found further support for the notion that men force women to engage in sexual behaviors because of the need to dominate them, or because they feel the need to show they have more power than them. Similarly, this is the result of maintaining traditional gender roles in which men are powerful and aggressive and women are passive and less assertive, especially sexually.

Feminist family theorists studying violence in families and intimate relationships have expanded the definitions of violence to include isolation, threats, and forced economic dependence (Thompson and Walker 1995). They have also reflected on the ways in which societal behaviors affect those already oppressed. For example, feminist family scholars have called attention to the fact that police officers sometimes refuse to interfere in domestic disputes or advise victims not to prosecute batterers. They have noted that our music has encouraged women to "stand by your man;" our cosmetic counters and lingerie departments have encouraged women to fulfill social prescriptions for femininity; and our junior high schools have stood by a tradition of relegating girls to supporting roles as cheerleaders while boys learn aggression on the sports field.

Although it is part of feminist family scholarship to identify the problems of oppression and inequities in our society, it is also imperative that feminist family scholarship generates alternatives and seeks ways to empower the oppressed and disenfranchised. Feminist family scholars identify issues and also seek ways to advocate on behalf of women and their families through education and support.

Disordered Eating

Using feminist theory to study disordered eating has been common for the last two decades. Some research suggests that as women gain power and status in society, they are pressured to conform to even more unrealistic appearance standards as a means of oppression. Jung and Forbes (2007) recently provided further support of this belief while also adding that although standards of beauty vary across cultures, they are used outside of the United States, in countries such as China and Korea to help the patriarchy maintain control.

Similarly, Mensinger, Bonifazi, and LaRosa (2007) found that societal changes are potentially responsible for the increased incidence of disordered eating among adolescent girls. Their research was based on the superwoman ideal which is the notion that women are feeling societal pressure to exhibit both feminine (i.e., appearance and appropriate dating behaviors) and masculine (academic excellence) traits in order to succeed in today's society. This pressure to excel, almost to the point of perfection, in both arenas has led to higher levels of disordered eating among adolescent girls. Both of these studies provide implications for our need to educate women about the importance of both self-fulfillment and maintaining realistic expectations while also striving to be the best they can possibly be.

CRITIQUE

Feminist family theory can be used to analyze certain aspects of family relations. It includes a wide range of "family types" within its definition of a "family unit." Other theories are narrower in their scope. Feminist family theory sheds light on other issues that are neglected or ignored by other theories, such as the male-oriented perspective of what was previously considered "objective" research. It attempts to lend more equal weight to women's issues in family interactions and to downplay the traditional gender roles of some other theories.

Feminist family theory is not without its critics, though. Feminism has been criticized as being oppressive to men by focusing only on issues that affect women. Feminist family scholars refute this by saying that issues that are important to women in families are important to men as well.

Feminist family theory has been criticized for working outside the parameters and paradigms of the traditional, scientific base of knowledge. Critics say that although science is not totally value-free, we should strive to present the information in the best and clearest way without becoming involved in the data. Feminist family scholars respond that because it is impossible to be truly objective, the most truthful thing is to admit our subjectivity and work hard to reflect on our role as researchers rather than deny its influence in the research process.

Feminist family theorists have also been criticized for their activist position. Social scientists, maintaining an objective stance, have frequently preferred being describers of events rather than facilitators of change. Feminist scholars argue that it is impossible to fully embrace and understand the oppression of the disenfranchised without being ethically bound to do something to alter that reality. Issues of inequity in relationships, such as division of labor in families, economic stability and support, and ways in which society devalues women's work and limits opportunities, should be addressed by those with power and privilege.

Feminist family theorists have also been criticized for working against traditional nuclear families. But the reality is that the traditional nuclear family is no longer the dominant norm. Feminist scholars argue that the inequality within families may actually lend itself to the dissolution of the traditional nuclear family as power differentials enter into the conversations, economy, and distribution of labor in American families.

Finally, some have challenged feminist family theory because, they claim, it pays too much attention to the oppression of one group—women—to the exclusion of other forms of oppression (e.g., by race, ethnicity, age, disability, religion, etc.). Although helping women find their voices is paramount in today's multicultural climate, exploring dynamics related to race, culture, class, and sexuality are also increasingly important (Ashner 2007). For example, standards for motherhood are often based on a White middle-class norm which leads to the oppression of working-class and working poor mothers in today's society (Jones 2007). Thus, while attempting to decrease the oppression of mothers, women of lower economic standing are simultaneously being oppressed. Race is another variable that needs to be disentangled. Black feminism has developed as a result of the need to recognize women who struggle with more than one type of oppression. It attempts to find a balance between raising consciousness based on race and raising consciousness based on gender (Few 2007). Exploring the diverse experiences of women across these many variables is a challenge worthy of our attention in the years to come.

APPLICATION

1. Alice and Bob Stephens seem to have a good marriage, a stable family, and two good jobs. In many ways, they are part of a privileged class. But it is clear that, at least on this night, there are two marriages—his and hers. Bob relies on Alice to take care of the "little things" that keep their family life going smoothly, yet Alice is troubled and feeling overwhelmed by keeping up with all those little things. Answer the following questions based on their situation:
   a. Compare Alice's experiences and Bob's experiences. What are some of the privileges they have? What are some of the inequities? Identify ways in which those inequities are intentional. Are there some inequities that are not intentional? If so, why do they exist?
   b. In what ways are their perspectives on their marriage different?
   c. How are Alice's and Bob's lives impacted by social norms and expectations?
   d. What social and/or historical contexts should be taken into account when attempting to understand the Stephens' family?
   e. Based on what you have learned studying feminist family theory, what recommendations for change might you suggest if Alice and Bob came in for counseling?
   f. If Bob and Alice were to divorce, how might the consequences of that divorce be different for each of them? What role would privilege play?
   g. If you wanted to study marriages like the Stephens', how might you design your research so that both Bob and Alice had equal voice in the study? What differences do you think you would find between the men and the women?

2. Katherine Allen talks about making the personal political in "Feminist Visions for Transforming Families: Desire and Equity Then and Now," which is provided under Sample Reading at the end of this chapter. Using this as a model, how can you do this in your own life?

REFERENCES

Allen, K. R. 1994. Feminist reflections on lifelong single women. In *Gender, families, and close relationships: Feminist research journeys*, ed. L. D. Sollie and L. A. Leslie, 97–119. Thousand Oaks, CA: Sage.

Allen, K. R., and K. M. Baber. 1992. Starting a revolution in family life education: A feminist vision. *Family Relations* 41: 378–384.

Ashner, N. 2007. Made in the (multicultural) U.S.A.: Unpacking tensions of race, culture, gender, and sexuality in education. *Educational Researcher* 36(2): 65–74.

Baber, K. M. 1994. Studying women's sexualities: Feminist transformations. In *Gender, families, and close relationships: Feminist research journeys*, ed. L. D. Sollie and L. A. Leslie, 50–73. Thousand Oaks, CA: Sage.

Baca Zinn, M. 2000. Feminism and family studies for a new century. *The Annals of the American Academy of Political and Social Science (AAPSS)* 571: 42–56.

Bernard, J. 1972. *The future of marriage*. New York: World Publishing.

Collins, P. H. 1998. It's all in the family: Intersections of gender, race, and nation. *Hypatia* 13: 62–82.

———. 2000. *Black feminist thought: Knowledge, consciousness, and the politics of empowerment*. 2nd ed. New York: Routledge.

Ferree, M. M. 1990. Beyond separate spheres: Feminism and family research. *Journal of Marriage and the Family* 52: 866–884.

Few, A. L. 2007. Integrating black consciousness and critical race feminism into family studies research. *Journal of Family Issues* 28: 452–473.

Gilligan, C. 1982. *In a different voice: Psychological theory and women's development*. Cambridge, MA: Harvard University Press.

Glazer, S. 2006. Future of feminism. *CQ Researcher* 16(14): 313–336.

Hines, D. A. 2007. Predictors of sexual coercion against women and men: A multilevel, multi-national study of university students. *Archives of Sexual Behavior* 36(3): 403–423.

Hochschild, A. R. 1989. *The second shift: Working parents and the revolution at home*. New York: Viking/Penguin.

Jones, S. 2007. Working-poor mothers and middle-class others: Psychosocial considerations in home–school relations and research. *Anthropology and Education Quarterly* 38(2): 159–178.

Jung, J., and G. B. Forbes. 2007. Body dissatisfaction and disordered eating among college women in China, South Korea, and the United States: Contrasting predictions from sociocultural and feminist theories. *Psychology of Women Quarterly* 31: 381–393.

Lorber, J. 1998. *Gender inequality: Feminist theories and politics*. Los Angeles: Roxbury.

MacDermid, S. M., and J. A. Jurich. 1992. Feminist teaching: Effective education. *Family Relations* 41: 31–39.

Mahoney, A. R. 1996. Children, families, and feminism: Perspectives on teaching. *Early Childhood Education Journal* 23: 191–196.

Mannino, C. A., and F. M. Deutsch. 2007. Changing the division of household labor: A nego-tiated process between partners. *Sex Roles* 56(5–6): 309–324.

Mensinger, J. L., D. Z. Bonifazi, and J. LaRosa. 2007. Perceived gender role prescriptions in schools, the Superwoman ideal, and disordered eating among adolescent girls. *Sex Roles* 57: 557–568.

Noonan, M. C., S. B. Estes, and J. S. Glass. 2007. Do workplace flexibility policies influence time spent in domestic labor? *Journal of Family Issues* 28: 263–289.

Okin, S. M. 1997. Families and feminist theory: Some past and present issues. In *Feminism and families*, ed. H. L. Nelson, 13–26. New York: Routledge.

Osmond, M. W., and B. Thorne. 1993. Feminist theories: The social construction of gender in families and society. In *Sourcebook of family theories and methods*, ed. P. G. Boss, W. J. Doherty, R. LaRossa, W. R. Schumm, and S. K. Steinmetz, 591–626. New York: Plenum.

Rutter, V., and P. Schwartz. 2000. Gender, marriage, and diverse possibilities for cross-sex and same-sex pairs. In *Handbook of family diversity*, ed. D. H. Demo, K. R. Allen, and M. A. Fine, 59–81. New York: Oxford.

Shehan, C. L., and K. C. W. Kammeyer. 1997. *Marriages and families: Reflections of a gendered society*. Needham Heights, MA: Allyn and Bacon.

Sollie, L. D., and L. A. Leslie. 1994. *Gender, families, and close Relationships: Feminist research journeys*. Thousand Oaks, CA: Sage.

Thomas, R. M. 2000. *Recent theories of human development*. Thousand Oaks, CA: Sage.

Thompson, L. 1992. Feminist methodology for family studies. *Journal of Marriage and the Family* 54: 3–18.

Thompson, L., and A. J. Walker. 1995. The place of feminism in family studies. *Journal of Marriage and the Family* 57: 847–865.

Walker, A. J. 1993. Teaching about race, gender, and class diversity in the United States families. *Family Relations* 42: 342–350.

Wood, J. T. 1998. Ethics, justice, and the "private sphere." *Women's Studies in Communication* 21: 127–149.

SAMPLE READING

Allen, K. R. 2001. Feminist visions for transforming families: Desire and equity then and now. *Journal of Family Issues* 22(6): 791–809.

This article looks at feminism from a social-historical perspective. Dr. Allen presents a model for analyzing your own life from a feminist perspective. She reviews feminist theories and political activism, while also showing how the personal is political.

SAMPLE READING

FEMINIST VISIONS FOR
TRANSFORMING FAMILIES
Desire and Equality Then and Now

Katherine R. Allen
Virginia Polytechnic Institute
and State University

Feminist visions for transforming families must be placed in social-historical context, consciously referencing the past, grounded in the present, and envisioning the future. In this article, I address topics that often run counter to prevailing assumptions about family development and change. The method I use to construct my argument is to rely on my own structural and processual connections to the ideologies and activism I describe. I weave in stories from my private life to illustrate a key principle of feminism, that the personal is political. What occurs in private life is a reflection of power relations in society. The analytic strategy I employ in this article is to reveal the connection between the personal and political by using my own life as a bridge for the transfer of feminist insights into family studies. My aim is to invite others into the conscious, reflexive practice of applying feminist knowledge to one's own life and scholarship. In reading these ideas, saturated with personal and political implications, I trust others will take the risk to incorporate their own resonances about private life and power relations. By inviting others into their own feminist journey from "silence to language to

Author's Note: *An earlier version of this article was presented as the closing plenary at the Groves 2000 Conference on Marriage and the Family, Asheville, North Carolina, June 17, 2000. Many thanks to Marilyn Coleman, Larry Ganong, Stacey Floyd-Thomas, and an anonymous reviewer for their helpful comments on this article.*

Using a social-historical perpective, the author provides a synthesis of key feminist ideas that have been influential in the lives of women and their families. The author addresses a variety of feminist theories and strategies for knowledge production. These ideas are illustrated with examples from her own life course as a way to demonstrate the transformative value of feminist insights for family studies.

JOURNAL OF FAMILY ISSUES, Vol. 22 No. 6, September 2001 791–809
© 2001 Sage Publications

action" (Collins, 1990, p. 112), I show one way that we as a community of scholars can produce more realistic perspectives about the families we study (Allen, 2000).

DEFINING FEMINISM

Like building a sandcastle on the beach, my working definition *of feminism* reflects the historical moment in which it is posed. In sharing this definition, I am aware of the elements that attempt to knock down my metaphoric sandcastle—to whisk it away with the daily flow of the tides or to flagrantly step on it as a mischievous child might do when no one is looking. Whatever the tide or the children do not level, the cleaning machines that rumble down the beach after dark surely will. Like sand fashioned into temporary figures, feminism can never be encapsulated in a singular treatise, and neither can it remain static after being printed on the page. In proposing a working definition *of feminism,* I take the risk of representing and misrepresenting in unique ways the ideas that fascinate me.

With these caveats in mind, I work toward an understanding of feminism that holds such constraints lightly and still has the courage to be stated. It is dangerous to speak seriously as a feminist scholar in a field in which feminist ideas continue to be marginalized (Thompson & Walker, 1995). Human perceptions and relationships are so fragile and tentative that the opportunities for misunderstanding are vast. The potential for connecting around the politicized inquiry associated with feminist family scholarship requires an inclusive, open mind and a patient, loving heart (Allen, 2000). The rewards for looking at family life through a feminist lens include a deepening connection between how we live and what we study. Feminism is against the status quo. It is an activist endeavor with the goal of social change.

Feminism is a way of being in the world (ontology), a way of investigating and analyzing the world (methodology), and a theory or model of how we know what we know about the world (epistemology) (for variations on these analytic categories, see Cook & Fonow, 1986; Harding, 1987; Hawkesworth, 1989; Riger, 1998). Feminism is not just an idea or a theory; it is also a *praxis,* the term that Marx used to "distinguish between what one does and what one thinks and to distinguish revolutionary practice from other types of activity" (Nielsen, 1990, p. 34). Praxis is "that continuous reflexive integration of thought, desire, and action" (Simon, 1992, p. 49). Nielsen (1990) further explained that praxis, originating with critical theory, is the active, reflective process that allows us to demystify and expose the real nature of the power relations that drive human interactions and transactions and motivate the desire for social change. Feminist praxis is a conscious, inclusive, and impassioned way of thinking about and operating in the world (Allen, 2000).

Feminism is a liberationist project emerging most recently from the civil rights movement for American Blacks in the 1950s and 1960s and spawning the gay liberation movement in the 1970s. The women's liberation movement, or second-wave feminism, was ignited in the mid-1960s as more and more women started to speak about what they were enduring under capitalist patriarchy, topics that until the publication of Friedan's (1963) *The Feminine Mystique* were still taboo to either name or discuss (Brownmiller, 1999). The grassroots attempt to emancipate women from oppression, starting in consciousness-raising (CR) groups, grew into a multitude of liberationist efforts (Christensen, 1997). In its current manifestations, feminism is joined with other ideologies and practices embraced by those on the margins to seek justice for all people exploited by global patriarchal capitalism (see Agger, 1998; Alexander & Mohanty, 1997; Ebert, 1996; White, 1991). Combining theory and praxis, then, feminism is a conscious action with the goal of unsettling the normativity (e.g., status quo) that gives unearned privileges to an elite few and exploits the labor, life, and desire of multiple others (Collins, 1990; Lorde, 1984; McIntosh, 1995). This exploitation occurs in systematic ways through the structural and ideological mechanisms of racism, sexism, heterosexism, classism, ethnocentrism, ageism, able-bodyism, and colonialism.

Feminism shares with other critical theories and practices a challenge to the oppressive conditions that contribute to the individual's alienation from self, other, and society by unfairly harming some and irrationally privileging others (Agger, 1998). There are countless varieties of feminism and, as in any liberationist movement, many internal and external debates. For example, Brownmiller (1999) chronicled the birth, growth, and transformation of the women's movement, addressing key feminist issues for the 30 years following 1968, including abortion, rape, heterosexuality and lesbianism, racial injustice, sexual harassment, and pornography. Also, in a recent exchange in the premier journal for feminist scholarship. *Signs: Journal of Women in Culture and Society*, Walby (2001a, 2001b), Harding (2001), and Sprague (2001) debated current ideas about the role of science in feminist scholarship. Each day, each conversation, each published work brings a new way to pose a feminist perspective of knowing, being, and acting in the world.

There are many feminist theories (for various accounts, see Ebert, 1996; Herrmann & Stewart, 1994; Jaggar & Rothenberg, 1984; Rosser, 1992; Spender, 1983), including some of the following. Feminism has a liberal slant, wanting to secure equal rights and help women get their fair share of the economic and legal pie. Feminism has a radical slant, characterized by the admonition to "get your laws and your hands off my body." Feminism has a lesbian slant, in which women choose a woman-centered private life in congruence with their politics as well as their desire (Rich, 1980). Feminism has a cultural slant of valorizing and celebrating women's unique and, to some, superior ways of being in the world, as in "men have had the power for so long, and look at what a mess they've made of things." Feminism has a multicultural slant, decentering what Morrison (1992) called *whitethings* as the unquestioned authority on agency and free space for all people, including people of color. Feminism has a critical slant, aimed at redistributing the means and ends of production so that "the hand that picks the grapes also gets to drink the wine."

LOCATING MYSELF IN FEMINISM

The feminisms from which I draw traverse all of these categories. As an educated, middle-class. White woman who came of age and into a radical consciousness in the second wave of feminist activity in the United States, I have certain unearned privileges that to an extent tolerate and even indulge my challenge of male dominance. When I am seeking equity in work, pay, and legal rights, I am aligned with liberal feminism (Rosser, 1992). When I came to realize that the feelings I had for another woman were passionate love—what women in the 19th century called "the love that dared not speak its name" (Faderman, 1991)—I claimed a lesbian life, aligning myself with lesbian feminism. The merger of lesbianism and feminism is a cohort phenomenon initiated by women who came of age in the late 1960s and early 1970s (Faderman, 1991). I am a lesbian feminist, then, in the sense that I found in feminism congruence between my lived reality of desiring an end to embodied oppression and my liberationist epistemology. I abandoned heterosexual privilege and let my career slow down to pursue this love that would change my standpoint or the way I looked at the world. When I am critical of feminist ideologies and practices in and of themselves or questioning of my own lesbian standpoint, I am a postmodern feminist (Elam & Wiegman, 1995; Gagnier, 1990).

I am also a critical antiracist White feminist (Frankenberg, 1993), which brings me to the work that ignites my passion now, interrogating my own race and class privilege, opening myself to a feminist politics in which I seek to understand how my identity as a middle-class White woman is complicit in the oppression of others (Allen, 2000). Antiracist feminism, with ties to radical-critical theory (Osmond, 1987), gives me the tools to deconstruct the ways that I am marked by the privilege and power of White patriarchal wealth (Alexander & Mohanty, 1997; Collins, 1990; Ellsworth, 1997; McIntosh, 1995). My praxis is to uncover how I manipulate and employ privilege for my own gain so that I can consciously oppose any participation in racist, classist, or sexist action. I wish to use my knowledge of how unearned privilege wounds those without it to challenge and redirect my impulse to reach for the choicest piece of pie.

Looking through the lens of diverse feminist perspectives on methodology (Harding, 1998), when conducting research in family gerontology, I am a feminist empiricist (Allen, Blieszner, Roberto, Farnsworth, & Wilcox, 1999). When combining my identity politics as an antiracist lesbian feminist, I am drawing from feminist standpoint theory (e.g., Allen, 2000). When applying postmodern theory to feminist family science as a reconstructionist of women's experiences in families (Baber & Allen, 1992), I am a feminist postmodernist. Feminists both critique and may incorporate any or all of the following perspectives on science: empiricist, standpoint, and postmodern (Harding, 1987; Hawkesworth, 1989; Riger, 1998; Rosser, 1992).

Feminism is a worldview, but it is also a home base. Feminism is a way of living in which I can struggle free from the alienating bonds of patriarchal expectations for a truncated life and envision and then become an authentic self even as I know that authenticity can never be fully realized (Sawhney, 1995). Feminism gives me a position from which to tell the truth, particularly to myself, even if it means speaking bitterness from my raised consciousness. Feminism gives me the courage to love those I desire with passion and without shame. Feminism is the place where my deepest connections are found. With an active feminist awareness, I can name my fears about the future, face my demons from the past, handle the assaults of an unforgiving world, and find joy in living through the process of becoming as fully conscious as my mind, heart, spirit, and body allow (see Krieger, 1996, for an elegant evocation of such a synthesis). This process, of course, has been called many things, from *conscientization* (Freire, 1970/1997), to *enlightenment* (Wilber, 1998), and even *salvation* or *serenity*. Feminists did not make it up, but at the same time, feminist scholars and activists have generated innovative ways to pursue the conscious desire for truth, justice, equality, integrity, and freedom in terms of exploring sexism (Morgan, 1970), materialism (Ebert, 1996), and racism (Christensen, 1997; Collins, 1990), among other manifestations of oppression. With this as background, I now illustrate feminist desire and equality in the past and present, constructing a sense of feminist history and its influence on family change.

LOVE AS EQUALS IN THE 19TH CENTURY

Consider the following passage describing "the beautiful friendship of two ladies" and the time frame in which it was written:

> In their youthful days, they took each other as companions for life, and this union, no less sacred to them than the tie of marriage, has subsisted, in uninterrupted harmony, for 40 years, during which they have shared each others' occupations and pleasures and works of charity while in health, and watched over each other tenderly in sickness...They slept on the same pillow and had a common purse, and adopted each others relations, and...I would tell you of their dwelling, encircled with roses...and I would speak of the friendly attentions which their neighbors, people of kind hearts and simple manners, seem to take pleasure in bestowing upon them. (Faderman, 1991, p. 1)

This passage was published in an American newspaper in 1843 by William Cullen Bryant, describing a trip to Vermont, where he met these unmarried women (e.g., "maiden ladies") who lived together. In the 19th century, female same-sex love, or *romantic friendship,* was a respected social institution in America. At the height of the Industrial Revolution, the worlds of White middle-class men and women were highly segregated. It was during this time that contemporary gender roles took root. Men worked outside the home in the business world, and women of means withdrew from the world of commerce to the female world of love and ritual (Smith-Rosenberg, 1975).

Gender-segregated marriage was a radical departure from the corporate family unit common in Colonial America over the previous two centuries, where the homestead was the center of life and survival (Hareven, 1991). In the 19th century, women were not yet full citizens. The U.S. Constitution enfranchised only one third of the population: White, landowning men. Women, native people, and people of color were excluded. Black males, in principle, gained the right to vote with the passage of the 15th Amendment in 1870, but in practice, the Black Codes and Jim Crow laws, particularly in the South, severely restricted full citizenship for those of African descent whose ancestors had been brought to this country by force (Bell, 1992; D'Emilio & Freedman, 1997). Women derived their rights through men; a woman had no sovereignty over her own body, children, or livelihood.

Perhaps because women were second-class citizens, their love for each other did not threaten the establishment. Women who loved other women were invisible (Faderman, 1981). There was no such thing as a lesbian until the late 19th century because women were not believed to be sexual. By the time the emerging discipline of modern sexology came into being, women who loved each other passionately were now considered deviant and labeled as *female sexual inverts* (D'Emilio & Freedman, 1997; Gagnon & Parker, 1995).

By the 20th century, women who realized they were lesbian had little chance to lead an authentic life (Faderman, 1991). They were forced to deny, repress, or hide their feelings because being *out* had serious consequences. Some women did sacrifice what little freedom they had throughout the past century. Despite being labeled as *other,* they carved out a life economically, socially, and sexually independent of men, creating a lesbian subculture, most notably among working-class butch or femme women, that never existed before love between women was defined as abnormal and unusual (Davis & Kennedy, 1986; Faderman, 1991). Their legacy for 21st-century women is that now some women find a lesbian identity viable, appropriate, and healthy (Baber & Allen, 1992). For some, it is a consciously chosen way of life.

In the 19th century, women of color experienced double and triple jeopardy in their struggle for full citizenship (Dill, 1988). The Chinese Exclusion Act of 1882 prohibited entry of Chinese women except as prostitutes or wives of merchants, teachers, and students. The bulk of Chinese immigrants were laborers, and their wives and daughters were not allowed to immigrate (Chow, 1998). By 1890, females comprised about 3% of the Chinese population in the United States. Most of these women had been sold to men in Hong Kong who later forced them into prostitution. Chinese women were not permitted to enter this country until 1943 when the Chinese Exclusion Act of 1882 was repealed (Chow, 1998). Consider, as well, the following quote from an older Black woman that reveals a profound understanding of female oppression in the context of race difference: "The black woman is the white man's mule and the white woman is his dog" (Collins, 1990, p. 106). One was forced to work much harder than the other, but both women were still the personal property of the master. Feminist historians have uncovered the reality of the constraints placed on women, retelling history from perspectives other than military and political events. They have uncovered ways that women of all backgrounds resisted and created their own lives in spite of the severe restrictions carved into law and everyday practice (Kerber & DeHart-Mathews, 1987).

FEMINIST EXPERIMENTS FOR RADICAL CHANGE IN THE 20TH CENTURY

After a 70-year struggle of organized activism on many fronts, women earned the right to vote in 1920 with the passage of the 19th Amendment. The next major historic milestone did not occur until half a century later when another significant female cultural revolution was ignited. Feminist essayist Robin Morgan, editor of the classic 1970 text *Sisterhood Is Powerful,* called the New Left and its student members "the little boys movement" because its leaders were White, middle-class young men who were challenging the hegemonic, militaristic, and capitalist values of their fathers. Yet few acknowledged their debts to the Black civil rights movement. Fewer recognized how they were repeating the very patriarchal privilege of the establishment males that they were rebelling against by using women only as sex partners and servants. Second-wave feminism arose out of women's dissatisfaction that they were often the invisible laborers in all the liberation movements in which they were involved. Male leaders and partners were not taking their quest for or right to emancipation seriously.

Women started rap groups, or CR groups, anywhere and everywhere—suburban kitchens, urban mental health centers, and church basements. I attended my first "speak out" in 1972 when I was a freshman at San Diego State University. I was alarmed by observing women who were speaking and acting with anger. I felt like I was witnessing something taboo, obscene, foreign, and wrong when I heard women speak their bitterness by naming and challenging the patriarchy that severely restricted their opportunities in life.

A year later, I transferred to the University of Connecticut and joined my first CR group. We were a collection of undergraduate and graduate students, faculty wives, women exploring their feelings for other women, and young mothers in turmoil over their seemingly isolated inability to be satisfied with the domestic monotony of their lives. I still have the mimeographed sheets of questions that were distributed in the CR group, which I reread periodically to remind myself that dialogue has always been a revolutionary self-help activity (Freire, 1970/1997). This early process of interrogating the social construction of gender steered me toward the qualitative methodologies I employ as a social scientist today.

We explored messages and expectations from childhood, puberty, and young adulthood. We addressed sex roles and perceptions of masculinity/femininity. We discussed what virginity meant to us and whether any of us still had it. We spent a lot of time discussing our bodies and self-image. We talked about sex, men, and men's bodies—our desire for them but our disappointment that men did not respond to us in the physical and emotional ways we wanted. We called ourselves *emotional lesbians* and wore buttons announcing "Together Women Together." Acknowledging that we felt more comfortable in female space but being too afraid to cross some imaginary line into an authentically embodied space, most of us were unable to transcend the rigid boundaries that heterosexism enforced on all of us from birth. We fought and challenged each other. It was in that context that I began to consciously practice the self-interrogation and rhetorical skills that I incorporate into my scholarship and teaching today.

As embarrassing as it is to tell, I take the risk to share the following story because only in our most vulnerable disclosures can we reveal the truth of how inauthenticity is internalized. Krieger (1991, 1996) explained that such theorized self-disclosure, in which one tells on oneself, is a particular window into the general phenomenon of structural oppression. One Tuesday night in 1975, I was in the midst of describing to my CR sisters how I no longer wanted to go out with a guy I was seeing because he was too nice. My friends pressed me for further information. Baffled by my own untheorized analysis of what was wrong with my partner, I mumbled something about his penis being too small. One of the older participants in the group—a woman in her late 40s who had raised five children and whose husband, a psychology professor, had a reputation for sleeping with students—challenged the absurdity of what I was saying: "What do you mean, 'too nice'?" "What do you mean, 'too small'?" She attacked these parroted gendered messages that I had internalized—messages that I needed a real man who was rough around the edges and well endowed underneath his clothes—to make me a woman. I broke into tears, I felt hatred for her, I shot back with something like, "You are a pathetic wife who puts up with your husband's infidelity in the name of love," but the truth is, she got to me. She broke through my denial, the distorted sexual script that had been spoon-fed to me by my sexist culture. She held up a mirror so that I could confront the convoluted fundamentals of heterosexuality that were motivating my behavior and poisoning any potential partnership with a man.

That CR group endured for the 3 years I spent as an undergraduate at Connecticut. In all its messy confusion and gut-wrenching challenges, it got me through young adulthood and paved the way for deepening my feminist consciousness through reading political texts—a process that taught me how to theorize my experience. Faderman (1991) explained that out of this CR context, a new vision of equality emerged.

In its purest form, it became the lesbian feminism of the 1970s and 1980s, before AIDS devastated the gay male community in the 1980s (Gagnon & Parker, 1995) and before the lesbian baby boom in the 1980s and 1990s (Patterson, 1994). Similar to the anomalous decade of the 1950s, with the majority of women staying at home, men in the workforce, and the baby boom in full force (Coontz, 1992), lesbian feminism as a political ideal is historically situated—a product of the late 20th-century liberation movements.

Lesbian feminism began with a radical separatist impulse. Women who loved women defined themselves in opposition to patriarchy and in opposition to the reformers in the National Organization for Women who wanted lesbians purged from the White middle-class women's movement (Brownmiller, 1999). But separatism is a project that is doomed to failure, at least on a large scale, as many of the alternative communities (e.g., Shakers, Oneidans, and Free Lovers) of the 1800s showed (D'Emilio & Freedman, 1997). Formed in reaction to male-dominated culture, separatism is fueled by negative energy to not do things, such as vote, interact with males, or support the patriarchy (Johnson, 1989). An us-versus-them mentality is responsible for the demise of many liberation movements and ideological feuds, such as the capitalists versus the communists, the men versus the women, the straight women versus the lesbians, the Blacks versus the Whites, the structural functionalists versus the symbolic interactionists, and the Hatfields versus the McCoys. These binary oppositions make neat boxes to dump our confusing thoughts into, but all they produce are scapegoats, heartache, and further oppression (Lorde, 1984). The challenge is to be for something without necessarily being against some arbitrary other.

Today, feminist desires for equality no longer freeze on gender as the only category. Black women, Latina women, Asian American women, working-class women, lesbians, old women, and men who love women, among others, have demonstrated that an analysis of gender alone is not sufficient to resist and transform oppressive social structures and processes. We must interrogate the intersections among gender, race, class, and sexual orientation by examining issues in all of their complexity. Bernice Johnson Reagon, a scholar, performer, and activist who organized the African American women's vocal ensemble *Sweet Honey in the Rock,* is unapologetic about the need for all of us, regardless of race, class, gender, ethnicity, or sexual orientation, to acknowledge our debt to the Blacks who started and sustained the civil rights movement and to correct our reluctance to recognize more than one form of oppression as primary (Christensen, 1997). Reagon (1983) uses her standpoint as a Black woman from which to begin any project and as grounds for reforming and redefining political expression:

> Black folks started it, Black folks did it, so everything you've done politically rests on the efforts of my people—that's my arrogance! Yes, and it's the truth; it's my truth. You can take it or leave it, but that's the way I see it. So once we did what we did, then you've got women, you've got Chicanos, you've got the Native Americans, and you've got homosexuals, and you got all of these people who also got sick of somebody being on their neck. And maybe if they come together, they can do something about it. And I claim all of you as coming from something that made me who I am. You can't tell me that you ain't in the Civil Rights movement. You are in the Civil Rights movement that we created that just rolled up

to your door. But it could not stay the same, because if it was gonna stay the same it wouldn't have done you no good. (p. 362)

FEMINIST VISIONS FOR NOW AND INTO THE FUTURE

World Traveling

Feminist scholars have demonstrated how inaccurate it is to treat gender as a separate and singular analytic category (Christensen, 1997; Hawkesworth, 1997). Yet in the discipline of family studies, even talking about gender is a taboo subject in many quarters (see the critique by Thompson & Walker, 1995). The dominant discourse about gender roles is still protected and rarely questioned (for an elaboration of how privilege and oppression operate in the theory and science of family studies, see recent analyses by Allen, 2000; Marks, 2000; Walker, 2000). But there is a progressive energy in family studies to acknowledge how the world is changing. Underscoring this energy is the spiritual ability to hold oneself responsible as a positive force for change (Allen, 2000). I desire social justice not just for myself and those I love but for anyone who is at risk. As we enter the 21st century, feminist theory is incorporating a renewed critique of the "exploitive relations of production and the unequal divisions of labor, property, power, and privilege these produce" (Ebert, 1996, p. xi) into the current postmodern trend in which a "localist genre of descriptive and immanent writing" (Ebert, 1996, p. xii) prevails. Both social critique and cultural analysis are needed to enable a transformative feminism "of transnational equality for all people of the world" (Ebert, 1996, p. xiii).

Feminist practice in family studies is active and ongoing, but still much more work needs to be done. We cannot just talk about how oppression has affected and made us into the women and men we are today. Feminist praxis is revolutionary. Thompson and Walker (1995) concluded that feminism has had a far greater effect on family pedagogy than on family research. Indeed, activist feminist teaching continues to inspire the discipline (for recent examples, see Allen, Floyd-Thomas, & Gillman, in press; Baber & Murray, 2001; Fletcher & Russell, 2001). We can make greater progress in terms of how we envision and study families by incorporating feminist lessons into our work. Lugones (1990) proposed the metaphor of world traveling to apply the principle of the personal is political to our practice in coming to value and respect the humanity of others. She described how we can bridge the span between our own experiences and those of others, thereby challenging traditional assumptions about individuals, families, and societies:

> There are worlds we enter at our own risk, worlds that have agon, conquest, and arrogance as the main ingredients in their ethos. These are worlds that we enter out of necessity and which would be foolish to enter playfully. But there are worlds that we can travel to lovingly and traveling to them is part of loving at least some of their inhabitants. The reason why I think that traveling to someone's world is a way of identifying with them is because by traveling to their world we can understand what it is to be them and what it is to be ourselves in their eyes.

Only when we have traveled to each other's worlds are we fully subjects to each other, (p. 401)

Building on Lugones's (1990) suggestion, we can adopt an attitude of careful curiosity toward the experiences of others (Thompson, 1995). What does it mean to travel to someone else's world? What can we gain by becoming "fully subjects to each other?" I offer a glimpse of this process in a story from my own life. I hope, like Hansel and Gretel in one of Grimm's fairy tales (Lang, 1969), that by leaving these stones, others can retrace their steps out of the forest of denial and into a place of renewed commitment to uncovering the realities of family life from the perspectives of those who live it.

Traveling to My Son's World

My son, at 14, has just experienced his mother's second divorce. The first one occurred when his father and I parted company after a long and difficult decision-making process, concluding that our marriage was never going to work out as planned. Matt was 2 at the time, and although I retained physical custody, his father has remained an active part of his life. After this divorce, I entered a lesbian partnership with another woman, who assumed most of the primary caregiving for our chosen family. Eventually, we had a second child (born to her), whose father was my brother's life partner. Our family seemed complete, and we proudly professed to the world how well our chosen family was working. Open in our community, we enjoyed the lesbian poster-family status we achieved, feeling protected and secure in how we presented ourselves to the world.

Then, the unfathomable happened, at least from my perspective. My former partner and I had just gotten a civil union in the state of Vermont, the first state in the United States to offer marriage-like benefits to gay and lesbian partners. We had also completed the legal work to add her last name onto Matt's name and to give me joint custody of our second child. It seemed that after 12 years in a committed partnership, we now had as many legal safeguards in place as possible. Yet soon after the civil union in Vermont, my partner found herself falling in love with another woman in our community, a divorced, heterosexual mother of two whose children also attended our children's school. In a matter of weeks, my partner confessed her newfound love and left our home and family to be with this woman and her children. She took our second child with her, leaving Matt and me behind.

Like most people who are left in marriage or other domestic partnerships, I experienced the abrupt ending of this relationship as a painful surprise (Chodron, 1997; Fisher & Alberti, 2000; Kingma, 2000; Murray, 1994). After all, we had just repeated our vows to love and care for each other for the rest of our lives. I was not prepared for her seemingly sudden change of heart, but after several months of denial, I had to admit to myself that she was gone. Almost overnight, the old definition of our family as headed by two lesbian mothers raising two young sons with several fathers in the picture was also over. I have had to play catch-up to my former partner in terms of coming to terms with the fact that the family I had staked my identity on no longer existed. What's worse, we were unable to negotiate a new family relationship. The odd branches we had sprouted on the family tree (Stacey, 2000), of which I had once been so proud, had been chopped off, and my ex-partner no longer resembled the person I once cherished.

As self-absorption with my own pain subsided, I started to notice my son's reactions to this ordeal. He seemed happier now that it was only the two of us. I was unprepared for his point of view on the family breakup:

> Now he finally had me, his mom, all to himself. He said that although he felt abandoned by my ex-partner, our home was much more relaxed without her rules and without having to share me with his sibling.

It has taken me a while to face up to the fact that my son's definition of our family was not the same as mine. My writings about chosen family ties and the careful construction of a lesbian family disintegrated under his scrutiny. As I experienced this unitarily constructed definition of my family crumble, like those grains of sand in my metaphoric sandcastle, I learned some painful lessons that are already in the family studies literature but were not yet real to me. I had not yet lived through the crucible in which I felt the heat of their truth. My son was a major teacher of these lessons.

He was taking the breakup of my partnership and our chosen family in stride. He was sorry that I was so sad to be left by someone I trusted and loved, but from his point of view, life was far easier with only one doting parent in his home. Having had two mothers was fine, he said, when he was little, but now that he was about to enter high school, he asked me, with a slight smile, if I would start dating guys until he graduated. The things that mattered to him were not really what I thought would matter. He wanted to be reassured that his standard of living would not decrease, that I would get the emotional support I needed from friends and therapy to still be a strong person, that I would have more time to spend with him in the ways he wanted me available (e.g., at home but not scrutinizing his activities too closely), and that I would continue to have my own life and not meddle in his. I thought he would be devastated by the loss of his other mother and his sibling, but to the contrary, he expressed relief.

In these conversations with and observations of my son, I saw that the person I was raising was thinking very differently than I. I saw that one loving and relatively well-functioning parent was enough for him to feel safe and secure. I witnessed something I had given lip service for years—that children need somebody to be intensely connected to them (Bronfenbrenner & Weiss, 1983). I saw that I needed to be as strong and healthy as I could and not give into my grief over being left because my primary responsibility was to raise this boy to adulthood. I saw that grief takes the course that all the self-help books say it does: at least 1 year to recover from the catastrophic exit of a life partner. I saw that despite the two divorces to which I had subjected my son, he was wise beyond his years and more loving toward me than I thought I deserved. Contrary to being the failure I felt I was in my own eyes, I was a capable and successful adult in his. He wanted me to know that nothing could take away his love for me, and I did not need a second adult in the home to cushion his transition to adulthood.

This experience has taught me the importance of social support, adequate economic resources, sobriety in thought and deed, and a deepening appreciation for a spiritual power beyond my own control. At midlife, I learned that although life can deal some devastating blows, it is possible to renew and rebuild. I could not have gained this perspective without traveling to my son's world or without the incredible support I received from friends in my private life and teachers in the books I read. A feminist vision for transforming families is one in which clear-sighted honesty for what is really going on takes precedence over the myths we tell ourselves of how things should function (Ruddick, 1989).

Traveling to Others' Worlds

In this article, I have activated my own experience to illustrate how feminist ideas can inform family scholarship because I am committed to the revolutionary project of social change. I want to see families taken seriously at all levels. To do that, we need clear-sighted vision, not cockeyed optimism or gloomy denial found in traditional family social science. Real life is the greatest teacher, and it is not surprising that some of the most profound and lasting insights have come from lived experience, as evident in the process by which Piaget's observations of his three children metamorphosed into an intellectual industry in the behavioral and social sciences.

To initiate one's own journey for a deeper consciousness about the families we study, I offer the following reflective inventory of questions. These questions are guides for making the personal-to-political connection, thereby facilitating the journey of discovering how what goes on in private life reflects what goes on in the world.

1. What is it about my personal experience that is unresolved? What do I not yet understand about myself? In what areas of my experience do I feel negative emotions (e.g., shame, doubt, guilt, and remorse)? In what areas of my experience do I feel positive emotions (peace, acceptance, joy, and happiness)? How are these emotions connected to my thoughts about families?

2. What are my motivations for doing this work? Who am I trying to impress? What would I rather be doing than working on this project? What do I hope to contribute to my own life and to family scholarship by pursuing this work?

3. What is my responsibility to the people whose lives I am studying? What do I owe them for giving me the opportunity to get inside their lives? What do I want to give back? What do I now understand about human existence (my own included) as a result of conducting this work? How can this work benefit the well-being of others?

By answering these questions, it will become clear that the process of reflecting on one's life and writing down the responses without self-censorship can be the kind of liberatory experience feminism promises. By freeing the writer within (Goldberg, 1986), we can replace our distanced stance from the subjects of our study with a critical eye toward the private-public connection. Taking these steps brings us closer to the revolutionary feminist praxis I have described in this article. In these ways, we can travel from silence to language to action (Collins, 1990), learning to theorize private experience in the service of creating a more just world.

REFERENCES

Agger, B. (1998). *Critical social theories*. Boulder, CO: Westview.
Alexander, M. J., & Mohanty, C. T. (1997). Introduction: Genealogies, legacies, movements. In M. J. Alexander & C. T. Mohanty (Eds.), *Feminist genealogies, colonial legacies, democratic futures* (pp. xiii–xlii). New York: Routledge.

Allen, K. R. (2000). A conscious and inclusive family studies. *Journal of Marriage and the Family,* *62*, 4–17.

Allen, K. R., Blieszner, R., Roberto, K. A., Famsworth, E. B., & Wilcox, K. L. (1999). Older adults and their children: Family patterns of structural diversity. *Family Relations, 48,* 151–157.

Allen, K. R., Floyd-Thomas, S. M., & Gillman, L. (In press). Teaching to transform: From volatility to solidarity in an interdisciplinary family studies classroom. *Family Relations.*

Baber, K. M., & Allen, K. R. (1992). *Women and families: Feminist reconstructions.* New York: Guilford.

Baber, K. M., & Murray, C. I. (2001). A postmodern feminist approach to teaching human sexuality. *Family Relations, 50,* 23–33.

Bell, D. (1992). *Faces at the bottom of the well: The permanence of racism.* New York: Basic Books.

Bronfenbrenner, U., & Weiss, H. B. (1983). Beyond policies without people: An ecological perspective on child and family policy. In E. F. Zigler, S. L. Kagan, & E. Klugman (Eds.), *Children, families and government: Perspectives on American social policy* (pp. 393–414). Cambridge, UK: Cambridge University Press.

Brownmiller, S. (1999). *In our time: Memoir of a revolution.* New York: Delta.

Chodron, P. (1997). *When things fall apart: Heart advice for difficult times.* Boston: Shambhala.

Chow, E. N-L. (1998). Family, economy, and the state: A legacy of struggle for Chinese American women. In S. J. Ferguson (Ed.), *Shifting the center: Understanding contemporary families* (pp. 93–114). Mountain View, CA: Mayfield.

Christensen, K. (1997). "With whom do you believe your lot is cast?" White feminists and racism. *Signs: Journal of Women in Culture and Society, 22,* 617–648.

Collins, P. H. (1990). *Black feminist thought: Knowledge, consciousness, and the politics of empowerment.* Winchester, MA: Unwin Hyman.

Cook, J. A., & Fonow, M. M. (1986). Knowledge and women's interests: Issues of epistemology and methodology in feminist sociological research. *Sociological Inquiry, 56,* 2–29.

Coontz, S. (1992). *The way we never were: American families and the nostalgia trap.* New York. Basic Books.

Davis, M., & Kennedy, E. L. (1986). Oral history and the study of sexuality in the lesbian community: Buffalo, New York, 1940–1960. *Feminist Studies, 12,* 7–26.

D'Emilio, J., & Freedman, E. B. (1997). *Intimate matters: A history of sexuality in America* (2nd ed.). Chicago: University of Chicago Press.

Dill, B. T. (1988). Our mothers' grief: Racial ethnic women and the maintenance of families. *Journal of Family History, 13,* 415–431.

Ebert, T. L. (1996). *Ludic feminism and after: Postmodernism, desire, and labor in late capitalism.* Ann Arbor: University of Michigan Press.

Elam, D., & Wiegman, R. (Eds.). (1995). *Feminism beside itself.* New York: Routledge.

Ellsworth, E. (1997). Double binds of whiteness. In M. Fine, L. Weis, L. C. Powell, & L. M. Wong (Eds.), *Off white: Readings on race, power, and society* (pp. 259–269). New York: Routledge.

Faderman, L. (1981). *Surpassing the love of men: Romantic friendship and love between women from the Renaissance to the present.* New York: William Morrow.

Faderman, L. (1991). *Odd girls and twilight lovers: A history of lesbian life in twentieth-century America.* New York: Penguin.

Fisher, B., & Alberti, R. (2000). *Rebuilding when your relationship ends* (3rd ed.). Atascadero, CA: Impact.

Fletcher, A. C, & Russell, S. T. (2001). Incorporating issues of sexual orientation in the classroom: Challenges and solutions. *Family Relations, 50,* 34–40.

Frankenberg, R. (1993). *White women, race matters: The social construction of whiteness.* Minneapolis: University of Minnesota Press.

Freire, P. (1997). *Pedagogy of the oppressed* (M. B. Ramos, Trans., New rev. ed.). New York: Continuum (Original work published 1970).

Friedan, B. (1963). *The feminine mystique*. New York: Norton.

Gagnier, R. (1990). Feminist postmodernism: The end of feminism or the end of theory? In D. L. Rhode (Ed.), *Theoretical perspectives on sexual difference* (pp. 21–30). New Haven, CT: Yale University Press.

Gagnon, J. H., & Parker, R. G. (1995). Conceiving sexuality. In R. G. Parker & J. H. Gagnon (Eds.), *Conceiving sexuality: Approaches to sex research in a postmodern world* (p. 316). New York: Routledge.

Goldberg, N. (1986). *Writing down the bones: Freeing the writer within*. Boston: Shambhala.

Harding, S. (1987). Introduction: Is there a feminist method? In S. Harding (Ed.), *Feminism and methodology* (pp. 1–14). Bloomington: Indiana University Press.

Harding, S. (1998). Subjectivity, experience, and knowledge: An epistemology from/for rainbow coalition politics. In M. F. Rogers (Ed.), *Contemporary feminist theory* (pp. 97–108). New York: McGraw-Hill.

Harding, S. (2001). Comment on Walby's "Against epistemological chasms: The science question in feminism revisited": Can democratic values and interests ever play a rationally justifiable role in the evaluation of scientific work? *Signs: Journal of Women in Culture and Society, 26*, 511–525.

Hareven, T. K. (1991). The history of the family and the complexity of social change. *American Historical Review, 96*, 95–124.

Hawkesworth, M. (1997). Confounding gender. *Signs: Journal of Women in Culture and Society, 22*, 649–685.

Hawkesworth, M. E. (1989). Knowers, knowing, known: Feminist theory and claims of truth. *Signs: Journal of Women in Culture and Society, 14*, 533–557.

Herrmann, A. C., & Stewart, A. J. (Eds.). (1994). *Theorizing feminism: Parallel trends in the humanities and social sciences*. Boulder, CO: Westview.

Jaggar, A. M., & Rothenberg, P. S. (1984). *Feminist frameworks: Alternative theoretical accounts of the relations between women and men* (2nd ed.). New York: McGraw-Hill.

Johnson, S. (1989). *Wildfire: Igniting the she/volution*. Albuquerque, NM: Wildfire.

Kerber, L. K., & DeHart-Mathews, J. (Eds.). (1987). *Women's America: Refocusing the past* (2nd ed.). New York: Oxford University Press.

Kingma, D. R. (2000). *Coming apart: Why relationships end and how to live through the ending of yours*. Berkeley, CA: Conari Press.

Krieger, S. (1991). *Social science and the self: Personal essays on an art form*. New Brunswick, NJ: Rutgers University Press.

Krieger, S. (1996). *The family silver: Essays on relationships among women*. Berkeley: University of California Press.

Lang, A, (Ed.). (1969). *The blue fairy book*. New York: Airmont.

Lorde, A. (1984). *Sister outsider: Essays and speeches*. Freedom, CA: Crossing Press.

Lugones, M. (1990). Playfulness, "world"-traveling, and loving perception. In G. Anzaldua (Ed.), *Making face, making soul: Haciendo caras: Creative and critical perspectives by feminists of color* (pp. 390–402). San Francisco: Aunt Lute Books.

Marks, S. R. (2000). Teasing out the lessons of the 1960s: Family diversity and family privilege. *Journal of Marriage and the Family, 62*, 609–622.

McIntosh, P. (1995). White privilege and male privilege: A personal account of coming to see correspondences through work in women's studies. In M. L. Andersen & P. H. Collins (Eds.), *Race, class, and gender: An anthology* (2nd ed., pp. 76–87). Belmont, CA: Wadsworth.

Morgan, R. (Ed.). (1970). *Sisterhood is powerful*. New York: Random House.

Morrison, T. (1992). *Playing in the dark: Whiteness and the literary imagination*. New York: Vintage.

Murray, N. P. (1994). *Living beyond your losses: The healing journey through grief.* Ridgefield, CT: Morehouse.

Nielsen, J. M. (1990). Introduction. In J. M. Nielsen (Ed.), *Feminist research methods* (pp. 1–37). Boulder, CO: Westview.

Osmond, M. W. (1987). Radical-critical theories. In M. B. Sussman & S. K. Steinmetz (Eds.), *Handbook of marriage and the family* (pp. 103–124). New York: Plenum.

Patterson, C. J. (1994). Children of the lesbian baby boom: Behavioral adjustment, self-concepts, and sex-role identity. In B. Greene & G. Herek (Eds.), *Contemporary perspectives on lesbian and gay psychology: Theory, research, and application* (pp. 156–175). Thousand Oaks, CA: Sage.

Reagon, B. J. (1983). Coalition politics: Turning the century. In B. Smith (Ed.), *Home girls: A Black feminist anthology* (pp. 356–368). New York: Kitchen Table Press.

Rich, A. (1980). Compulsory heterosexuality and lesbian existence. *Signs: Journal of Women in Culture and Society, 5*, 631–660.

Riger, S. (1998). Epistemological debates, feminist voices: Science, social values, and the study of women. In D. L. Anselmi & A. L. Law (Eds.), *Questions of gender: Perspectives and paradoxes* (pp. 61–75). New York: McGraw-Hill.

Rosser, S. V. (1992). Are there feminist methodologies appropriate for the natural sciences and do they make a difference? *Women's Studies International Forum, 15*, 535–550.

Ruddick, S. (1989). *Maternal thinking: Toward a politics of peace.* Boston: Beacon.

Sawhney, S. (1995). Authenticity is such a drag! In D. Elam & R. Wiegman (Eds.), *Feminism beside itself* (pp. 197–215). New York: Routledge.

Simon, R. I. (1992). *Teaching against the grain: Texts for a pedagogy of possibility.* New York: Bergin & Garvey.

Smith-Rosenberg, C. (1975). The female world of love and ritual. *Signs: Journal of Women in Culture and Society, 1*, 1–29.

Spender, D. (Ed.). (1983). *Feminist theories: Three centuries of key women thinkers.* New York: Pantheon.

Sprague, J. (2001). Comment on Walby's "Against epistemological chasms: The science question in feminism revisited": Structured knowledge and strategic methodology. *Signs: Journal of Women in Culture and Society, 26*, 527–536.

Stacey, J. (2000). The handbook's tail: Toward revels or a requiem for family diversity. In D. H. Demo, K. R. Allen, & M. A. Fine (Eds.), *Handbook of family diversity* (pp. 424–439). New York: Oxford University Press.

Thompson, L. (1995). Teaching about ethnic minority families using a pedagogy of care. *Family Relations, 44*, 129–135.

Thompson, L., & Walker, A. J. (1995). The place of feminism in family studies. *Journal of Marriage and the Family, 57*, 847–865.

Walby, S. (2001a). Against epistemological chasms: The science question in feminism revisited. *Signs: Journal of Women in Culture and Society, 26*, 485–509.

Walby, S. (2001b). Reply to Harding and Sprague. *Signs: Journal of Women in Culture and Society, 26*, 537–540.

Walker, A. J. (2000). Refracted knowledge: Viewing families through the prism of social science. *Journal of Marriage and the Family, 62*, 595–608.

White, S. (1991). *Political theory and postmodernism.* Cambridge, UK: Cambridge University Press.

Wilber, K. (1998). *The marriage of sense and soul: Integrating science and religion.* New York: Broadway.

Biosocial Theory

Ross and Roberta, both single parents in their early thirties, live across the hall from each other, and their children attend the same school. One day they were sitting with some other single parents as they watched their children play a soccer match. They started talking about how difficult it is to find a person to marry in today's society. After all, here are four adults who are attractive, funny, intelligent, and could date all they wanted if they had the time. The problem seems to be that none of them can find long-term relationships that are satisfying and can lead to eventual remarriage and having more children. Roberta stated that the problem was that men are raised differently than women and that they just don't understand what women want and need in a relationship.

Ross, being a scientist, said that mate selection as it currently exists is the result of thousands of years of evolution and the natural selection of traits that will allow the strongest of each species, in this case humans, to survive. Thus, for men to attempt to survive it is better to have multiple mates to increase their chances of reproducing. For women, however, because they have to invest more time and energy in reproductive activities simply because they are the ones that give birth, it is imperative for them to choose their mates wisely on the basis of who will provide the most resources. From this, Ross concluded that women have a greater need to select a good mate and marry than do men, which is why women are desperate to marry and men are desperate to avoid commitment and simply attempt to reproduce with multiple women. And men certainly don't want to use their time and resources on other men's children! Lisa replied:

> OK, I don't understand everything you just said, but I do know that if men would simply wake up and smell the java, they would realize what a great person I am and fall madly in love with me. I mean, really, what's not to love about me? Or any of us, for that matter? And how could they not love my child once they spent some time with him? The real problem is we just don't understand each other.

So, who's right? Are the women correct in assuming that society has created the differences between genders that lead to problems in mate selection, or is Ross correct in assuming that the problems that exist today are related to a genetic predisposition to certain personality characteristics that is born from years of evolutionary selection and change? These questions and more will be addressed in this chapter.

HISTORY

The history of biosocial theory is difficult to discuss with any certainty because there are so many variations. Variations that combine the ideas and beliefs of people from many disciplines are typical of a theory in its formative years, but they are also what make this theory both unique and exciting. Because there are many theories that are similar to biosocial theory—such as evolutionary psychology (Cosmides, Toby, and Barkow 1992), ethology and sociobiology (Thomas 1996), and psychobiology (Cloninger, Svrakic, and Przybeck 1993)—what you read here may not be the same as the treatment of this material in another text.

Whereas biosocial theory is in its beginning stages, it is based on ideas that have been around for some time. One of the earliest publications concerning evolution was *The Origin of Species* by Charles Darwin (1859). In this book, Darwin suggests that there is a struggle for survival among species, with nature "selecting" those individuals who are best adapted to the environment. This process occurs over generations, and as individuals are changing to fit the environment, the environment is also changing. Until the last several decades, Darwin's ideas were left basically untapped by social scientists in their understanding of human social behavior. In fact, there was a bias against his principles, with many in this area believing that biology and society were such opposites that they would never have a place in the same discussion.

Because of this opposition, much of the early work in this area was done in the medical arena as biologists sought to discover biological causes of individual behaviors, as well as by ethologists who studied animal or human behavior from an evolutionary perspective. Perhaps the first to move the discussion of selection from biological predetermination to possible influences of the environment was W. D. Hamilton (1964a, 1964b). Hamilton believed in the concept of inclusive fitness, which means not only that individuals change and adapt over time in order to survive but also that fitness includes those individuals who surround or are related to the individual. In other words, because we inherit our genetic material, it is in our best interest to support those we are related to, because this promises the survival of our own genes as well. This would help to explain such things as parental investment in children. This idea led other social scientists to consider the genetic nature of human relationships as they exist within a social environment.

Perhaps the most influential writing in this area was by Edward Osborne Wilson, who in 1975 published the book, *Sociobiology*. In this writing, he posited that evolution was evident in people across time and that genes influence individual behaviors that have evolved in order to ensure survival. While many in the field did not agree with his ideas, the book did generate a great deal of discussion and research concerning the role of genetics in human behavior. Similarly, Hans J. Eysenck (1967; Eysenck and Eysenck 1985) sought to explain the role of genetic predisposition in introversion/extraversion and stability/neuroticism and used this biological basis to explain how individuals interacted differently based on the social situation. These principles have been expanded upon in recent decades to explain human behavior in many areas, including mate selection, parenting, child development, behavioral and mental disorders, and the mind–body connection in the treatment of medical diseases. It is important to remember that this brief historical review is far from comprehensive but simply seeks to point out that the ideas of Darwin have been expanded upon and used to understand modern behavior, although there is still disagreement in the social sciences as to which is more powerful—nature or nurture.

BASIC ASSUMPTIONS

Because the assumptions of the theory depend on which version or writing you are discussing, it is important to note that these twelve assumptions are being taken verbatim from a chapter on biosocial perspective written by Troost and Filsinger (1993).

"Humans have an evolutionary origin." This is based once again on the ideas of Darwin and the principle of natural selection. As Mayr (1991) states, "Change comes about through the abundant production of genetic variation in every generation. The relatively few individuals who survive, owing to a particularly well-adapted combination of inheritable characteristics, gives rise to the next generation" (37).

"The family has played an important role in human evolution." Because survival of the individual is dependent on survival of the family, the existence of families across time has helped individual family members adapt and thus survive. An example of this is that people everywhere across cultures live in families of some sort, raise children, and attempt to make a living or a means to survive. These similarities are seen as a result of our specific evolutionary history (Fox 1989).

"The evolutionary origin of humans has an influence upon families today." Human behavior today is based upon the genetic and social adaptation of individuals and families since time began. Thus, reactions to current social issues such as parental investment in children and gendered behavior all have their basis in evolution.

"Proximate biology has an influence on the family, and the family has an influence on proximate biology and the health of its members." Proximate, as will be discussed shortly after, refers to interaction between genetic predisposition and social interactions. This simply means that individuals are predisposed to some diseases or medical conditions, which influences how they interact within the family. Maybe they are frequently tired and thus are not as active in family activities. In turn, the behaviors of family members influence the health of other family members (e.g., smoking, increased stress, physical abuse, or violence).

"Biosocial influences are both biological and social in character." One cannot discuss the social influences on behavior without also addressing the biological components.

"The biosocial domain is concerned with three factors: the biological, biosocial, and social." Although most social scientists do not as of yet have accurate ways to measure each of these factors, the best model is one that would take each of them into consideration. Problems come when you try to disentangle one from the other.

"Human biological and biosocial variables do not determine human conduct but pose limitations and constraints as well as possibilities and opportunities for families." It is important to distinguish between biology driving human behavior and influencing human behavior. The premise of this theory is that genetics sets the stage for certain behaviors but does not necessarily determine how or even if they will be exhibited.

"A biosocial approach takes an intermediate position between those who emphasize the similarity between humans and other animals (Wilson 1975) and those who emphasize the differences (Charon 1989; Mead 1964)." While most who utilize this theory would agree that humans have evolved throughout time, most would also support the notion that we are also a unique species with our own culture and interactions. The reality lies somewhere in the middle.

"Adaptation is assumed to have taken place over a vast period of time. The hundreds to thousands of generations to reach Hardy–Weinberg equilibrium in adaptive evolutionary biology (Birdsell 1981) are vastly different than, for example, human ecology.... Conjectures about biological adaptation in the span of one generation or over the course of the twentieth century or the computer age are dubious assertions." The Hardy–Weinberg law is the idea that if a system is at equilibrium, or in balance, the genetic distribution of alternative forms of a gene are also stable. In other words, genetic transitions do not take place until that system is no longer stable. At that point, genes may mutate or change so that some become more dominant than others. This is the basic principle of natural selection. Some mutation takes place to allow for greater fitness or to ensure adaptation that is necessary for survival. Because this process takes a great deal of time, it would be absurd to think we could study this change across just one or two generations; to understand behavior today you must also understand the behavior of our ancestors.

"Adaptations in physiology or conduct vary by environment." Whereas we are born with our genetic structure (our *genotype*), the way that we express those genetic tendencies (our *phenotype*) will vary across different environments and situations. Further, the interaction between our genotype and our phenotype necessitates a great deal of diversity across individuals, families, and cultures. This means that two different individuals with the same genetic composition, but entirely different environments, would probably exhibit entirely different behaviors.

"Extant features of human biology can be used to reveal aspects of our adaptation in the past (see Troost 1988a; Turke 1988)." Obviously we cannot go back in time and examine how people in other eras lived their lives on a day-to-day basis, although we do have a good deal of archaeological evidence that provides us with some clues as to what their lives must have been like. Despite this inability to witness their experiences for ourselves, this theory posits that we can trace current features to their historical roots for at least a glimpse into why those biological features were adaptive at one point in time.

"Proximate, distal and ultimate levels of interpretation can be approached separately; ideally they will be integrated." Definitions of proximate, distal, and ultimate levels will be given in the next section. At this point it is important to note that while you can focus on one piece of the equation at a time, the most fruitful explanations will come from an analysis of all three levels at the same time because it is difficult to determine where one begins and the next one ends.

PRIMARY TERMS AND CONCEPTS

Because this theory is called *biosocial*, the most logical place to start when discussing primary terms and concepts is with the theory title itself. As mentioned earlier, biosocial describes the relationship between the biological and the social. Each component is seen as acting on its own behalf while also working together to produce human experience. The family is a perfect example of a biosocial entity because its members share some genetic structure as well as a social environment, with the purpose of advancing its individual members and unified entity (Lovejoy 1981).

Adaptation

Based on these ideas, the family has come about because of adaptation. According to the principle of *ultimate causation*, the family has helped to reproduce the species because it provides the support or framework in which adaptation takes place. *Adaptation* is the ability to change or increase the level of fitness in order to increase the chances of survival through greater numbers of offspring.

Fitness

Fitness refers to the ability to fit within the environment. Generally, one would consider the fitness of an individual. However, Hamilton (1964a, 1964b) argued that we should also include the fitness of that individual's relatives as being important, which he referred to as *inclusive fitness*. For example, based on the idea of *reciprocal altruism*, individuals work together to better meet the needs of each person. An example of this is parenting, as it is in the best interests of both the mother and the father to work together to bear children and raise them until the children are old enough to have their own offspring. This process ensures survival of the genetic and social structures of all parties involved. Therefore, the ultimate cause of families today is a history of adaptation that has led to the successful reproduction of fit children, which is best done within some sort of family unit. Simply, you cannot analyze families today without recognizing this evolutionary past.

Proximate Causes

On the other end of the continuum are proximate causes. Proximate causes, literally meaning nearby or in close proximity, are the day-to-day interactions that take place during regular family life. This includes the interplay of biological and social forces such as learning, language, and culture. If ultimate causes represent the past, and proximate causes represent the present, then *distal* or *intermediate causes* represent how the two interrelate. It should be noted, however, that not all who subscribe to this theory add this distal component. Rather, many assume that behaviors exhibited today are by necessity an interaction between some feature from the past that has been adapted and the current biological and social conditions. As noted above, perhaps it would be most productive to approach studies or topics with the assumption that all three levels should be analyzed and/or considered.

Natural Selection

It is through natural selection that these terms and concepts come together. Natural selection explains our evolutionary past because it is through adaptation that those genes most able to ensure survival will be passed along to the next generation. This is known as *survival of the fittest*. In addition, it is through this evolutionary process that modern individuals behave as they do. An individual's genetic material must still interact with the environment. For example, although at conception the genetic material that is transferred controls the development of things such as the central nervous system, muscles, and other body functions and organs that influence behavior, how these genes develop also depends on the environment, such as proper vitamins, minerals, and nutrients; lack of exposure to harmful toxins, gases, or drugs; and a harm-free environment. Thus, one cannot state that the biological is more important than the social, or vice versa because both must work together to ensure that survival and adaptation take place.

As has been stated numerous times, biosocial theory has many forms and similar areas of research. Whereas this chapter covers terms most commonly seen across readings concerning a biosocial perspective, it is by no means an exhaustive listing of terms often associated with a biosocial approach. However, it is a comprehensive listing of those terms which seem most necessary in order to have a working knowledge of this theory.

COMMON AREAS OF RESEARCH AND APPLICATION

Although it may seem from our discussion thus far that the research in this field will pertain mostly to evolution or perhaps family formation, the reality is that there is a great deal of research done in the past few decades using a biosocial approach to explain topics at both the individual and family level. For example, temperament and personality development have been studied, as well as a variety of gender issues such as the genetic basis of gender differences, theories of incest and rape, and mate selection and sexual interest. As the Sample Reading at the end of this chapter suggests, researching the role of hormones such as testosterone is part of the cutting-edge work being done, which utilizes a biosocial perspective. For that reason, we will discuss briefly a few studies done since that decade review article was written, which demonstrates the strength of the biosocial model. We will first review some of the areas mentioned earlier and discuss other ways this theory is currently being applied, particularly in the medical and family therapy fields.

Temperament

Richter, Eiseman, and Richter (2000) have used a biosocial theory to determine the influence of genetic and environmental factors on personality development, especially temperament. Temperament, our automatic response to stimuli, is thought to be genetically predetermined. However, the environment in which one is raised, or the stimuli to which one has to react, influences how that temperament is displayed. Thomas and Chess (1980) support this idea through cross-cultural research on temperament. For example, they suggest that children will attempt to match their temperament to the standards of the culture in which they reside. Thus, while they may have a genetic predisposition toward certain behaviors, they will not engage in those behaviors because they are not seen as socially acceptable.

Udry (1994) did similar work on temperament, but in this case, he was studying adolescent problem behaviors. Whereas traditionally researchers assessed delinquency and other adolescent problem behaviors by studying the current environment, such as family and social situations, Udry suggests you must also consider biologically based individual differences such as temperament. In fact, he states that "you can make good predictions of who will use marijuana at age 14 by personality and environmental factors measured in the same children at age 4" (104). This is because children with different temperaments choose different environments that match those genetic predispositions.

The work previously mentioned by Eysenck (1967) is another example of using a biosocial perspective at the individual level. His earlier work (Eysenck 1967) was focused on developing a typology of personality that details the various traits and habits of different components of the personality. At this time, he identified two primary personality types: introversion/extraversion and stability/neuroticism. He later added the dimension of impulse control/psychoticism (Eysenck 1982). His first step was to identify these dimensions, then to develop a test to measure them, and finally to develop a theory to explain why people have different levels of each of these traits. He did this by using brain research that showed how different people's brains reacted differently to the same stimuli. For example, whereas extroverts have brains that respond more slowly and weakly to stimuli, introverts have brains that react more quickly and strongly. Because of this, extroverts seek environments that provide a good deal of stimulation, whereas introverts seek to avoid chaotic environments (Ryckman 2000). Thus, the genetic predisposition of the personality trait, introversion/extraversion, is displayed differently depending on the social environment.

Eysenck (1997) continued to develop these ideas in order to utilize a biosocial approach. His current research assumes that biosocial influences are a given upon which additional empirical research should build. He supports the movement within psychology of the acceptance of the mind–body connection as a standard from which to develop more scientifically based research. Although this idea has not been accepted by everyone within the field, it has spurred further research into the notion of basing future research on biosocial ideals (Brody 1997).

Gender

Another area of research that commonly utilizes a biosocial approach is that of the development of gendered behavior and sexual interest. Whereas there are many avenues explored in this general area, we'll discuss a few studies concerning the construction of gender, sexual interest, and the rape and incest theories. For example, Udry (2000) has used a biosocial model to explain how hormones, both present at birth and produced throughout adulthood, combine with the social expectations of each gender to form gendered behavior. By this he means that whereas males and females are genetically driven at birth, the effects of these hormones can be either strengthened or weakened based on the environment and the social beliefs about what's masculine and feminine. While you've probably all heard about this with regard to the importance of hormones during adolescence, and can probably remember what it felt like to experience those peaks and valleys of hormone surges, Udry takes this one step further by suggesting that the environment also influences how these hormones effect us.

Specifically, in one study Udry measured hormone levels of females during early adolescence and then again when they were between the ages of twenty-seven and thirty. He also asked them questions about the types of behaviors their parents encouraged with regard to masculinity and femininity. What he found was that "if a daughter has natural tendencies to be feminine, encouragement will enhance femininity; but if she has below average femininity in childhood, encouraging her to be more feminine will have no effect" (Udry 2000, 451). Thus, although hormones obviously drive some of our behavior, it is also important to consider the social environment when trying to discover why some people are more feminine or masculine than others.

Sexuality

Baldwin and Baldwin (1997) also conducted research on gender, but they focused on sexual interest. It is similar to the work of Udry (1994) in that it suggests that using an either/or approach to study gender is inappropriate: Both nature and nurture are important. Baldwin and Baldwin believe that whereas females are more interested in the romantic or love-based notion of sexuality, males are more concerned with the physical pleasure or enjoyment of sexual activities. Biologically it is in the best interest of the male to enjoy sexual activity and to share this with multiple partners in order to increase his chances of producing offspring. However, many believe that sexual interest is controlled by the social or cultural norms that exist. In contrast, Baldwin and Baldwin found that both biological drives and social norms work in concert to produce a diverse range of interests in sexual activity.

Taking this idea of sexual interest in another direction, there has also been a good deal of research which seeks to explain rape and incest from a biosocial perspective. For example, Hendrix and Schneider (1999) stated that because it would be to the detriment of families to inbreed, we have a biological predisposition toward sexual inhibition, starting during early childhood, that makes mating with family members unattractive. This will help determine survival of the fittest. In addition, most societies also have cultural taboos against incest, which reinforces this genetic inhibition. They believe that for some cultures the biological drive is stronger, whereas for others the incest taboo is more important. These two pieces together explain why most cultures do not support incest; it will weaken their genetic traits while also going against cultural standards.

Similarly, Ellis (1991) has used both biological and social reasons to explain rape. He believes that the desire to rape is driven by both sex drive and a desire to control and possess, neither of which are learned. In addition, men are genetically predisposed to a stronger sex drive because of natural selection or the need to procreate with multiple partners. Although the drive for sex is inborn, the means for meeting this need is learned through social experience. Finally, there are hormonal explanations for why some people are more prone to committing rape than others. These hormones not only increase the sex drive and the need to possess and control but also decreases the person's concern for the suffering of others. Thus, through this combination of biological and social experiences, men are more likely to rape than women, and the urge is greater in some men than in others. It is hoped that this discovery will lead to the ability to reduce the risks of rape by manipulating the hormonal and social influences on men predisposed toward rape.

These are just a few of the many areas of research that have benefited from acknowledging both the biological and social influences on behavior. Several fields of study, such as family medicine and family therapy, also take a biosocial approach. There are many reasons this would be helpful in family medicine, including the importance of genetic risk factors for some diseases (such as alcoholism and some types of cancer), the importance of family involvement in individual compliance with medical treatment, and the effects of stress on both the individual and the family. As has been found with parents who have chronic kidney disease, the illness of one family member also affects the entire family because that parent is no longer able to maintain his or her predisease family roles (Smith and Soliday 2001). In this case, limitations caused by the biological disease affect the social interactions of all those involved. Thus, it is easy to see that medical professionals could benefit from recognizing the mind–body connection for a wide variety of reasons.

As Campbell (1993) suggested, family therapists or other professionals who deal with the family could also benefit from a biosocial approach. When patients come to a therapist with a problem, such as depression, it is important to recognize that this has both a biological component that can be treated with medication and a social component that can be addressed with therapy. This allows for more comprehensive treatment of the problem.

The Role of Testosterone

Booth et al. (2003) studied the relationship between testosterone, child and adolescent adjustment, and parent–child relationships. This is easier to do now that testosterone can be measured using a saliva sample, which is simple to collect. While there is some research on the relationship between testosterone and behavioral problems in adults, research on children is in the beginning stages. Interestingly enough, it was found that high levels of testosterone alone did not create increased risk behavior or symptoms of depression in children. However, the quality of the parent–child relationship did affect those variables. Thus, when the quality of the parent–child relationship was high, this was able to minimize testosterone-related adjustment problems. This is important because it tells us that one has to include social context when trying to understand the relationship between hormones and behavior.

Rowe et al. (2004) found similar evidence of the existence of biosocial interactions in their study of adolescent boys. They found that testosterone is related to social dominance for boys during adolescence, particularly if they do not have deviant peers. This interaction between hormones and behavior is once again influenced by social context (who they associate with).

Finally, Booth, Johnson, and Granger (2005) looked at the relationship between testosterone and marriage. Previous research found that married men have lower levels of testosterone than divorced men (Mazur and Michalek 1998). Current research suggests that testosterone can encourage both positive and negative behavior depending on the social context. For example, in this study testosterone was not shown to affect marital quality by itself. However, when you add the social context of men who feel overloaded by their work and family roles, those with higher levels of testosterone reported lower marital quality than did men with lower levels of testosterone. Because we have stated that testosterone levels are now easier to measure, we would predict that the influence of testosterone will be increasingly studied across topics in the family field. It should be noted, however, that it is difficult, if not impossible, to establish a cause–effect relationship, or to disentangle the roles of biology, social context, and behavior.

CRITIQUE

The fact that there are many critics of biosocial theory perhaps also means that there are many things one would suggest to be limitations of a biosocial theory. However, the following items are based on the assumption that you support the notion of the importance of both biology and environment in human behavior. That said, one valid critique of biosocial theory is that there is disagreement over the basic tenets of the theory and which principles are most important. As was mentioned in the Basic Assumptions section, where you get your information will determine what items are mentioned as being of primary importance. While this is perhaps not a huge stumbling block, it does make it more difficult than using structural functionalism—for example, everyone agrees as to what that means. The relative newness of this theory is one reason for this disagreement, so we would suggest this will change over time.

Another problem with this theory is that while it makes intuitive sense that both nature and nurture are important, it is very difficult to disentangle the two in research designs. In fact, in some cases it may even be unethical to attempt to determine genetic influences due to the intrusive and perhaps even experimental nature of that research. Thus, we are constrained by the measures that are currently available. Not only that, just imagine telling participants to give some blood and urine samples; it may not go down well with the participants because they may not anticipate such requests in a study that they think deals only with personality. Hence, in research of this nature, it may be more difficult to find and retain participants.

As you could probably guess from reading this chapter, theory cannot explain everything. Some research, and some human behavior for that matter, contradicts what we would genetically predict. An example of this is the fact that families today are moving toward having fewer rather than more children, to the extent of not having enough children to replenish the population. How does this fit with the evolutionary need to carry on your genetic material? Although there is a great deal of speculation, we don't exactly know.

Finally, there is a tendency to confuse a genetic predisposition with a value judgment—that is, it is easy to say that because there is a genetic tendency toward a certain trait, then a certain behavior should follow. An example of that is the genetic and hormonal differences between males and females. While we have said that women have more to be concerned with when it comes to mate selection than do men because they are physically responsible for bringing a child into this world, it doesn't mean that women should automatically be responsible for the care of that child for the rest of its life. While our cultural beliefs may suggest that to be true, it is not entirely biologically based, as some have suggested.

Similarly, while research from this theoretical perspective suggests rape is biologically driven, this does not mean that individuals should not be held accountable for such behavior. Remember, one of our assumptions stated that human biological or biosocial drives do not determine human behavior. In other words, even though an individual may have the genetic predisposition toward rape, this does not mean that he or she must act on that drive. Further, we have strict social norms and laws that guard against this behavior, thus indicating that individuals will benefit by not engaging in such acts. Instead, we should use this information when we treat offenders or engage in prevention efforts. Recognizing the biological or social drives that possibly guide such behavior can provide another avenue of exploration as we strive to decrease its incidence.

Thus, while most social scientists would support the use of a biosocial perspective when researching and explaining human behavior, there is still much work to be done in the development of this theory. This does seem, however, to be the wave of the future.

APPLICATION

1. Refer to the scenario with the group of single parents discussed in the vignette provided at the beginning of this chapter. According to biosocial theory, who is right—Ross or the other women?

2. It's exam week, and a friend comes to you saying she's not sure she's going to make it through the next exam because she doesn't feel well. She needs to maintain a 3.5 GPA to keep her scholarship and has been studying very hard. You ask her what hurts and she replies, "I don't know, everything!" How would you use a biosocial approach to help her?

3. Think about the role of hormones in your life. What have you learned or been told about how they influence you physically? What about emotionally? Socially? How can you use a biosocial perspective to understand how hormones influence your behavior as well as how your environment can effect your hormones?

4. List ways that you are like one of your parents or a sibling. Now go through your list and write ways that each of these could be genetic or socially constructed. How can the interaction between genetics and your family environment be responsible for these similarities?

5. Again, think about the story at the beginning of the chapter. How does biosocial theory explain why adults are willing to raise nonbiological children?

6. Which of the research areas from the Sample Reading section do you find most interesting and why? Which application do you find most unbelievable and why?

REFERENCES

Baldwin, J. D., and J. I. Baldwin. 1997. Gender differences in sexual interest. *Archives of Sexual Behavior* 26(2): 181–210.

Booth, A., D. R. Johnson, and D. A. Grander. 2005. Testosterone, marital quality, and role overload. *Journal of Marriage and Family* 67: 483–498.

Booth, A., D. R. Johnson, D. A. Granger, A. C. Crouter, and S. McHale. 2003. Testosterone and child and adolescent adjustment: The moderating role of parent–child relationships. *Developmental Psychology* 39(1): 85–98.

Brody, N. 1997. Dispositional paradigms: Comment on Eysenck (1997) and the biosocial science of individual differences. *Journal of Personality and Social Psychology* 73: 1242–1245.

Campbell, T. L. 1993. Applying a biosocial perspective on the family. In *Sourcebook of family theories and methods: A contextual approach*, ed. P. G. Boss, W. J. Doherty, R. LaRossa, W. R. Schumm, and S. K. Steinmetz, 711–713. New York: Plenum.

Cloninger, C. R., D. M. Svrakic, and T. R. Przybeck. 1993. A psychobiological model of temperament and character. *Archives of General Psychiatry* 50: 975–990.

Cosmides, L., J. Toby, and J. H. Barkow. 1992. Introduction: Evolutionary psychology and conceptual integration. In *The adapted mind: Evolutionary psychology and the generation of culture*, ed. J. H. Barkow, L. Cosmides, and J. Toby, 3–15. New York: Oxford Univ. Press.

Ellis, L. 1991. A synthesized (biosocial) theory of rape. *Journal of Consulting and Clinical Psychology* 59(5): 631–642.

Eysenck, H. J. 1967. *The biological basis of personality*. Springfield, IL: Charles C. Thomas.

———. 1982. *Personality, genetics, and behavior: Selected papers*. New York: Praeger.

———. 1997. Personality and experimental psychology: The unification of psychology and the possibility of a paradigm. *Journal of Personality and Social Psychology* 73: 1224–1237.

Eysenck, H. J., and M. W. Eysenck. 1985. *Personality and individual differences: A natural science approach*. New York: Plenum.

Fox, R. 1989. *The search for society: Quest for a biosocial science and morality*. New Brunswick, NJ: Rutgers Univ. Press.

Hamilton, W. D. 1964a. The genetical evolution of social behavior. I. *Journal of Theoretical Biology* 7: 1–16.

———. 1964b. The genetical evolution of social behavior. II. *Journal of Theoretical Biology* 7: 17–52.

Hendrix, L., and M. A. Schneider. 1999. Assumptions on sex and society in the biosocial theory of incest. *Cross-Cultural Research* 33(2): 193–218.

Lovejoy, C. O. 1981. The origin of man. *Science* 211: 341–450.

Mayr, E. 1991. *One long argument: Charles Darwin and the genesis of modern evolutionary thought*. Cambridge, MA: Harvard University Press.

Mazur, A., and J. Michalek. 1998. Marriage, divorce, and male testosterone. *Social Forces* 77(1): 315–330.

Richter, J., M. Eiseman, and G. Richter. 2000. Temperament, character and perceived parental rearing in healthy adults: Two related concepts? *Psychopathology* 33(1): 36–42.

Rowe, R., B. Maughan, C. M. Worthman, E. J. Costello, and A. Angold. 2004. Testosterone, antisocial behavior, and social dominance in boys: Pubertal development and biosocial interaction. *Biological Psychiatry* 55:546–552.

Ryckman, R. M. 2000. Eysenck's biological typology. In *Theories of personality*. 7th ed., 349–390. Belmont, CA: Wadsworth.

Smith, S. R., and E. Soliday. 2001. The effects of parental chronic kidney disease on the family. *Family Relations* 50(2): 171–177.

Thomas, R. M. 1996. Ethology and sociobiology. In *Comparing theories of child development*, ed. R. M. Thomas. 4th ed., 394–412. Pacific Grove, CA: Brooks/Cole.

Thomas, A., and S. Chess. 1980. *The dynamics of psychological development*. New York: Brunner/Mazel.

Troost, K. M., and Filsinger, E. 1993. Emerging biosocial perspectives on the family. In *Sourcebook of family theories and methods: A contextual approach*, ed. P. G. Boss, W. J. Doherty, R. LaRossa, W. R. Schumm, and S. K. Steinmetz, 677–710. New York: Plenum.

Udry, J. R. 1994. Integrating biological and sociological models of adolescent problem behaviors. In *Adolescent problem behaviors: Issues and research*, ed. R. D. Ketterlinus and M. E. Lamb, 93–107. Hillsdale, NJ: Lawrence Erlbaum.

Udry, J. R., 2000. Biological limits of gender construction. *American Sociological Review* 65(3): 443–457.

Wilson, E. O. 1975. *Sociobiology: The new synthesis.* Cambridge, MA: Belknap.

SAMPLE READING

Booth, A., K. Carver, and D. A. Granger. 2000. Biosocial perspectives on the family. *Journal of Marriage and the Family* 62(4): 1018–1034.

This decade review article provides a topical summary of areas of research that have benefited from the principles of a biosocial perspective. How much has been done in such a short period of time will probably amaze you.

SAMPLE READING

BIOSOCIAL PERSPECTIVES
ON THE FAMILY

Alan Booth, Karen Carver, and
*Douglas A. Granger**
Pennsylvania State University

New theoretical models conceptualize families as systems affected by, and effecting change in, reciprocal influences among social, behavioral, and biological processes. Technological breakthroughs make noninvasive assessment of many biological processes available to family researchers. These theoretical and measurement advances have resulted in significant increases in research on family processes and relationships that integrate knowledge from the fields of behavioral endocrinology, behavior genetics, and, to a lesser degree, evolutionary psychology. This review covers a broad spectrum, including the topics of parenthood, early child development, adolescent and middle child development, parent-child relations, courtship and mate selection, and the quality and stability of marital and intimate relations. Our intention is to introduce, by example, the relevance of the biosocial approach, encourage family researchers to consider the application of these ideas to their interests, and increase the participation of family researchers in the next generation of studies.

Key Words: *child development, evolution, family relations, genetics, hormones.*

This is the first appearance of a decade-in-review article devoted to biosocial perspectives on the family. There are several decades of research examining the links between biology and individual development (e.g., perception, memory, maturation), but it is only recently that research has focused on families. Although the information is still fragmented, we now have enough to devote an article to biosocial research as

Department of Sociology, 211 Pennsylvania State University, University Park, PA 1602 (axb24@ psu.edu).

*Biobehavioral Health Department Pennsylvania State University, University Park, PA 16802.

it pertains to families. By biosocial we mean concepts linking psychosocial factors to physiology, genetics, and evolution. This article is a prelude to an explosion of biosocial research related to families anticipated over the next decade. We offer a hint of things to come and hope to perhaps encourage readers to start their own biosocial research project.

Early social scientists, such as William James (1842–1910), assumed that physiological processes were critical components of the behavioral and social phenomena they were studying. Until recently, however, the influence of those assumptions on scientific thinking was limited by significant gaps in knowledge. The nature of many physiological processes was largely unknown, and the technology necessary to operationalize physiological variables was in its infancy. Given these limitations, it is not surprising that research on human development and the family largely focused on the interface between the social environment and individual behavior. Many of those who did study physiological processes looked for simplistic models in which reductionist principles could be applied to reveal "the biological determinants" of behavior. The application of this focus led to clearly drawn boundaries between the social and biological sciences, the exceptions being studies of individual prenatal, infant, and adolescent development.

In the last 2 decades, significant effort has been focused on reversing this trend. Technical and conceptual advances have begun to break down disciplinary walls. Specifically, advances that enable noninvasive and inexpensive measurement of many physiological processes have given behavioral and social researchers new opportunities to integrate biological measures into their programs (Granger, Schwartz, Booth, & Arentz, 1999). In parallel, a series of paradigm shifts have occurred in scientific thinking about the relative contributions of both nature and nurture to behavioral phenomena (McClearn, 1993) and individual development (Gottlieb, 1992).

Dynamic models have replaced the simple reductionist ones of the past. They can best be described as systems models positing that individuals and families are best understood as the product of reciprocal influences among environmental (primarily social), behavioral, and biological processes (e.g., Cairns, Gariepy, & Hood, 1990; Gottlieb, 1991, 1992). In these models, biological functions set the stage for behavioral adaptation to environmental challenge. At the same time, environmental challenges may induce behavioral change that in turn affects fast-acting (e.g., hormone secretion) and slower-responding (gene expression) biological processes. Biological activities that facilitate a particular behavioral response, and behavioral activities that set the stage for changes in biological processes, may be stimulated or attenuated by environmental challenges (immediately or at some earlier stage in the individual's life). Evidence suggests that these interacting factors are capable of affecting differences in developmental trajectories, even for individuals with the same genetic constitution (e.g., identical twins).

Hereafter we focus on topics addressed by family scholars for which methodologically sound biosocial research has advanced knowledge on the topic and for which further research has the potential to yield new information. We focus primarily on behavioral endocrinology and behavioral genetics but briefly cover studies from evolutionary psychology and behavioral pharmacology. Following a primer on each biological topic, this article is organized around the family themes of parenthood, early child development and parent-child relations, adolescents and parent-child relations, courtship and mate selection, and marital and intimate relations. We conclude with notes on next steps in biosocial research and on how family scholars can become involved.

PRIMER ON BIOLOGICAL CONNECTIONS

Behavioral Endocrinology

The endocrine system produces several hundred hormones and releases them in response to signals from the brain, either nerve signals or other blood-borne chemical messengers. Hormones are chemical messengers that regulate, integrate, and control bodily functions by turning gene expression (influences) on or off. Hormones mediate both short-term processes, such as immediate responses to stress (e.g., fight or flight), and longer-term processes, such as growth, development, and reproduction. Researchers are interested in basal as well as reactive levels of hormones. Behavioral endocrinology is in the forefront of the integration of biological measures into studies of children and families because recent research has shown that hormones may play an integral role in furthering our understanding of individual differences in developmental trajectories, family relationships, and factors that mediate these processes. One of the reasons behavioral endocrinology is at the forefront is that technical advances have made possible the assessment of many important hormones in saliva (Kirschbaum, Read, & Hellhammer, 1992). For introductory reading on the operation of the endocrine system and its role in regulating many aspects of human biology and behavior, we recommend Nelson (1999). The following hormones are discussed in this review.

Testosterone is one of several androgens produced by the endocrine system. Men produce levels several times higher than do women. In women, the primary sources are the ovaries and the adrenal glands, whereas in men the sources are the testes and the adrenal glands. The hormone is implicated in the development of secondary sexual characteristics, reproduction, dominant behavior (which is sometimes antisocial and aggressive), and interest in activities that are traditionally masculine. It also plays an important role in men's competitive activities that involve gaining, maintaining, and losing social status (Mazur & Booth, 1998).

Dehydroepiandrosterone (DHEA) is a hormone produced by the adrenal glands that has a wide range of effects and is a precursor of other hormones. Preliminary studies indicate a possible association with health risk behavior (i.e., alcohol use and smoking), cognitive abilities, and emotionality. There are dramatic developmental differences in DHEA; levels are very low until about age 6 (adrenarche), and then it increases through age 15. In prepubertal children and in females, peripheral conversion of DHEA is the major pathway for testosterone production and may be an early marker for physiological development (McClintock & Herdt, 1996).

Oxytocin affects a variety of cognitive, grooming, affiliative, sexual, maternal, and reproductive behaviors. It is known to be important in parturition and lactation and may be implicated in maternal-infant interactions (Turner, Altemus, Enos, Cooper, & McGuinness, 1999).

Estradiol is the primary female reproductive hormone. It is implicated in the onset of puberty, menstruation, sexual and reproductive capacity, pregnancy, and menopause. It is associated with maternal behavior and may be important to general social affiliative behavior as well (Fleming, Ruble, Krieger, & Wong, 1997).

Cortisol is an endocrine product that enables individuals to adapt to the vicissitudes of life and to environmental changes. Men and women produce the same amount of cortisol. Cortisol regulates metabolism, the fight-flight response, immune activity, sensory acuity, and aspects of learning and memory. Cortisol is particularly interesting because its levels are affected by a variety of environmental processes (the amount of social, physical, and immune stimuli; Stansbury & Gunnar, 1994).

Behavioral Genetics

Behavioral genetics is the study of the relative contribution of genes and the environment to individual differences in behavior. The amount of genetic influence may be derived from the correlation of a behavioral measurement within pairs of siblings with known differences in genetic relatedness. For example, the correlation of antisocial behavior within pairs of identical (monozygotic) twins, who share 100% of their genes, is compared with the correlation within pairs of fraternal (dizygotic) twins, who share 50% of their genes. In one study (Reiss, 1995), the correlation for identical twins was .81, whereas for fraternal twins it was .62. To estimate the genetic influence, the difference between the two correlations is multiplied by 2 ($2 \times .19 = .38$). In this example, 38% of the variance in antisocial behavior may be attributed to genetic influences. Studies typically employ multiple sibling pairs (full siblings, half siblings, adopted siblings, siblings from blended families), multiple measures of the same phenomena (child estimates, parent estimates, teacher estimates), and structural equation modeling to determine the fit between genetic relatedness and measures of behavior (Neale & Cardon, 1992; Plomin, 1994).

Environmental contributions are parceled out to those shared by siblings (e.g., home, parents, family wealth, parents' education) and those not shared and which make siblings from the same family different from one another (e.g., parental treatment, sibling gender and age, peers, teachers). The distinction between shared and nonshared environment is important because the influence of the latter is stronger and increases throughout the life course. The portion of variance that is shared can be obtained by subtracting the heritability estimate from the identical twin correlation. In the above example, 43% of the variation would be from shared factors (.81 − .38). The remaining variance (19%) would be the effect of the influence of the nonshared environment. A powerful method of estimating genetic influence involves estimating differences in behavior among identical twins who have been reared together versus those who have been reared apart. With a few exceptions, results across methods are similar (Rowe, 1994).

Knowledge about the ways genes influence behavior is limited. Complex sets of genes are instrumental in influencing such things as intelligence and antisocial behavior. Nonetheless, it is unlikely that genes are specifically coded for IQ or criminal behavior. Rather, genes affect such things as memory or speed of processing in the case of intelligence, and impulse control and sensation seeking in the case of antisocial behavior. Some genetic influence is passive, derived from the fact that parents and children share genes. Smart kids live in parent-designed, intellectually challenging environments. Some genetic influence is reactive, stemming from the way parents and others respond to genetically influenced behavior. Antisocial behavior may cause parents to be less affectionate. Finally, some genetic influence is active, that is, genetically influenced behaviors cause children to seek and create environments that in turn affect their behavior. The risk-taking child may seek like-minded individuals as friends.

Two lines of research are of interest to family researchers: one focuses on genetic contributions to measures of family environments (stemming from reactive and active processes); and the other focuses on the way in which environmental factors moderate the expression of genetically influenced behavior. In the former, variance in such independent variables as the home environment, parenting styles, offspring's television viewing, and characteristics of peer groups are subject to genetic influences—especially as the child matures and exercises more control over his or her environment (Scarr & McCartney, 1983). Research on the factors that moderate by amplifying and reducing genetic influences include historical and cohort variables, as well as parenting practices. For example, authoritative parenting may reduce genetic influences, whereas laissez faire practices may increase them.

There are two reasons for introducing genetics into family studies. The first is to correctly identify the source of change in variables such as cognitive development and antisocial behavior to avoid attributing genetic influences to environmental ones and vice versa. The clinical and programmatic significance of this knowledge is that intervention strategies can be targeted to those aspects of the environment that can be altered. The second reason to consider genetic variables is to develop better fitting models to explain dependent variables. Those interested in expanding their understanding of behavioral genetics should read articles by Reiss (1995) and Plomin (1995).

Evolutionary Psychology

Evolutionary psychology focuses on (a) behavior that has enhanced genetic replication in past generations and (b) the way in which contemporary behavior effects reproductive success. In humans, women tend to invest more in offspring than do men and tend to be more selective in their choice of mates—mostly on the basis of men's willingness and ability to make a parental contribution. Men tend to invest less in parenting and may increase their chances of passing on their genetic material by being more promiscuous and concerned about the fidelity of their mates. One example of such behavior is the finding that when compared with biological offspring, stepchildren elect to leave or are "pushed out" of their home earlier (White & Booth, 1985). This may be attributable to the stepparent's lack of desire to invest in children who do not have his or her genetic material.

Theory and research on evolutionary psychology interests family scholars because there is evidence that it affects virtually every aspect of family life. Mate selection and offspring-parent relations, as well as topics such as the quality and stability of stepfamilies, family violence, incest, and the impact of the support capability of the environment, are all considered under the rubric of evolutionary psychology. For introductory reading, we suggest Buss and Schmitt (1993), Daly and Wilson (1983), and Davis and Daly (1997).

Behavioral Psychopharmacology and the Family

Progress made in describing the biological processes involved in regulating behavior has led to breakthroughs in the design and availability of drugs that stimulate or attenuate those processes. Examples include hormone-replacement therapies (i.e., testosterone, estradiol) to resolve midlife changes in negative moods, attitudes, and behavior; Viagra to address impotence and sexual dysfunction; Prozac for affective disorder; and Ritalin for disruptive behavior disorders of childhood. With the exception of Ritalin (Barkley, 1989), little is known about the effect of these agents on family relationships. Although space limitations prevent us from dealing with this topic, family researchers should be on alert for novel opportunities to test and develop theoretical models by studying the impact of the behavioral, cognitive, and attitudinal changes induced by these medications within the broader social ecology of the family.

One of the challenges facing biosocial research is that investigators in each of the fields involved (behavioral endocrinology, behavioral genetics, evolutionary psychology, behavioral psychopharmacology) tend not to be concerned about the other. Their practitioners rarely cite one another. Moreover, they seldom draw on the other fields to help explain the imponderables in their own work. The biosocial sciences can benefit from heeding Wilson's (1998) call for greater unification of the social and biological sciences.

PARENTHOOD

Biosocial research has focused on numerous aspects of becoming a parent. Evolutionary psychology is implicated in establishing a mating relationship. Hormones are examined with respect to the decision to have children, as well as decisions about the timing of sexual intercourse and parenting behavior following birth.

Establishing a Stable Sexual Relationship

To ensure survival, a period of several years of intense parental care is required. By the time they are age 3 or 4 children stand a good chance of reaching adulthood, and the need for intense care wanes. Humans ensure the needed care by establishing monogamous relationships, whereas most other primates do so through other forms of social organization. Compared with men, women are much more discriminating because future investment in offspring will be higher. Women select mates partly based on the resources they control and partly on the resources they can bring to bear on the support of the mother and her offspring (Daly & Wilson, 1983).

Cashdan (1995) added another dimension to reproductive strategies by taking into account women's dominance, status, and access to resources, some of which are associated with the hormone testosterone. Cashdan's research indicated that women with higher testosterone-associated dominance are less in need of a partner and are less selective in the sense they have more sexual partners and are less likely to agree with the statement, "I would not want to have sex with a man unless I am convinced that he is serious about a long-term commitment." On the other hand, women with low testosterone levels who expect or need partner involvement will be more selective and engage in behavior that is more likely to attract a man, such as minimizing assertiveness and sexual activity to assure the man that her offspring are his.

The Decision to Have Children

The decision to have a child is not well understood socially or biologically. Testosterone may be implicated. In a study explaining a wide range of gendered behavior in 250 women aged 27–30, Udry, Morris, and Kovenock (1995) found high testosterone related to a wide range of nontraditional behaviors related to the family, including not marrying, assigning a lower priority to marrying, having fewer children, and enjoying childcare activities less. It would appear that women's decisions to have a child may be related, in part, to basal levels of testosterone.

Not yet examined is whether female engagement in more competitive, aggressive, independent, or solitary activities, or activities with unrelated men, further increases testosterone. If so, it suggests a feedback mechanism that may help explain participation in parenting. Furthermore, the role of estradiol and other hormones related to reproduction remain to be explored as factors influencing decisions to have children. Whether testosterone or some other hormone influences men's decisions to have children is unknown.

Research supports a moderate heritable component for fertility expectations and desires. Rodgers and Doughty (in press) used the National Longitudinal Study of Youth to investigate ideal, desired, and expected family size. Findings suggest that both fertility expectations and completed fertility have a heritable component, although expectations have a higher level of genetic influence than do outcomes.

Timing of Sexual Intercourse

The role of biological processes in the timing of sexual intercourse is central to parenting. Females of all nonhuman mammals exhibit hormonally related signs of receptivity (visual, pheromonal, behavioral, and combinations of these) at the time of ovulation. The research on humans has been less consistent, mostly because of the difficulty in collecting enough data throughout the menstrual cycle. The only study showing that all the links are present (Van Goozen, Weigant, Endert, Helmond, & Van de Poll, 1997) focused on sexually active, normally, and regularly menstruating women who were not on the pill. Blood samples were obtained every other day, as were measures of sexual activity and mood. Testosterone and estradiol were highest at the ovulatory phase, as were female-initiated sexual activity and interest in sexual activity. It appears that hormones and sexual activity are greatest when women were most likely to conceive. Still, much has to be learned about signals linking the hormones and sexual behavior. Potentially contributing to the functioning of this intricate pattern of linkages between hormones and behavior is interest in having children, early experience with infants or young children, or harsh environments that threaten infant viability. These topics warrant research.

Parenting Behavior Following Birth

Parenting behavior shortly after birth is linked to biological factors. During pregnancy, many hormones are elevated to levels much higher than at any other time in life. Within weeks of birth mothers' hormone levels decline to normal levels. In cases where postpartum decline in estradiol is gradual, mothers report a greater feeling of attachment to their infants (Fleming, Ruble, Krieger, & Wong, 1997). This may be because estradiol triggers the production of oxytocin (Uvnas-Moberg, 1997), which appears to be implicated in mother's preoccupation with their infant children (Lechman & Mayes, 1998) and in their calm feelings while breast-feeding (Altemus, Deuster, Galliven, Carter, & Gold, 1995). Apparently, breastfeeding itself is a factor in the amount and quality of mother-child interaction. A comparison study indicated that mothers exposed to sucking during skin-to-skin contact shortly after birth talked to their babies more and spent more time with them than did mothers just experiencing skin-to-skin contact (Widstrom et al., 1990). Thus, the links among oxytocin, breast-feeding, and maternal care appear to be important in parent-child relations. Another study implicates the hormone prolactin, as well as oxytocin. Comparisons of women 4 days postpartum and a control group indicated these hormones were associated with lower levels of muscular tension, anxiety, and aggression (Uvnas-Moberg, Widstrom, Nissen, & Bjorvell, 1990). In men, a drop in basal testosterone immediately following the birth of a child has been noted (Storey, Walsh, Quinton, & Wynne-Edwards, in press). This may increase feelings of nurturing on the part of the father. Whether these biological factors continue to play a role as the child develops is not known.

Progress has been made in identifying important biosocial relationships in many phases of becoming a parent. Evolutionary factors that contribute to producing viable offspring have been identified in mate selection. Genetic influences have a role in fertility preferences. Hormones may be important in establishing unions that increase the chances of offspring survival, creating interest in having children, setting the timing of sexual intercourse, and shaping the quality of infant care. The research to date is largely descriptive, however, and little is known about direction of effects or pathways of influence.

EARLY CHILD DEVELOPMENT AND PARENT-CHILD RELATIONS

Hormonal and genetic factors are implicated in the development of gendered behavior and other aspects of cogitative development. They also are linked to the development of the parent-infant bond.

Gendered Behavior

Prenatal testosterone production (and perhaps other androgens) during the second trimester of pregnancy affects gendered behavior in adult female offspring in their late 20s (Udry et al., 1995). Gendered behavior refers to one in which males and females differ. More than 20 different measures were used to examine gendered behavior, including such things as marriage, number of births, domestic division of labor, feminine appearance, vocational interests, employment in male-dominated occupations, and personality measures. In this bipolar concept of gender, the higher the score, the more feminine the individual. Using this same data, Udry (2000) found that the greater the mother's testosterone, the smaller the effect of daughter's testosterone on adult-gendered behavior. Moreover, the greater the prenatal (mother's) testosterone, the less sensitive the female child was (during the teen years) to the mother's socialization efforts with respect to feminine behavior. This is probably because the early androgen exposure permanently organizes the brain. Female adolescents with low exposure to prenatal androgen were much more responsive to parental socialization efforts.

The development of gender differences in young children is clear and predictable, with boys preferring aggressive rough and tumble play and traditionally masculine toys and girls preferring more sedentary activities and gender-specific toys. Androgens appear to be implicated in defining the behavior. Most of the research linking hormones and play comes from studies of children with hormone-related disorders (e.g., females with congenital adrenal hyperplasia are exposed to very high levels of androgens from their adrenal glands, and males with idiopathic hypogonadotropic hypogonadalism generate very low levels of androgens). These studies are valuable because they represent essentially natural experiments that randomly assign an affected child and a control sibling to experimental and control conditions. Nonetheless, they may not represent how these processes occur in the population at large (see Collaer and Hines, 1995, for detailed review of the research).

Cognitive Development

A study of genetic influences on the home environment and on its relationship with cognitive development in 1- and 2-year-old children reveals substantial influences (Braungart, Fulker, & Plomin, 1992). The study compares adopted sibling pairs with a matched sample of sibling pairs living with biological parents. The home environment was measured by the Home Observation for Measure of Environment (HOME) scale, which estimates the intellectual resources (e.g., books and other stimulating resources along with material responsiveness and stimulation) available in the home. Cognitive development was measured by the Mental Development Index (MDI). More than one third of the variance in the HOME scores was accounted for by genetic influences, and approximately half the HOME-MDI relationship was mediated by genetic influences. Thus, offspring genetics plays an important role in the family intellectual environment, even in infancy.

Parent-Child Attachment

Research suggests that infant and early childhood experiences alter short- and long-term patterns of cortisol production. Maternal separation, for example, affects the threshold for cortisol production as well as the size of the cortisol increase (Gunnar, Mangelsdorf, Larsen, & Herstgaard, 1998). Young children with histories of child abuse tend to have atypical cortisol profiles throughout the day (Hart, Gunnar, & Cicchetti, 1995). Even cultural differences in care-giving and child-rearing practices (such as maternal emphasis on emotional expression, consistency in daily schedules, and degree of stimulation) are linked to cortisol profiles in infants (Super, Harkness, & Granger, preliminary data). Studies of institutionalized Romanian orphans indicate that severe social and tactile deprivation in early childhood may result in disruption of the circadian pattern of cortisol production (Carlson & Earls, 1997).

In middle childhood, traumatic events within the family are significant sources of cortisol activation for children. Children from families with high levels of conflict, punishment, serious quarreling, and fighting tend to have the highest cortisol levels (Flynn & England, 1995). Cortisol production increases in response to changes in family composition, such as men migrating in and out of the household for seasonal work opportunities, as well as for children living with a stepfather or distant relatives (Flynn & England, 1995).

The patterns of cortisol production noted above (e.g., basal level, response threshold, size of increase, and daily pattern) have the potential for affecting numerous aspects of child development. Children's cortisol increase resulting from parent-child conflict is associated with high levels of offspring social difficulties, withdrawal, anxiety, and a low sense of control-related beliefs (Granger, Weisz, & Kauneckis, 1996). In addition, cortisol increases are associated with internalizing behavior problems, symptoms of anxiety disorders, and negative patterns of control-related beliefs (Granger, Weisz, McCracken, Ikeda, & Douglas, 1996). Children's low basal cortisol also is associated with maternal dysfunction and psychopathology and parenting stress, and interrelationships between mother and child cortisol levels (Granger et al., 1998). Taken together, these studies suggest that the individual differences in children's cortisol response to features of the family environment contribute to children's behavioral adjustment and development.

No doubt part of the relationship between cortisol response and family relationships has genetic origins. For example, genetic influences have been observed for several measures of parenting behavior that would affect mother-child attachment. They include parental warmth (Braungart, 1994), affection, punitive parenting (Plomin, Reiss, Hetherington, & Howe, 1994), expressiveness (Plomin, McClearn, Pedersen, Nesselroade, & Bergeman, 1988), and inconsistency (Braungart, 1994). Most of these findings are from twin studies.

Evolutionary psychology also suggests how parental interest in reproductive success influences parent-child attachment in infants. There is evidence that parents are reluctant to invest in newborns if the offspring is of poor quality and unlikely to survive or there is little food or few other resources such that infant care would threaten the reproducing pair or older children. Fathers are reluctant to support newborns if they have doubts about the paternity of the child. Stepparents who have no genetic investment in the child are more inclined to abuse their children than are biological parents (Daly & Wilson, 1988).

Both hormones and genetic influences on measures of the family environment are implicated in the cognitive development of infants. Cortisol has a major role responding to and defining the parent-child bond, as well as offspring internalizing and externalizing behavior. An intergenerational component appears to be in evidence. Behavioral genetic research indicates that offspring genes influence numerous aspects of the family environment. Evolutionary psychology helps us understand aspects of the dark side of parent-child bonds. Given the range of biological influences, integrated studies are needed to understand how early development is linked to the three biological models.

LATER CHILD DEVELOPMENT AND PARENT CHILD RELATIONS

Adolescent dominance, aggression, and sexual behavior, along with antisocial behavior and depression, appear to have biological links. Special attention is given to gender differences in the link between testosterone and behavior. In addition to children's genetic effects on the environment, we also consider the way environment moderates genetic influences.

Sexual Development

Although puberty is evident around age 12 for girls and age 14 for boys—a time when gonadal development is clearly apparent—the organization of the process is established prenatally. Recent research suggests the early stages of puberty begin at age 6, when the adrenal cortex begins to mature and secrete low levels of the hormone DHEA. The metabolism of DHEA leads to the production of both testosterone and estradiol (McClintock & Herdt, 1996). By age 10, DHEA production is significant and corresponds with children's first sexual attraction, sexual fantasy, and sexual activity. DHEA is a much-overlooked marker with a wide range of behavioral, cognitive, and neural effects. As a precursor to potent hormones such as estradiol and testosterone, its effects may be much larger than current research suggests.

Dominance and Aggression

The period of adolescence is marked by physiological changes, in addition to a withdrawal (sometimes estrangement) from the family of origin, increased involvement with peers, and an increase in dominance and aggression for both boys and girls. Much of the testosterone and estradiol production goes toward organizing physiological development but some is manifested in behavior. One study of boys in childhood and early adolescence (ages 6 to 13) suggests that taking body mass as well as testosterone into account differentially predicts dominance and aggression (Tremblay et al., 1998). Increasing testosterone and body mass predict dominance, but only body mass predicts physical aggression. Thus, the relation between testosterone and physical aggression in this age group (and perhaps others) may be moderated by body mass. Boys with greater body mass may elicit aggression or find it easier to deal with individuals by being aggressive. Further research is needed to determine whether the relationship holds true for girls.

There remains the question of whether it is hormones or some other variable that produces changes in dominance (and possibly aggression). Evidence that hormones produce the change may be found in a randomized, double-blind, placebo-controlled crossover study of 35 boys and 14 girls who were in treatment for pubertal delay. Administrations of hormones to males and females were followed by an increase in physically aggressive behaviors and impulses but not verbal aggression (Finkelstein et al., 1997). It is noteworthy, however, that there is substantially less information regarding the link between testosterone and dominance in female subjects.

Sexual Behavior

Testosterone change in boys is also associated with changes in sexual behavior. A longitudinal study of 82 boys 12–13 years of age assessed over three years linked normal changes in testosterone with changes in sexual behavior. Monthly changes in saliva testosterone and weekly reports of sexual activity revealed that increases in testosterone were associated with coital initiation, frequency of coitus, and the rising incidence of other sexual behavior (Halpern, Udry, & Suchindran, 1998). Noteworthy is another study of this same sample that found serum testosterone collected semiannually and cumulative reports of sexual behavior over a 3-year period were unrelated. The more frequent collection of testosterone in saliva (which represents an estimate of the biologically active hormone in blood that is available to affect behavior) and improved measure of sexual activity detected changes not revealed in the earlier study. This suggests that longitudinal studies of behavior should make frequent assessments and measure free testosterone so that specific changes can be linked to alterations in behavior close to the time at which they occur.

A behavioral genetics study indicated a moderating effect of environmental factors on the heritability of the age of onset of sexual intercourse. Dunne et al. (1997) showed that genetic factors explained more of the variance in age at first sexual intercourse for a younger cohort (born 1952–1965) of twins than for an older cohort (born 1922–1952). Effects were interpreted to mean that parents of younger twins exercised less social control over offspring behavior.

Sex Differences

It is clear that there are marked gender differences in the link between testosterone and risky or nonconforming behavior. Although androgens result in increased interest in such behavior, Udry (1988) demonstrated that social controls (father presence and participation in sports) reduced the relationship between testosterone and sexual activity among adolescent girls, whereas these same controls had little impact on the testosterone-sexual behavior link among boys. The differential impact of social controls on boys and girls suggests that although there are similarities in the hormone-behavior link (e.g., interest in sex and masculine behavior), there are important differences that require exploration.

Nowhere is this more evident than in studies of competition among male subjects. Testosterone is shown to rise in anticipation of competition. Following competition, testosterone remains high or climbs further in winners but drops in losers (Booth, Johnson, & Granger, 1999), a finding that has been replicated numerous times. Nonetheless, testosterone does not have the same role in female competitors. There is no anticipatory rise in female competitors, nor does winning and losing affect testosterone production (Mazur, Susman, & Edelbrock, 1997). In a pilot study (Booth & Dabbs, 1996), it appears that cortisol was implicated in the preparation for and outcome of competitive events. Although untested, DHEA also may have a role in female competition because it is a precursor of testosterone.

The relevance of competition studies to families is that family members confer and take away status from one another. For example, the preferential treatment of one child over another is a way of giving status to one and taking it away from another. Children who receive more favorable treatment may experience an increase in testosterone, which is then expressed in more dominating behavior toward the less favored sibling. Giving and withholding support from spouse in family problem solving is another way status is gained and lost that, in turn, could affect hormone production and may then affect the quality of subsequent family interaction. Given the paucity of research on competing women, it is uncertain how and which hormones may be involved in the conferring and taking away of status from female family members.

Parental Relations, Adolescent Depression, and Antisocial Behavior

Genetically influenced characteristics of children also affect aspects of adolescent family environment. Significant genetic influences were found for children's and parents' ratings of positive factors (such as warmth, support, empathy, and mutual involvement in enjoyable activities), as well as for negative factors (such as frequency and intensity of disputes and feelings of anger). No influence was observed for control as assessed by monitoring offspring activities (Plomin et al., 1994; Rowe, 1981, 1983). Significant nonshared influences also were noted.

In an analysis of the impact of parents' negativity (anger, coercion, and conflict) on adolescent depression (as assessed by three scales) and antisocial behavior (measured from the Behavioral Problems Index antisocial scale), significant nonshared environment, as well as genetic contributions, were observed for the independent variable and the dependent variables (Pike, McGuire, Hetherington, Reiss, & Plomin, 1996). The nonshared environment contribution was modest in comparison with the genetic influence, accounting for nearly two thirds of the contribution. Moreover, the genetic influence accounts for most of the relation between parents' negativity and adolescent adjustment.

Genetic studies also reveal that environmental factors moderate the genetic influence on adolescent depression and antisocial behavior. Among adopted twins without a biological risk of antisocial behavior (as measured by having a biological parent without an antisocial personality disorder), the correlation between the family environment and becoming antisocial was trivial among those growing up in an adverse family environment. In contrast, among twins with a biological risk, there was a strong correlation between an adverse family environment and antisocial behavior (Cadoret, Yates, Troughtoh, Woodworth, & Stewart, 1995). In other words, children without genetic risk for antisocial behavior do not manifest such behavior, even in adverse environments, whereas children with a genetic predisposition are much more likely to display antisocial behavior in adverse environments than in more positive environments. A similar finding was observed among twins with and without a biological risk of depression. In this case, the interaction was between being at risk for depression and experiencing stressful life events (Kendler et al., 1995).

Transition to Adulthood

Studies have illustrated the implications of hormone production in youth for problems in adulthood. Numerous adolescents engage in antisocial or deviant behavior. For a few, it extends into adulthood; for others, it is limited to adolescence (Moffitt, 1993). One study revealed that adolescent boys who had been expelled or suspended from school, ran away from home, fought, stole, or were arrested were far more likely to commit a crime as an adult if they had high levels of testosterone than if their testosterone production was average or below (Booth & Osgood, 1993). Social factors such as marriage and full-time employment tended to dampen the impact of testosterone on adult male antisocial behavior. Another study using the same sample of men demonstrated that high testosterone is related to low occupational status and periods of unemployment (Dabbs, 1992). Testosterone-related low occupational success was attributable in part to testosterone-related antisocial behavior during adolescence that got the young men into trouble at school.

Still another study suggests that father's testosterone may be linked to parent-child relationships. Julian, McKenry, and McKelvey (1990) found that fathers with low testosterone had a better quality relationship with offspring 12–18 years of age than did high-testosterone men. Thus, part of the research agenda facing us is to address the issue of why testosterone is related to antisocial behavior in some individuals but not in others. What personal experiences and environmental factors explain the differential impact of the hormone?

One of the few areas of study that combines behavioral endocrinology, genetics, and evolutionary psychology stems from an investigation by Belsky, Steinberg, and Draper (1991), which proposes that early family relationships that are harsh, rejecting, and opportunistic (versus sensitive, supportive, and rewarding) result in an earlier onset of puberty that leads to a precocious and promiscuous reproductive strategy. Although early studies produced mixed results, recent longitudinal studies have clarified the causal paths. There is a genetic influence in that mother's early marriage and childbearing accounts for part of the early onset of daughter's puberty (Ellis & Garber, in press). This study reveals that the mother's low quality romantic relationship with the biological father, stepfather, or boyfriend has an independent effect on the early onset of puberty, as does the presence of a stepfather or boyfriend. The authors suggest that the effect of the presence of an unrelated man may be similar to that observed in studies of other mammals in which pheromones produced by the unrelated adult male accelerate female pubertal maturation (Sanders & Reinisch, 1990). A second longitudinal study suggests that positive care giving from the biological father plays a unique and pivotal role in delaying pubertal development (Ellis, Dodge, Pettit, & Bates, in press). Mother's care giving was found to be redundant of paternal involvement. Further research is needed to clarify the mechanisms involved and to more precisely estimate genetic influences on pubertal maturation.

Hormones have a particularly strong influence on adolescent development. They are related to social dominance and reproductive behavior but seem to have different effects on boys and girls. Testosterone appears to influence behavior that is eventually expressed in adult antisocial behavior and poor socioeconomic achievement. Environmental factors are found to be important moderators of genetic influences on adjustment. Studies combining biosocial models add to our understanding of the onset of female puberty and subsequent promiscuous behavior.

COURTSHIP AND MATE SELECTION

Among the most fascinating—but also puzzling—recent findings are those that suggest an association between a basic feature of the immune system and the process of selecting a mate. Immunologists long ago identified basic features of our cells that enable the immune system to recognize self versus other and subsequently eliminate potentially damaging molecules it determines as other. The basic feature of this part of the immune system is proteins found on cell surfaces called human leukocyte antigens (HLA) or the major histocompatibility complex (MHC). Put simply, the MHC defines for each person a unique "immunological fingerprint." Recent findings suggest that interpersonal cues signal information about individual differences in MHC. Humans can detect individual differences in odors (sweat) associated with MHC, which influence decisions regarding mate selection and perceived attractiveness (Wedekind, Seebeck, Bettens, & Paepke, 1995). In other words, mate selection might be influenced by olfactory or other cues that signal immunological differences. The greater the immunological differences, the greater the chances of producing a viable infant. Inbreeding avoidance may be the most important function of MHC-associated mating preferences (Potts, Manning, & Wakeland, 1994). Studies of mice suggest that MHC preferences come about through imprinting (Yamazaki et al., 1988). Infants learn how their own MHC type smells, and evolutionary forces have evolved a preference for dissimilar types.

It is of interest that scores of studies find behavioral and social similarity important to understanding mate selection. Winch, Ktsanes, and Ktsanes's (1954) theory of complementary needs never received much support (e.g., Udry, 1964). The MHC studies draw family scholars back to exploring complementarity, albeit in a different form, as an explanatory variable.

This preference for immunological differences would certainly help to explain mate selection studies of Kibbutz marriages and Chinese arranged marriages. Shepher (1971) studied mate selection in Israel Kibbutz where from the time of birth, children were raised in child-care facilities. Parents saw them a few hours a day, but most of the time they were with the care providers and other children. Shepher observed that, upon reaching adulthood, individuals never married someone from the same facility. Wolf (1995) studied arranged marriages in China that took place in the early part of this century. Marriages were often arranged when children were very young. In some communities, the female child would go to live in the male's home where she was treated as one of the children. In other communities, the female remained with the birth parents until mature, whereupon she moved to the male's family. Compared with those who did not reside together until maturity, the couples who lived together as children had unsuccessful marriages. Many were never consummated, and few had children. Men were consistently unfaithful and had children with mistresses. For MHC preferences to be the explanatory mechanism in these studies, we would need evidence of imprinting (akin to the mouse studies) to explain the rejection of kibbutz-mates and sons of foster families.

Family researchers should find this work of interest not only because of its relation to mate preferences and incest avoidance, but also because of its relation to birth outcomes. For example, HLA similarity has been associated with repeated spontaneous abortions (Thomas, Harger, Wagener, Rabin, & Gill, 1985), and lower birth weight (Ober et al., 1987).

Students of contraceptive use also will find the HLA studies of interest. Estradiol reduces women's ability to discriminate immunological differences among potential mates. High estradiol may be found among pregnant women and women on "the pill." A modern contraceptive method may be resulting in poor mate selection from the standpoint of producing children who are less likely to survive. The inability of these women to detect appropriate mates may affect the stability of courtship relationships. Cohabiting pill users have significantly higher rates of union dissolution (controlling for a wide assortment of suspected covariates) than other nonhormonal-based contraceptors (Carver, 1998).

Developments in another line of research bear watching because of their relevance to mate selection. Faces judged to have above average symmetry are regarded as more attractive. Facial symmetry may be associated with greater immunological competence and increased gene variation, which means that mating with such individuals would increase the chances of infant survival (Gangestad & Buss, 1993; Gangestad & Thornhill, 1998; Grammar & Thornhill, 1994; Mitton, 1993; Thornhill & Gangestad, 1993). Preference for masculine facial features has been observed to vary during the phase of the menstrual cycle. When conception is most likely, women prefer less masculine faces than during the rest of the menstrual cycle (Penton-Voak et al., 1999). The masculine faces may signal immunological competence, whereas the less masculine faces may indicate paternal interest and investment in offspring. Gangestad and Simpson (in press) integrate these findings into a theory that suggests women vary their reproductive strategy according to the harshness of the environment. When the environment is difficult, women place more weight on indications of genetic fitness than they do when the environment is less demanding. How these findings, if borne out by subsequent studies, would play out in mate selection or extra-pair sexual relationships is deserving of study.

The integration of measures of basic features of the immune system into mate selection and courtship research serves to increase understanding of incest avoidance, contraceptive use, and unstable courtship relations as they relate to the evolutionary need to produce viable offspring.

RELATIONSHIP QUALITY AND STABILITY

Testosterone's links to marrying and divorcing are considered first, followed by reports of research on the relationship between marital quality and testosterone. Genetic influences on divorce are considered, as is the association between marital conflict and immunity.

Marital Status

In the preceding section, several biological mechanisms were suggested that may define marital relationship quality and stability. Insight is obtained from evidence that testosterone levels in men drop after they marry. In a 10-year longitudinal study of Air Force officers who underwent four physical exams over that period of time, Mazur and Michalek (1998) were able to compare changes in testosterone with changes in marital status. Unmarried men's testosterone levels were high, but following marriage, they decreased. One scenario is that single men are mostly in the company of other men, and everyday competition (some of which may be over women) keeps testosterone levels elevated (e.g., Booth, Shelley, Mazur, Tharp, & Kittok, 1989). Once married, exposure to other men declined, and the need to compete for women disappeared. Another scenario is that the marriage itself lowered testosterone—similar to what was observed after the birth of an infant. Wives expect men to behave in supportive and nurturing ways, and lowering testosterone may be crucial to successfully enacting the caring spousal and parent roles. Alternatively, biological messages (e.g., pheromones) having to do with sex or reproduction may cause testosterone to decrease.

Relationship Quality

Even though marriage is accompanied by a drop in testosterone, hormones may still be related to marital quality. An analysis of men from a representative sample of 4,462 former military servicemen between the ages of 33 and 42 showed that men with higher testosterone production were less likely to marry in the first place; once married, they were more likely to divorce (Booth & Dabbs, 1993). The likelihood of never marrying was 50% higher for men whose testosterone levels were one standard deviation above the mean compared with those whose testosterone levels were one standard deviation below the mean. Similarly, men at the higher level were 43% more likely to divorce than were those at the lower level. Once married, men with higher testosterone levels were 31% more likely to leave home because of a troubled relationship with their wife, 38% more likely to have extra-marital sex, and 13% more likely to report hitting or throwing things at their spouse. In addition, high-testosterone men were more likely to report low-quality marital interaction, a finding supported by Julian and McKenry (1989). These findings were net of other social variables such as low socioeconomic status or deviant behavior in other arenas. It is important to note, however, that substantial numbers of men with high testosterone had excellent marriages. The mechanism that explains this differential marital success is unknown. There is also the caveat that cross-sectional studies do not clarify whether conflictual marriages raise testosterone.

On the other hand, marriage does play a protective role with respect to the link between testosterone and antisocial behavior and depression. Men with high testosterone levels are at risk of committing a crime and being depressed. Marriage, along with steady employment, reduces the likelihood of both (Booth, Johnson, & Granger, 1999; Booth & Osgood, 1993). Because these studies are based on cross-sectional data, it is not possible to estimate the causal ordering of the variables. The work of Mazur and Michalek (1998) and Gubernick, Worthman, and Stallings (1991) has suggested that marriage may reduce the likelihood that high-testosterone men commit crimes and get depressed. The nature of the mechanism is unclear, however.

We know little about hormones and women's marriages. Having low levels of testosterone may be important to relationship quality, or quality may be associated with hormones associated with reproduction, such as estradiol or oxytocin. Equally important is dyadic research on marital partners to see how hormone-behavior links in one individual are related to hormone-behavior links in the spouse.

Genetics and Divorce

Given that divorce rates are so consistent from society to society (Goode, 1993), it is not surprising that a number of studies have shown genes to influence divorce. Estimates of the heritability of divorce have ranged from .26 (Turkheimer, Lovett, Robinette, & Gottesman, 1992) to .53 (Jockin, McGue, & Lykken, 1996; McGue & Lykken, 1992). Jockin et al. (1996) hypothesized that personality traits play a key role. They demonstrated that between 30% and 42% of the heritability of divorce risk comes from genetic factors affecting personality. This finding is supported by a study of the association between parent and offspring divorce indicating that behavior problems mediate a significant share of the link (Amato, 1996). Analysis is needed that combines methods used by family researchers (survival analysis) with behavior genetics methods to explain the genetic mediation of divorce (e.g., Meyer, Eaves, Heath, & Martin, 1991).

The consequences of divorce for children may also have genetic origins. In a large-scale study of divorce, Block, Block, and Gjerde (1986) and Cherlin and colleagues (1991) both demonstrated that boys' elevated risk for behavior problems observed after divorce disappeared when behavior problems many years before divorce were controlled. Although Cherlin, Chase-Lansdale, and McRae (1998) demonstrated in a later study that the gap between children from divorced and nondivorced families widened as children moved into young adulthood, there remains a significant amount of unexplained variance. It is possible that the behavior problems of the boys before and after divorce are related because of underlying enduring personality characteristics and not because a high-conflict marital relationship generates the problems. This is an example of a finding that could be greatly informed by including a genetic component in the study.

Marital Conflict, Immunity, and Health

Data from large epidemiological studies suggest that poor personal relationships are a major risk factor for morbidity and mortality (House, Landis, & Umberson, 1988). The search for mechanisms has revealed substantial evidence regarding the role of immune function. Kiecolt-Glaser, Glaser, Cacioppo, and Malarkey (1998) demonstrated that abrasive marital interactions have important endocrine and immunological correlates. In general, marital separation or divorce, higher marital conflict, and lower marital satisfaction are associated with lower immune function. Such stress-related immuno-logical changes may be a pathway through which close personal relationships influence health (e.g., infectious diseases, cancer, wound healing).

Testosterone is related to poor union quality and stability, as are genetic influences. In contrast, evidence that environmental factors influence hormone levels involves the finding that testosterone declines when men marry. Marital conflict and instability may compromise the immune system, which in turn affects health.

FUTURE DIRECTIONS

Recent Research Advances

The biosocial research community is now poised to construct and test multivariate and latent models of the interacting effects of genetic, endocrine, environmental, histori-cal, and behavioral factors that will increase our understanding of family relationships and processes, as well as developmental outcomes (Susman, 1998). Researchers have cleared several major hurdles that now make such advances possible. First, we have reliable and valid noninvasive methods to obtain measurements of biological systems with direct relevance to biosocial research. Second, gene mapping is progressing at a rapid rate, which will advance our ability to disentangle genetic and environmental influences. Third, large public use data sets are now, or soon will be, available that contain biological markers, as well as representative samples of household pairs (twins, siblings, and unrelated adolescents residing in the same household) needed to more accurately estimate genetic variance. The National Longitudinal Study of Adolescent Health (Bearman, Jones, & Udry, 1997), rich in biological, behavior, social, and contextual data, is the premiere study in this category.

Increased Involvement in Biosocial Research by Social and Behavioral Scientists

Contemporary social and behavioral scientists have expressed renewed interest in how the factors they study influence and are influenced by physiological and genetic processes. A content analysis of articles in three journals that publish family research revealed a substantial growth in the number of articles per issue involving biological variables. Issues from 1990 to mid-1998 were compared to issues from 1980 to 1989. For Journal of Marriage and the Family, the number per issue increased by 47% (.76 to 1.12), for Social Forces, 121% (.28 to .62), and for Journal of Personality and Social Psychology, 18% (1.10 to 1.30).

Development of Infrastructure Support

The National Institutes of Health have established new priorities that designate "studies on the interactions between biological and behavioral processes" as being of "high program relevance." The National Science Foundation's Division of Social, Behavioral, and Economic Research has as one of its goals to advance fundamental knowledge about "biological factors related to human behavior." In short, there is now a national agenda to facilitate the integration of biosocial perspectives into research on child and adult well-being and development within the context of the family.

How to Get Involved

This does not mean that family scholars must become biologists to take an active role in this line of research. Rather, we envision family researchers and trainees learning enough biology to become part of an interdisciplinary scientific team. This team approach contrasts with the notion of training one investigator who "knows all" about several fields of knowledge. The latter scenario seems problematic because ultimately depth of knowledge in any one field may be sacrificed to breadth of knowledge. We expect future family researchers to have specialized skills in traditional disciplines but also to have the practical and theoretical biological training needed to speak the common language and facilitate collaboration between investigators who represent different disciplinary perspectives. Family researchers may obtain that knowledge by reading references cited here, attending the meetings of scholarly groups such as the International Society for Psychoneuroendocrinology, Society for Behavioral Medicine, Behavior Genetics Association, and International Workshop on Methodology of Twin and Family Studies.

NOTE

We are indebted to Paul Amato, Jay Belsky, Ann C. Crouter, Daniel Lichter, J. Richard Udry, Susan Welch, and Lynn White for very helpful comments on earlier versions of this manuscript. This research is supported in part by the Pennsylvania

State University Population Research Institute, with core support from the National Institute of Child Health and Human Development, grant 1-HD28263.

REFERENCES

Altemus, M., Deuster, P., Galliven, E., Carter, C., & Gold, P. (1995). Suppression of hypothalamic-pituitary-adrenal axis responses to stress in lactating women. *Journal of Clinical Endocrinology Metabolism, 80,* 2954–2959.

Amato, P. (1996). Explaining the intergenerational transmission of divorce. *Journal of Marriage and the Family, 58,* 628–640.

Baker, L. A., & Daniels, D. (1990). Nonshared environmental influences and personality differences in adult twins. *Journal of Personality and Social Psychology, 58,* 103–110.

Barkley, R. (1989). Hyperactive girls and boys: Stimulant drug effects on mother-child interactions. *Journal of Child Psychology and Psychiatry, 30,* 336–341.

Bearman, P. S., Jones, J., & Udry, J. R. (1997). *The National Longitudinal Study of Adolescent Health: Research design.* Available at: *http://www.cpc.unc.edu/projects/addhealth/design.html*

Belsky, J., Steinberg, L., & Draper, P. (1991). Childhood experience, interpersonal development, and reproductive strategy: An evolutionary theory of socialization. *Child Development, 62,* 642–670.

Block, J., Block, J., & Gjerde, P. (1986). The personality of children prior to divorce: A prospective study. *Child Development, 57,* 827–840.

Booth, A., & Dabbs, J. (1993). Testosterone and men's marriages. *Social Forces, 72,* 463–477.

Booth, A., (1996). *Cortisol, testosterone, and competition among women.* Unpublished manuscript.

Booth, A., Johnson, D., & Granger, D. (1999). Testosterone and men's depression: The role of social behavior. *Journal of Health and Social Behavior, 40,* 130–140.

Booth, A., & Osgood, D. (1993). The influence of testosterone on deviance in adulthood. *Criminology, 31,* 93–117.

Booth, A., Shelley, G., Mazur, A., Tharp, G., & Kittok, R. (1989). Testosterone, and winning and losing in human competition. *Hormones and Behavior, 23,* 556–571.

Braungart, J., Fulker, D., & Plomin, R. (1992). Genetic mediation of the home environment during infancy: A sibling adoption study of the HOME. *Developmental Psychology, 28,* 1048–1055.

Braungart, J. M. (1994). Genetic influences on "environmental" measures. In J. C. DeFries, R. Plomin, & D. W. Fulker (Eds.), *Nature and nurture during middle childhood* (pp. 233–248). Oxford, U. K.: Blackwell.

Buss, D. M., & Schmitt, D. P. (1993). Sexual strategies theory: An evolutionary perspective on human mating. *Psychological Review,* 100, 204–232.

Cadoret, R., Yates, W., Troughtoh, E., Woodworth, G., & Stewart, M. (1995). Genetic-environmental interaction in the genesis of aggressive and conduct disorders. *Archives of General Psychiatry, 52,* 916–924.

Cairns, R., Gariepy, J., & Hood, K. (1990). Development, microevolution, and social behavior. *Psychological Review,* 97, 49–65.

Carlson, M., & Earls, E. (1997). Psychological and neuroendocrinological sequelae of early social deprivation in institutionalized children in Romania. In C. Carter, I. Lederhendler, & B. Kirkpatrick (Eds.), *The integrative neurobiology of affiliation* (pp. 419–428). New York: New York Academy of Sciences.

Carver, K. (1998). *The effect of hormonal contraceptive use on the risk of union dissolution in the United States.* Unpublished manuscript.

Cashdan, E. (1995). Hormones, sex, and status in women. *Hormones and Behavior, 29,* 354–366.

Cherlin, A., Chase-Lansdale, P., & McRae, C. (1998). Effects of parental divorce on mental health throughout the life course. *American Sociological Review, 63*, 239–249.

Cherlin, A., Furstenberg, F. F., Chase-Lansdale, P. L., Kiernan, K., Morrison, D. R., & Teitler, J. (1991). Longitudinal studies of effects of divorce on children in Great Britain and the United States. *Science, 252*, 1386–1389.

Collaer, M., & Hines, M. (1995). Human behavioral sex differences: A role for gonadal hormones during early development? *Psychological Bulletin, 118*, 55–107.

Dabbs, J. (1992). Testosterone and occupational achievement. *Social Forces, 70*, 813–824.

Daly, M., & Wilson, M. (1983). *Sex, evolution, and behavior*. Boston: Willard Grant Press.

———. (1988). Evolutionary social psychology and family homicide. *Science, 242*, 519–524.

Davis, J., & Daly, M. (1997). Evolutionary theory and the human family. *The Quarterly Review of Biology, 72*, 407–435.

Dunne, M. P., Martin, N. G., Statham, D. J., Slutske, W. S., Dinwiddie, S. H., Bucholz, K. K., Madden, P. A., & Heath, A. C. (1997). Genetic and environmental contributions to variance in age at first sexual intercourse. *Psychological Science, 8*, 211–216.

Ellis, B., Dodge, K., Pettit, G., & Bates, J. (in press). Quality of early family relationships and individual differences in the timing of pubertal maturation in girls: A longitudinal test of an evolutionary model. *Journal of Personality and Social Psychology*.

Ellis, B., & Garber, J. (in press). Psychosocial antecedents of variation in girls' pubertal timing: Marital depression, stepfather presence, and marital and family stress. *Child Development*.

Finkelstein, J., Susman, E., Chinchilli, V., Kunselman, S., D'arcangelo, R., Schwab, J., Demers, L., Liben, L., Lookingbill, G., & Kulin, H. (1997). Estrogen or testosterone increases self-reported aggressive behaviors in hypogonadal adolescents. *Journal of Clinical Endocrinology and Metabolism, 82*, 2433–2438.

Fleming, A., Ruble, D., Krieger, H., & Wong, P. (1997). Hormonal and experiential correlates of maternal responsiveness during pregnancy and the puerperium in human mothers. *Hormones and Behavior, 31*, 145–158.

Flynn, M., & England, B. (1995). Childhood stress and family environment. *Current Anthropology, 36*, 854–866.

Gangestad, W. W., & Buss, D. M. (1993). Pathogen prevalence and human mate preferences. *Ethology and Sociobiology, 14*, 89–96.

Gangestad, W. W., & Simpson, J. A. (in press). The evolution of human mating: Trade offs and strategic pluralism. *Behavioral and Brain Sciences*.

Gangestad, W. W., & Thornhill, R. (1998). Menstrual cycle variation in women's preferences for the scent of symmetrical men. *Proceedings of the Royal Society of London, B, 265*, 927–933.

Goode, W. J. (1993). *World changes in divorce patterns*. New Haven, CT: Yale University Press.

Gottlieb, G. (1991). Experiential canalization of behavioral development: Theory. *Developmental Psychology, 27*, 4–13.

———. (1992). *Individual development and evolution: The genesis of novel behavior*. New York: Oxford University Press.

Grammar, K., & Thornhill, R. (1994). Human *(Homo sapiens)* facial attractiveness and sexual selection: The role of symmetry and averageness. *Journal of Comparative Psychology, 108*, 233–242.

Granger, D. A., Schwartz, E. B., Booth, A., & Arentz, M. (1999). Salivary testosterone determination in studies of child health and development. *Hormones and Behavior, 36*, 18–27.

Granger, D. A., Serbin, L. A., Schwartzman, A. E., Lehoux, P., Cooperman, J., & Ikeda, S. (1998). Children's salivary cortisol, internalizing behavior problems, and family environment: Results from the Concordia Longitudinal Risk Project. *International Journal of Behavioral Development, 22*, 707–728.

Granger, D. A., Weisz, J. R., & Kauneckis, D. (1996). Neuroendocrine reactivity, internalizing behavior problems, and control-related cognitions in clinic-referred children and adolescents. *Journal of Abnormal Psychology, 103*, 267–276.

Granger, D. A., Weisz, J. R., McCracken, J. T., Ikeda, S., & Douglas, P. (1996). Reciprocal influences among adrenocortical activation, psychosocial processes, and clinic-referred children's short-term behavioral adjustment. *Child Development*, 67, 3250–3262.

Gubernick, D., Worthman, C., & Stallings, J. (1991). *Hormonal correlates of fatherhood in man.* Unpublished manuscript.

Gunnar, M., Mangelsdorf, S., Larsen, M., & Herstgaard, L. (1998). Attachment, temperament, and adrenocortical activity in infancy: A study of psychoendocrine regulation. *Developmental Psychology, 25*, 355–363.

Halpern, C., Udry, J., & Suchindran, C. (1998). Monthly measures of salivary testosterone predict sexual activity in adolescent males. *Archives of Sexual Behavior, 27*, 445–465.

Hart, J., Gunnar, M., & Cicchetti, D. (1995). Salivary cortisol in maltreated children: Evidence of relations between neuroendocrine activity and social competence. *Development and Psychopathology*, 7, 11–26.

House, J. S., Landis, K. R., & Umberson, D. (1988). Social relationships and health. *Science, 241*, 540–545.

Jockin, V., McGue, M., & Lykken, D. T. (1996). Personality and divorce: A genetic analysis. *Journal of Personality and Social Psychology, 71*, 288–299.

Julian, T., & McKenry, P. (1989). Relationship of testosterone to men's family functioning at mid-life: A research note. *Aggressive Behavior, 15*, 281–289.

Julian, T., McKenry, P., & McKelvey, M. (1990). Mediators of relationships stress between middle-aged fathers and their adolescent children. *Journal of Genetic Psychology, 152*, 381–386.

Kendler, K., Kessler, R., Waiters, E., Maclean, C., Neale, M., Heath, A., & Eaves, L. (1995). Stressful life events, genetic liability, and onset of an episode of major depression in women. *American Journal of Psychiatry, 154*, 1398–1404.

Kiecolt-Glaser, J. K., Glaser, R., Cacioppo, J. T., & Malarkey, W. B. (1998). Marital stress: Immunological, neuroendocrine, and autonomic correlates. *Annals of the New York Academy of Sciences*, 840, 656–663.

Kirschbaum, C., Read, G. F., & Hellhammer, D. H. (1992). *Assessment of hormones and drugs in saliva in biobehavioral research.* Kirkland, WA: Hogrefe & Huber.

Lechman, J., & Mayes, L. (1998). Maladies of love—An evolutionary perspective on some forms of obsessive-compulsive disorder. In D. Hann, L. Huffman, I. Lederhendler, & D. Meinecke (Eds.), *Advancing research on developmental plasticity: Integrating the behavioral science and neuroscience of mental health* (publication 98, pp. 134–152). Washington, DC: National Institute of Mental Health.

Mazur, A., & Booth, A. (1998). Testosterone and dominance in men. *Behavioral and Brain Sciences, 21*, 353–363.

Mazur, A., & Michalek, J. (1998). Marriage, divorce, and male testosterone. *Social Forces, 77*, 315–330.

Mazur, A., Susman, E., & Edelbrock, S. (1997). Sex differences in testosterone response to a video game contest. *Evolution and Human Behavior, 18*, 317–326.

McClearn, G. (1993). Behavior genetics: The last century and the next. In R. Plomin & G. McClearn (Eds.), *Nature, nurture and psychology* (pp. 27–51). Washington, DC: American Psychological Association.

McClintock, M., & Herdt, G. (1996). Rethinking puberty: The development of sexual attraction. *Current Directions in Psychological Science*, 5, 178–183.

McGue, M., & Lykken, D. T. (1992). Genetic influence on risk of divorce. *Psychological Science*, 3, 368–373.

Meyer, J. M., Eaves, L. J., Heath, A. C., & Martin, N. G. (1991). Estimating genetic influences on the age at menarche: A survival analysis approach. *American Journal of Medical Genetics*, 39, 148–154.

Mitton, J. B. (1993). Enzyme heterozygosity, metabolism, and developmental stability. *Genetica,* *89*, 47–66.

Moffitt, T. (1993). Adolescence-limited and life-course-persistent antisocial behavior: A developmental taxonomy. *Psychological Review, 100*, 674–701.

Neale, M. C., & Cardon, L. R. (1992). *Methodology for genetic studies of twins and families.* The Netherlands: Kluwer Academic.

Nelson, R. J. (1999). *An introduction to behavioral endocrinology.* New York: Sinauer.

Ober, C., Simpson, J. L., Ward, M., Radvany, R. M., Andersen, R., Elias, S., Sabbagha, R., & The DIEP Study Group. (1987). Prenatal effects of maternal-fetal HLA compatibility. *American Journal of Reproductive Immunology and Microbiology, 15*, 141–149.

Penton-Voak, I. S., Perrett, D. I., Castles, D. L., Kobayashi, T., Burt, D. M., Murray, L. K., & Minamisawa, R. (1999). Menstrual cycle alters face preference. *Nature, 399*, 741–742.

Pike, A., McGuire, S., Hetherington, E., Reiss, D., & Plomin, D. (1996). Family environment and adolescent depressive symptoms and antisocial behavior: A multivariate genetic analysis. *Developmental Psychology, 32*, 590–603.

Plomin, R. (1994). *Genetics and experience: The interplay between nature and nurture.* Thousand Oaks, CA: Sage.

———. (1995). Genetics and children's experiences in the family. *Journal of Child Psychology and Psychiatry, 36*, 33–68.

Plomin, R., McClearn, G., Pedersen, G., Nesselroade, J., & Bergeman, C. (1988). Genetic influence on adults' ratings of their current family environment. *Journal of Marriage and the Family, 51*, 791–803.

Plomin, R., Reiss, D., Hetherington, E., & Howe, G. (1994). Nature and nurture: Genetic influence on measures of family environment. *Developmental Psychology, 30*, 32–43.

Potts, W. K., Manning, C. J., & Wakeland, E. K. (1994). The role of infectious disease, inbreeding and mating preferences in maintaining MHC genetic diversity: An experimental test. *Philosophical Transactions of the Royal Society of London, Series B: Biological Sciences, B, 346*, 369–378.

Reiss, D. (1995). Genetic influence on family systems: Implications for development. *Journal of Marriage and the Family, 57*, 543–560.

Rodgers, J. L., & Doughty, D. (in press). Genetic and environmental influences on fertility expectations and outcomes using NLSY kinship data. In J. L. Rodgers, D. C. Rowe, & W. B. Miller (Eds.), *Genetic influences on fertility and sexuality.* Boston: Kluwer Academic.

Rowe, D. C. (1981). Environmental and genetic influences on dimensions of perceived parenting: A twin study. *Developmental Psychology, 17*, 203–208.

———. (1983). A biometrical analysis of perceptions of family environment: A study of twin and singleton sibling kinships. *Child Development, 54*, 416–423.

———. (1994). *The limits of family influence: Genes, experience, and behavior.* New York: Guilford Press.

Sanders, S., & Reinisch, J. (1990). Biological and social influences on the endocrinology of puberty: Some additional considerations. In J. Bancroft & J. Reinisch (Eds.), *Adolescence and puberty* (pp. 50–62). New York: Oxford University Press.

Scarr, S., & McCartney, K. (1983). How people make their own environments: A theory of genotype→environment effects. *Child Development, 54*, 424–435.

Shepher, J. (1971). Mate selection among second generation Kibbutz adolescents and adults: Incest avoidance and negative imprinting. *Archives of Sexual Behavior, 1*, 293–307.

Stansbury, K., & Gunnar, R. (1994). Adrenocortical activity and emotion regulation. In N. Fox (Ed.), The development of emotion regulation: Biological and behavioral considerations. *Monographs of the Society for Research in Child Development, 59*, 108–134.

Storey, A. E., Walsh, C. J., Quinton, R. L., & Wynne-Edwards, K. E. (in press). Hormonal correlates of paternal responsiveness in new and expectant fathers. *Evolution and Human Behavior.*

Susman, E. (1998). Biobehavioral development: An integrative perspective. *International Journal of Behavioral Development, 22*, 671–679.

Thomas, M. L., Harger, J. H., Wagener, D. K., Rabin, B. S., & Gill, T. J. (1985). HLA sharing and spontaneous abortion in humans. *American Journal of Obstetrics and Gynecology, 151*, 1053–1058.

Thornhill, R., & Gangestad, S. W. (1993). Human facial beauty: Averageness, symmetry and parasite resistance. *Human Nature*, 4, 237–269.

Tremblay, R., Schaal, B., Boulerice, B., Arseneault, L., Soussignan, R., Paquette, D., & Lauret, D. (1998). Testosterone, physical aggression, dominance and physical development in early adolescence. *International Journal of Behavioral Development, 22*, 753–777.

Turkheimer, E., Lovett, G., Robinette, C. D., & Gottesman, I. I. (1992). The heritability of divorce: New data and theoretical implications [abstract]. *Behavior Genetics, 22*, 757.

Turner, R. A., Altemus, M., Enos, T., Cooper, B., & McGuinness, T. (1999). Preliminary research on plasma oxytocin in normal cycling women: Investigating emotion and interpersonal distress. *Psychiatry: Interpersonal & Biological Processes, 62*, 97–113.

Udry, J. R. (1964). Complementarity in mate selection: A perceptual approach. *Marriage and Family Living, 25*, 281–289.

———. (1988). Biological predispositions and social control in adolescent sexual behavior. *American Sociological Review, 53*, 709–722.

———. (2000). Biological limits of gender construction. *American Sociological Review*, 65 (3), 443–457.

Udry, J. R., Morris, N., & Kovenock, J. (1995). Androgen effects on women's gendered behavior. *Journal of Biosocial Science, 27*, 359–369.

Uvnas-Moberg, K. (1997). Physiological and endocrine effects of social contact. In C. Carter, I. Lederhendler, & B. Kirkpatrick (Eds.), *The integrative neurobiology of affiliation* (pp. 146–163). New York: New York Academy of Sciences.

Uvnas-Moberg, K., Widstrom, A., Nissen, E., & Bjorvell, H. (1990). Personality traits in women 4 days postpartum and their correlation with plasma levels of oxytocin and prolactin. *Journal of Psychosomatic Obstetrics and Gynaecology, 11*, 261–273.

Van Goozen, S., Weigant, V., Endert, E., Helmond, F., & Van de Poll, N. (1997). Psychoendocrinological assessment of the menstrual cycle: The relationship between hormones, sexuality, and mood. *Archives of Sexual Behavior, 26*, 359–382.

Wedekind, C., Seebeck, T., Bettens, F., & Paepke, A. J. (1995). MHC-dependent mate preferences in humans. *Proceedings of the Royal Society of London, B, 260*, 245–249.

White, L., & Booth, A. (1985). The quality and stability of remarriages: The role of stepchildren. *American Sociological Review, 50*, 689–698.

Widstrom, A., Wahlbert, V., Matthiesen, A., Eneroth, P., Unvas-Moberg, K., Werner, S., & Winberg, J. (1990). Short-term effects of early sucking on maternal behavior and breastfeeding performance. *Early Human Development, 21*, 153–163.

Wilson, E. O. (1998). *Consilience: The unity of knowledge.* New York: Knopf.

Winch, R. F., Ktsanes, T., & Ktsanes, V. (1954). The theory of complementary needs in mateselection. *American Sociological Review, 19*, 241–249.

Wolf, A. (1995). *Sexual attraction and childhood association.* Stanford, CA: Stanford University Press.

Yamazaki, K., Beauchamp, G. K., Kupniewski, D., Bard, J., Thomas, L., & Boyse, E. A. (1988). Familial imprinting determines H-2 selective mating preferences. *Science, 240*, 1331–1332.

Reprinted from: Alan Booth, Karen Carver, and Douglas A. Granger, "Biosocial Perspectives on the Family." In *Journal of Marriage and Family*, 62(4), pp. 1018–1034. Copyright © 2000 by The National Council on Family Relations. Reprinted with permission.

EPILOGUE

In the Introduction to this book, we asked you to consider some fundamental questions about how individuals and families functioned—"Why do families do that?" and "Why do they behave that way?" In this book, we have explored nine different ways in which family scholars have explained family functioning. Each theory provides a unique set of lenses through which to examine family functioning and offers different explanations as to why families behave the way they do.

The following figure "Summary of family theories" provides a basic comparison between the nine family theories that have been covered in this book. We have covered how families may be seen from both a broad, "macro" perspective as social institutions that function to maintain society and from an individual level to the specific "micro" perspective of individual analysis within the family system.

The purpose of social science is not to suggest there is only one truth about individuals and families but rather to discover the many layers of their complex lives. Thus, depending on the question, the situation, and the outcome needed, the theoretical perspective that is most useful will vary. In addition, knowing many theories gives us a multitude of options to choose from in order to assess, analyze, and understand a family better. Theories evolve over time, and these theories will continue to change and develop as research continues to challenge our understanding about families, increasing our knowledge of family issues, confronting our assumptions about how we define families, and expanding our perceptions of the complexities of family life.

The importance of knowing multiple theories can be seen in this example. Let's say that you are investigating the factors individuals consider when choosing an intimate partner, with a specific focus on the importance of social practice. As a result, structural functionalism or biosocial theory provides a sufficient framework for your research questions. However, if you want to look at how particular couples make their decisions about becoming life partners, or how individuals choose one person over another, then you can probably get a better understanding by using the theory of social exchange. Conflict theory or even feminism would also help you decide why individuals choose the person they do. Each theory would provide you with different ways to focus your questions, which would in turn reshape your answers to those questions.

Let's say that you want to know not only why people pick the partners they choose but also why they choose them at that particular time. In other words, if you had met this same person two years ago, would you still have fallen in love? The previously

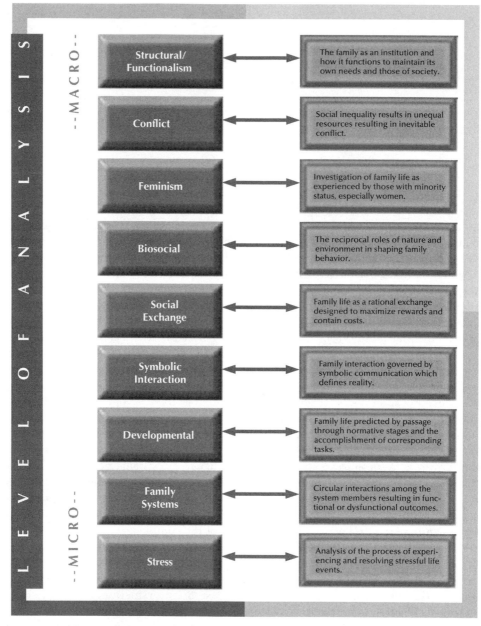

Summary of family theories.

mentioned theories will not be as useful in answering this new question. Instead, you might turn to family development, symbolic interaction, or even family systems theory to guide your research. Finally, you now decide that the most interesting questions have to do with the disagreements or tensions in relationships once they form. This results in turning to conflict, feminist, or stress theory to best answer your new questions.

Knowing which theory to use is often a matter of preference, can be dictated by the situation, and sometimes is simply based on guessing. Theories speak to us because they resonate with what we believe to be important. Because of this, you may have found, as you read these chapters, that you preferred some theories over others. That is a fairly typical experience. If you continue to work in this field, you will find that your colleagues will reflect theoretical orientations, either by training or by preference, in their work. The important thing is to remember that each theory has its usefulness. You may find, for example, that one theory explains 85 percent of the families with whom you work. However, there will inevitably be situations when that one theory will not explain a family as well as another theory might, and when you are faced with that family, in your office or in your life, it is always useful to have other theories in your repertoire.

Because a theory can change the way we view and understand the world—and families—theories can also help us know how to intervene. When we approach families in a systematic way, we can be certain that we have considered all possible avenues of understanding families, and therefore, the most effective ways of helping families achieve their best selves.

USING THE THEORIES

You have had the chance in this book thus far to consider each theory in its own historical context. It is important to practice using the theories in a more comprehensive way, to determine how each theory provides a focus for family issues. These theoretical lenses will give you a different perspective about a family's strengths, weaknesses, struggles, issues, challenges, and potentials.

Below is a complex case study of a three-generation family. Imagine that you are a helping professional, perhaps a family life educator or counselor, assigned to work with the family described below. Try to understand their situation and dynamics using each of the theoretical frameworks explained in this text.

Using each theory in the book, outline the major issues or crises facing the family from that perspective. Consider the strengths and weaknesses from that perspective. Find examples of basic assumptions and examples from the case study. What roles do the family members play, if any? How do they enact their roles? How are the societal or individual issues played out in the family?

After having considered each theory separately, consider them as a group. Which theories seem to be most useful to you in understanding the Maldonado family? Why did you prefer one over another? What is it about their perspective that you find more reasonable or useful for the kind of work that you would eventually like to do with families? Thus, use this application experience to illustrate not just the context of the theories but their applicability to your future career.

THE MALDONADO FAMILY

Juan and Maria Maldonado have been married for fifteen years. They were both born in Mexico and immigrated to the United States five years ago. Life was difficult for them in Mexico. Juan worked very long, labor-intensive days in the factory for little pay, which was barely enough to support his four children and wife. Maria worked as a nurse in the local village hospital. Despite all their hard work, they were still poor and did not see much hope for their future. Because they could not see a way out of their economic situation, they decided to move to the United States in hopes of finding a better life for themselves and, in particular, for their children. Maria's aunt, who was already living in the United States, offered to help Juan find a job there. While they were filled with sadness at leaving their extended family behind, the Maldonados moved their family to the United States full of hope for a brighter future.

Since they have come to the United States, things have improved a little. Their children have learned English very well, although Juan and Maria still struggle with the language, which makes them depend a great deal on Marco, their eldest, for translation. Because Juan found a good job at a factory, their economic lives have improved. Maria cannot work as a nurse because she cannot speak English. As a result, she cleans houses to make some extra money. Granted, they will probably never be able to buy Nikes and fancy cars, but the children have clothes, shoes, medical care, and a dental plan.

Once Juan and Maria settled in the United States, both of their mothers came to live with them. The townhouse they rent is cramped with eight people living in it, but the two youngest children don't mind sleeping on the floor, and life is easier on Maria now that the older women are there, because they do all the cooking and cleaning for the family. She is free to do more housecleaning and to take English classes at the community college. Juan and Maria felt that bringing the grandparents to live with them was important. They missed the closeness of the family in Mexico, and they wanted their children to know their grandparents. They felt very sad that both of their fathers had died since they had left Mexico and they could not afford to go to their funerals. Having their mothers nearby meant they could also ensure that they had the best childcare. And Maria's mother could now be nearer to her own sister, who had been so instrumental in getting the Maldonado family to move to the United States in the first place.

Despite an improved living situation, the Maldonado family still has many problems. Both Juan and Maria worry about what will happen if Juan loses his job. They know that their inability to speak English puts them both at risk with employment. Maria really wants a job at a hospital, but it costs money to take the special "English for Nurses" classes required to work at the hospital. Besides, the classes are taught at night, when she needs to be at home with the boys helping them with their homework. Marco, who is now fourteen-years old, and his brother, Phillip, twelve-years old, are very little help around the house and seem to be getting into trouble more and more in the neighborhood. They used to come straight home from school, but now they hang out with friends Maria doesn't know and seem to defy her authority. Juan, who is working the night shift, is either sleeping or at work and sees his sons only on the weekends. Katrina, who is ten-years old, is a very quiet girl and is very pleasing to everyone. She quietly does her homework, and stays with her grandmothers when Maria must go out. Everyone thinks Katrina is a wonderful little girl, but secretly Maria worries that perhaps Katrina is a little too withdrawn.

Recently, Juan and Maria were called in for a parent–teacher conference to discuss Rosina, their eight-year-old daughter. They had to take Marco to be their translator. The school offered to provide one, but they felt more secure with Marco. But they were embarrassed by Marco's attitude when they got to the school because he was rude to the teacher instead of being respectful. He said it was because the teacher "talked bad" about Rosina. According to her teacher, Rosina's grades, which have never been great, were getting even worse. They found out that Rosina had also been talking a lot in class and was frequently disruptive. They also discovered that other children in class teased her because of her clothes and her accent. When this happened, she yelled at them and once even attempted to hit another child, which is ultimately what prompted this conference. The teacher suggested that perhaps Rosina needed to see the school counselor for some help. That apparently is what made Marco angry, causing him to be rude to the teacher because he believed that Rosina was provoked, and therefore, did not need any help from a school counselor. The teacher suggested that perhaps Marco needed some help as well. Juan and Maria went home from the conference very upset and didn't really know what to think.

In addition, Juan and Maria have been fighting more than usual since their parents came to live with them. When Juan and Maria first invited their mothers to live with them, they imagined the extended family in only positive ways—the larger family festivities, the holidays with grandmothers present, the traditional foods being taught to their daughters, the sense of honor to women that the older women would instill in their sons. Both Maria and Juan know that their mothers are happy to be with them, but they also know that they miss Mexico. Although Maria appreciates their help around the house, she still feels overwhelmed with having to take care of four children while also working and going to school. She has to do all of this while under the watchful eyes of her elders and never seems to do anything up to their level of standards. She feels that they do not see the value of the sacrifices that she and Juan make for the sake of their children. For example, Juan works the night shift so he can earn more money. In fact, he wishes that Maria didn't have to work at all. He feels that he should earn enough money to care for her and the family. But his mother says that he should work while his children are in school, like his father did, so he can be *un papa verdadero*—a real father—to them in the evenings and set *un buen ejemplo*—a good example—to them. Maria and Juan never seem to have any time alone together.

Trying to meet the expectations of their parents while establishing new goals for their own family is difficult for Juan and Maria. Even though they see each other only between shifts or on weekends, those times are often spent arguing about the children or which bills to pay this month and which things can wait a little longer. Occasionally, Maria thinks about the times in Mexico when she was poorer but had more family to support her, had more social status in the village, and fought less with Juan. She wants her children to have every opportunity, but she also wants her family to be happy. Perhaps they should consider moving back to Mexico and give it another try there?

Author Index

Note: Some author names may not appear in a particular page referred, as they are comprised in et al.

Subject Index

Note: Page numbers in *italics* denote tables or figures.

ABC-X model of family stress, 96, 103
  and ambiguous loss, 114, 119
  definition of the situation, 98–99
  family resources, 97–98, 100–101
  and Lipman-Bluman criteria, 96–97
  stress and crisis, 99
  stressor events, 96–97
Abuse, 127, 195
  child abuse, 281, 282
  detrimental relationships and, 194
  domestic violence, 126, 129, 173, 177, 240
  in family, 172–173
  sibling violence, 173
  spousal abuse, 195, 206, 237
Acculturation, 155
  discussion and interview about, 143
  gaps, 141, 142, 156, 157
  research, 141
  stress, 141, 142, 158
Adaptability, 95, 97, 133, 163
Adaptation, 16, 43, 45, 164, 263, 265, 276
  for adolescents, 102
  of behaviorism, 202
  cross-institutional, 85
  of family, 71, 73, 77, 101, 133, 264
  Family adjustment and adaptation response (FAAR)
      model, 106–107
  and family crisis, 106
  and human behavior, 262
  of ideals, 91
  to U.S. cultural traditions, 155
Adolescents, 68, 72, 130, 143, 148, 283.
      See also Parent–Adolescent relationships
  in absence of family members, 146, 148, 151
  ambivalence of, 152
  antisocial behavior, 285
  as cultural brokers, 155
  coping, 102
  depression, 285
  families with, 72
  familism, 153–154
  and hormone impact on, 267, 286

  nostalgia, 148, 149, 151
  peer group system, 57
  prenatal androgen impact on, 281
  problem behavior of, 266
  sharing of responsibilities, 72
  testosterone impact on, 268
Adulthood, 251, 255, 266, 287, 290
  transition to, 285–286
Adults, 67, 113, 129, 255, 206
  access to resources, 166
  aged, 74, 166
  childless, 78
  conflict in relationships, 128
  divorce and, 45
  families with young, 73
AFDC grant, 182, 188, 197
Age, 72, 87, 91, 166, 191, 192–193, 283
Aggression, 164, 169, 237, 240, 281, 282, 283
"Aim-inhibited sex idea", 51
Ambiguous loss, 100, 111
  and absence of rituals, 115
  characterisitcs of, 111–116
  effects on families, 116–118
  and narrative therapy, 118–120
  stress, exacerbating, 113–114
  types of, 112
American Sociological Association, 123
Anthony, Susan B., 230
Antiracist feminism, 248
Aristotle, 4, 5
Assertion, 169, 223
Assumptions, in theories, 3
Attractiveness, 202, 215, 218
Attribution theory, 197
Avoiders, 170–171
Axial coding, 144

Bad luck, 180, 190–191, 195
Bargaining, 168–169, 213, 214, 222
Behavior, 5, 12, 27, 35, 67, 91, 115,
      125–126, 233–234, 262, 270, 274.
      See also individual entries